THE COMPLETE
VEGAN
KITCHEN

JANNEQUIN BENNETT

Foreword by Carl Lewis

Photography by Double Image Studio

Thomas Nelson
Since 1798

NASHVILLE DALLAS MEXICO CITY RIO DE JANEIRO BEIJING

Published in Nashville, Tennessee. Thomas Nelson is a trademark of Thomas Nelson, Inc.

Color photographs by Double Image Studio, Richmond, Virginia

Photograph on page vii by Tim Alexander

Illustration on page 38 by Janet Brooks

More information about Carl Lewis can be found on his website www.carllewis.com.

Library of Congress Cataloging-in-Publication Data

Bennett, Jannequin, 1956–
    Very vegetarian / Jannequin Bennett ; introduction by Carl Lewis.
        p. cm.
    Includes index.
    ISBN-10 1-4016-0347-5 (paperback)
    ISBN-13 978-1-14016-0347-2 (paperback)
    ISBN-10 1-55853-952-2 (hardcover)
    ISBN-13 978-1-55853-952-5 (hardcover)
    1. Vegan cookery. I. Title.
TX837 .B463 2001
641.5'636—dc21   2001004336

Printed in the Singapore
09 10 11 — 5 4 3

To

Lois Florence Bennett,
mother, mentor, inspiration,

and

Gordon Clowe Bennett,
father, editor, counselor

■ ■ ■

Contents

Introduction
Carl Lewis

Can a world-class athlete get enough protein from a vegetarian diet to compete? I've found that a person does not need protein from meat to be a successful athlete. In fact, my best year of track competition was the first year I ate a vegan diet. Moreover, by continuing to eat a vegan diet, my weight is under control, I like the way I look (I know that sounds vain, but all of us want to like the way we look), I enjoy eating more, and I feel great. Here's my story.

When I grew up in New Jersey, I always enjoyed eating vegetables and was influenced by my mother, who believed in the importance of a healthy diet even though we ate meat regularly because my father wanted it. At the University of Houston I ate meat and tried to control my weight the wrong way—by skipping meals. Frequently I would skip breakfast, eat a light lunch, and then have my fill at dinner—just before I went to bed. Not only is skipping meals the wrong way to diet, but the way I did it is the worst way because your body needs four hours to digest its food before you go to sleep.

In May of 1990 I decided to change the way I ate when I realized that controlling my weight by skipping meals was not good for me. Within the space of a few weeks, I met two men who changed my way of thinking and eating. The first was Jay Cordich, the Juice Man, whom I met at the Houston radio station where I worked in the early morning. He was there to talk about his juicer, which makes fresh juice from fruits and vegetables. He said that drinking at least sixteen ounces of freshly squeezed juice each day will increase a person's energy, strengthen the immune system, and reduce the risk of disease. A few weeks later while doing publicity for a track meet in Minneapolis, I met Dr. John McDougall, a medical doctor who teaches about the link between good nutrition and good health and was promoting his latest book. Dr. McDougall challenged me to make a commitment to eating a vegetarian diet and then to just do it.

I remember vividly making the decision in July of 1990 to become a vegan. I was competing in Europe and ate a meal of Spanish sausage on a Saturday and on the following Monday started eating vegan. The hardest thing for me was changing my eating habits from skipping meals to eating throughout the day—which is much healthier. I also missed salt, so I substituted lemon juice for flavor.

In the spring of 1991—eight months after beginning to eat vegan—I was feeling listless and thought I might need to add protein from meat to my diet. Dr. McDougall, however, explained that my listlessness was due to my needing more calories because I was training so many hours each day, not because I needed more animal-based protein. When I increased my calorie intake, I regained my energy. I was drinking twenty-four to thirty-two ounces of juice a day. I ate no dairy products. And I had my best year as an athlete ever!

You have total control over what you put in your body. No one can force you to eat what you don't want to eat. I know that many people think that eating a vegetarian diet—and especially a vegan diet—will require sacrifice and denial. Jannequin Bennett demonstrates in this book that eating vegan does not have to be tasteless and boring. As she says, "vegan eating is a truly indulgent way of life, as vegans regularly partake of the very best foods that nature has to offer." Here are recipes that will excite your taste buds. By the way, a few of my own recipes are included.

Keep in mind that eating vegan does require a commitment to being good to your body and to acting responsibly toward the world around you. Most of us are not aware of how much damage we do to our bodies and to our world by the way we eat. I challenge you to write down everything you eat and drink for one week. You will probably be amazed at the amount of snacks you eat, the different ways in which milk and cheese are a part of your diet, and—worst of all—how much fast food you consume.

Most snacks such as cookies, chips, candy, French fries, and soft drinks are highly processed foods that have lost many of their useful nutrients. Worse still, most of these foods are loaded with fat, salt, and chemicals. For instance, a 1.5-ounce bag of barbeque potato chips has the same number of calories as a medium baked potato, but 70 times the amount of fat and 20 times the amount of salt. Cheese and other dairy products are loaded with artery-clogging saturated fat and cholesterol. Most cheeses get 70 to 80 percent of their calories from fat.

You have to be especially careful when you eat in fast food restaurants. As the consumption of unhealthy fast food has increased, so has obesity, which is now second only to smoking as a cause of death in the U.S. Eric Schlosser reported in *Fast Food Nation* that the rate of obesity among American children is twice as high today as it was twenty-five years ago. Moreover, it seems that wherever people eat unhealthy fast food, waistlines start to expand. Between 1984 and 1993, for instance, the number of fast food restaurants in Great Britain roughly doubled. And so did the obesity rate among adults. Overweight people were once a rarity in Japan. Fast food restaurants arrived there thirty years ago, and today one-third of all Japanese men in their thirties are overweight.

Your body is your temple. If you nourish it properly, it will be good to you and you will increase its longevity. Being good to your body, however, requires diligence and determination. I began eating vegan for health reasons and continue primarily because of that. Others eat vegan for ethical or spiritual reasons. Whatever your reasons are for eating a plant-based diet, *Very Vegetarian* will help you do it with style and taste.

More information about Carl Lewis can be found on his website www.carllewis.com.

Acknowledgments

I would like to thank the entire staff at the Jefferson Hotel for their generous support, especially Pat Manning, Assistant General Manager and Food and Beverage Director; Joseph Longo, General Manager; and the staff of TJ's, in particular my peeps Angel Fields, Charlie Peebles, and Marion Coe. Thanks also go to David Bunger, Amber Marchant, Jackie Chan for his enthusiasm about seitan, and Melanie Schoof for getting the ball rolling.

I would also like to thank my family: my sister Kyryn for planting the cookbook-writing seeds years ago, my brother Christian for our earliest experiments in the kitchen, my brothers Damian and Gregg, and my sisters Liane, Hilary, and Meaghan for being my first taste testers.

I am grateful to my friends: Laura Southerland for her vintage seventies cookbook collection and interest in all things edible, Cheryl Stockton for her unflagging hospitality and strong coffee, Lorraine Kendrick for her good spirit and for being a model of perseverance, Janet Dix and Sue Washko for tolerating my literary hibernation, and Bev and Jim Southerland for being my culinary tour guides to Washington, D.C, and environs.

In addition, I thank Larry Stone, publisher at Rutledge Hill Press, for initiating this project; Jennifer Greenstein for her patient editing; and Gordon Bennett for being my mentor and sharing his editorial insights.

I thank Villeroy and Boch for the use of china, Lois Bennett for her vintage serving pieces, and Susan Delgado and Nicolas Timmons for their props and good natures.

My thanks also go to my culinary mentors Sinath Phae and Sambeth Enn, the staff at Rococo's in Charlottesville for their consistent warmth, Susan O'Reilly, Richard Kelsey for his enthusiastic forays into vegan baking, and all the wonderful cooks, dishwashers, owners, and servers I've had the pleasure of working with through the years.

Getting Started
Choosing a Vegan Diet

Vegan food is, quite simply, an indulgence. When you indulge, you give yourself permission to enjoy the very best. Vegan eating is a truly indulgent way of life, as vegans regularly partake of the very best foods—the most nutritious, appealing, and tasty—that nature has to offer. As you'll find when you explore the recipes in this book, vegan food is enticing and exciting. A well-crafted vegan plate offers a festival of flavors, textures, and colors that makes every meal an aesthetic celebration.

You may be surprised to read about indulgence in a vegan cookbook. You may even think of a vegan diet as Spartan or odd. Indeed, vegan diets are still uncommon in many circles. But vegan/vegetarian eating is no longer on the cultural fringe. Today we have more information on the vital link between diet and health. Our shrinking world invites us to rub elbows with more cultures and experience their cuisines. Our concern about the condition of our environment grows and our frantic lifestyles send us in search of simplicity. Today, eating a vegan diet makes more and more sense for those who seek to make personal choices that have a positive impact on their own lives and on the world at large. Good health and feeling good about our choices enable us to be more effective in our relationships and our work. When we treat ourselves to a healthy and thoughtful lifestyle, we have the energy to tackle tasks large and small with renewed vigor. Sometimes a little indulgence goes a long, long way.

For those readers for whom vegan eating is a new idea, this book will provide a variety of reasons for giving it a try. For all readers, including experienced vegetarians and vegans, we offer exciting recipes to whet your appetite for food and life even further. The bottom line is that vegan eating is about living well—in health, harmony, and joy.

What Is a Vegan Anyway?

Simply stated, vegans (pronounced VEE-guns) are vegetarians who do not eat any food that comes from animals. Obviously, that means they don't eat beef, chicken, pork, or fish. It also means that dairy products, eggs, and even honey aren't on the menu.

What Do Vegans Eat?

Years of eating meals that shine the spotlight on meat and relegate vegetables and grains to supporting roles have limited our awareness of their nutritional talent. On the vegan table, barley, bulgur, and millet share billing with the more familiar rice and wheat. The healthy vegan demands full lusty performances from all grains.

The palette of produce offered is varied as well. Green beans, corn, peas, and white potatoes—vegetables of our childhood table—now share billing with a host of other options, creatively and enticingly prepared.

Legions of legumes—lentils, beans, and peas—grace many a vegan plate. And soy, so frequently touted in medical circles and the media today, is, in its varied forms, an increasingly important part of vegan cuisine.

Though you may not have thought about it, you've probably been eating vegan foods all your life. Perhaps they never took center stage, but they have been there in the background. If your family never ate green beans without fatback, potatoes without sour cream, or salads without mayonnaise, you are in for a treat when you try vegan renditions of these foods. Even if you've been a vegetarian for years, chances are you have relied on cheese, butter, and eggs to a large extent, often allowing them to overpower the other elements in the meal. The recipes in this book are designed to showcase the essence of the vegetables, grains, beans, and fruits that go into them. You will be amazed at the results that can be obtained with just these ingredients.

So, while vegans may be defined in conversation by what they don't eat, healthy vegan living is all about what they do eat. Vegan eating isn't about deprivation—it's about fulfillment.

Why Vegan?

Vegans choose to eat as they do for a variety of reasons. Good health is a big reason. Ethical, ecological, and spiritual reasons come into play as well. This chapter offers information and reflections on these issues, along with basic nutritional guidelines, shopping tips, and strategies for changing eating patterns. But the main feature here is the recipes. This is, after all, a cookbook! We're dishing up food that is delicious, healthy, and inviting, for anyone who is hungry for really great food.

Nutritional Issues

You don't need this book to tell you about the importance of eating healthy foods. Powerful voices such as the American Cancer Society and the American Heart Association have weighed in on the link between nutrition and health. The shift toward highly refined foods, with little fiber and more fat, combined with our more sedentary lives, has taken a toll on our health. As our diets and lifestyles have changed dramatically over the last one hundred years, heart disease and cancer become closer to all our lives.

Much of the increase in fat consumption comes with hefty support from the meat and dairy industries. In the typical diet of developed nations, slightly more than a quarter of the fat comes from meat, a quarter from butter and margarine, a quarter from milk and cooking fats, and a quarter from cheese and the fats in sweets. Cheese consumption in the United States has risen 300 percent since 1970, making cheese the leading source of saturated fat in the American diet. (For more information on saturated fats, see page 25.)

The foods we eat have often been processed in a way that reduces fiber and vitamin content. A potato is rich in complex carbohydrates, fiber, folate, and vitamin C before its transformation into French fries. Potatoes destined for the fryer are often aged in warehouses so the complex carbohydrates become simple sugars. This helps the potatoes become brown and crunchy. The peeling, washing, frying, and salting dramatically change the nutritional profile. One serving of French fries, about 10 to 15 (who really eats only 10 to 15?), has almost 4 times the calories of a medium baked potato but only one-quarter of the vitamin C and fiber, one-half of the iron and carbohydrates, and 180 times as much fat and 25 times as much sodium.

Processing takes away and, unfortunately, it adds as well. A wide variety of chemicals not naturally found in our food—pesticides, preservatives, artificial flavor, and color additives—are added regularly for preservation and presentation. And when we eat "futher up the food chain" to include animal products in our diets, we consume not only the chemicals used to process and preserve these foods, but also the chemicals fed to the animals, such as growth hormones, antibiotics, and the pesticides sprayed on the plants they eat, which all concentrate in animal fat. We also add items that we should be limiting, such as salt, fat (especially hydrogenated fat), and sugar.

Choosing a vegan diet won't magically shield you from nutritional and chemical pitfalls. But changing your eating pattern to exclude animal products and embrace whole foods can go a long way toward preserving your health. When you say goodbye to animal products and highly processed foods, you remove all of the cholesterol and much of the saturated fat from your diet. Your total fat intake will fall from the 36 to 40 percent consumed by the typical American omnivore to about 30 percent or less. Most of the fats you do consume (and yes, fat is necessary for overall health) will actually be good for you!

The fiber content of your diet will increase as well, providing defense against cancer and heart disease. Increased fiber intake helps regulate blood sugar levels (a particular benefit if you are hypoglycemic or diabetic). Fiber consumption also helps you maintain a healthy weight: because fiber makes us feel full, we actually may take in fewer calories.

A wide range of vitamins and minerals, including cancer-fighting antioxidants, will find their way into your body, and not just in pill form. The traces of hormones, steroids, antibiotics, and other chemicals fed to animals to speed up maturation or increase body size will disappear from your diet. If you choose primarily organic foods, your intake of trace amounts of pesticides and agri-chemicals will decrease as well.

In short, if you decide to change to a vegan diet, if you do away with animal products and choose varied and less-processed foods, you'll do your health a favor.

Ethical Considerations

Though many vegans choose their diet on the simple premise that killing is wrong, the ethical issues that surround vegan eating are really quite complex. Concern for the ethical treatment of animals starts well before the slaughterhouse. Inhumane practices designed to meet the massive demand for all animal products are rampant throughout agribusiness—mistreatment of which the average consumer is often quite unaware.

The Saga of the Dairy Cow

Think your life is stressful? Forty years ago the life expectancy of a dairy cow was twenty years. Today, Bossie can expect to live only four years—four very hard years. Modern industry practices keep the cows in a nearly continual state of pregnancy through artificial insemination. Rarely allowed to roam free, Bossie and her bovine companions are fed synthetic hormones to increase milk production by as much as 40 percent, which necessitates frequent milking. She is also subjected to a steady diet of antibiotics and animal refuse (the latter linked to mad cow disease). These "advancements" in dairy cow productivity have created a glut of milk, which, in turn, has generated increased marketing campaigns to create demand.

Bossie's calves are removed from her side very shortly after birth and shipped to veal factories. There they are chained in a stall, fed a diet without roughage or iron to ensure nicely textured and colored meat, and injected with hormones and antibiotics to support survival until the calf is large enough to slaughter. The old standard for veal was a calf, six months or younger, fed exclusively mother's milk. The modern farm industry is able to raise a calf almost to maturity, resulting in higher profits from a larger animal whose flesh is like that of a newborn.

Productivity at Great Cost

Cows aren't the only ones to suffer. Chickens are often caged so tightly that they can hardly stretch their wings. Packed in tightly with others, they tend to peck and claw in desperation—so producers cut off their beaks. Extreme lack of exercise causes brittle bones that break with the slightest stress. Wire mesh floors cause foot deformities. Starvation forces molting, which renews egg production. As a result of pressure from animal rights activists, in 2000, McDonald's agreed to stop buying chicken from suppliers that debeak or starve, and required that each egg-laying hen have an eight-by-nine-inch cage. Recently McDonald's and Denny's have committed to supporting growers who use controlled atmosphere killing (CAK), which is thought to be the most humane way to harvest the birds. In this method, nitrogen or other gas replaces a normal atmosphere and the chickens are said to die with much less trauma. While this represents a step toward more reasonable treatment, the end can hardly be called compassionate or humane. Hard to believe that these guidelines represent improvements!

In the business of agriculture, animals are fed, kept, and medicated with an eye to increased production, not their well-being. And the conditions under which animals are shipped to slaughterhouses and put to death are far from humane. When we consume animal products, we lend support to these practices.

Sharing the Wealth, Maintaining Our Treasures

Raising animals for food is an inefficient use of our world's resources. Grain is the primary source of nutrition for most of the world's population. Of the land that is used to produce grain, about a quarter provides feed for livestock. Furthermore, acres and acres of tropical rain forests—forests vital to the health of our planet—are being destroyed daily to make room for cattle to graze. Chemical and biological waste runoff from livestock production pollutes our waterways. When you add up the costs to humanity, raising livestock for food is a losing proposition.

Spiritual Reflections

We rarely think of food as spiritual, but there is a strong spiritual aspect to eating. This is because food is, at its very essence, life giving. The fact that food is spiritually significant plays out in religions across the human spectrum. In the Roman Catholic tradition, Benedictine monks and Carmelite nuns maintain vegetarian diets in conjunction with their contemplative lives. Orthodox Christian sects require abstinence from animal products during the Lenten season, a time of prayer and penitence. Many sacred scriptures instruct their followers to avoid senseless killing. The best known connection between vegetarianism and religion is ahimsa, or the ideal of harmlessness, which is common to Buddhism, Jainism, and Hinduism.

Deciding to pursue a vegan diet can be an active choice to do what is good. In seeking to do no harm—to ourselves, to other beings, and to the earth—we draw from the spirit and feed the spirit.

The Bottom Line

There are myriad reasons to embrace a vegan diet. A vegan diet will improve your health. It is healthier for the environment. Eating only plant-based food speaks against the cruelties often perpetrated against other beings for the sake of commerce. Eating vegan is a peaceful choice, one that may feed us spiritually and improve our lot as human beings. Vegan eating is also delicious. It introduces a creative aspect to the act of eating, enriching our day-to-day existence. At the very basis of the choice of a vegan diet is respect: respect for your own life and the lives of others. Inherent in the choice is a desire to live mindful of the consequences of our daily decisions, and an acknowledgment of the connection linking humans, animals, and the earth.

All the rhetoric and arguments aside, veganism is a joyous celebration of life. A decision to live in a healthful and compassionate fashion feeds not just the body but the soul. Surround yourself with what you need to continue on this journey to health and wholeness.

Eating Vegan with Ease: Seasoned Advice

Living vegan in a meat and dairy world sometimes seems like a tough fit. Dinner parties, dinners out, even a foray to the local grocery store may at times seem daunting to the unpracticed. Planning meals may present particular challenges to those long accustomed to offering vegetable "sides" to accompany a meat-based main dish. Furthermore, vegans often find themselves explaining their food choices to others. Vegan eating should be a celebration, not a chore. Here are some simple tips to help the novice or seasoned vegan fully enjoy the vegan celebration.

Learning to Think Vegan

If a vegan diet is new to you, allow yourself time for transition. It takes time to change your perception of what a meal should include. It takes time to master the nutritional knowledge that allows you to fully benefit from the foods you choose. Changing a lifetime of eating habits will not happen overnight. Identifying why you want to change your eating habits can help you stay motivated when those familiar temptations arise. People come to this dietary lifestyle for a wide variety of reasons. Your goal may be as general as "I'd like to feel better" or as specific as "I'd like to reduce my risk of heart disease, cancer, and Type II diabetes." Being clear on why you want to make this change can help you stay focused should the going get rough.

Setting specific goals for yourself can give a sense of accomplishment. If all your meals currently contain meat, you may want to declare one day "meatless." If you don't eat meat but have dairy products every day, you will need a plan to wean yourself from them. Clearly stated reasoning and goals can help ensure success.

In the beginning, you may want to stick with familiar foods that you know you like. Some people like to start off with meat substitutes. This may be helpful in keeping your resolve, but keep in mind that some of these are highly processed. When you can, check out other cuisines. In many cultures, meat is scarce and reserved for special occasions and whole cuisines have been built on the bedrock of beans and grains.

Liberate yourself from seeing a meal as a main dish and sides. Instead, think about enjoying an assortment of foods rich in nutrients at each meal. Think balanced, appetizing, and satisfying. A vegan meal, from preparation to presentation to consumption, provides an aesthetic experience that is nourishing to both body and spirit.

Revel in the preparation. Read cookbooks. Experiment. Taste and smell and touch. Use the freshest ingredients you can find, including fresh herbs. Broaden your culinary horizons by introducing yourself to unfamiliar produce and seasonings. (Have you enjoyed an artichoke lately?)

Shopping for the Vegan Kitchen

Eating Close to Home

Most of us have no difficulty finding a wide selection of produce. More and more grocery stores are offering organic selections that provide a healthy foundation for your meals. Look for "USDA Organic" on the label.

An even fresher approach is to "eat close to home." Consider growing your own kitchen garden featuring your favorite vegetables and a wide variety of herbs. In a number of areas around the country, small organic farms are sprouting up—big enough to serve the immediate community, but not big enough to market broadly. Buying from one of these small-scale organic farmers not only puts great-tasting and wholesome food on your table, but also helps to reduce the quantity of pesticides that seep into the ground and water near your home.

You can find local organic farmers at area farmers' markets, open from early spring and into the fall in most areas. Make the trip to the farmers' market a special treat in your week. Sniff and touch ripe produce, and buy a fresh-cut flower or two. Take in the colors and sights and sounds of people enjoying the earth's bounty. Try to find a vegetable with which you are unfamiliar, and give it a try. Talk with the growers— ask questions about varieties, storage, and even cooking. If you find a grower whose wares you particularly like, see if there is a way to buy from him or her on other days of the week.

You may be able to buy local produce through Community Supported Agriculture (CSA). With this arrangement, farmers take "subscriptions" or offer consumers a "share" of their crops. As the crops come in, you receive produce in season, fresh from the field. No matter how you approach it, eating close to home is healthier, tastier, less expensive, and bushels of fun.

Grocery Store Logic

You'll be amazed at how many convenience foods are available at your grocery store to get you started as you learn how to put together meatless meals. Most supermarkets have a health food section that makes it easier for you to find things. Make sure to look there and in the produce section when searching out soy products.

One of our local stores has begun to keep plain and flavored tofu near the organic produce and sprouts, along with seitan, vegan cheeses, and fresh Asian noodles.

Next to the vegan cheeses are the almost-vegan products—the tofu cheeses with casein, the margarines with whey. You may already be an inveterate label reader. Perhaps before you concentrated on the nutrition data; now you will want to look for animal products masquerading as chemical additives. By far the most common are albumin (egg white protein), whey (milk derivative), lactose (milk sugar), casein (isolated milk protein), and gelatin. Lard and suet are obviously from meat, but stearic acid, a saturated fat, can come from beef or cocoa butter. There are plenty of other additives, but it's best to avoid foods whose ingredient lists read like the index to a chemistry text. Try to find the least-processed foods possible. Avoid items with the words "hydrogenated," "modified," or "artificial." Some foods will state on the packaging if they are vegetarian, which usually means they contain some egg and/or dairy products, or vegan. While there may be a few new terms to learn—such as carrageenan (a thickener made from Irish moss) and inulin (a sweetener made from vegetable starch)—the labels on the foods you choose should be easy to understand, with ingredients you recognize as food.

Once you've explored your grocery store, locate the local health food store or natural foods market. The selection of organic produce, flours, sweeteners, and soy foods is usually extensive. Don't be afraid to ask questions. If the shopper next to you seems experienced, ask his or her advice if you're confused. People love to talk about food.

Off the Beaten Path

Don't forget the little specialty market down the street. Cuisines from other cultures are an exciting source of great vegan food, and shopping at the local source is an enriching experience. Larger cities will offer a variety of such adventures: Asian, Indian, Middle Eastern, Latin American, and more. And you never know what is just around the corner in smaller communities. Take a walk! You may discover a culinary treasure.

Leaving Home Without Your Lunch Box

Adopting a vegan diet does not mean the end to eating in restaurants or going to parties. A little planning can help prevent awkward or embarrassing situations.

Restaurant Savvy

The restaurant industry has become increasingly attuned to its vegetarian diners. Many restaurants have vegetarian dishes on the menu, though they often feature dairy or eggs. With the proliferation of different dietary regimes in the last few years, most restaurants have grown accustomed to accommodating guests' requests for special diets. You are paying for the food and should be able to have a dish prepared to your liking. Restaurants want happy guests, so if you are courteous and patient, your server and the cooks will most likely treat you to an enjoyable dining experience. Here are some tips for selecting a meal and communicating your needs:

- Many people in the restaurant industry are not familiar with the word "vegan." If you merely describe yourself as vegan, you run the risk of being misunderstood. Gently stating your needs to the server makes it easier on everyone. Inform your server that you don't eat any meat, fish, eggs, or dairy products.
- Ask the server to recommend something. Many restaurants train their servers to know which dishes are vegetarian or can be easily adapted to accommodate different diets.
- Make sure to ask about hidden ingredients. Often chicken broth or butter are the clandestine components. Lard is sometimes an issue in Mexican restaurants, and Indian food may be cooked with ghee, a type of clarified butter. Japanese, Vietnamese, Thai, and Chinese dishes often include fish, clam, or oyster sauce. If you ask whether a dish contains animal products and your server says he doesn't think so or isn't sure, ask politely, "Would you check on that for me, just to make sure?" A polite request is almost always greeted willingly, and may help to communicate just how serious you are about avoiding animal products. Many dishes can be easily adapted to vegan standards, and most restaurants are willing to do so.
- Many dishes are prepared only when ordered by a guest. Look for menu items with lots of ingredients and determine which ones might be tasty without the meat, fish, or dairy. For instance, penne tossed with grilled chicken, roasted vegetables, and red pepper sauce is great without the chicken—or the cheese that may be sprinkled on top. Filet mignon served with roasted fingerling potatoes, fiddlehead ferns, and grilled spring onions is wonderful without the filet—as long as the potatoes are not roasted in butter. In restaurants with elaborate accompaniments, I often ask for a plate of just the accompaniments to a dish. Otherwise, I will pick and choose from side dishes listed with various menu items and ask for a vegetable plate.
- If your server has no suggestions, and the menu gives no clue what might be available, determine what you want to eat. It is helpful to let the kitchen know what you may be in the mood for—a huge plate of grilled vegetables; a bowl of pasta with broccoli and garlic; rice with steamed vegetables, soy sauce, and ginger; a burrito with refried beans and spinach, topped with pico de gallo. The more guidance you give, the easier it will be for the server and the kitchen to put together a satisfying meal.

- Understand that your request may take some extra time. Kitchen crews spend hours each day preparing ingredients for specific menu items. Special requests may be a challenge to accommodate, especially at busy times.

Don't forget to reward your server for the extra effort by saying a genuine "thank you," and leaving a healthy tip.

You can avoid a lot of discussion at the table if you call ahead before you dine. Simply phone the restaurant and ask if they can accommodate a vegan diet. If the person who answers seems confused, you might want to ask to speak to the manager or chef. Make sure that the person to whom you are speaking understands that you don't eat any animal products. Try calling early in the day to allow the chef to plan.

Get to know the food ingredients and options at restaurants you frequent. When some crafty server or chef comes through with a delicious variation on a standard menu item, make that specific variation part of your next order.

Though more and more people today are choosing foods that truly nourish them, your order may be met with more than a little bit of curiosity on the part of your waiter. Be ready for questions and field them politely. You may be helping the next vegan diner who comes in the door.

What about fast food?

While fast food chains are probably not your first choice for eating out, there are times when circumstances may find you waiting in line with your friends or family, wondering what you can possibly eat. Fast food chains have increasingly tried to make provisions for their vegetarian customers. Your best bets in the fast food world are salads (not Caesar, though) and salad bars, baked potatoes, tostadas or tacos with vegan refried beans, subs with only vegetables, and "burgers" with no meat or cheese—just the bun and all the fixings. Be aware that salad dressings may contain gelatin, flour tortillas may contain dairy products, rolls and buns may contain eggs or egg whites, and beans may contain lard. Do not expect the counter people to be able to answer questions reliably about vegan options. Many of the larger chains have vegetarian information on their websites. While these foods may be vegan, do not expect healthful preparations. Ultimately, a little planning can eliminate the need to depend on fast food. For specific information, check out the website for the Vegetarian Resource Group (www.vrg.org). They offer a state-by-state guide of vegetarian and vegan friendly restaurants along with a thirty-two-page guide to vegetarian menu items at restaurant and fast food chains.

Parties

Food plays a central role in the way we traditionally celebrate life's milestones, but the food is not the reason for the gathering. There will be times when the menu doesn't match your needs, but go—and enjoy the celebration for the main event, not the culinary sideline.

Casual get-togethers and cookouts are perhaps the easiest settings to manage. If each guest is bringing a dish to share or meat to grill, you can share a large bowl of vegan potato salad or a platter of hummus and veggies, or bring your own veggie burgers—just make sure to be the first one at the grill.

If the invitation is to a dinner party at someone's home, after telling that host how delighted you are at the invitation, slip in a gentle reminder that you are a vegan. You might want to assure your host that a plate of the side dishes or a large salad is sufficient. If you know your host well enough, offer to bring a dish to share with the entire group. My hosts have welcomed contributions from my own kitchen (who refuses food from a chef, after all?) and have appreciated the opportunity to try something new.

Food plays a central role in more formal gatherings such as wedding receptions, so these occasions often pose a quandary. It would be a shame to miss a lovely occasion because the menu doesn't meet your needs. If you have been invited to a banquet or catered event, contact your host or the facility in advance so a meal may be prepared for you. This will save you and your host embarrassment during the function.

Celebrating in Your Own Home

Serving a Crowd

Those of us who love to entertain know sharing a meal with friends is one of life's greatest pastimes. Inviting a casual acquaintance over to eat is a great way to establish a true friendship. Cooking for "meat eaters" can be great fun because you get a chance to introduce them to the tantalizing flavors, colors, and textures of vegan food. Share what you love and serve it with style. Your guests will come back for more—again and again.

Eating at Home

Don't forget that the most important meals you cook and share are those you enjoy with your family. Giving loving attention to whole, hearty, and satisfying vegan meals can make a world of difference in the well-being of those you love.

A Guide to Vegan Nutrition

Choosing to embrace a vegan diet requires careful consideration. Carrying out that decision is a thoughtful process as well. The healthy diner—vegan or otherwise—must know something about nutrition in order to plan nourishing and enticing meals. The information in this section will provide you with a wealth of information that you can use to make sound nutritional decisions.

The USDA introduced the food pyramid in 1992 as a graphic depiction of dietary guidelines. The latest version can be found at www.mypyramid.gov, where recommendations are given based on age, gender and activity level. There are specific suggestions in the Tips and Resources section for those following vegetarian diets. Whatever the guidance, each plan is built on a strong foundation of complex carbohydrates, fruits, and vegetables.

Many of us are familiar with the term RDA, Recommended Dietary Allowance. This was the intake level of a particular nutrient that was deemed adequate for all the known needs of healthy people. In 1995, this was expanded to incorporate a broader understanding of the role that nutrition has in preventing chronic disease, promoting health and performance.

So the RDA has been replaced by the DRI, Dietary Reference Intakes. This number is comprised of four different reference values and is thought to give more accurate guidelines for nutrients in a wider range of settings and personal circumstances.

In 1997 the American Dietetic Association officially endorsed vegetarian diets, and vegan diets specifically, as being nutritionally sound and providing health benefits in the prevention and treatment of certain diseases. Vegans take in significantly higher amounts of fiber, vitamin C, potassium, magnesium, vitamin B-6, and folate than even lacto-ovo-vegetarians. A sound vegan diet, however, must be planned to meet specific nutritional requirements. Guidelines for vegans include 6 to 11 servings of grains (including breads, pastas, and cereals); 3 to 5 servings of vegetables; 2 to 4 servings of fruit; and 4 to 5 servings of beans, legumes, seeds, and nuts. The ADA recommends that special attention be paid to getting enough iron, vitamin B-12, vitamin D, calcium, and zinc. Iodine consumption may be a concern as well. While these nutrients may concern dietitians, the question most often asked by those considering changing to a vegan diet is, "Will I get enough protein?"

What's in a Serving?				
For one serving of grain, you might eat . . .	1 slice bread	$1/2$ cup cooked pasta	1 ounce dry or $3/4$ cup cooked cereal	2 tablespoons wheat germ
For one serving of vegetables, you might eat . . .	1 cup salad greens	$1/2$ cup cooked vegetable	1 medium carrot	$3/4$ cup vegetable juice
For one serving of fruit, you might eat . . .	1 medium orange, banana, or apple	2 apricots or plums	$1/2$ cup cooked or fresh fruit	$3/4$ cup juice
For one serving of beans or legumes, you might eat . . .	1 cup soymilk or $1/2$ cup soft or medium tofu	1 cup lentil soup	$1/2$ cup hummus or cooked beans	2 tablespoons peanut butter

Getting All You Need

Protein

We all know how important proteins are: they build muscle, repair cells, and make the enzymes responsible for basic bodily functions like eating, breathing, and moving. It is not necessary to consume animal products to get adequate protein into your diet. What many people don't realize is that they get plenty of protein from grains, beans, and vegetables.

Between 23 and 54 percent of the calories in beans and legumes (lentils and tofu, for example) come from protein. Spinach is 49 percent protein, and wheat germ, 31 percent. If you are eating enough calories and a varied diet, you are almost guaranteed to be getting enough protein.

Protein Providers

1 cup cooked lentils	18 grams
1 cup cooked chickpeas	14.5 grams
1 cup cooked brown rice	5 grams
2 tablespoons peanut butter	8 grams
1 baked potato	4.5 grams
$1/2$ cup firm tofu	20 grams
$1/3$ cup soy nuts	12 grams

Many plant foods, however, do not contain all the essential amino acids, the building blocks of proteins. Most grains, for example, lack the amino acids lysine and threonine, while many beans lack methionine. This is why a varied diet is so important. When all essential amino acids are consumed throughout the day, the body uses the protein more efficiently, meaning that less overall protein needs to be consumed.

The daily reference intake (DRI) of protein is 56 grams for men and 46 grams for women. Pregnant women are encouraged to increase their intake to 50 grams and lactating women to 60 grams per day. Your individual needs may vary depending on your body size and activity level. Considering the rich assortment of foods in the vegan diet, meeting protein needs is a snap.

Iron

Most of the iron in our bodies is found in hemoglobin, which ferries oxygen from our lungs to our cells. Anemia results when daily iron requirements are not met and the body's iron stockpile is depleted. The DRI for iron is 8 milligrams for men and 18 milligrams for women (8 milligrams after menopause). The problem in vegan diets is not the amount of iron consumed, but the amount of iron the body absorbs. While "heme iron" from animal sources is readily absorbed by the body, nonheme iron is much more temperamental. For example, a cup of tea can cut iron absorption by half, whereas a glass of orange juice can increase absorption fourfold. Phytates, chemicals found in whole grains, bind iron so tightly that it is all but unavailable to the body, but vitamin C largely counteracts the action of phytates. Phytates are also destroyed by cooking or fermenting, as in yeast breads.

You probably naturally pair foods that optimize your body's uptake of iron: cream of wheat with strawberries, five-bean chili with tomatoes, a soymilk smoothie made with pineapple and kiwi, whole grain bread with a slice of tomato. Eating these foods in combination, and saving your coffee and tea for other times, can help your body make efficient use of these iron-rich foods.

Vitamin B-12

This water-soluble vitamin is unique because it is stored in the body. In fact, most of us are walking around with a five-year supply in our livers. Our bodies treat vitamin B-12 as a precious commodity, reabsorbing about 70 percent of what we use every day. (Vitamins are cofactors—they assist in chemical reactions but are not used up by them.) As a result, our vitamin B-12 requirements are very small—perhaps as little as 1 microgram a day, although the DRI is 2.4 micrograms. This is a good thing, since neither plants nor animals can synthesize vitamin B-12.

Many plant-based foods—tofu, greens, legumes, seaweed, and tempeh—contain a form of B-12 slightly different from the one our bodies can use. To ensure optimum health, vitamin B-12 should be supplemented in the vegan diet.

The most reliable vitamin B-12 supplement is cyanocobalamin. The cyanide ion stabilizes the vitamin until we put it in our mouths, where enzymes remove the cyanide and attach to the cobalamin. Vitamin B-12 is then escorted through the digestive tract, changing partners along the way until it reaches the small intestine where it can be absorbed. This is why chewable and sublingual tablets are more effective supplements than pills that are swallowed.

You will need to choose a reliable source of vitamin B-12. Fortunately, many common foods are now supplemented. Check the nutrition labels of soymilk, veggie burgers, and breakfast cereals. It's best if the label specifies cyanocobalamin so you know that you are getting an active form of the vitamin. (When checking nutritional labels on cereals, be sure to read the values for cereal alone, *without* milk.)

The most fun source of active vitamin B-12 is nutritional yeast. This handy kitchen helper has a toasted, nutty taste perfect for sprinkling on popcorn, stirring into hummus, mixing into lentil stew, or making into mushroom gravy. Try mixing it with ground almonds and a little salt to make a Parmesan cheese substitute. Nutritional yeast is often used to impart a cheesy flavor (see, for instance, Macaroni and Cheeze, page 193).

Red Star Vegetarian Support Formula (T6635+) is the only brand of nutritional yeast that guarantees the active form of vitamin B-12. Half a tablespoon contains enough vitamin B-12 to meet the daily nutritional needs of two people. As a bonus, you'll also get zinc, selenium, protein, and the full complement of B vitamins. The yeast is grown on cane and beet molasses and is certified kosher (except during Passover when no yeast may be consumed). For those concerned, Red Star nutritional yeast is inactive and guaranteed to contain no *candida albicans*, a yeast that can cause debilitating infections.

Vitamin D

If vitamin D worked in corporate America, its title might be CEO of Calcium Uptake and Relocation. There would be branch offices all over the body and corporate headquarters located in the intestines, regulating the absorption of calcium and phosphorus. The central office would then allocate the minerals to the branches for deposit in bones and teeth.

Vitamin D is produced in our skin when we are exposed to sunlight. A light-skinned person can meet vitamin D requirements with just ten to fifteen minutes of exposure two or three times a week in the summer. Darker skin requires up to six times more exposure for similar results. However, smog and sunscreen prevent vitamin D production. In high-fiber diets, the vitamin D found in fortified foods may be ushered right through our system without being absorbed. So even though we could theoretically store enough vitamin D in the summer to carry us through a long, dark winter, it's best to look for supplementation.

While rickets is not as common as it once was, this vitamin D deficiency disease is still reported, especially in elders and home-bound individuals. A breakfast of fortified soymilk and granola would start your day off right by providing 5 micrograms, your entire day's requirement, of vitamin D. Fortified breakfast cereals are other good bets. If you choose to take a supplement, 200 IU (international units) will provide the 5-microgram requirement. Because vitamin D is fat soluble and is readily stored in the body, you should be very careful not to exceed the Tolerable Upper Intake Level (UL) for Vitamin D, 50 micrograms or 2000 IU. Overloading on vitamin D can cause calcium deposits in soft tissues, including the kidneys (ouch! kidney stones) or the eardrum (which may cause deafness).

Calcium

Calcium is well known as the builder of strong bones and teeth. But did you know that calcium is also necessary for the transmission of nerve impulses and for muscle movement? The good news is that vegans tend to absorb and retain calcium better than non-vegans do. Some good sources of calcium are green leafy vegetables (kale, mustard greens), tahini, tofu (when prepared with calcium salts), almonds, figs, and sunflower seeds. In addition, there are several calcium-fortified foods that make it easy to meet the RDA of 1,000 milligrams. Most soymilk is enriched with calcium, providing 300 to 400 milligrams in just 1 cup. Tofu processed with calcium salts can provide 300 milligrams in a 1/2 cup serving.

Calcium-Rich Foods

You need 3 to 5 servings of calcium rich foods every day. Here are some great choices:

1 cup fortified soymilk (350 mg)
1 cup calcium-fortified orange juice (300 mg)
5 figs (258 mg)
2 cups raw or 1/2 cup cooked collards (178 mg)
2 tablespoons sesame seeds (176 mg)
1/2 cup edamame—green soybeans (130 mg)
1/2 cup cooked navy beans (128 mg)

Some dark leafy greens (spinach, beet greens, Swiss chard) contain oxalates that bind calcium (and iron), making it unavailable to the body. Salt, caffeine, and phosphorus can also inhibit the assimilation of calcium. While clearly there is value to spinach, going easy on salt, salty snacks, and caffeinated beverages is a good general practice.

Zinc

Zinc, a trace mineral, is involved in the metabolism of carbohydrates, proteins, and fats, and the basic processes of bodily repair and maintenance: cell reproduction and tissue growth and recovery. Children have a particularly critical need for zinc in order to maintain normal growth and development.

The USDA's recommended daily allowance of zinc is 11 milligrams for men, 8 milligrams for women (11–12 milligrams during pregnancy and lactation), and 3 milligrams for toddlers, 5 for children 4 to 8 years old and 8 milligrams after 9 years of age).

Eating foods high in zinc is just the beginning of getting enough. The amount of zinc your body actually absorbs can vary from 8 to 38 percent of what makes it to your belly. The zinc intake of the average person with a diet including animal and dairy products is 8.6 to 14 milligrams per day. In such a diet, 70 percent of the zinc comes from animal sources. Furthermore, with a diet high in animal products and low in fiber, a large percentage of the zinc that is consumed is absorbed.

Plant-based diets, emphasizing whole grains, may actually contain more than the recommended amount of zinc, but much of it is not in a form that the body can use. Phytates, a compound found in whole grains, and fiber both bind zinc and other minerals, making them inaccessible to the body.

You may say to yourself, "I'll just keep eating dairy if animal sources are a good source of zinc." Actually, a diet high in calcium makes phytates bind minerals more effectively, so lacto-ovo vegetarians may need more zinc than vegans.

Zinc Sources	
1 cup bran flakes	5 milligrams
1⅓ cups Special K	3.7 milligrams
¾ cup Nutrigrain	3.7 milligrams
½ cup Grape-nuts	1.2 milligrams
2 tablespoons toasted wheat germ	3.2 milligrams
2 tablespoons peanuts	1.8 milligrams
2 tablespoons pumpkin seeds	1.2 milligrams
2 tablespoons tahini	1.3 milligrams
½ cup cooked chickpeas	1.3 milligrams
½ cup cooked tempeh	1.5 milligrams
½ cup cooked TVP (texturized vegetable protein)	1.4 milligrams

Zinc lozenges aren't the answer, either. Zinc is more effectively absorbed in small doses. Large doses of zinc may elevate cholesterol by affecting the balance of LDL and HDL proteins, the bad and good lipo-proteins that regulate cholesterol. Excess zinc can also cause copper deficiency by out-competing copper for its binding sites, which in turn can impair immune function. Besides, many zinc lozenges contain compounds such as mannitol, sorbitol, and citrate that actually bind the zinc, keeping it inaccessible.

Many high-fiber foods contain a correspondingly high amount of zinc, so while much of the zinc isn't available, a reasonable amount makes it to the bloodstream. Also, phytates are fairly easy to circumvent. Cooking and fermentation destroy phytates, making the zinc available to the body. So yeasted whole grain breads are excellent sources of zinc. Only 5 percent of the zinc may be absorbed from an unprocessed whole grain cereal, but once two-thirds of the phytates are destroyed through fermentation, 20 percent of the zinc is absorbed. Some cereals also may be malted, increasing the availability of the minerals in the grains. Fermented soy foods—miso, tempeh, soy sauce—are good sources of trace minerals with high bio-availability.

To be safe, the USDA is now recommending that vegetarians get one-and-a-half times the RDA of zinc—making the requirements 22 milligrams for men, 18 milligrams for women, and 15 milligrams for children—since we don't know precisely how the body handles zinc from plant sources. What a great excuse to eat some of the great-tasting and satisfying foods high in zinc.

Iodine

Since the introduction of iodized salt in 1924, little notice has been given to this essential trace mineral. The incidence of endemic goiter, an iodine-deficiency disease, had dropped dramatically in this country. Infant formulas were supplemented with iodine beginning in the 1960s. Iodized oils have been introduced in countries where salt isn't commonly used. The RDA for iodine, set at 150 micrograms, is well below the 250 and 170 micrograms that American men and women, respectively, consume every day.

All was quiet on this salty front until the USDA was deciding whether foods containing soy proteins could make special health claims. Soy contains compounds that can prevent the body from using iodine, an integral part of thyroxin, a thyroid hormone that helps regulate your body's energy usage.

After careful consideration, the USDA observed that no link has been demonstrated between soy consumption and thyroid disorders, as long as sufficient quantities of iodine are included in the diet. Persons with low thyroid function or marginal iodine intake may want to consult a doctor, dietitian, or nutritionist.

Raw flaxseeds also contain a substance known to inhibit the use of iodine by the thyroid. Cooking inactivates these compounds, so baked goods containing flaxseeds are not a cause for concern. It is advised that no more than 3 tablespoons of raw flaxseeds be consumed each day.

The most secure way to address these health concerns is to make sure you are eating an iodine-rich diet. One-half teaspoon of iodized salt provides 200 micrograms of sodium, or 133 percent of the RDA. Sea vegetables have very high levels of iodine—and they are tasty, too. Kelp powder is widely available in natural foods markets. Gomaiso, a Japanese blend of seaweed and sesame seed, can be found in Asian markets.

Soy!

Everybody's talking about soy . . . with good reason. In October 2000, the USDA determined that consuming 25 to 30 grams of soy protein each day as part of a diet low in saturated fat and cholesterol may reduce the risk of heart disease. Clinical studies have shown that soy protein reduces total LDL cholesterol ("bad" cholesterol) levels. Intriguingly, researchers have found that in Asian countries, where soy foods have been a staple of the daily diet for centuries, incidences of heart disease, breast cancer, and unpleasant menopausal symptoms are significantly lower than in the United States. Soybeans contain some interesting phyto-chemicals (plant chemicals) called isoflavones. These molecules have structures similar to estrogen, a hormone produced by the ovaries, and may play a significant role in protecting women's health. Additional protection against disease is believed to be provided by isoflavones' antioxidant properties.

Soybeans contain 42 percent protein and eight essential amino acids. They also contain high concentrations of fiber and minerals. While the nutritional benefits of soy are clear, the disease-fighting mechanisms are not yet clearly understood. Research is underway on several fronts, including prostate cancer, breast cancer (where there is controversy about whether soy provides a benefit or a harm), diabetes, and kidney disease.

What is well understood is that soy is a tasty, healthful food available in a style to suit almost every taste. Here is an overview of soy products available. For recipes and details on how to prepare these products, see "Soy Foods" (page 241).

Edamame (ə-da-MA-may) is the name given to soybeans when they are eaten fresh. Similar in size to a butter bean, fresh soybeans have a crunch and sweet taste something like English peas. They have a very high protein content, so they do not have the grainy, starchy texture of lima beans. Sold shelled or in the pod, edamame should be briefly blanched (page 205), then refreshed in cold water before use. A good addition to salads and stir-fries, edamame can also be used much like English peas or fava beans—tossed into rice for a quick pilaf, strewn over a salad, or puréed. For edamame recipes, see pages 249–250.

Lecithin, extracted from soybean oil, is used as an emulsifier, that is, a substance that allows fats to be evenly distributed in foods. Lecithin extends the shelf life of many processed foods by helping them remain moist and preventing spoilage.

Miso, a fermented soybean paste, is a staple of Japanese cuisine. Made from soybeans, grain, or beans and sea salt, miso is inoculated with a mold, fermented, then aged for six months to three or more years. Unpasteurized miso contains natural digestive organisms, like *Lactobacillus*, the culture found in yogurt. There are three main varieties of miso: blond, red, and brown. Blond miso is made with rice, barley, or soybeans only and has a mild nutty flavor and moderate saltiness. Red miso is made with adzuki beans for a slight sweetness but sturdy flavor. Dark miso has been aged longer and has a sharper saltiness and full-bodied flavor.

Each tablespoon of miso has 35 calories and contains 2 grams of protein along with vitamin A, folate, niacin, and potassium. Use miso as you would bouillon cubes or mixed with water in place of homemade stock. Because miso contains live cultures, it should be added to dishes after cooking is finished. Lighter miso may be whisked into hummus or added to creamy sauce or salad dressings. Darker miso can be added to veggie burgers, stews, or hearty sauces.

All miso is very high in salt, so wait until after miso has been added to adjust the final seasonings in any recipe.

Natto, made from fermented cooked whole soybeans, is used in miso soup and sushi and as a topping for rice or vegetables. Sometimes compared to blue cheese in pungency, natto has a very strong flavor to which the Western palate is not accustomed. Natto has a nutritional profile similar to miso, but with a lower sodium content.

Okara is the pulp left after the initial processing stage of tofu or soymilk production. While it has less protein than whole soybeans, the protein is more digestible and of higher quality. Okara is high in fiber, with a slightly sweet flavor. It is used to make sandwich patties and is added to granola, cookies, or other baked goods. It is also used in soy sauce and as the basis for TVP, a trademarked brand of soy protein.

Soybean oil is extracted from whole soybeans. This widely used oil is low in saturated fat (15 percent) and high in unsaturated fat (61 percent polyunsaturated, 24 percent monounsaturated). As with all highly unsaturated oils, soybean oils are often hydrogenated to extend shelf life. Soybean oil's mild flavor makes it suitable for salad dressings or sautéing.

Soy cheese is made from soymilk and can be found in a variety of flavors.

Soy flour is a high-protein, low-gluten flour made from toasted soybeans. Available in de-fatted and full-fat versions, the full-fat type should be refrigerated to ensure the freshness of the oils. Soy flour may be substituted for up to 25 percent of wheat flour in most recipes without further adjustments. Because of its high fat content, full-fat soy flour will cause baked goods to brown more quickly.

Soy grits are made from soybeans that have been toasted and cracked into pieces. While normally not eaten by themselves, soy grits can be added to rice, grains, casseroles, and stews or substituted for flour in some recipes.

Soy yogurt is made from soy milk, live active cultures, evaporated cane juice, and flavorings with a small amount of thickener, usually tapioca or cornstarch. Soy yogurt is creamy and satisfying, though a bit thinner than cow's milk yogurt.

Soy isoflavones are isolated phytochemicals sold as dietary supplements. It is uncertain whether any benefit is derived from these compounds by themselves. Your best bet is to consume these powerful antioxidants in their natural state as a part of some other soy product.

Soymilk is made by grinding soybeans into a thick paste with water. Boiling water is added to the paste, the mixture is cooked, and the soymilk strained off. Much homemade soymilk (mine included) has a decidedly beany flavor. Commercial soymilks have overcome this and are produced in a wide range of flavors and richness. Most soymilk is fortified with vitamin D and calcium. Some soymilk is further fortified with isolated soy protein and thickened with carrageenan. There is even soymilk coffee creamer that won't curdle when it hits the hot coffee.

Soymilk can be found in aseptic packaging on a shelf in the health food section or in the dairy case. The producers of refrigerated soymilks have made an effort to replicate the flavor, consistency, and nutrition of cow's milk. Most brands of soymilk are good enough to drink cold, straight out of the carton—but make your mom happy and use a glass. Warming the soymilk, either in coffee, cocoa, or sauces, tends to underscore its beany beginnings.

Use soymilk as you would cow's milk. You can even curdle it with lemon juice for a reasonable substitute for buttermilk.

Powdered soymilk is available in whole-fat or low-fat versions. It is best used rehydrated in smoothies, puddings, or cooked dishes as it has a raw, beany flavor when consumed plain.

Soy nuts are a high-protein, low-fat snack made from whole soybeans that have been soaked and then baked or roasted. Soaking the soybeans makes the proteins more easily digestible. Soy nuts can be found plain in most bulk-foods departments or packaged in plain, smoked, or barbecue flavors.

Soy nut butter is made from crushed, roasted soy nuts blended with soy oil to produce a smooth peanut butter substitute.

Soy protein can include okara, the pulpy by-product of tofu or soymilk production, or simply be processed soy flour. Either coarse or fine, all formulations are high in protein and fiber. Also called TSP (texturized soy protein) or TVP (texturized vegetable protein), this meat substitute is easily rehydrated with boiling water and used in chilies, burgers, lentil loaf, or spaghetti sauce. Manufacturers are increasingly inventive with their formulations, which include tofu hot dogs, pepperoni, sliced tof-urkey, and sausage.

Soy protein concentrates are highly refined, containing about 70 percent protein (compared to 38 percent for soybeans). These were designed as a food additive and can be found in many packaged foods. The processing removes many of the isoflavones.

Soy protein isolates are a more refined product than concentrates, containing 90 percent protein in a very digestible form. A highly fractionated food, protein isolates have not been shown to have the same health benefits as eating whole soy foods.

Soy sauce, a liquid made from okara or fermented soybeans, is available in three main types: tamari (soy by-product of miso production), shoyu (soy sauce and wheat blend), and teriyaki (soy sauce plus sugar, vinegar, and spices).

Soy sprouts are packed with protein and vitamin C. They are fairly delicate and are best eaten raw or quickly sautéed.

Tempeh, originally from Indonesia, is a fermented soy food. The beans in tempeh are kept whole, giving it a substantial texture that can withstand most cooking methods. Use tempeh as you might portobello mushrooms. It is particularly good barbecued and served with rice and grilled vegetables. For tempeh recipes, see pages 251–252.

What do I do with tofu?

"But tofu doesn't have any flavor," is a familiar refrain. Of course, tofu has a flavor; it is just subtle. This is what makes it so versatile. You can use it in hearty entrées to show off intense spices or blend it with fresh fruit to make a tasty, nutritious smoothie. You can fashion it into meatballs, mix it with ground nuts for a reasonable cheese substitute, or enjoy it very simply, marinated with soy sauce, sesame oil, ginger, and garlic. (For recipes and details on how to prepare tofu, see pages 243–248.)

You will find tofu refrigerated in the produce section of the grocery store, or in aseptic packaging on the shelves of the health food section or the Asian food aisle. The refrigerated tofu has an expiration date. Once you get it home, remove it from its packaging and change the water. The tofu tastes fresher if the water is changed every day. (I realize that almost no one does this, but it really does help.)

Asian markets and health food stores often sell fresh tofu in bulk. This tofu is often made locally or at least close by. Make sure the tofu is immersed in clean water, not sitting out in the air. The tofu should have a clean, white appearance.

There are three basic types of tofu. Note that any tofu can be made firmer by pressing it for a few hours or overnight to remove some of the water (for instructions, see page 244).

Soft or silken: Silken tofu is soft, with a creamy texture that melts in the mouth. Use it for dressings, dips, shakes, puddings, and sauces. It substitutes for yogurt, sour cream, or milk. When used in baked goods, it helps keep them moist.

Regular or medium-soft: The all-around tofu, medium is used for fillings, cheesecakes, pies, and salads, or whenever you want a firm texture.

Firm: The sturdiest tofu, firm is used in soups, on the grill, marinated and roasted, in casseroles, and on sandwiches. It retains its shape through many cooking methods.

With the explosion in the soy foods industry, you can now find barbecued, jerked, fried, and other flavors of tofu in vacuum-sealed packages. Some of these are delicious; you'll have to discover your preferences by trial and error. Look for products that have been minimally processed and have the fewest possible chemical additives.

Does tofu grow on trees?

Tofu is made by soaking soybeans in water. Soaking the beans activates enzymes that begin to break down the proteins and carbohydrates, making the beans more digestible. The beans are then ground, cooked, and kneaded with water to extract the soymilk. The water extracts much of the protein, phytochemicals, and isoflavanoids, and some of the carbohydrates. The soymilk is boiled, and then curdled with salt or acid. Calcium and magnesium salts are most common. The delicate curds are gently placed in a large flat sieve, which allows the whey to drain. The curds are then pressed. The more the tofu is pressed, the denser it becomes. Some silken tofu is not pressed at all and has the consistency of yogurt. Firmer tofu is more caloric but more nutritious.

Some tofu manufacturers have begun to add soymilk powder to the whey. This process increases the nutrient level and improves shelf life. It does, however, impart a slightly off flavor detectable by tofu aficionados. Baked goods, salad dressings, and the like do not suffer from its addition, though.

The Skinny on Fat

While most of us need to reduce fat in our diets, it is important not to cut fat out completely. Fats serve many functions vital to our health. Sixty percent of our nervous systems, including our brains, are made of fats. Fat-soluble vitamins, white blood cells, and cell membranes rely on fat for proper functioning.

Our bodies can make most of the fats we need for all of these functions except for two: alpha-linolenic acid (Omega-3 fatty acid) and linoleic acid (Omega-6 fatty acid). Since we must get these two fats from our diets, they are called Essential Fatty Acids (EFAs). Omega-6 fatty acids are found in seeds and legumes, such as corn, peanuts, and soybeans. Omega-3 fatty acids are found in pumpkin seeds, walnuts, flaxseeds, and leafy vegetables.

So how much fat do you need every day? Chances are that you would consume sufficient fat if you never added any to the food you prepare. Most whole grains and beans contain fats of various types. Nuts and nut butters, soybeans and soy foods, sesame seeds and tahini, corn, and coconut are also sources of fat in our diets. Using the USDA standard of 30 percent of all calories from fat, a 2,000-calorie diet should include 600 calories from fat, or 67 grams. A low-fat diet that has only 10 percent of calories coming from fat would include only 200 calories from fat, or 22 grams.

Saturated, Unsaturated, Hydrogenated: A Chemistry Lesson

A little bit of chemistry can be helpful in understanding the differences in oils. All oils are fats. All fats are made of fatty acids, long chains of carbon and hydrogen atoms with an acidic group at one end, attached to a chemical backbone called glycerol. Simple fats, or triglycerides, are formed when three fatty acids combine with one glycerol molecule.

When the carbon atoms are full of hydrogen, the fat is called "saturated." When one or more of the carbon atoms has an extra bond to another carbon atom instead of a hydrogen atom, the fat is called "unsaturated." A fat with one carbon double bond is mono-unsaturated; with more than one, poly-unsaturated.

The saturated fats have long, straight chains that are easy to pack and are usually solid at room temperature. Palm kernel oil and cocoa butter are examples of naturally occurring highly saturated fats. Saturated fats raise blood cholesterol levels, one of the risk factors for heart disease. Saturated fats promote high levels of low-density lipoproteins, or LDLs. These compounds transport cholesterol to the arterial walls and body tissues. This is why LDLs are referred to as "bad" cholesterol.

Unsaturated fatty acids have bends in the carbon chains at the double bonds, which make them difficult to pack. These fats tend to be liquid at room temperature, so we call them oil. Unsaturated fats reduce the production of cholesterol and LDLs. Olive and canola oil are excellent sources of mono- and polyunsaturated fats.

Super-poly-unsaturated oils have the highest concentration of essential fatty acids. These oils are found refrigerated in opaque containers. They are very sensitive to heat and light and react with oxygen very quickly. Flaxseed, primrose, and borage oils are all excellent sources of EFAs.

While it is important to consume both Omega-3 and Omega-6 fatty acids, it is important that they be in the proper ratio. Primitive diets probably contained equal amounts of these essential fatty acids, but today we may consume ten times more Omega-6 than Omega-3. This is important, since these compounds compete in the body. High levels of alpha-linolenic (Omega-3) acid are thought to reduce the risk of heart disease. However, a high level of linoleic acid (Omega-6) relative to alpha-linolenic acid has been associated with increased incidence of cancer.

Most vegetable shortenings and margarines contain oils that have been hydrogenated, that is, the carbon-carbon double bonds are broken and hydrogen atoms are added. Hydrogenation of oils reduces their polyunsaturated nature and produces trans–fatty acids. Trans–fatty acids raise LDL levels and reduce HDL levels, much as saturated fats do. It is generally thought that these isomers, normally found in insignificant quantities in oils, have damaging effects on cell membrane integrity and immune function.

However, there are some solid vegetable shortenings with no hydrogenated fats. These products usually contain palm or coconut oil. (see glossary following) To make matters more confusing, some shortenings claim to have 0 grams of trans fat yet still contain hydrogenated oil. The catch here is that the level of trans-fatty acids is low and the amount per serving is considered negligible so the manufacturer can legally claim that there are no trans fat per serving. This does not mean that they're not there!

The best way to avoid trans–fatty acids is to eat a low-fat diet and minimally processed foods. Hydrogenated oils must be listed separately on the ingredients list of packaged foods. By law, ingredients are listed by weight, so the lower down the list of ingredients hydrogenated oil appears, the less the product contains. This will be of importance when you are shopping for margarine. Another good rule of thumb is that the harder the margarine, the more hydrogenated the oil.

Know Your Oils

Supermarket shelves are painted with a delicate palette of oils, from almost clear peanut oil to pale canola oil, straw-colored sunflower oil, sun-bright corn oil, and deep green olive oils. Fats and oils enrich and lubricate foods, make us feel full, and help control appetite.

Each oil has a distinct profile, but which oil you use and how are largely a matter of personal preference. The only exceptions are the oils meant for flavoring. Walnut, hazelnut, toasted sesame and extra virgin olive oils lose their fragrance and become slightly bitter when heated. Since these are significantly more expensive than oils meant for cooking, there should be little temptation to misuse them. Certain oils sold as dietary supplements, such as flaxseed oil, should never be heated. Try adding these to grain salads, salad dressings, and smoothies.

Canola oil is a light, pleasant-tasting oil derived from rapeseed, a member of the mustard family. The tangy mustard flavor, from erucic acid, was selectively bred out of the rapeseed plant to obtain the canola plant.

Canola was bred specifically to produce a favorable fatty acid profile: 6 percent saturated fat, 62 percent monounsaturated fat, and 32 percent polyunsaturated fat. Of these, 10 percent is alpha-linolenic (Omega-3), 24 percent is linoleic (Omega-6), and 60 percent is oleic (Omega-9).

Canola oil can be used at medium-high heat for sautéing, roasting, baking, and some stir-frying.

Coconut oil has a pleasant flavor and may be used for either cooking or baking. It is often used to give a rich mouth feel reminiscent of butter. While the fact that it is 87 percent saturated fat concerns some, others believe that the high lauric acid content and medium chain triglycerides have health benefits.

Corn oil is pressed from corn kernels and has medium weight, with 13 percent saturated, 24 percent monounsaturated, and 59 percent polyunsaturated fat, and a high concentration of Omega-6 fatty acid. Corn oil has a light taste and is excellent for frying.

Flaxseed oil has a high concentration of EFAs and a delicate nature. It is used as a dietary supplement. Find flaxseed oil in the grocery or health food store. Never heat flaxseed oil. Use it as a healthful addition to salad dressings, on popcorn, in cereal, in smoothies, or straight out of the bottle. This oil has a wheaty, slightly bitter flavor. Because it is highly polyunsaturated, it can become rancid and smell fishy. Use flaxseed oil within 2 months of opening.

Grapeseed oil is virtually tasteless, with 72 percent polyunsaturated fat and 68 percent linoleic acid (Omega-6). Its high vitamin E content protects it from oxidation and increases the shelf life. Its bland background makes it perfect for infusion with truffles or herbs. Grapeseed oil can be used over medium-high heat or in cold cuisine. Some manufacturers claim a smoke point as high as 425°, but experience says 350°. Grapeseed oil is more expensive than most general cooking oils.

Hazelnut oil is an excellent source of vitamin E. It has a delicate flavor that is destroyed by heating. Use it as a flavoring in salad dressings or drizzle it on cooked vegetables, grains, beans, or stews just before serving. It is rich in monounsaturated oils, and 1 tablespoon contains half of the RDA of vitamin E.

Olive oil is pressed from the fruit of the olive tree, which was a gift from the goddess Athena to the people of Athens and has been cultivated for 5,000 years. I am tempted to believe that there would be no civilization without olive oil and garlic.

This is an unreasonably biased view, but olive oil, high in monounsaturates, has been implicated in the good health of Mediterranean peoples.

Cold-pressed olive oil is produced without the benefit of steam or chemical solvents. As the name implies, simple physical force is used to press the oil from the olives.

Extra virgin olive oil is made from the first cold pressing of olives, which yields a deep green oil with a full, fruity flavor. Extra virgin olive oils should not be heated to high heat, since the delicate fragrance will be diminished. Try weaning yourself from bread with butter by combining extra virgin olive oil, sliced garlic, salt, and pepper as a dip for bread. Extra virgin oil is used like a nut oil, drizzled over raw or cooked vegetables, grains, beans, or stews just before serving.

Many countries require olive oils to carry the acid content on their labels since this is the way olive oils are distinguished. Acidity contributes a bitter flavor and hastens rancidity. Extra virgin olive oil may be no more than 1 percent acid.

Virgin olive oil is 1 to 3 percent acid and also comes from the first pressing of the olives. Virgin olive oils include a wide variation in color and flavor, from deep green and fruity to light yellow and mild.

Olive oil can mean a mixture of virgin oil and oil refined through steaming or chemically processing the olives.

Light olive oil has been filtered to produce an oil with a light fragrance.

Pomace oil is a low-grade oil produced by treating the seeds and pulp of olives after most of the oil has already been extracted, with steam or chemical solvents. It can have a slightly bitter, chemical taste.

Palm oil should not be confused with palm kernel oil. This is a pure white, neutral shortening with many uses. Palm oil is 50 percent saturated fat, 38 percent mono-unsaturated fat and 12 percent polyunsaturated, giving it a healthier profile than butter!

Palm kernel oil, sometimes used in the Caribbean for frying, rivals coconut oil in saturation. This strong-flavored fat has little to recommend it.

Peanut oil is versatile, with 17 percent saturated, 46 percent monounsaturated, and 32 percent polyunsaturated fats. It is excellent for high-heat frying or stir-frying. Its light flavor makes it adaptable for both cold and hot dishes. It is an excellent source of vitamin E.

Safflower oil would be the nutritional heavyweight, with its 75 percent polyunsaturates, but it lacks vitamin E. Safflower oil remains fluid when refrigerated, which makes it excellent for salad dressings. It can also take high heat without smoking, making it a good choice for frying.

Sesame oil, whether raw or toasted, is high in polyunsaturates. The raw oil is light in color, with a high smoke point, making it suitable for frying and most culinary applications. Nutty brown toasted sesame oil imparts a delightful flavor to Asian dishes, as well as dishes from other cuisines. Use it only for flavoring, adding it to hot dishes at the last minute. Never use toasted sesame oil for sautéing. It is also called "dark" or "Asian" sesame oil.

Sunflower oil is highly polyunsaturated and smokes at very low temperatures, making it suitable for low- to medium-temperature cooking and salad dressings. Sunflower oil is very high in vitamin E.

Vegetable oil, a term used on many labels, often means soy oil. Soy oil is high in polyunsaturates (38 percent), alpha-linolenic acid (Omega-3), and vitamin E. This is a good general cooking oil. It can stand medium-high heat but also has a light enough flavor for salad dressing.

Walnut oil is one of the best plant sources of EFAs, especially alpha-linolenic acid (Omega-3). Walnut oil may be added to salad dressings or drizzled over vegetables, grains, beans, or stews just before serving.

Blended oil is the name given by oil packaging companies to oils that are a combination of varieties. Oils are blended to improve their nutritional and cooking profiles. I prefer a blend of 75 percent canola and 25 percent virgin olive oil as my general cooking oil. Manufacturers will normally explain the advantages of each blend on the bottles. There are even blends of supplemental oils, with flaxseed oil mixed with pumpkin seed oil and others to produce a favorable blend of essential fatty acids.

Cocoa butter is a fat extracted from cocoa beans during the processing of chocolate. It is particularly useful in vegan baking to simulate the texture of butter. Cocoa butter is highly saturated and not recommended for general consumption.

Margarine was developed in the late 1800s as a butter substitute. While there are some brands of both stick and tub margarine made entirely of naturally occuring fats, most margarines contain hydrogenated or partially hydrogenated oil. Generally, the harder the fat, the more hydrogenated it is. Many margarines are fortified with vitamins, particularly A and D. Milk solids and whey are often added to improve the flavor profile of margarine; check the label carefully if you want to avoid these. For all the applications in this book, a softer, stick margarine will work well. Find a brand with oil listed before hydrogenated oil and few additives. Try replacing tub, whipped, and liquid margarines with olive oil, hummus, or white bean spread, or simply omit it from pancakes and waffles.

Shortening is fat which is solid at room temperature and can stand relatively high heats. Spectrum and Earth Balance both produce shortenings made entirely of naturally occurring fats. However, most shortening is made from highly hydrogenated oil. White and virtually flavorless, shortening does not have the water inherent in butter and added to margarine. When substituting, add 2 tablespoons of water along with 1 cup of shortening to replace 1 cup of margarine or butter.

Fat replacers, such as tofu, applesauce, or mashed banana, contribute a rich flavor and maintain moisture in low-fat baked goods. Your choice of fat replacer depends on the recipe.

How Sweet It Is: Choosing Sweeteners

Taste buds for sugar are located at the tip of the tongue. Perhaps this accounts for the primacy of sweetness in our cravings and the heated debates that spring up around our choices of sweeteners. Sucrose, a disaccharide composed of one glucose molecule and one fructose molecule bound together, is commonly referred to as sugar. White sugar is processed from either sugar cane—a large, bamboo-like plant grown in tropical climates—or sugar beets, a root vegetable that can be grown in a wider range of climates. Our bodies use various minerals and B vitamins to metabolize sugar. While some of these nutrients are found in the cane or beet, refining sugar removes these. In the refining process, char from animal bones may be used to filter out impurities from the sugar, so vegans generally try to avoid this form of sweetener.

Fortunately, a wide range of sweeteners is available, some with interesting flavors and more substantial nutrition than refined sugar.

Barley malt syrup is processed from fermented grain. It has an attractive nutritional profile of soluble complex carbohydrates, maltose, and small amounts of glucose and fructose.

Brown rice syrup has a mild, butterscotch flavor that is very pleasant in baked goods. The nutritional composition—soluble complex carbohydrates, maltose, and a small amount of glucose—is not believed to cause the swings in blood sugar associated with simple mono- and disaccharides. Brown rice syrup is made by fermenting rice to break down the starches, straining the liquid from this process, and boiling it to the desired consistency.

Brown sugar is a widely used name for many sugars that are not white. Much of the brown sugar sold commercially is refined white sugar with molasses sprayed on it to give it a deeper flavor and light tan color.

Concentrated fruit juice is higher in complex carbohydrates than refined sugar. White grape juice, while acidic, has a mild, tart flavor and can be used in recipes where leavening is not required. Other concentrated fruit juices make good bases for smoothies, sorbets, or seltzer drinks. Some fruit juices can be found dehydrated, in powdered form.

Confectioners' sugar is a finely ground refined sugar used to make frostings and for dusting baked goods. In the United States, the sugar is mixed with cornstarch to prevent clumping. In the United Kingdom, it is called "icing sugar" and has no cornstarch.

Date sugar is made from ground dates and is composed primarily of fructose. The flavor is deep and not suitable to all applications.

Demerara sugar is a raw sugar from Guyana that is light brown and has a mild taste.

Evaporated cane juice is made by dehydrating freshly pressed cane juice then milling the resulting crystals to provide a uniform product. This requires much less processing than traditional white sugar while retaining more of the essential vitamins and minerals. Turbinado, Demerara, and light tan sugar crystals are more refined than evaporated cane juice. Evaporated cane juice retains the vitamins and minerals found in cane juice.

Fructose, also called fruit sugar, is a monosaccharide. This simple sugar is more easily absorbed by the body than sucrose or glucose. Sometimes found refined in crystal form, fructose is sweeter than sugar, but loses some of its sweetening power when heated.

High fructose corn syrup (HFCS) is made by an enzymatic process that changes the glucose in regular corn syrup to fructose. It has become the sweetener of choice for most sodas, candy, and snack foods. Because fructose is a simple molecule, easily absorbed by the body, it is readily converted into fat when its carbohydrates are not used immediately for energy. There are many consumer advocate groups trying to ban HFCS from school lunch programs, cereals, and snacks. Some health food stores will not carry products made with it. Does yours?

Glucose is a monosaccharide that does not easily form crystals, making it especially useful in jams, preserves, baked goods, candies, and frozen desserts. Corn syrup is composed primarily of glucose. Light corn syrup has been refined and has a mild flavor. Dark corn syrup has added caramel flavor and coloring; its taste is stronger.

Honey, the product of our industrious apiary inhabitants, is not considered vegan. It is composed of roughly equal amounts of the simple sugars fructose and glucose.

Maltose, a disaccharide, is a natural product of the fermentation of grains, making it important to the brewing industry.

Mannitol is found naturally in small amounts in fruits. It is made by processing sucrose, glucose, or starch to make a sugar with good sweetening power and fewer calories. These sugars are not easily digestible and may cause stomach cramping or diarrhea. Mannitol is not generally sold for home use, though it is included in many processed foods, particularly reduced-calorie products.

Maple syrup is the boiled down sap of the maple tree. To make 1 gallon of maple syrup, 20 to 40 gallons of sap are needed. This pleasant-tasting, amber syrup is graded according to color and flavor intensity: AA is the lightest and mildest, A is a medium amber and fuller flavored, B is dark and hearty, and C is a deep brown-black with a molasses-like quality. Maple sugar is also available. Both maple syrup and maple sugar are significantly sweeter than refined white sugar.

Molasses is the liquid that remains when sugar crystals are extracted from cane juice. When sugar cane has been allowed to ripen in the sun, the juice is merely clarified and concentrated, producing unsulfured molasses. Unsulfured molasses is the mildest and most highly prized. Green or immature sugar cane requires treatment with sulfur fumes to extract the sugar. The juice is boiled once to remove sugar, then a second time. The molasses obtained from the first boil has a higher sugar content and is milder. Both forms of molasses are called sulfured. The molasses left after the third boiling of the syrup is called blackstrap molasses. This very dark, bitter syrup is used primarily for cattle feed and industrial uses, though it is sometimes recommended as a good source of iron, magnesium, or potassium. Blackstrap molasses can add interesting dimensions to hearty breads and desserts when used prudently.

Raw sugar is a name often applied to products inaccurately. Raw sugar is a by-product of sugar production. It is the residue left when both refined sugar and molasses have been removed from the sugar cane juice. Raw sugar can be full of bacteria and is not legally used or sold in the United States. The term "raw sugar," however, is often used to refer to any of the light tan to brown sugars on the market today.

Sorbitol, see Mannitol.

Substituting for Sugar

1 cup sugar equals:

1 cup Succanat

1$\frac{1}{3}$ cups brown rice syrup. When used in baking, reduce the total amount of liquid in the recipe by $\frac{1}{4}$ cup and increase the baking powder by $\frac{1}{4}$ teaspoon.

1$\frac{1}{2}$ cups barley malt syrup. When used in baking, reduce the total amount of liquid in the recipe by $\frac{1}{4}$ cup and increase the baking powder by $\frac{1}{4}$ teaspoon.

$\frac{2}{3}$ cup maple syrup. When used in baking, reduce the total amount of liquid in the recipe by $\frac{1}{4}$ cup and increase the baking powder by $\frac{1}{4}$ teaspoon.

1 cup date sugar. When used in baking, dissolve date sugar in the liquid called for in a recipe to ensure even distribution.

$\frac{2}{3}$ cup powdered fructose

$\frac{1}{2}$ cup blackstrap molasses and $\frac{1}{2}$ cup mild syrup such as brown rice or corn

1 cup turbinado, Demerara, or light brown sugar

$\frac{1}{2}$ cup corn syrup. When used in baking, reduce the total amount of liquid in the recipe by $\frac{1}{4}$ cup.

Stevia and concentrated fruit juice will vary widely in sweetening power, depending on the form you use. Follow the manufacturers' instructions or experiment before committing a recipe's outcome to the sweetener.

Stevia is called the sugar plant, because its leaves are 150 to 400 times sweeter than sugar and impart no calories to the foods to which they are added. Found as a plant, liquid extract, pure powder, and a powder mixed with extenders to give a profile closer to that of sugar, stevia is suitable for cold dishes and for adding to coffee or tea. It is not recommended for baking as it turns bitter on heating.

Succanat is the brand name for a popular sweetener made by mixing sugar and molasses back together after initial processing. The resulting brown granules mix very easily and have a full, mellow flavor, a sucrose content lower than that of refined sugar, and trace elements found in sugar cane.

Sugar is the common name for sucrose, a sugar both reviled and loved.

Turbinado sugar is a raw sugar that has been washed to remove the surface molasses, making it closer to refined white sugar. Turbinado sugar is light tan in color with a mild taste.

At Your Fingertips: The Efficient Vegan Kitchen

It's been a long day for everyone, and dinnertime is just around the corner. What will you eat? A well-stocked pantry, efficient equipment, and a little know-how can make preparing healthy vegan meals a snap and a pleasure. Here are some tips for setting up a kitchen that will work for you.

Preparing the Pantry

You'll want to have a rich assortment of ingredients on hand. I'm not suggesting that you buy everything on this list—you'd probably have to move to a bigger place—but buy enough to keep meals lively and you prepared.

Canned Goods	
Canned beans are essential for spontaneity at mealtimes. Canned tomatoes and tomato sauce can also make meals happen quickly.	Vegetable broth, low sodium
	Pasta sauces
	Tomato sauce
	Diced tomatoes
Chickpeas	Diced tomatoes with chilies
Kidney beans	Roasted red peppers
Vegetarian baked beans	Chipotle chilies
Refried beans, vegetarian	Coconut milk
Lentil soup	Artichoke hearts
	Hominy

Grains

Start with grains you know you like, and then get adventurous. Buying grains from the bulk section lets you test in small amounts.

Rice	Barley	Corn Grits
Millet	Bulgar	Wild rice
Quinoa	Polenta	

Oils

Choose one or two oils for cooking, then accumulate small bottles of oils for flavoring. (See pages 26–29 for descriptions of oils.)

Canola oil

Olive oil

Extra virgin olive oil

Walnut, flaxseed, or hazelnut oil

Hot chili oil

Toasted sesame oil

Dried Beans/Legumes

Make sure to have some quick-cooking beans like lentils and split peas. Look for smooth unblemished surfaces.

Lentils	Chickpeas
Black-eyed peas	Pinto beans
Black turtle beans	Split peas

Fruits/Juices/Teas

Applesauce

Canned fruit in juice

100 percent fruit concentrates

Green tea

Mint tea

Condiments

There's only so much room in the door shelves of the refrigerator, so buy in small quantities that you can use in a reasonable amount of time. Yeast, vinegar, and soy sauces do not require refrigeration.

Nutritional yeast	Raspberry vinegar
Ketchup	Red wine vinegar
Mustard	Tarragon white
Pickles	wine vinegar
Salsa	Soy sauce
Salsa verde	Mushroom soy
Barbecue sauce	sauce
Hot sauces	Garlic chili sauce
Balsamic vinegar	Red curry paste
Rice wine vinegar	Green curry paste
Apple Cider vinegar	

Noodles/Pasta

If you are new to Asian pasta, start with whole wheat or buckwheat ramen noodles. (See pages 196–197.)

Ramen

Rice noodles, broad and slender

Cellophane noodles

Penne

Orecchiete

Spaghetti

Angel hair

Fettucine

Couscous

Soy, Nut, and Grain Milks

Plain

Vanilla, coffee, chocolate, etc.

Coffee creamer

6-ounce "juice" boxes

Sea Vegetables

If you have a friend who uses seaweed regularly—or who has some sitting on a shelf—ask to borrow some to experiment. A little seaweed goes a long way. Asian markets generally have better prices on seaweed. Store seaweed in a cool, dry place away from direct sunlight.

Hijiki	Kombu	Kelp
Wakame	Dulse	

Nuts

Hazelnuts
Pumpkin seeds
Pine nuts
Pecans
Pistachios
Sunflower seeds
Sesame seeds
Almonds /almond butter
Peanuts/peanut butter
Cashews/cashew butter
Soy nuts/soy nut butter

Dried Fruits

Apricots	Raisins
Dates	Prunes
Cranberries	Sun-dried
Cherries	tomatoes

Spices

Buy spices you plan to use and store them in a cool, dry place— not above the stove, please. Spices have a limited shelf life, so don't ruin your best cooking efforts with ingredients well past their prime.

Baking Essentials

All-purpose flour	Cornmeal
Whole wheat	Cornstarch
pastry flour	Potato starch
Whole wheat flour	Tapioca starch
Wheat germ	Baking powder
Wheat bran	Baking soda
Soy flour	Cocoa
Oat bran	Chocolate
Egg Replacer	Gluten-free
	Baking Mix

Sweeteners

There are so many sweeteners! If possible, buy them in small quantities from the bulk section to see which you prefer. (For more on choosing sweeteners, see pages 29–32.)

Brown rice syrup	White sugar
Malted barley	Demerara
Blackstrap molasses	(turbinado) sugar
Succanat	Evaporated cane juice
Stevia	Maple syrup
Corn syrup	All-fruit preserves
Brown sugar	

Snacks

For the cost of one brand name package of microwave popcorn, you can buy two pounds of bulk popping corn and fifty brown paper lunch bags, which should keep you in popcorn for quite some time. Then you can toss the popcorn with a teaspoon of olive oil and sprinkle with nutritional yeast.

Pretzels	Flatbreads
Corn for popping	

Freezer	Refrigerator
Frozen foods can save your sanity on a busy day. Frozen fruits are convenient for making smoothies with intense flavors. While a steady diet of meat analogues would get tiresome, they are perfect for quick dinners.	*Be careful not to stuff the refrigerator so full that some precious vegetable gets lost in the hinterlands. Pre-cut vegetables either from the salad bar or the produce section can reduce preparation time dramatically, especially if you are not so adept with a knife.*

Vegetables	Veggie burgers	Fresh vegetables	Bread
Fruit	Veggie sausage	Fresh fruit	Rolls
Juice concentrates		Prepared vegetables	Fresh pasta
		Seitan	Soy foods

Asian Ingredients

A number of recipes in this book call for Asian ingredients that may be unfamiliar to you.

Black beans are dried, fermented black soybeans. They have a salty, pungent, slightly sweet and nutty flavor.

Black bean sauce is a spicy reddish brown sauce made with chilies, garlic, and black beans. It can be chunky with whole soybeans or puréed.

Chili oil is a light sesame oil infused with very hot, red chilies. Use it sparingly as a flavoring agent only, never for sautéing.

Chili paste with garlic is a spicy mix of soybeans, chilies, and garlic. A little bit goes a long way.

Coconut milk in this book always refers to the unsweetened kind used as a base for Thai curries. (Sweetened cream of coconut contains dairy products.) Look for brands with as few ingredients as possible. The coconut milk will separate in the can, so shake the can vigorously before opening.

Five spice powder is a mixture of fennel, star anise, cloves, cinnamon, and Szechuan peppercorns.

Fresh ginger has a unique flavor. Look for ginger with an unblemished, light tan skin. If the ginger is withered at the ends, it is old and will not give much flavor. Peel ginger with a standard vegetable peeler or scrape the peel off with a spoon. To slice ginger, cut crosswise to shorten the tough fibers. To sliver, cut the slices into matchsticks. To grate ginger, use a ginger grater or the finest side of a box grater. If you are grating a large quantity, clean the grater of the fibers periodically.

Hoisin sauce is made with soy beans, chilies, garlic, and spices to produce a thick, slightly sweet, slightly spicy sauce. Hoisin is nice to have around for spontaneous stir-frying.

Miso is a thick fermented soy bean paste used as a base for soup. See pages 20–21 for further information.

Mushroom soy sauce, also called dark or thick soy sauce, is Chinese soy sauce with molasses mixed in. It is used much like Kitchen Bouquet to add color and deepen flavors. Use sparingly—too much imparts a burnt flavor to the dish.

Rice wine vinegar has a mild flavor and is less sharp than cider or white vinegar.

Seitan is a concentrated form of wheat gluten often used as a meat substitute. Wheat flour is kneaded with water and rinsed repeatedly until most of the starch is washed out, leaving a ball of dough. The dough is then boiled in broth for at least forty minutes and sometimes a few hours, until it is tender. The spongy texture of seitan allows it to absorb the sauce used in its preparation.

Sesame oil in this book means toasted sesame oil, an amber oil with a nutty flavor used for seasoning, never for sautéing.

Soy sauce is a generic term for the dark, salty sauce central to Asian cuisine. Though we tend to think of Chinese and Japanese styles of soy sauce, Indonesia and Korea also make distinctive versions.

Shoyu is a Japanese soy sauce brewed with more wheat than Chinese soy sauce. It is less salty than Chinese soy sauce, with a hint of sweetness.

Tamari is a thick, Japanese soy sauce brewed with no wheat.

Wonton skins are small squares or circles of pasta. Sold fresh or frozen in packs of three dozen, wonton skins will keep well wrapped in the refrigerator several days after opening. If fresh, the extras can be wrapped tightly and frozen. Wonton skins make excellent ravioli without the fuss of making fresh pasta.

Equipment: The Right Stuff

No special gadgets are needed to prepare fabulous plant-based meals, but good equipment makes the job easier. A restaurant supply store or specialty kitchen shop will carry the less familiar utensils.

This is not a complete list, just a few items you may find particularly useful when making the recipes in this book. Plan on acquiring equipment as you acquire skills.

Knives: Most cooks can survive with just three good knives: a chef's knife, a paring knife, and a serrated slicer. The chef's knife should be large enough to handle big jobs like acorn squash, but small enough for everyday onion dicing. The paring knife should be able to handle delicate tasks like peeling a kiwi and small cutting tasks like dicing a shallot. The slicer should cut tomatoes and bread with equal ease.

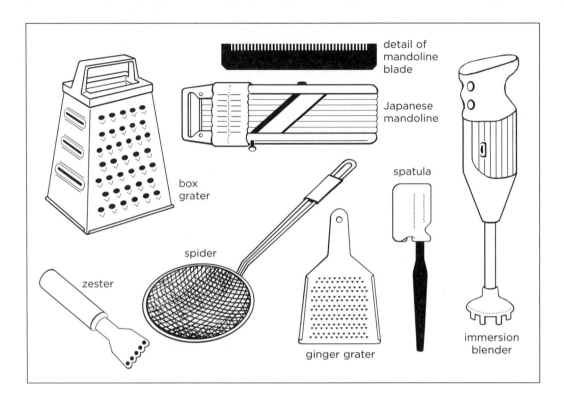

detail of mandoline blade

Japanese mandoline

box grater

spatula

spider

zester

ginger grater

immersion blender

Zester: These small devices quickly and efficiently remove only the zest, the colorful part of a citrus skin, leaving the bitter pith behind. They do have a sharp cutting surface and will dull if thrown into the jumble of a kitchen drawer.

Ginger grater: These small, hand-held graters have lots of little barbs that catch the ginger fibers but let the pulp and juice run free. They can be ceramic or steel.

Box grater: This old standby is quite versatile. One side can be used to grate nutmeg or lemon zest, another for slicing thin planks of vegetables, and the other two for coarse or fine grating.

Japanese mandoline: This is just for fun. Similar to a box grater, but more versatile, these vegetable "planers" come with three blades to make different size shreds. Long thin "noodles" can be cut from cucumbers, zucchini, or carrots.

Heat-resistant spatula: When this rubber utensil was first introduced, a colleague of mine threw one into the fryer at 375°. After 3 or 4 minutes, he removed it, rinsed it off, and indeed, it was a bit greasy but still like new. While I don't recommend this trial by fryer, these rubber spatulas will become an indispensable part of your kitchen arsenal. Heat-resistant spatulas, or "high heat scrapers," while not cheap, last for years—much longer than regular rubber spatulas—even with constant use. They are particularly helpful when reheating soups and stews, making sauces or puddings, or making thick soups or stews. More efficient than a spoon, these effectively scrape the bottom and edges of pots for more even cooking with fewer lumps and less burning.

Spring-loaded tongs: Most professional cooks cannot imagine life without tongs. It's an extension of the hand, turning foods on the grill or in the fryer, removing vegetables from boiling water, pulling pans out of the oven, and snapping emphatically at other cooks who may have gotten too rowdy. Tongs are available in different weights and lengths. Eight to ten inches is a good general length; twelve to sixteen inches is normal for use on the grill. Some models have a small ring around them that keeps them closed when they are in the drawer.

Spider: The original spiders were round sieves whose wires resembled a spider web. Whether round or square, these almost-flat strainers are perfect for removing tomatoes from boiling water, pears from their poaching liquid, or falafel from a fryer. Use a spider when tongs might bruise or break an item. A "skimmer" or "wok strainer" will also do the job.

Nonstick saucepan: A good nonstick skillet with a heavy-duty surface lets you use very little oil and prevents waste, since food can't adhere to the bottom of the pan. Nonstick surfaces should not be heated dry over high heat or they will degrade.

Cast-iron skillet: This pan retains an even heat longer and better than stainless steel or cast aluminum ones. Cast-iron can be heated dry at high heat, making it perfect for quick searing with very little oil. Once seasoned, the surface is almost nonstick as long as it is not scoured with abrasive scrub pads.

Soup pot/Dutch oven: A heavy bottom is essential for the long cooking times that soups and stews require. An eight-quart capacity is sufficient for most home purposes. It is important that you have enough room to stir the soup without its splashing. A Dutch oven can double as a casserole, allowing you to do all the prep work on the top of the stove, then cover it and slide it into the oven.

Immersion blender: This device looks a little bit like the workings of a milk shake machine encased in plastic and made portable. Use it to purée soups and sauces, or to make rice milk.

Food processor: No other appliance does a better job of processing tofu into its myriad incarnations. Tofu mayonnaise, puddings, and baked goods all benefit from the food processor. And of course it's also great for slicing, grating, and puréeing other ingredients.

Coffee grinder: Reserve one of these for grinding spices and grains. The most basic models are strong enough to process barley into flour, or most spices into powder. Peppercorns are better off in a peppermill.

Rice cooker: Everyone has some cooking task that defeats even the best effort. I can't make toast, even with a toaster. If making perfect rice is an insurmountable challenge for you, invest in a rice cooker. It miraculously produces perfect rice every time you follow the simple instructions. Rice cookers are also great for those with limited space on the stovetop.

Cutting Vegetables: A Little Know-how

Cutting vegetables into different shapes provides visual and textural interest. Here are some basic techniques used in preparing vegetables.

Dice: to cut into uniform cubes. A fine dice is $\frac{1}{4}$ inch; medium, $\frac{1}{3}$ to $\frac{1}{2}$ inch; and large, $\frac{1}{2}$ to 1 inch.

To dice an onion: Peel the onion and cut the root end off. Cut the onion in half from stem to root. Place each half flat on a cutting board. Securely holding the top of the onion, make several cuts parallel to the cutting board. Make similar cuts perpendicular to the cutting board to create a checked pattern on the onion. Holding the stem end, cut across the onion, making perfect little squares. Use this same basic technique when dicing other vegetables.

Chop: to cut in an irregular fashion. This is done when dicing would be a waste of effort. For example, chopping is used for large greens that will be cooked or soup ingredients that will be cooked and then puréed.

Mince: to chop in an irregular pattern until the pieces are very small. This technique is used when the pieces of food must be small enough to fit on a small space, such as vegetables on a soup spoon, or salsa ingredients on a chip.

Cut on a bias: to cut long vegetables diagonally. This cut is particularly good for zucchini, carrots, asparagus, celery, and peeled broccoli stems.

Matchstick: to cut into long, square pieces. Slice the vegetable evenly on the diagonal. Cut the slices into thin strips. This is a stylish alternative to shredding carrots.

Julienne: to cut into long strips. This cut is very similar to the matchstick but is more widely applied. For example, one can julienne green peppers without first cutting them on a diagonal.

Chiffonade: to cut leaves into thin, uniform shreds. This is the way iceberg lettuce is cut for tacos, to use a familiar example. Stack the leaves on top of each other, and then roll them up. Using a sharp knife, cut widthwise slices off the roll, no more than $\frac{1}{4}$ inch thick.

appetizers & snacks

Dips and Spreads

Tuscan White Bean Spread

Black Bean Dip

Refried Bean Dip

Curried Lentil Dip

Guacamole

Skordalia

Caponata

Baba Ganoush

Artichoke Dip

Pâtés and Terrines

Roasted Vegetable Terrine

Vegan Chopped Liver

Pancake-Like Appetizers

Tostones

Sweet Potato Falafel

Spinach and Mushroom Quesadillas

Panelle (Italian Chickpea Patties)

Spicy Corn Blini with Red Peppers and Shiitakes

Filled Appetizers

Phyllo Triangles with a Choice of Fillings

Vegan Chilies Rellenos

Fresh Spring Rolls

Bruschetta

Bruschetta with Sun-Dried Tomato Pesto and Portobello Mushrooms

I t's fine to whirl together some tofu and onion soup mix and serve it with potato chips as an appetizer or snack. But why not explore the world of possibilities for beginning a meal? Fancy restaurants serve a very small dish at the start of a meal called an amuse bouche, or amuse the mouth. This small bite whets the appetite for the feast to come. As you begin to choose your food more consciously, you will grow to treasure the little gems proffered before a main meal. In the Middle East, many small dishes, or mezze, are presented as gifts to guests, demonstrating the generosity of the host. Often these *are* the meal.

Once you remove meat from the center of the plate and allow yourself to conceive of an "entrée" as a vegetable-based creation, the whole notion of appetizer becomes fuzzy. You could serve most of these dishes in larger portions as the centerpiece of a meal, or you could conceive an entire meal around a number of small dishes—even moving from cuisine to cuisine, should you choose.

DIPS & SPREADS

Tuscan White Bean Spread

This recipe benefits from a very fruity olive oil. If fat content is not a concern, you may want to add an extra couple of tablespoons for a fuller flavor. I also like to add some raw garlic to this for a little extra bite. You may want to add a little of your favorite hot sauce, too.

For an easy but elegant appetizer, spread this on some good Italian bread and top with some roasted red peppers, fresh tomato slices, or grilled portobellos. Use fresh sage leaves as a garnish.

2 cups cooked white
    beans
    (Great Northern or
    cannellini)
1 teaspoon oil
2 small onions, thinly sliced
4 cloves garlic, thinly sliced
1 tablespoon lemon juice
2 tablespoons extra virgin
    olive oil
1 tablespoon chopped
    fresh sage
Sea salt

Purée the beans in a food processor. Put the oil in a saucepan over high heat. Add the onions and garlic, and stir constantly until the onions develop a light, golden brown color. To the puréed beans in the food processor, add the cooked onions and garlic, lemon juice, and olive oil. Purée all the ingredients. Add sage and sea salt to taste. Adjust the seasonings. Adjust the thickness with water.

Makes about 2 cups.

Black Bean Dip

Chipotles are dried, smoked jalapeños that add a hot, smoky dimension, complementing the deep, earthy flavors of the black beans. If you prefer a milder flavor, the recipe works well without them, too.

2   cups cooked black beans
1   teaspoon oil
1/4   teaspoon cumin seeds
1   small onion, diced
1   or 2 cloves garlic, minced
1/4   teaspoon chili powder
1/2   chipotle chili, canned or
     dried, or 1/4 teaspoon
     chipotle powder
2   tablespoons lime juice
2   tablespoons chopped
     fresh cilantro
Sea salt

Mash or purée the beans in a food processor. Heat the oil in a saucepan over medium heat. Add the cumin seeds, onion, and garlic, and cook until the onion just begins to soften. Add the chili powder and mix well. Cook just until the onion is soft. Add the mixture to the beans along with the chipotle, lime juice, and cilantro. For a smoother dip, purée the mixture. Add sea salt to taste and adjust the seasonings. Adjust the thickness with water.

Makes about 2 cups.

Refried Bean Dip

2   cups cooked pinto beans
2   teaspoons oil
4   cloves garlic, minced
1   medium onion, diced
1   jalapeño, fresh or
     canned, minced
1/2   teaspoon ground cumin
1/4   teaspoon ground
     coriander
1/2   teaspoon chili powder
1/2   medium red bell pepper,
     diced
1   medium green bell
     pepper, diced
1   tablespoon lemon juice

Mash the beans either in a food processor, with a potato masher, or with the back of a wooden spoon. Reserve. Heat the oil in a saucepan over medium-high heat. Sauté the garlic, onion, and fresh jalapeño just until the onion begins to soften. Add the cumin, coriander, and chili powder. Sauté until the spices are fragrant and the onion is soft. Add the peppers to the pan and stir until they are coated with the spices. When the peppers are hot, reduce the heat to low, add the beans to the pan, and mix well. Add the lemon juice and adjust the consistency with water. Cook until the beans are hot. Taste and adjust the seasonings. Serve warm or at room temperature.

Makes about 2 cups.

Curried Lentil Dip

2   teaspoons oil
1   small onion, diced
4   cloves garlic, minced
2   teaspoons grated fresh
    ginger
1   teaspoon curry powder
½   teaspoon ground cumin
¼   teaspoon ground
    coriander
⅛   teaspoon dried mustard
    or ¼ teaspoon crushed
    red pepper
⅛   teaspoon white pepper
2   cups cooked yellow
    or red lentils
2   tablespoons lemon juice
2   tablespoons tahini
Sea salt

Heat the oil in a saucepan over medium-high heat. Add the onion, garlic, and ginger. Cook just until the onion begins to soften. Add the spices and cook at least 3 minutes or until the spices begin to release their fragrance. Remove from heat. Add the lentils to the pan and mix thoroughly. If the lentils are cold, warm them slightly. Mash the lentils with a potato masher or pulse in a food processor until coarsely mashed. Stir in the lemon juice and tahini. Taste and season with sea salt.

Makes about 2½ cups.

Guacamole

There are endless variations on guacamole. I prefer the simple approach to allow the flavor of the avocado to shine through. However, some chopped fresh tomatoes do add a nice touch. If you want to stretch the guacamole, add some soy mayonnaise.

4   ripe avocados
2   tablespoons lemon juice
2   cloves garlic, minced
½   small onion or 4 green
    onions, thinly sliced
1   small jalapeño, fresh or
    canned, minced
1   tablespoon chopped
    fresh cilantro
Sea salt

Mash the avocados against the side of a small mixing bowl. Add the rest of the ingredients. Taste, add salt, and adjust the seasonings.

Makes about 2½ cups.

Skordalia

Garlic and potatoes—two of the most versatile foods—are combined to make a pungent sauce good with raw vegetables or toasted pita triangles. For those who enjoyed mashed potato sandwiches as a kid, it can also be used as a base for a sandwich, with some thinly sliced red onion and grilled vegetables.

2   cups mashed potatoes
1   tablespoon minced garlic
½   cup extra virgin olive oil
2   tablespoons white wine
    vinegar or lemon juice
Salt and pepper

Mix all the ingredients in a medium mixing bowl. Taste the mixture and adjust the seasonings with salt and pepper.

Makes 2½ cups.

Caponata

I wish more people loved eggplant as much as Sicilians do! Perhaps this recipe will help convert a few more. Although traditionally green olives are used, I prefer kalamatas. If you can't get good fresh tomatoes, use diced canned tomatoes.

1   pound eggplant, cut into
     1-inch cubes
4   to 6 teaspoons oil
2   stalks celery, cut on the
     diagonal into ½-inch pieces
1   medium onion, chopped
3   cloves garlic, chopped
½   cup red wine vinegar
1   tablespoon sugar
1½ cups seeded, diced tomatoes
1   tablespoon capers
2   tablespoons pitted,
     slivered kalamata olives
⅛   teaspoon freshly ground
     black pepper
1   tablespoon pine nuts,
     lightly toasted
2   tablespoons minced fresh
     parsley (optional)
1   tablespoon coarsely chopped
     fresh basil (optional)
Salt

Generously salt the eggplant cubes and place them in a colander. Allow the eggplant to drain for 30 minutes. The eggplant should have released a fair amount of light brown liquid. Rinse the eggplant briefly under cold water and pat dry.

Heat 2 teaspoons of the oil in a large sauté pan over medium-high heat. Add the celery, onion, and garlic and sauté until the onion is just softened. Remove the onions and celery from the pan and reserve in a large mixing bowl. Heat 2 more teaspoons of the oil in the pan over medium-high heat. Add the eggplant cubes in a single layer and cook until they are lightly browned, about 8 minutes. Cook the eggplant in batches if necessary. If you overcrowd the pan, the eggplant will not cook evenly. Add the eggplant to the bowl with the onions and celery.

Add the vinegar and sugar to the sauté pan, bring to a boil, and reduce the mixture by half. Pour the vinegar mixture over the eggplant mixture and toss until the vegetables are coated. Let the mixture cool slightly. When the mixture is still warm, add the remaining ingredients. Taste and adjust the seasoning with salt. Let the caponata stand for at least 30 minutes or overnight (refrigerate if letting stand more than 30 minutes). Serve chilled or at room temperature.

Makes 4 to 5 cups.

Baba Ganoush

A vegetarian classic, baba ganoush is a good vehicle for introducing the glorious eggplant into your diet. Serve this with warm pita triangles (for Whole Wheat Pita Bread, see page 271).

2   medium eggplants, about 3 pounds
Oil
¼ cup tahini
1   teaspoon minced garlic
2   tablespoons lemon juice
2   tablespoons extra virgin olive oil
1   tablespoon minced fresh parsley
Salt and pepper

Preheat the oven to 400°. Prick the skins of the eggplants with a fork. Lightly oil the eggplants and place them on a baking sheet. Roast the eggplants in the oven until they look withered and the flesh is soft, about 30 to 45 minutes. Remove the eggplants from the oven and let them cool.

When the eggplants are cool enough to handle, remove the pulp from the skins. Squeeze the pulp gently to remove excess water. Chop the pulp very fine. Combine with the remaining ingredients in a medium mixing bowl. Taste the mixture and adjust the seasonings with salt and pepper.

Makes 3 cups.

Artichoke Dip

This dip can be eaten cold or hot. You can easily extend it by adding ½ cup of cooked spinach or 8 ounces of chopped tofu.

½ cup sliced almonds
3   cloves garlic, minced
1   14-ounce can artichoke hearts, drained
1   small onion, diced
⅔ cup soy mayonnaise
2   tablespoons lemon juice
2   tablespoons snipped fresh dill
1   tablespoon minced fresh parsley
Pinch white pepper
Sea salt

In the bowl of a food processor, coarsely chop the almonds. Add the garlic and pulse a few more times until well blended. Gently squeeze any excess water from the artichoke hearts. Add the artichoke hearts to the almond mixture and pulse until coarsely chopped. Add the remaining ingredients and mix well. Taste and season with sea salt.

Alternatively, chop the almonds with a chef's knife. Gently squeeze any excess water from the artichoke hearts and chop them fine. In a mixing bowl, mix the almonds, artichoke hearts, and remaining ingredients. Taste and season with sea salt.

Makes about 2½ cups.

PÂTÉS AND TERRINES

Roasted Vegetable Terrine

Plan ahead to dazzle your guests with the jeweled layers of this special treat. The techniques used in this recipe are basic, but the result is stunning. The leeks provide a frame for the lines of color. Substitute seasonal vegetables as you like: asparagus, sorrel, sweet onions, or sugar snap peas in spring; eggplant, portobellos, or red peppers in summer; cauliflower, fennel, or celery root in fall. In winter, thin slices of sweet potatoes, white potatoes, rutabagas, and beets can be layered in a pan, seasoned as the terrine, baked slowly, and pressed to make a beautiful side dish.

2 or 3 medium leeks, green and white parts
2 teaspoons salt, divided
1 pound young green beans or asparagus, trimmed
2 medium zucchini
2 medium yellow squash
½ cup seasoned oil, approximately
½ pound shiitake mushrooms
Salt and pepper
¼ cup chopped garlic chives or green onions
¼ cup chopped fresh tarragon
1 cup roasted red peppers
Tomato-Tarragon Dressing (page 115) or Roasted Red Pepper Coulis (page 131)
Tarragon leaves or garlic chives for garnish

Preheat the oven to 375°. Trim any browned or dried leaves from the leeks. Cut the leeks into halves lengthwise, leaving the roots attached. Wash the leeks well under running water, being careful to remove any sand between the leaves.

Carefully put the leeks into a Dutch oven or a soup pot, curling the leeks around the edges. Add enough cold water to the pot to cover the leeks by 2 inches. Add 1 teaspoon of salt to the water. Bring the water to a boil over high heat. Reduce the heat to medium and simmer the leeks until tender, about 6 minutes. Drain the leeks and cool under gently running cold water. When the leeks are cool enough to handle, remove the root end and separate the leaves. Reserve.

In the same pot, bring two quarts of water with 1 teaspoon of salt to boil. Add the green beans or asparagus to the water and blanch them for 2 minutes. Using a slotted spoon or a pair of tongs, remove the beans or asparagus from the pot and cool under gently running cold water. Reserve.

Cut the zucchini and yellow squash lengthwise into ¾-inch strips. Brush the squash strips with seasoned oil. Lightly salt and pepper the squash as desired. Place in a single layer on either a baking sheet covered with parchment paper, a nonstick baking sheet, or a baking sheet sprayed with nonstick cooking spray. Roast the vegetables for 10 minutes. Carefully turn the vegetables and roast for 5 minutes longer or just until tender.

While the squash are roasting, remove the stems from the shiitakes. Brush any dirt from the mushrooms, but do not rinse the mushrooms with water. In a medium bowl, toss the mushroom caps with $\frac{1}{4}$ cup of seasoned oil and salt and pepper to taste. Place the mushroom caps, gill side up and in a single layer, on either a baking sheet covered with parchment paper, a nonstick baking sheet, or a baking sheet sprayed with nonstick cooking spray. Roast the mushrooms for 10 to 15 minutes or until they are tender. Drain in a colander placed over a bowl. (Save any liquid in the bowl for making stock, if you wish.) Reduce the oven temperature to 325°.

Oil a 9x5-inch loaf pan. Line with parchment paper or waxed paper. Using the longest leek leaves, lay them widthwise in the loaf pan, making sure to line the bottom of the pan evenly and leaving a 2-to-3-inch overhang on each side. You should have a single layer of leek leaves covering the width of the pan. Beginning in the middle of the pan, lay leek leaves lengthwise to cover the ends of the pan, leaving a 2-to-3-inch overhang. Repeat until you have two layers of leeks completely covering the ends. If you have extra, add another layer of leeks to the width of the pan.

Combine the garlic chives and tarragon in a small bowl. Sprinkle 1 tablespoon of the herb mixture over the leeks. Layer half of the shiitakes in the bottom of the loaf pan. Top with half the zucchini, then half the yellow squash, then half the red peppers. Sprinkle 1 tablespoon of the herb mixture over the red peppers. Layer on all of the green beans or asparagus. Sprinkle with 1 tablespoon of the herb mixture. Layer the remaining vegetables: peppers, yellow squash, zucchini, and shiitakes. Sprinkle the shiitakes with the remaining tablespoon of herb mixture. Fold the overhanging leeks over the terrine to cover.

Cover the terrine with parchment paper or waxed paper, then with aluminum foil. Place the loaf pan in a larger roasting pan. Place the pans in the oven and pour enough hot water into the bottom pan to come 1 to 2 inches up the sides of the loaf pan. Bake for 40 minutes. Remove from the oven and let cool, covered.

When the terrine is cool, keeping the covers on, place another loaf pan on top of it. Stack jam jars, cans, potatoes, or bricks in the top loaf pan to weight it. Place the terrine in a small baking dish to catch any liquid. Refrigerate, covered, for 12 hours or more. Liquid will accumulate on the top of the terrine. To prevent a mess in your refrigerator, keep the terrine in a baking dish to catch any overflow. Drain any liquid from the terrine as it accumulates.

Remove the foil and waxed paper. Invert the terrine onto a cutting board or flat platter to unmold it. Using a sharp knife, carefully cut the terrine into 8 slices. To serve, place 2 tablespoons of Tomato-Tarragon Vinaigrette or Roasted Red Pepper Coulis on each plate. Place the terrine in the center of the plate and garnish with whole tarragon leaves or garlic chives.

Makes 8 servings.

Vegan Chopped Liver

If you are concerned with fat content, reduce the oil to 1 teaspoon and omit the olive oil. Be careful not to over-process this dish. The slightly coarse texture is pleasing—better than that of the original chopped liver!

2   teaspoons oil
1   medium onion, sliced
2   cloves garlic, minced
1   cup sliced button mushrooms
½   teaspoon dried basil
⅛   teaspoon dried marjoram
½   teaspoon sea salt
¼   teaspoon white pepper
½   cup dry red wine
½   cup walnut pieces
2   cups green beans, cooked until just soft
¼   cup minced fresh parsley
8   ounces tofu
½   cup matzoh meal or breadcrumbs
2   tablespoons extra virgin olive oil, or 1 tablespoon flaxseed oil and 1 tablespoon extra virgin olive oil
1   tablespoon lemon juice

Heat the oil in a large sauté pan over high heat. When the oil begins to smoke, add the onion and garlic. Cook, stirring every minute or two, until the onion is a deep golden brown. Add the mushrooms, basil, marjoram, salt, and pepper. Cook until the mushrooms have released their liquid. Continue cooking until the mixture is dry. Add the wine to the hot pan and cook until the liquid is reduced by half. Add the walnuts and cook until the mixture is dry. Remove the pan from the heat.

Coarsely chop the green beans and parsley in a food processor. Add the mushroom mixture and process until well blended but still coarsely chopped. Crumble the tofu into the mixing bowl. Add the matzoh meal, olive oil, and lemon juice. Pulse until all the ingredients are well mixed and the texture is slightly coarse. Taste and adjust the seasonings.

Makes 4 cups.

PANCAKE-LIKE APPETIZERS

Tostones

If you are not accustomed to working with plantains, you should know that there are no bad plantains. (Okay, the moldy ones are probably too far gone.) When they are green and somewhat hard, they can be fried as tostones (fritters) or plantain chips, or baked and mashed like potatoes. Just about anything that you might want to do with a potato can be done with a plantain. When the skin turns to yellow-brown, they can be sautéed and served as a side dish that combines a fruity sweetness with the starchiness of a potato. When they are black, plantains make some marvelous desserts. Look for them in the produce section with Latin American items.

4 plantains, yellow-green and somewhat hard
Oil for frying
Sea salt
Chipotle Ketchup (page 121), Pico de Gallo (page 137), or prepared salsa

To peel the plantains, remove the top and bottom with a sharp paring knife. Cut long slits down the plantain just deep enough to go through the peel. You may prefer to cut the plantain into halves or thirds before trying to peel it.

Heat ½ inch of oil in a wide skillet over medium-high heat. (If you have a thermometer or are using a fryer, adjust to 350°.) Cut the plantains into 1-inch slices. Fry the plantains in a single layer, turning once, for about 2 to 3 minutes on each side. Remove the plantains to a paper towel and drain.

Flatten the plantain slices using the flat side of a meat mallet (what are you going to do with it now, anyway?) or a small, heavy pan. The flattened slices should be about ½ inch thick. If the plantains crumble when flattening, they are not cooked enough and should be refried, roasted, or microwaved until they become a little softer.

Return the slices to the skillet or fryer, and fry until golden brown and crispy. Season with sea salt. Reserve in a warm oven or serve immediately with Chipotle Ketchup, Pico de Gallo, or prepared salsa.

Makes 4 to 6 servings.

Sweet Potato Falafel

This is a quick and easy recipe using falafel mix, which you can find in the health food section of most grocery stores. The sweetness of the sweet potato begs for a hot, spicy foil, such as Chipotle Salsa, Harissa Dipping Sauce, or Meshwiya.

1 cup falafel mix
1 tablespoon chopped fresh cilantro
1 teaspoon ancho chili powder
½ teaspoon ground cumin
¼ teaspoon cayenne
1 teaspoon lemon juice
1 cup mashed sweet potatoes
Salt and pepper
2 tablespoons oil
Chipotle Salsa (page 137), Harissa Dipping Sauce (page 139), or Meshwiya (page 139)

Pour 1 cup of boiling water over the falafel mix in a medium bowl. Cover and let stand for 15 minutes or until all the water is absorbed and the ground chickpeas in the mix are relatively soft. Add the cilantro, chili powder, cumin, cayenne, and lemon juice to the falafel mix and mix well. Add the sweet potatoes. Taste the mixture and adjust seasonings with salt and pepper.

Heat 1 tablespoon of the oil in a wide, heavy skillet or nonstick pan over medium-high heat. Drop the falafel mix by heaping tablespoons into the pan. Flatten the falafel with a metal spatula to ensure even cooking. These are more delicate than regular falafel, so do not crowd them in the pan or they will be difficult to turn. Cook the patties on one side until golden brown, about 4 minutes. Turn the patties with a metal spatula and cook the other side for 3 more minutes. Repeat with remaining oil and falafel mixture. Season with salt and pepper. Serve immediately, reserve in a warm oven, or refrigerate and reheat later. Serve with Chipotle Salsa, Harissa Dipping Sauce, or Meshwiya.

Makes 24 patties.

Caponata (page 46), Tuscan White Bean Spread (page 43).

Tofu Boursin (page 154), Tofu Boursin Lavosh (page 154).

Sun-Dried Tomato and Lentil Burgers (page 155), Macaroni and Cheeze (page 193).

Next page, clockwise from top: Corn Chowder (page 81), Spicy Sweet Potato Soup (page 73), Vegetable Soup with Lemon and Dill (page 79).

Spinach and Mushroom Quesadillas

Quesadillas without queso? (That's Spanish for cheese.) While you can substitute vegan cheese for cow's milk cheese, why not try using one of the delicious bean dips given on pages 43–44 to hold the ingredients together inside the tortilla?

Quesadillas lend themselves to many variations—usually depending on what's left over in the fridge. Have fun with them! Served with a bowl of black bean soup, these can make a very hearty meal.

4   teaspoons oil
1   pound spinach, washed,
     brown or wilted leaves
     discarded
2   teaspoons minced garlic
Pinch salt
1   medium onion, sliced
     or diced
8 ounces mushrooms, sliced
1/2 cup plus 1 tablespoon
     Black Bean Dip
     (page 44)
     or refried beans
6 10-inch flour tortillas
     (choose those made
     without lard)
Pico de Gallo (page 137),
     or prepared red or
     green salsa

Heat 1 teaspoon of the oil in a wide (11 or 12 inch), heavy skillet over medium-high heat. Add spinach and 1 teaspoon of the garlic. Season with a pinch of salt. Cook until the spinach wilts. Remove the spinach to a colander and reserve.

Heat another teaspoon of oil in the pan, and add the remaining 1 teaspoon of garlic, onion, mushrooms, and salt. Sauté the vegetables until the mushrooms release their liquid, and then cook the mixture until it is dry.

Squeeze the spinach dry and combine with the mushroom mixture. Sauté for another minute to ensure that the mixture is dry. Place the vegetable mixture in the colander.

Wipe the skillet clean and heat 1 teaspoon of oil until it is quite hot. Soften each tortilla by heating it in the skillet for about 10 to 15 seconds on each side. Remove the skillet from the heat while you assemble the quesadillas.

Spread 1½ tablespoons of Black Bean Dip or refried beans on each tortilla. Place ⅙ of the vegetable mixture on half of the tortilla. Fold the tortilla in half so you have a half moon shape. Repeat until all the tortillas are filled.

Return the skillet to high heat. Heat 1 teaspoon of oil in the skillet. Lightly brown each quesadilla on both sides. Reserve in a warm oven or cut each quesadilla into 3 wedges and serve immediately with Pico de Gallo or prepared green or red salsa.

Makes 6 servings.

Panelle (Italian Chickpea Patties)

1 cup chickpea flour (also called gram flour)
½ teaspoon salt
2 tablespoons chopped fresh parsley
Oil for frying
Salsa Cruda (page 138), Caponata (page 46), Roasted Red Pepper Coulis (page 131), or Aioli (page 120)

In a medium saucepan, whisk 3 cups of cold water into the chickpea flour and salt, making sure that no lumps form. Place the pan over medium-high heat and bring the mixture to a boil, stirring constantly. Reduce the heat to medium-low and continue cooking the mixture until it pulls away from the sides of the pan, about 30 minutes. Stir in the parsley.

Spread the mixture in a greased jellyroll pan so you have an even layer about ½ to ¾ inch thick. This will not fill the entire pan. Allow the mixture to cool completely. Cut into 8 squares and then cut each square into 2 triangles.

Heat the oil in a wide saucepan. You can use a minimum of oil or ½ inch of oil. The more oil you use, the crisper the panelle will be. Over medium-high heat, fry the panelle in a single layer until they are golden brown. Drain on paper towels. Repeat until all the panelle are fried. Serve immediately or reserve in a warm oven. Serve with Salsa Cruda, Caponata, Roasted Red Pepper Coulis, or Aioli.

Makes 5 servings.

Spicy Corn Blini with Red Peppers and Shiitakes

The heat in the blini is balanced by the sweetness of the red peppers. You could serve these little pancakes with Sweet Onion Caviar (page 229).

½ cup fine cornmeal
½ cup flour
2 teaspoons baking powder
¼ teaspoon baking soda
¼ teaspoon ancho chili powder
⅛ teaspoon cayenne
Pinch ground cumin
¼ teaspoon sea salt
¼ cup corn, fresh or frozen (not canned)
1 tablespoon oil
½ cup soymilk
1¼ teaspoons rice wine vinegar or cider vinegar
1 tablespoon chopped fresh parsley
2 tablespoons sliced green onions
4 ounces shiitake mushrooms
1 large red pepper, washed, seeds and pith removed
1 teaspoon minced garlic
1 tablespoon julienned fresh basil

Sift the cornmeal, flour, baking powder, baking soda, chili powder, cayenne, cumin, and salt together in a medium bowl. Coarsely chop the corn with a knife or in a food processor. In a small bowl, beat together the corn, oil, soymilk, vinegar, and 2 tablespoons of water. Combine the wet and dry ingredients and mix well. Stir in the parsley and green onions.

Choose a skillet that is good for making pancakes. Heat the skillet over medium heat and add ½ teaspoon of oil. Tilt the skillet to evenly distribute the oil. Drop the blini batter by scant tablespoons into the hot skillet. Cook the blini until small bubbles appear around the outer edge on the top, about 1 to 2 minutes. Flip the blini and cook on the other side until the blini has puffed up and the second side is golden brown, about 1 minute. Remove the blini from the pan and reserve on a platter. Cover with a clean kitchen towel if you will use immediately, or reheat later in a warm oven.

Slice the shiitakes as thinly as you can. Cut the red pepper into very thin strips. Heat another teaspoon of oil in the skillet. Add the garlic and shiitakes. Sauté the mixture until the mushrooms begin to release their liquid, about 4 minutes. Add the peppers to the pan and cook until the mixture is mostly dry. Do not overcook or the peppers will begin to fall apart. Stir in the basil.

To serve, place a small amount of the mushroom mixture on top of each warm blini. Serve immediately.

Makes 18 to 24 blini.

FILLED APPETIZERS

Phyllo Triangles with a Choice of Fillings

Greek cuisine is a natural source for vegan dishes because during the Lenten season, the eating of animal products is prohibited. The following recipe includes two filling variations. The basic technique of making triangles can be used for any reasonably dry filling. A soggy filling will result in flimsy phyllo.

1 **pound phyllo leaves**
About 1 cup fruity
   olive oil
Spiced Seitan Filling,
   or Artichoke and
   Spinach Filling
   (recipes follow)

Thaw the phyllo for 8 hours or more in the refrigerator.

Preheat the oven to 375°. Clean your work surface and dry thoroughly. Any residual moisture will make the phyllo stick. Pour the oil into a bowl and have handy a 2-inch pastry brush. Have the baking sheet(s) at hand. You will need to work quickly so the phyllo does not dry out and become brittle.

Unroll or unfold the phyllo leaves. Carefully remove one sheet and place it on the work surface. Cover the remaining phyllo with plastic wrap. (Some books recommend a damp kitchen towel, but this can make the leaves soggy and the towel tends to dry out in the course of making the triangles.) Brush the phyllo lightly with oil. You do not want to soak the phyllo. It is not necessary that every inch of phyllo be covered. Cover the first sheet with a second and brush it with oil.

Cut the phyllo leaves into thirds lengthwise. Put 1 teaspoon of filling 1 inch from the end of the strip. Lift one corner near the filling and fold it over the filling so that the other corner has come to a point. Continue folding the pastry over, flag-style, keeping the edges even. You should now have a cute little triangle.

Place the triangles seam-side down on an ungreased baking sheet. Brush the tops lightly with oil. Place the triangles about 1 inch apart (in case they split while cooking). Bake the triangles for 20 minutes or until they are golden brown.

Makes 36 triangles.

Spiced Seitan Filling

1 pound prepared seitan
1 teaspoon oil
1 minced shallot
¼ cup red wine
½ cup currants or coarsely chopped raisins
½ teaspoon ground cinnamon
¼ teaspoon ground nutmeg
Pinch of black pepper
Sea salt to taste
1 teaspoon cornstarch dissolved in 1 tablespoon water
2 tablespoons pine nuts

Coarsely chop the seitan. Heat the oil in a saucepan over medium heat. Add the shallot and cook for 1 to 2 minutes or just until it begins to soften. Add the seitan and warm through. Add the wine, currants, and spices. Cook until the liquid is reduced by half. Add the cornstarch and cook until thickened. Stir in the pine nuts. Cool.

Makes enough for 36 triangles.

Artichoke and Spinach Filling

1 pound fresh spinach or 1 10-ounce package frozen spinach
1 teaspoon oil
1 medium red onion, diced
2 teaspoons minced garlic
1 cup canned artichoke hearts, well-drained and coarsely chopped
Zest of 1 lemon
2 tablespoons chopped fresh dill
½ to 1 cup breadcrumbs
Sea salt and pepper

If you are using frozen spinach, thaw it completely. Squeeze as much water out of it as you can with your hands. Put it into a clean, sturdy kitchen towel (not terry cloth) and twist it until all the water has come out.

Heat the oil in a skillet over medium heat. Add the onion and the garlic. Sauté the mixture for 3 or 4 minutes or until the onion begins to soften. Add the spinach and cook just until it is wilted. Remove from the heat. Drain any liquid that has accumulated in the pan. Add the artichoke hearts, lemon zest, dill, and breadcrumbs, using only ½ cup of breadcrumbs to start. If the mixture still seems wet, add more breadcrumbs. Taste the mixture and season with salt and pepper.

Makes enough for 36 triangles.

Vegan Chilies Rellenos

This is a low-fat version of a perennial favorite. For a more traditional version, you can stuff the peppers with vegan cheese, dredge them in flour, then soymilk, then flour, and fry them in oil.

18 jalapeño peppers or
     6 poblano peppers
½ cup slivered almonds
1 teaspoon minced garlic
1 tablespoon nutritional
     yeast
¾ cup mashed potatoes
Salt and pepper
Oil
Mild Tomato Sauce
     (page 185), Pico de Gallo
     (page 137),or prepared
     salsa

Preheat the oven to 350°. Cut a slit down the side of each pepper. Cook the peppers in a pot of boiling salted water for 3 to 6 minutes or just until they are tender. Drain and cool under gently running water. Cut a slit down the length of each pepper. Wearing gloves, cut or scrape the seeds and pith from the peppers.

Grind the almonds in a food processor or spice mill, or cut them very fine with a knife. Mix the garlic, yeast, and potatoes with the almonds. Season with salt and pepper.

Fill each pepper with the mixture. Place the peppers in an oiled glass baking dish. Brush the tops of the peppers lightly with oil. Bake the peppers for 25 minutes or until the filling is bubbly. Serve with Mild Tomato Sauce, Pico de Gallo, or prepared salsa.

Makes 6 servings.

Fresh Spring Rolls

If you know how to roll a burrito, you can make spring rolls. This version uses a delicate rice paper wrapper which can be served fresh or fried.

Unless you really like working with your knife, a Japanese mandoline or food processor with a variety of discs comes in handy here. You can use a good box grater if you are careful.

1   ounce mung bean
    threads (glass noodles)
1   teaspoon sesame oil
2   ounces shiitake
    mushrooms
    (about 4 medium)
1   teaspoon canola oil
1   teaspoon minced garlic
1   teaspoon grated fresh
    ginger
4   ounces inari, or dried or
    smoked tofu
3   green onions, thinly
    sliced
2   small carrots, shredded
    into long threads
2   tablespoons chopped
    Thai basil, or 1
    tablespoon chopped
    sweet basil and 1
    tablespoon chopped mint
1   tablespoon toasted
    sesame seeds
12 rice papers, 6 to 8
    inches in diameter or
    square
Simple Soy Dipping Sauce
    (page 138), Sweet and
    Sour Dipping Sauce
    (page 138), or
    Vietnamese Lime
    Dipping Sauce (page 139)

Put the bean threads into a small bowl. Cover with 3 cups of boiling water. Cover the bowl and let the noodles stand for about 15 minutes. Drain the noodles in a colander and rinse under gently running cold water. Dry the bowl. Return the noodles to the bowl and season with the sesame oil.

Remove the stems from the shiitakes. Slice the mushroom caps as thinly as possible. Heat the canola oil in a skillet over medium heat. Add the mushrooms, garlic, and ginger and sauté for 3 minutes. Cut the block of tofu so it is half as thick. Cut each piece into long, thin strips. Add the tofu to the shiitakes and cook for 1 minute more. Do not worry if the tofu breaks up a little. Remove from the heat. Add the green onions, carrots, basil, and sesame seeds to the mushroom mixture. Reserve.

Fill a large wide bowl with cold water. Dip 2 or 3 rice papers in the water for an instant. Lay the rice papers on your work surface. When they are pliable, place a line of the noodles in the lower third of the paper within an inch of the edge. Top the noodles with some of the mushroom mixture. Fold the bottom third of the paper over the filling and roll just enough to enclose the filling. Fold the two sides in over the bottom of the rice paper. Roll up the rice paper to form a tight cylinder. Moisten the last flap of the rice paper with water to seal the spring roll. Remove the finished rolls to a platter and cover with plastic wrap to keep them moist while you finish making the other spring rolls. Should the rice paper become brittle while working with it, brush it with some cold water and wait a minute for it to become pliable again. Serve with dipping sauce.

Makes 12 spring rolls.

Fried Spring Rolls: For each spring roll, use 2 wrapping papers instead of 1 (use a total of 24 wrapping papers). Fry in oil at 375° until golden.

BRUSCHETTA

Bruschetta with Sun-Dried Tomato Pesto and Portobello Mushrooms

1   loaf good Italian-style
     bread
1 or 2 cloves garlic, peeled
2   tablespoons olive oil,
     preferably a fruity
     extra virgin
1   5-inch portobello cap or
     2 3-inch portobello caps
Olive oil
Salt and pepper
2   tablespoons Sun-Dried
     Tomato Pesto (page 128)
12   basil leaves for garnish
     (optional)

Cut the bread at a 45° angle to make slices about ¾ inch thick. Cut 12 slices and reserve the rest of the bread. Slice one garlic clove in half lengthwise. Rub the garlic on the bread. Using your fingers or a pastry brush, rub a little olive oil on the bread also.

Heat a large flat-bottom sauté pan over medium-high heat. Lightly spray pan with nonstick cooking spray or coat with olive oil. Drain any excess oil from the pan. Place the bruschetta in the pan, putting in only as many as fit comfortably. Brown the bruschetta, first on the garlic side, then on the other. Repeat as necessary. (You can also toast the bread under a broiler, watching carefully. But preparing the bruschetta on the stovetop ensures a soft, creamy inside and thin crisp crust.) Reserve.

Brush the top of the portobellos lightly with olive oil. Very lightly brush the gills (or underside) of the mushrooms. Salt and pepper the mushrooms. In a sauté pan over medium-high heat, place the mushrooms, top down, in the pan. Occasionally shake the pan to ensure that the mushrooms aren't burning. Allow the mushrooms to cook until water begins to collect in the gills. Turn and cook for 1 minute longer. Alternatively, broil or roast the seasoned mushrooms until they are cooked through. Remove from pan and place on a plate. When the mushrooms are cool enough to handle, cut into 12 very thin strips.

Spread ½ teaspoon of the pesto over the garlic side of the bruschetta. Lay a strip of portobello on each bruschetta. If possible, twist the strip. Not only will this give you a convenient place to anchor a basil leaf garnish, but it will also add visual interest to your presentation. Arrange attractively on a platter and serve.

Makes 12 bruschetta.

soups

Stocks

Vegetable Stock
Roasted Vegetable Stock
Green Vegetable Stock
Mushroom Stock
Asian Broth
Japanese Seaweed Broth (Kombu Dashi)

Hot Soups

Microwave Miso Soup for One
Miso Soup
Hot and Sour Soup with Glass Noodles
Thai Vegan Tom Yum Gong
Spicy Sweet Potato Soup
Onion Soup
Caldo Verde (Portuguese Green Soup)
Harvest Vegetable Soup
Chunky Polish Borscht
Potato Soup: Four Variations
Grilled Eggplant and Roasted Red
Pepper Soup

Vegetable Soup with Lemon and Dill
Four Mushroom and Barley Soup
Corn Chowder
Jary (Algerian Vegetable Soup)
Black Bean Soup
Tuscan White Bean Soup
Tomato, Fennel, and White Bean Soup
Curried Yellow Split Pea Soup
Lentil and Spinach Soup
Escarole and White Bean Soup

Chilled Soups

Two Melon Soup with Plum Wine
Blueberry and Red Wine Soup
Strawberry Soup with Almond Milk
Korean Seaweed Soup
Avocado Soup
Chilled Spring Pea Soup with Tarragon
Gazpacho: Two Variations
Chilled Beet and Cucumber Soup

Soup is the ultimate comfort food. It evokes childhood memories of steaming bowls meant to soothe and heal. As adults, we continue to nourish our bodies and spirits with soup. Thick, thin, simple, complex—soup is an emotionally and gastronomically satisfying experience.

Soup making is one of the more contemplative culinary tasks. It requires the use of all the senses in making subtle judgments about balancing flavors and textures. Since ingredients do vary—an April onion is not like a September onion—we are called on to adjust the sweet, salty, sour, and bitter tastes until we have a potion that satisfies the taste buds, nourishes the body, and comforts the spirit.

Think of the recipes in this chapter as guidelines, as jumping-off points for your own resourcefulness and creativity. The following section explains some of the techniques involved in soup making.

Selecting a stock: Stocks provide a nuanced backdrop for the featured ingredients in soup, so the stock you use for a soup must complement the soup's main components. For instance, a roasted vegetable stock would overpower the delicacy of spring peas, and a light green stock would be lost in a spicy sweet potato soup. Soups that don't require stock usually require more vegetables in the soup itself.

Preparing mirepoix: The heart and soul of many soups and sauces, mirepoix (pronounced mere pwah) is a combination of carrots, onions, and celery, all finely diced and sautéed in oil, perhaps with a few herbs added. If you don't know what kind of soup you want to make, just begin by cutting some mirepoix and generally an inspiration will hit before you are done.

Puréeing soup: Process soup in a food processor in batches until it is smooth. In some cases it's best to first strain the stock from the solids, purée the solids by pulsing until they are coarsely chopped, and then add some of the stock back to the mixture until the desired texture is reached.

For chunky soups, strain the stock from the solids, use a potato masher to reduce the solids to pulp, and then combine the stock and solids.

Immersion blenders also work well for puréeing soup. However, take care when blending soups with fibrous vegetables, such as Chilled Spring Pea Soup with Tarragon (page 91), to make sure the blades are not bound by fibers wrapped around the armature.

Making creamy soups with no cream: There are many ways to thicken soup. Most of them not only improve the texture of a soup but also add some nutritional kick. Mashed potatoes and puréed white beans both give you a creamy consistency. Barley is an excellent thickener. Rice can also be overcooked then mashed or puréed and added to soup, though the consistency can be a bit grainy. Roux, that classic mixture of fat and flour, will work for soups whose acidity isn't too high, such as Corn Chowder (page 81). Browning the flour in the fat gives a rich, deep flavor to the soup. The rule of thumb for roux is 1 tablespoon of oil and 1 tablespoon of flour to 1 cup of stock, soymilk, or water. This quantity will be sufficient to thicken a soup, although it will take some time. If you are in a hurry, use 2 tablespoons of flour and 2 tablespoons of oil to 1 cup of stock, soymilk, or water.

Puréed tofu can also be added to soups to give a creamy richness and a protein and calcium boost.

Cutting vegetables: If a soup is going to be puréed, cutting the vegetables into small pieces will speed up the cooking and make puréeing easier. For chunky soups, keep in mind the size of the bowls and spoons that you will be using. It can be awkward to encounter something in your soup bowl that is larger than your soup spoon. If you are using flat, wide soup bowls, small vegetables sink to the bottom and their visual effect is lost. Larger chunks of vegetables rise from the soup like an iceberg, promising more underneath. A variety of shapes and textures improves the soup-eating experience through heightened visual appeal.

Flavoring with miso, bouillon powder, and Spike: If you are not able to make stock, these provide a reasonable substitute. All of these are salty and most of them contain some form of nutritional yeast. Try to find the "no salt added" kind. (Besides, you can always add salt, which is much cheaper than these packaged powders.) Bouillon powder and Spike also contain dehydrated vegetables. Some bouillon powders may contain animal fat or MSG, so as always, read the labels carefully.

Miso is your best bet for a fast soup stock. The darker the miso, the saltier it is— and with as much as 630 milligrams of sodium in 1 tablespoon, it is salty. (Use a lighter miso if you are concerned with your salt intake.) Despite the salt, miso provides good amounts of protein, calcium, phosphorus, magnesium, and potassium. Depending on the soup, use anywhere from 1 tablespoon to 1/4 cup of miso per quart of water. See pages 20–21 for more information on miso.

If you don't care to use any of the above, try using tomato juice or the water from cooking vegetables or beans, or just doubling the amount of mirepoix in the soup.

STOCKS

Restaurants use the ends, scraps, and peelings of vegetables for stock. It would be wasteful to throw them away. The various combinations of vegetable trimmings that are used give the stocks different characters. Where will you get these myriad vegetable scraps? From your freezer! Keep a large, airtight plastic bag or container in your freezer and add vegetable scraps as they accumulate. Zucchini trimmings, the woody ends of asparagus or lemongrass, carrot ends, basil stems, fennel stalks, mushroom stems, celery hearts, and cucumber ends can all find new life as soup stock.

If you are buying organic produce, then the peelings of carrots, cucumbers, and potatoes may be used also. There are a few things you may not want to use: onion skins will turn the stock a dark brown color; seeds and pith (the white part) from peppers will turn bitter in stock, as will tomato seeds; the waxy coating of rutabagas and turnips is unpleasant; cabbage and broccoli can overpower the stock if allowed to boil for too long.

Use your judgment. If you would never want to see that many carrots on your plate, don't put them in your stock. The combination of vegetables should be one you like.

Leaving the stock unsalted allows you to use it for many different recipes. It can be used as a base for miso soup; reduced, flavored, and thickened for a sauce; or used to cook lentils or split peas.

If you are making the stock for a specific recipe, add a small amount of the herbs in the soup recipe to the stock. Don't overdo it, though. The long simmering time of the stock will give the flavors plenty of time to develop.

Patience is essential for successful stocks. Do not rush the process. Most of the recipes here take at least an hour to simmer. If the broth tastes weak, let it simmer longer. Your perseverance will be amply rewarded by richer, fuller flavors.

Vegetable Stock

3   medium onions, peeled and cut into quarters
8   whole cloves (optional; do not substitute ground cloves)
10 cloves garlic, smashed
4   celery stalks, cut into 2-inch pieces, or the heart of 1 bunch celery, cut into 2-inch pieces
4   carrots, cut into halves lengthwise, then into 2-inch pieces
2   to 4 cups reserved vegetable trimmings
2   bay leaves
4   sprigs fresh thyme (optional)
4   black peppercorns

Stick the cloves into the onions. Place all ingredients in a large soup pot with 5 quarts of cold water. Put the pot on the stove on high heat. When the water is just about to boil, turn the heat to medium. Partially cover the pot and simmer the stock for about an hour or until all the vegetables are falling-apart soft. Taste the broth. If it seems weak, simmer for another 30 minutes or so.

To make a thin stock, strain the stock through a colander or large-holed strainer. Press on the vegetables to extract all the liquid.

To preserve some of the vegetable fibers and thicken the stock, before straining it, purée with an immersion blender. Strain the stock through a colander or strainer to catch the stringy, inedible fibers.

If you want a more intense flavor, return the stock to the pot and reduce it to half its original volume. Do this over low heat to preserve the delicate flavors.

Makes about 1 gallon.

Roasted Vegetable Stock

Vegetables that lend themselves to roasting are eggplant, fennel, onions, tomatoes, carrots, and potatoes. Asparagus ends, broccoli trimmings, and mushrooms work well also. Try to cut the vegetables into pieces that will cook at the same rate. Onions and carrots will need to be a bit smaller than zucchini. Potatoes and broccoli stems need to be cut so they roast in about the same time as a clove of garlic. Generally, the harder a vegetable is, the smaller the chunk for purposes of roasting.

Roasting the vegetables at a low temperature (275°) prevents charring and develops the sweetness of the vegetables more intensely. For a thick stock, roast white potatoes or sweet potatoes with the vegetables.

This stock is particularly good for puréeing and using later to make sauces. (See Vegan Demi-glace, page 143.)

3 medium onions, peeled and cut into eighths

10 whole cloves garlic

4 celery stalks, cut into 2-inch pieces

4 carrots, cut into halves lengthwise, then into 2-inch pieces

4 cups reserved vegetable trimmings, or 1 zucchini, 1 eggplant, and 2 tomatoes, cut into 1-inch cubes

3 tablespoons oil

2 bay leaves

4 black peppercorns

Preheat the oven to 350°. In a large mixing bowl, toss the vegetables with the oil. Arrange the vegetables in a single layer, if possible, on 2 baking sheets lined with parchment paper or sprayed with nonstick cooking spray. Roast for 20 minutes. Stir the vegetables and rotate the pans. Roast for another 15 to 20 minutes or until they are tender to the touch. It is not necessary that they be cooked all the way through.

Discard any charred or blackened vegetables. Transfer the vegetables to a soup pot and add 5 quarts of water, the bay leaves, and the peppercorns. Turn the heat to high. When the water is just about to boil, turn the heat to medium. Partially cover the pot and simmer the stock for about 1 hour or until all the vegetables are falling-apart soft.

To make a thin stock, strain the stock through a colander or large-holed strainer, discarding the bay leaves. Press on the vegetables to extract all the liquid.

To preserve some of the vegetable fibers and thicken the stock, before straining it, purée the stock with an immersion blender. Strain the stock through a colander or strainer to catch the stringy, inedible fibers.

If you want a more intense flavor, return the stock to the pot and reduce it to half its original volume. Do this over low heat to preserve the delicate flavors.

Makes about 1 gallon.

Green Vegetable Stock

This stock is ideal for soups featuring the first vegetables of spring, such as asparagus and peas. It's also good as a base for miso soup. Use the trimmings from romaine lettuce (don't freeze these), the ends of asparagus, basil stems, green beans that are past their prime, broccoli stems, bok choy trimmings (no head cabbage, though, please), and the like to flavor this delicate broth.

1	gallon reserved trimmings from green vegetables or 1 head romaine lettuce, cut into 2-inch squares
4	green onions, cut into 4-inch lengths
½	bunch parsley
2	cloves garlic
2	bay leaves

Cover the vegetables and bay leaves with cold water in a soup pot. Turn the heat to high. When the water is just about to boil, turn the heat to medium. Simmer the stock, uncovered, for 20 minutes. Turn off the heat and let the stock stand for 25 minutes.

Strain the stock through a colander or large-holed strainer. Gently press on the vegetables to extract all the broth. (Do not purée this stock.) Discard the solids.

Makes about 1 gallon.

Mushroom Stock

When saving mushroom stems, remove all the dirt from the stem before placing it in the freezer. You may want to save mushroom stems separately so you can accumulate enough for this hearty stock. The darker the mushrooms, the deeper the flavor of the stock.

2	teaspoons oil
2	medium onions, diced
2	teaspoons minced garlic
4	cups reserved mushroom stems or 3 cups sliced shiitake, portobello, cremini, or button mushrooms
4	celery stalks, cut into 2-inch pieces, or the heart of 1 bunch celery, cut into 2-inch pieces
2	cups reserved vegetable trimmings (optional)
4	sprigs fresh thyme
½	ounce dried mushrooms (optional)
2	bay leaves

Heat the oil in a wide skillet over high heat. When the oil is hot, add the onions, then the garlic and mushroom stems or mushrooms. Cook without stirring for 1 minute or until the onions develop a golden brown color. Reduce the heat to medium. Cook the mixture, stirring occasionally, until the mushrooms have given up their liquid and are dry, about 15 to 25 minutes.

Put the mushroom mixture into a soup pot along with the remaining ingredients and 8 cups of water. Place the soup pot over high heat. When the water is just about to boil, turn the heat to medium. Partially cover the pot and simmer the stock for about 1 hour. Taste the broth. If it seems weak, simmer for another 30 minutes or so.

Strain the stock through a colander or large-holed strainer. Press on the vegetables to extract all the broth. (Do not purée this stock if using mushroom stems.) Discard the solids.

Makes about 1½ quarts.

Asian Broth

There is nothing mysterious about Asian broth. Our lack of experience with certain ingredients makes them seem intimidating, but with a little practice you can achieve marvelous results. Add or subtract ingredients depending on the cuisine. If you are planning to make a Thai-style soup, add the tough, woody tops of lemongrass and the roots and stems of cilantro. For a Chinese soup, add some star anise. For a spicy broth, add some extra chilies or Szechuan peppercorns.

4	dried shiitake mushrooms
6	cloves garlic
5	green onions
3	$1/4$-inch slices of fresh ginger
1	carrot, sliced lengthwise
1	small chili, fresh or dried
1	teaspoon whole peppercorns

Cover the dried mushrooms with $1\frac{1}{2}$ cups of boiling water. Cover and let stand for 20 minutes. Remove the mushrooms from the water and cut into $1/4$-inch strips. Strain the soaking liquid into a medium pot. Add the remaining ingredients and 3 cups of cold water. Place the pot over medium heat and simmer for about 40 minutes or until the broth is fragrant. For a richer flavor, allow the broth to sit off-heat for an additional hour before straining. Strain the broth.

Makes 1 quart.

Japanese Seaweed Broth (Kombu Dashi)

The simplest dashi (broth) involves kombu seaweed soaked overnight in water, but for our purposes, a slightly more elaborate recipe is given. Seaweed is a good source of iodine, which may be a concern for some people on vegan diets. For an earthy-tasting broth, add 1 or 2 dried shiitake mushrooms per cup of water. The kombu that is soaked for the broth can be saved, cut into strips, and stir-fried with tofu or vegetables, or added back into a soup at the end of cooking.

1	4-inch piece kombu seaweed or dulse
2	$1/4$-inch slices fresh ginger
$1/4$	cup soy sauce
2	tablespoons sake or dry sherry (optional)
1	tablespoon mirin or 1 tablespoon sugar (optional)

Gently wipe the kombu with a dry paper towel to remove dirt. (Do not rinse with water or you will lose much of the flavor.) Soak the kombu in 4 cups of cold water in a pot for 8 hours or more. Remove the kombu and reserve for another use. The stock can be used at this point to make a light miso soup.

Alternatively, soak the kombu in 4 cups of cold water for 1 to 2 hours. Heat on medium-low. Just before the water boils, remove the kombu. Reserve the kombu for another use.

Add the ginger, soy sauce, sake or sherry, and sugar (but not mirin) to the pot. Bring the mixture to a boil. Lower the heat and simmer for 10 minutes. Add the mirin. Taste the broth and adjust the seasonings.

Makes about 4 cups.

HOT SOUPS

Microwave Miso Soup for One

I am a lazy cook at home. Often I don't even want to dirty a pot. This version of miso soup allows me the comforts of hot soup with very little fuss. In the winter I add extra garlic and ginger for their warming properties and to ward off colds and sniffles. You can also add just about any leftover steamed vegetable, scraps of leafy greens, or small bits of seaweed. (I often add leftover Edamame with Hijiki and Brown Rice, page 249.)

1 tablespoon light miso
1¼ cups water or Japanese Seaweed Broth (page 68)
¼ teaspoon minced garlic
¼ teaspoon grated fresh ginger
1 1-inch square dulse, wakame, or other seaweed (optional)
1 green onion, thinly sliced
1 shiitake mushroom, thinly sliced
2 ounces tofu, diced (optional)

Put the miso in the bottom of a large soup cup (not a shallow soup bowl). Slowly add the water or light stock and mix well so there are no lumps of miso. Add the garlic, ginger, and seaweed. Heat on high in the microwave until fairly warm but not hot, about 2 minutes. Add the rest of the soup ingredients. Heat for an additional minute or until it is quite hot but not boiling. Remove the cup from the microwave and cover with a small plate. Allow the flavors to blend for 3 or 4 minutes.

Makes 1 serving.

Miso Soup

This is a slightly more involved version, but all miso soups are very fast to make. They are traditionally eaten for breakfast in Japan and provide a good protein and calcium boost to start the day.

Dark miso is saltier than light miso, so adjust the flavoring with soy sauce as necessary. Generally, I like light miso in spring and dark miso in winter.

4   cups water or Japanese Seaweed Broth (page 68)
1   teaspoon minced garlic
1/2 medium onion, thinly sliced
1 1/2 teaspoons grated fresh ginger
1/2 cup matchstick-cut carrots
1   cup thinly sliced shiitake or button mushrooms
1   3-inch piece of wakame, dulse, or other seaweed (optional)
2   green onions, thinly sliced
1   cup thinly sliced seasonal vegetables (asparagus, green beans, watercress, dandelion greens)
4   tablespoons miso
8   to 10 ounces tofu, cut into small cubes

Combine the water or light stock, garlic, onion, ginger, carrots, mushrooms, and seaweed in a soup pot. Bring the mixture to a boil over high heat. Reduce the heat to medium and simmer until the carrots are barely tender, about 5 to 10 minutes. Add the green onions and seasonal vegetables. Simmer for 5 more minutes or until those vegetables are crisp-tender. In a small bowl, slowly add 1 cup of the soup broth to the miso and whisk until there are no lumps left. Add the miso and tofu to the soup. Turn off the heat and cover the pot. Let the soup steep for 3 to 4 minutes. (If you own covered soup bowls, you can ladle the soup into the bowls and cover them.)

Makes 4 entrée servings or 8 appetizer servings.

Hot and Sour Soup with Glass Noodles

This is a decidedly easy version of a classic dish from northern China. The glass noodles add the same textural element that eggs normally do, and tofu replaces the usual pork.

5   dried wood ear mushrooms
1   teaspoon peanut or canola oil
1   teaspoon grated fresh ginger
2   teaspoons minced garlic
10 shiitake mushrooms, cut into ¼-inch strips
4   cups Asian Broth (page 68)
¼ cup rice wine vinegar
2   tablespoons soy sauce, or 1 tablespoon soy sauce and 2 teaspoons mushroom soy sauce
1   ounce glass noodles (mung bean threads)
2   tablespoons cornstarch (optional)
8   ounces tofu, cubed
2   teaspoons sesame oil
1   teaspoon black pepper
4   green onions, trimmed and thinly sliced on the diagonal

Cover the dried mushrooms with 1½ cups boiling water. Cover and let stand for 20 minutes. Remove the mushrooms from the water and cut into ¼-inch strips. Strain the soaking liquid and reserve.

Heat the oil in a 4-quart pot. Sauté the ginger, garlic, and shiitakes together for 1 to 2 minutes. Add the stock and the reserved soaking liquid. Bring the broth to a boil. Add the vinegar, soy sauce, glass noodles, and reserved mushrooms. Bring the broth to a boil again. When the broth just begins to boil, reduce the heat to low. Allow the soup to simmer over low heat for 3 minutes or just until the glass noodles are done.

Mix the cornstarch with 2 tablespoons cold water. Slowly pour this into the soup, stirring constantly. Cook for 3 minutes longer or until the soup is slightly thickened. Add the tofu, sesame oil, pepper and green onions. Taste and adjust the seasonings.

Makes 6 servings.

Thai Vegan Tom Yum Gong

This is a refined and refreshing soup. Make sure your stock is redolent of ginger and lemongrass. While lime leaves and tamarind soup base can be hard to find, they are worth the effort. No doubt, when you do discover a market that sells them, you'll find innumerable other treasures there also. Tofu substitutes for the traditional shrimp.

1	stalk lemongrass or 2 teaspoons sliced, dried lemongrass
6	cups Asian Broth (page 68)
1/2	package Knorr tamarind soup base
4	kaffir lime leaves, fresh or frozen, or 1 tablespoon grated lemon zest
1/2	cup quartered button mushrooms
1	tablespoon fresh lime juice
1	teaspoon Thai chili paste
1	tablespoon light soy sauce
8	ounces tofu, cut into 1/2-inch cubes
2	green onions, cut on the diagonal into 1/4-inch slices
2	green Thai chilies, very thinly sliced
3	tablespoons coarsely chopped fresh cilantro
1	ounce fresh enoki or straw mushrooms
Whole cilantro leaves	

If using fresh lemongrass, trim the end. Cut slices from the root end, 1/4 inch thick, on a sharp diagonal. Stop cutting when the stalk seems woody or when the thin reddish band is no longer visible. Remove the woody center from the slices. If you can't bear to throw away the rest of the lemongrass, cut the top of the stalk into 3-inch lengths and crush them with the side of your knife. In a soup pot, bring the broth and the tamarind soup base to a boil with the lemongrass slices and stalk pieces and the lime leaves. Add the button mushrooms and simmer for 20 minutes. Remove the lemongrass stalk pieces. Add the lime juice, chili paste, and soy sauce to the broth. Adjust the seasonings.

Just before serving, add the tofu, green onions, chilies, and chopped cilantro. Let the flavors blend for 3 minutes. Ladle into bowls and garnish with enoki and whole cilantro leaves.

Makes 8 to 10 servings.

Spicy Sweet Potato Soup

Hearty whole-grain bread is an especially good accompaniment to this soup.

2   teaspoons cumin seed
    or 1 teaspoon ground
    cumin
1   tablespoon oil
3   medium onions, cut into
    a medium dice
4   cloves garlic, thinly
    sliced, or 2 teaspoons
    garlic purée
1/2 bunch celery, cut into
    a medium dice
2   medium carrots, cut
    into a medium dice
1 1/2 teaspoons ancho chili
    powder
2   teaspoons grated fresh
    ginger (optional)
8   cups water or Roasted
    Vegetable Stock
    (page 66)
3   pounds sweet potatoes,
    peeled, cut into 1- to
    2-inch cubes
1   small dried chipotle
    or 1/2 canned chipotle,
    drained
1/4 cup fresh lemon or lime
    juice
Salt and pepper
1/4 cup pumpkin seeds
Fresh cilantro leaves,
    whole or coarsely
    chopped

If you are using cumin seeds, toast them gently in a soup pot over medium heat just until they begin to brown. Add the oil and raise the heat to medium-high. Add the onions, garlic, celery, and carrots. Cook without stirring until the vegetables brown slightly. (This will take some patience and restraint.) When the vegetables have begun to brown, add the chili powder, ginger, and ground cumin, if not using seeds. Cook this mixture until a heady aroma rises from the pot and vegetables are fairly soft.

Add the stock and the sweet potatoes. Cook until the sweet potatoes are very soft, just about falling apart, about 40 minutes. Taste the soup and add chipotles accordingly. Remember that the heat of the chipotle will continue to develop over the next day or so, so if you are heat-averse, be conservative at this point.

Purée the soup and return it to the pot. Add the lemon juice and season with salt and pepper. If the soup is too spicy, a bit of sugar will tone it down a little. If the soup is too mild, a little more chipotle will add some kick.

Toast the pumpkin seeds either in a sauté pan over low heat on top of the stove or in a medium oven, until they begin to pop and plump up.

Ladle the soup into bowls. Top with toasted pumpkin seeds and cilantro.

Makes 8 to 10 servings.

Onion Soup

This soup may satisfy those who are nostalgic for French onion soup. Feel free to top the soup with a large crouton and some vegan cheese.

1 tablespoon oil
3 yellow onions, cut into halves and sliced ¼ to ½ inch thick
3 cloves garlic, thinly sliced, or 2 teaspoons minced garlic
¼ teaspoon dried thyme or 2 teaspoons fresh thyme leaves
4 cups Mushroom Stock (page 67)
1½ teaspoons Spike or similar seasoning, or 1 tablespoon dark miso
Sea salt and pepper

In a large soup pot, heat the oil over medium heat. When the oil begins to smoke, add the onions, garlic, and dried thyme. Cook without stirring until the onions develop some color, 1 to 2 minutes, and then stir. Cook, stirring every 1 to 2 minutes, until onions are a deep brown color. The aroma should be pleasant. (If any of the onions blacken and smell burned, discard all the onions and oil and start again, as the resulting soup will taste burned.) When most of the onions have taken on a rich brown color, add the stock, fresh thyme, and Spike. Raise the heat to high and bring to a boil. Reduce the heat to medium. Taste the soup and adjust the seasonings.

Makes 6 to 8 servings.

Caldo Verde (Portuguese Green Soup)

This soup is ubiquitous in Portugal. Every café on every street corner sells its own version of caldo verde, the national soup. Traditionally, chorizo, or spicy sausage, is added in small quantities as a flavoring agent, but the soup does not suffer from its omission.

This potato soup is thinner than you might expect, giving the greens a chance to costar with the potatoes.

1 tablespoon oil
1 medium onion, finely diced
1 clove garlic, minced
6 Idaho potatoes, peeled and thinly sliced
1½ teaspoons salt
½ teaspoon white pepper
1 pound kale, chard, or collards, washed and trimmed

In a large soup pot over medium-high heat, heat the oil. Add the onions and garlic and sauté for 3 minutes. Add the potatoes and sauté, stirring constantly, for 3 more minutes. Add 2 quarts of cold water and bring the soup to a boil. Reduce the heat to medium and cover the pot. Simmer the soup for another 10 minutes or until the potatoes are falling apart. Purée the soup. Season with salt and white pepper. Return the soup to medium heat and warm. Stack the kale leaves, roll them into a thick "cigar," and cut the cigar into slices to yield neat shreds. Add the shredded greens and simmer for 5 minutes or until the greens are bright green and tender.

Makes 6 to 8 servings.

Harvest Vegetable Soup

This soup showcases the flavors of those fabulous root vegetables we wouldn't eat as children. Modify the mixture of vegetables based on what looks good in the market. No oil or stock is used, giving this soup a clean, straightforward flavor. For a more intense flavor, roast the vegetables in the oven until they are about half cooked and then proceed as the recipe directs.

Peeling root vegetables and winter squash can be difficult. Make sure your peeler or knife is sharp so it won't jump off the vegetables. This soup is puréed, so don't waste a lot of energy cutting your vegetables really small. It does help to cut the vegetables into roughly the same size so they cook at the same rate.

Because this soup takes some time to cook, you can use its appealing aroma to motivate you while you do household chores.

1	very large rutabaga, peeled and diced
4	parsnips, peeled and diced
2	medium turnips, peeled and diced
1	medium butternut squash, peeled and diced
3	carrots, peeled and diced
2	Idaho potatoes, peeled and diced
2	large sweet potatoes, peeled and diced
1	bunch celery, diced
3	medium onions, diced, or 2 large leeks, cleaned and sliced

Sea salt

Place all ingredients in a large soup pot. Add enough cold water to cover the vegetables by 4 inches. Turn the heat to medium-high. Allow the mixture to just barely come to a boil, and then reduce the heat to a medium simmer. If you cook this soup at too high a temperature, it will darken. Cook until the vegetables are quite soft. This may take some time, so patience is required. Add water to the pot as necessary.

Purée the soup. Adjust the thickness with water. Season with sea salt. (Pepper is not recommended for this soup as it may muddy the flavors of the vegetables.)

Makes 8 to 10 servings.

good but not worth the trouble

Chunky Polish Borscht

Fermented beet juice, or kvas, adds a distinctive taste to most borscht. For those desiring a really authentic flavor, the recipe follows. The rest of us can use a mixture of white vinegar and lemon juice.

1   tablespoon oil
1   large onion, diced
1   clove garlic, minced
4   stalks celery, diced
2   medium carrots, peeled
     and cut into $1/2$-inch cubes
2   medium potatoes, peeled
     and cut into $1/2$-inch cubes
4   medium beets, peeled
     and cut into $1/2$-inch cubes
$2^{1}/_{2}$ cups shredded green
     cabbage
4   green onions, thinly sliced
     on the diagonal
3   tablespoons white vinegar
2   tablespoons fresh lemon
     juice or $1/2$ cup Kvas
     (recipe follows)
2   tablespoons chopped fresh dill
1   teaspoon salt
$1/4$ teaspoon white pepper
1   cup cooked white beans
     (Great Northern or cannellini)
Vegan sour cream (optional)

In a large soup pot over medium heat, heat the oil and sauté the onions, garlic, celery, and carrots for 4 minutes or just until they begin to soften. Add the cubed potatoes and beets and cook for 10 minutes longer, taking care that the vegetables do not brown.

Add 6 cups of water. Cover the pot and simmer over medium-low heat for 15 minutes. Add the cabbage and cook for 15 more minutes or until the vegetables are tender. Add the green onions, vinegar, lemon juice, dill, salt, and pepper. Taste and adjust seasonings.

To serve, place $1^{1}/_{2}$ to 2 tablespoons of white beans in the bottom of each soup bowl and ladle the borscht over them. Garnish with vegan sour cream, if desired.

Makes 8 to 10 servings.

Kvas (Fermented Beet Juice)

3   medium beets, peeled and
     cut into 1-inch cubes

Place the beets in a sieve and wash them under cold water. Put the beets into a crock or ceramic container. Add enough warm water to cover them by at least 2 inches. Cover the container with its lid, or seal it with aluminum foil, and set aside at room temperature for 5 to 7 days, until the liquid ferments and tastes sour.

Strain the mixture through a sieve lined with a double thickness of cheesecloth and set over a large bowl. Discard the beets and refrigerate the kvas, tightly sealed, until you are ready to use it as a flavoring agent.

Makes 1 cup.

Potato Soup: Four Variations

Potatoes provide us with a ready palette for many different flavor variations. Chef's potatoes, those irregular, round potatoes sold in netted bags, are an inexpensive choice for soup. If you want to splurge, try Yukon Gold, with their waxy yellow flesh, in the Potato and Roasted Garlic Soup variation. Idaho russets, with their creamy white flesh, work well in the Potato and Leek Soup. Save your fingerling and red skin potatoes for salads and roasting.

Basic Potato Soup

For this soup, I prefer to mash the potatoes before puréeing them. This prevents the potatoes from becoming gummy and adds complexity to the soup's texture.

2   tablespoons oil, or
      vegan margarine
2   medium onions, diced
1   teaspoon minced garlic
      (optional)
3 to 4 pounds potatoes,
      peeled and cut into
      1- to 1½-inch cubes
1½ teaspoons sea salt
1   quart full-bodied
      soymilk

In a large soup pot over medium heat, melt the margarine or heat the oil. Add the onions and garlic and sauté until the onions are translucent. Do not brown the onions. Add the potatoes, salt, and enough cold water to cover by 3 inches. Raise the heat to high and bring the soup to a boil. Lower to a simmer and cook until the potatoes are quite soft. Drain the vegetables, reserving the liquid, and mash them, adding the soymilk and the reserved cooking water. Purée the vegetables. Add more water or soymilk as desired. Return the soup to the stove and warm before serving.

Makes 8 to 10 servings.

Potato and Roasted Garlic Soup: Add 1 head of Roasted Garlic (page 223) to Basic Potato Soup.

Potato and Watercress Soup: Prepare Basic Potato Soup without garlic. When it is ready to be rewarmed, add 1 bunch of chopped watercress. Allow the soup to warm with the watercress for 10 minutes to allow flavors to meld. Alternately, purée the watercress with the potatoes.

Potato and Leek Soup: Replace 1 onion with 1 large or 2 medium leeks, white parts only. Wash the leeks well, cut into halves lengthwise, and cut into ¼-inch slices. Sauté the leeks with the garlic and onion and proceed as the recipe directs.

Grilled Eggplant and Roasted Red Pepper Soup

This soup has a hearty, surprisingly "meaty" texture, especially when the eggplants are grilled over mesquite chips or charcoal. The eggplants, peppers, and onions may be grilled a day in advance— perhaps late on a summer evening when you just don't want to leave the grill and go back inside.

2   large or 4 small eggplants
Salt
Seasoned oil
2   large red bell peppers
Oil
2   large onions, cut into
    $\frac{1}{2}$- to $\frac{3}{4}$-inch slices
1   small onion, diced
6   cloves garlic, very thinly
    sliced
4   stalks celery, diced
$1\frac{1}{2}$ teaspoons dried basil,
    or $\frac{1}{4}$ cup shredded
    fresh basil
$\frac{1}{2}$ teaspoon dried thyme
    or 2 teaspoons fresh thyme
6   cups Roasted Vegetable
    Stock (page 66)
1 24-ounce can diced
    tomatoes or $1\frac{1}{2}$ cups diced
    fresh tomatoes
Salt and freshly ground
    pepper

Cut the eggplants into 1-inch-thick slices. Liberally salt each side and lay the slices in a colander. Allow the eggplants to drain for half an hour. When the eggplants have released a fair amount of liquid, rinse each slice under cold water and pat dry.

Brush the eggplant slices sparingly with the seasoned oil. On an outdoor grill over medium heat or on a grill pan on the stovetop, grill the eggplant until it is about half cooked, about 3 to 6 minutes on each side, depending on your cooking method. Reserve the grilled eggplant in a baking dish or bowl deep enough for the juices to collect.

Rub the red peppers with oil and grill them, turning occasionally, until the skins begin to blister. When most of the skin has blistered, place the peppers in a bowl and cover the bowl with plastic wrap or a plate to steam the peppers.

Brush the onion slices with seasoned oil and grill until about half cooked, 3 to 5 minutes on each side, depending on your cooking method.

When cool enough to handle, cut the eggplant and onion slices into 1-inch chunks. Reserve them along with any juices that may have accumulated.

Remove the black skin, seeds, and pith from the peppers. Chop the peppers coarsely and reserve.

Heat 1 tablespoon of oil in a soup pot over medium-high heat and sauté the diced onion, garlic, celery, and any dried herbs. Sauté this mixture until the onion begins to color and is soft. Add the stock. When the stock is hot, add the tomatoes, grilled vegetables, and any liquid that may have accumulated.

Cook until heated through. Add fresh herbs, salt, and freshly ground pepper. Taste the soup and adjust the seasonings.

Makes 8 to 10 servings.

Vegetable Soup with Lemon and Dill

This is a versatile soup that can accommodate most green vegetable scraps you may have hanging around in your refrigerator. Asparagus, escarole, and artichokes would all do nicely, as would cauliflower, fennel, and even mushrooms.

Because warm lemon zest can become bitter on standing, the yield of this soup is smaller so it can be consumed in one day.

1   tablespoon oil
1   medium leek, white part only, washed, cut into halves lengthwise, and cut into 1/4-inch semicircles
2   cloves garlic, minced
1   medium carrot, diced
3   stalks celery, plus the heart, diced
4   cups Green Vegetable Stock (page 67)
1/3 cup jasmine rice
1   teaspoon salt
1/8 teaspoon white pepper (optional)
2   medium zucchini, cut into 1/2-inch semicircles
1/2 pound green beans, cut on the diagonal into 1/2-inch pieces
Zest and juice of 1 lemon
1 tablespoon chopped fresh dill

Heat the oil in a soup pot over medium-high heat. Add the leeks, garlic, carrot, and celery and sauté just until the vegetables begin to soften, about 3 minutes. Add the stock and bring the soup to a boil. Add the rice, stir, and reduce the heat to low. Cook for 10 to 15 minutes, just until the rice is al dente. (To test for this, cut a rice grain into halves. It should have a little white dot in the middle.) Add the salt and pepper.

Raise the heat to medium. Add the zucchini, green beans, and any other vegetable you are using. Cook for 4 or 5 minutes, just until the vegetables are tender. Add the lemon zest, juice, and dill and mix well. Taste and adjust the seasonings.

Makes 4 to 6 servings.

Four Mushroom and Barley Soup

It takes some time and patience to develop all the rich flavors of the mushrooms in this soup, but the result is well worth the effort. Use half the barley if you are not planning on eating the soup right away, because barley has a tendency to swell.

8 ounces button mushrooms
2 large portobello mushrooms
4 ounces shiitake mushrooms
4 ounces cremini, hedgehog, oyster, or other exotic mushrooms
1 tablespoon oil
3 medium onions, diced
1 tablespoon minced garlic
4 stalks celery, diced
1 teaspoon dried thyme or 1 tablespoon fresh thyme
2 teaspoons salt
8 cups warm Mushroom Stock (page 67)
1 cup pearl barley
1/4 teaspoon black pepper (optional)

If the stems on the button mushrooms are tough, remove them. Cut the mushrooms into bite-size pieces. Remove the stems from the portobellos. Trim any dirt from the stems and reserve the stems for stock. Cut the caps into halves and cut into 1/8-inch pieces. Remove the woody stems from the shiitakes and reserve for stock. Cut the caps into 1/4-inch pieces. Prepare the exotic mushrooms, removing any woody stems and dirt, then cutting the caps into bite-size pieces. Reserve.

In a large soup pot, heat the oil over high heat. When the oil begins to smoke, add the onions, garlic, celery, and dried thyme. Cook without stirring until the onions develop some color, 1 to 2 minutes. Cook, stirring every 1 or 2 minutes, until half of the onions are brown, about 6 minutes. Watch them carefully—if they are blackening and smell like they are burning, remove them from the heat.

Add the salt and mushrooms to the onions. Reduce the heat to medium-high. Cook the mixture, stirring, until the mushrooms release all their liquid, about 25 minutes. This part takes some patience and restraint. Cook the mixture until most of the mushroom liquid has evaporated and the mixture is almost dry. This ensures a deep mushroom flavor.

Add the stock, raise the heat to medium-high, and bring the soup to a boil. Add the barley. Reduce the heat to medium and cook for 15 to 30 minutes, or until the barley is tender. Add the pepper. Taste and adjust the seasonings.

Makes 8 to 10 servings.

Corn Chowder

This colorful soup highlights the bounty of late summer, when corn is plentiful, peppers are fully ripe, the potato harvest is beginning, and the nights have begun to have a little chill to them.

Fresh corn is ideal in this recipe because you can use the cobs for stock. Try using leftover grilled corn on the cob for an added flavor note. Cooking the potatoes separately ensures even doneness.

8   small red skin potatoes, peeled and cut into ½-inch cubes
¼   teaspoon salt
¼   cup vegan margarine or oil
2   medium onions, diced
1   teaspoon minced garlic
4   stalks celery, diced
2   medium carrots, diced
½   teaspoon ground cumin
⅛   teaspoon cayenne
⅛   teaspoon dark chili powder
3   tablespoons flour
8   cups warm Vegetable Stock (page 65)
1   tablespoon oil
1   large red bell pepper, cut into ½-inch squares
1   large yellow bell pepper, cut into ½-inch squares
2   medium green bell peppers, cut into ½-inch squares
4   cups corn kernels
1   teaspoon salt
¼   teaspoon white pepper
2   tablespoons chopped fresh cilantro
Diced tomatoes (optional)
Whole cilantro leaves (optional)

Cover the potatoes with water in a small pot. Add the salt. Bring the water to a boil. Boil for three minutes or until the potatoes are tender. Remove the pot from the heat, drain the hot water, and rinse the potatoes with cold water until they are cool. Reserve.

In a large soup pot over medium heat, melt the margarine or heat the oil. Add the onions, garlic, celery, carrots, and spices. Sauté until the vegetables soften, about 8 minutes. Add the flour, stirring vigorously so no lumps develop. Cook the flour for 2 minutes to eliminate the raw taste. Remove the pot from the heat. Slowly add 1 cup of the warm vegetable stock. Stir until the stock is fully incorporated and the mixture is smooth. Add 1 more cup of the stock and mix well. Add the remaining stock and mix well. When the mixture is smooth, return the pot to medium heat. Stir occasionally as the soup comes to a boil, making sure there is no scorching on the bottom of the pot. When the soup just begins to boil, lower the heat and cook for another 15 minutes or until the soup thickens.

While the soup is cooking, heat the oil in a skillet over medium-high heat. Add the peppers and sauté until they are tender. Add the corn, peppers, potatoes, salt, pepper, and chopped cilantro to the soup. Taste and adjust the seasonings.

Garnish with diced fresh tomatoes and cilantro leaves, if desired.

Makes 8 to 10 servings.

Jary (Algerian Vegetable Soup)

This soup gets its body from bulgur, the major ingredient in tabbouleh (for more on bulgur, see page 170). The use of fresh green herbs is characteristic of soups from several Middle Eastern cuisines. This soup is traditionally eaten at sunset to break the day's fast during Ramadan. You may omit the puréeing step for a much chunkier soup.

2   tablespoons oil
1   onion, diced
2   stalks celery, diced
1½ teaspoons minced garlic
1   teaspoon paprika
Pinch cayenne
¼   cup tomato purée
4   cups Vegetable Stock
     (page 65)
¼   cup fine bulgur
½   cup chopped fresh parsley
½   cup chopped fresh cilantro
½   cup chopped fresh mint
½   cup cooked chickpeas
1   to 2 tablespoons fresh
     lemon juice
Salt

In a large soup pot over medium-high heat, heat the oil and sauté the onion, celery, garlic, paprika, and cayenne until the onion is soft, about 6 minutes. Add the tomato purée and stock. Bring to a simmer and then stir in the bulgur. Reduce the heat, cover, and simmer for 30 minutes, stirring occasionally, until the bulgur is tender.

Purée the soup. Add the herbs and purée again. Stir in the chickpeas and reheat the soup. Add the lemon juice and salt to taste.

Makes 4 servings.

Black Bean Soup

Cooking the carrots and peppers separately from the beans retains their vibrant colors and gives the soup a festive confetti look. Chili powder and cayenne may be added to give this soup some heat, but leaving them out allows the robust flavor of the black beans to shine through. Fresh cilantro leaves and diced tomatoes make a lovely garnish.

2   cups black beans
1¹/₂ tablespoons whole
    cumin seeds
2   tablespoons chopped
    garlic
1   medium red onion, diced
1   bay leaf
2   carrots, diced or cut
    into ³/₈-inch-thick
    semicircles
2   tablespoons oil
1   large green bell pepper,
    cut into ¹/₂-inch squares
1   red bell pepper, cut into
    ¹/₂-inch squares
1   yellow bell pepper, cut
    into ¹/₂-inch squares
1¹/₂ tablespoons fresh
    lemon juice
2   teaspoons juice from
    pickled jalapeños
    (optional)
¹/₂ teaspoon ground
    coriander
¹/₂ teaspoon ground cumin
1¹/₂ teaspoons salt
Diced fresh tomatoes
    (optional)
Whole cilantro leaves
    (optional)

Wash the beans in a large colander, checking thoroughly for small stones. Use the quick- or long-soaking method (page 163) to shorten the cooking time. In a large soup pot over medium-high heat, toast the cumin seeds until they become slightly brown and release their fragrance. Add the beans, garlic, onion, and bay leaf to the pot along with 6 cups of water. Do not salt the water. Raise the heat to high and bring the beans to a boil, stirring occasionally. Reduce the heat and simmer the beans until soft. The time may vary, but it should take from 30 to 45 minutes.

In a separate pan over medium-high heat, sauté the carrots in the oil for 2 minutes. Add the peppers and sauté until crisp-tender, about 3 minutes.

Add the vegetables to the soup, along with the lemon juice, spices, and salt. Remove and discard bay leaf. Let the soup simmer over low heat for 30 minutes before serving to allow the flavors to meld. Garnish with diced tomatoes and cilantro leaves, if desired.

Makes 4 to 6 servings.

Tuscan White Bean Soup

Making this soup from scratch with dried beans gives it a clean flavor that canned beans simply can't match.

1½ cups dried white
    beans (Great Northern or
    cannellini)
2   tablespoons oil
2   medium onions, cut into
    ¼-inch slices
4   garlic cloves, thinly sliced
Salt and pepper
1   tablespoon finely sliced
    fresh sage
¼   cup extra virgin olive oil,
    plus extra for drizzling
Fresh sage leaves

Wash the beans in a large colander, checking very carefully for stones. Use the quick- or long-soaking method (page 163) to shorten the cooking time. Place the beans in a 6-quart pot and cover with 6 cups of cold water. Bring the beans to a boil over high heat. Reduce the heat to medium and simmer the beans until they are soft, about 40 minutes. Skim any foam that develops. Add more water as necessary. The cooked beans should be covered by 2 to 4 inches of cooking liquid. Reserve the beans and the cooking liquid.

In a large soup pot, heat the oil over high heat. When the oil begins to smoke, add the onions and garlic. Cook without stirring until the onions develop some color, about 1 or 2 minutes, and then stir them. Cook, stirring every 1 or 2 minutes, until the onions turn a deep brown color. If the onions are blackening and smell like they are burning, reduce the heat to medium-high and watch closely.

When the onions are nicely caramelized, add the beans and their cooking liquid. If the beans are not quite soft, cook the soup over medium heat until they are. Purée the soup. Adjust the thickness with water. Add salt and pepper to taste. Stir in the sage and olive oil. Let the soup stand for 15 minutes to allow flavors to blend.

To serve, ladle the soup into bowls, drizzle with more extra virgin olive oil, and sprinkle with sage leaves.

Makes 8 to 10 servings.

Tomato, Fennel, and White Bean Soup

1   cup dried white beans or 1 16-ounce can white beans (Great Northern or cannellini)
1   large fennel bulb
2   tablespoons oil
3   medium onions, diced
4   cloves garlic, thinly sliced, or 2 teaspoons minced garlic
1   teaspoon fennel seeds
4   stalks celery, diced
1   teaspoon dried basil
1/2 teaspoon dried thyme
6   cups Vegetable Stock (page 65), or 3 cups tomato juice and 3 cups water
2   cups diced tomatoes, canned or fresh
Salt and pepper

If using dried beans, wash them in a colander, checking thoroughly for small stones. Place the beans in a 2-quart saucepan along with 1 quart of cold water. Cook the beans on medium-high heat for about 1 hour or until they are tender. If using canned beans, rinse them well in a colander and reserve.

To prepare the fennel, cut off the bottom and the long stalks, reserving the stalks for stock and the feathery leaves for garnish, if desired. Cut the bulb into halves. Remove the core by cutting toward the middle of the bulb on either side of the core. Pop out a triangular piece of core. Trim away any core you may have missed. Cut the fennel into 1/4-inch slices. Cut the flat slices from each end into strips.

In a large soup pot, heat the oil over medium-high heat. Add the onions, garlic, and fennel seeds and sauté for 3 minutes. Add the fennel, celery, basil, and thyme and sauté for 5 minutes longer. Raise the heat to high and add the vegetable stock. Bring the soup to a boil and turn it off. Add the diced tomatoes and reserved beans. Adjust the seasoning with salt and pepper. Reheat the soup if necessary. Garnish with whole or chopped fennel leaves.

Makes 4 to 6 servings.

Curried Yellow Split Pea Soup

1 tablespoon oil
1 medium onion, diced
2 teaspoons minced garlic
2 medium carrots, diced
2 stalks celery, diced
2 teaspoons grated fresh ginger
2 teaspoons medium curry powder or garam masala
1/2 teaspoon ground cumin
1/2 teaspoon ground coriander
2 1/2 cups yellow split peas
1 teaspoon sea salt
1/4 teaspoon white pepper
1 teaspoon oil
1 large red bell pepper, diced
2 Granny Smith or other tart apples, diced
Whole cilantro leaves (optional)

Heat 1 tablespoon of oil in a soup pot over medium-high heat and sauté the onion, garlic, carrots, celery, ginger, and spices until the vegetables begin to soften and the spices give up their fragrance, about 10 minutes. Add the split peas and 2 quarts of water to the pot. Raise the heat to high and bring the soup to a boil. Lower the heat to a simmer and cook until split peas are falling apart, 15 to 25 minutes. Taste and add salt and pepper.

In a small pan over medium heat, heat 1 teaspoon of oil and sauté the bell pepper until crisp-tender. Add half the diced apples and cook for 1 minute. Add the sautéed peppers and apples to the soup and stir gently.

Ladle the soup into bowls and garnish with the remaining apples and, if desired, cilantro leaves.

Makes 8 servings.

Lentil and Spinach Soup

I prefer to make this soup with water instead of stock so the flavor of the lentils really comes through.

1 tablespoon oil
2 medium onions, diced
1 teaspoon minced garlic
4 stalks celery, plus hearts, diced
2 medium carrots, diced
1 1/2 teaspoons dried basil
1/2 teaspoon dried thyme
1 large bay leaf
2 cups brown lentils, washed
1 teaspoon salt
1/4 teaspoon black pepper
4 cups spinach leaves, washed and chopped coarsely

Heat the oil in a soup pot over medium-high heat and sauté the onions, garlic, celery, carrots, and dried herbs until the vegetables begin to soften. Add the lentils and 2 quarts of water to the pot. Raise the heat to high and bring the soup to a boil. Lower the heat to a simmer and cook for 15 to 25 minutes, until the lentils are done.

Add the salt, pepper, and spinach and mix well. Remove and discard bay leaf. Taste the soup and adjust the seasonings. Serve immediately.

Makes 6 to 8 servings.

Escarole and White Bean Soup

¾ cup dried white beans or
1½ cups canned white
beans (Great Northern or
cannellini)
1 tablespoon oil
2 medium onions, diced
5 cloves garlic, thinly sliced
4 stalks celery, plus hearts,
diced
1 teaspoon dried basil
½ teaspoon dried thyme
2 medium bay leaves
6 cups Vegetable Stock
(page 65)
1 24-ounce can diced
tomatoes with juice
1 teaspoon salt
¼ teaspoon black pepper
1 pound escarole, cleaned,
trimmed, and chopped
½ cup chopped fresh basil
(optional)

Wash the dried beans in a large colander, checking very carefully for stones. Use the quick- or long-soaking method (page 163) to shorten the cooking time. Place the beans in a 2-quart pot and cover with 4 cups cold water. Place over high heat and bring to a boil. Reduce the heat to medium and simmer until the beans are soft, about 40 minutes, skimming any foam that develops. The cooked beans should be covered by a scant inch of cooking liquid when done. Add more water as necessary. Reserve the beans and the cooking liquid.

If using canned beans, rinse well in a colander and reserve.

Heat the oil in a soup pot over medium-high heat and sauté the onions, garlic, celery, and dried herbs until the vegetables begin to soften. Add the stock to the pot, raise the heat to high, and bring the soup to a boil.

Add the beans and their cooking liquid, tomatoes and their juice, salt, and pepper and mix well. Taste and adjust the seasonings. Warm the soup over medium heat. Remove and discard bay leaves.

Just before serving, add the escarole and cook for 4 minutes or until the escarole is tender. Add the fresh basil.

Makes 8 to 10 servings.

CHILLED SOUPS

Two Melon Soup with Plum Wine

This soup is extremely easy to make. If you'd like to simplify the recipe even further, use just one type of melon. The sea salt brings out the sweetness of the melons, and the pepper provides a nice piquant counterpoint along with the dried ginger. Make this soup the night before you plan to serve it to allow the flavors to develop completely.

The soup shows to best advantage in shallow soup bowls with wide rims. Consider using a thin slice of sweet carambola (star fruit) or strawberry as a garnish. For a dramatic presentation, reserve one slice of each melon, slice the melon with a mandoline into long ribbons, and interweave the ribbons on top of the soup bowls.

1   ripe honeydew or 4
    cups honeydew cubes
1   ripe cantaloupe or 4
    cups cantaloupe cubes
½   teaspoon dried ginger
    (preferably Jamaican)
2   teaspoons grated fresh
    ginger
1   cup Japanese plum wine
2   pinches sea salt
2   pinches white pepper

Peel, seed, and chop each melon into pieces small enough for a food processor or blender. Purée each melon separately and reserve in medium bowls. Into each bowl whisk ¼ teaspoon of dried ginger, 1 teaspoon of fresh ginger, and ½ cup of plum wine. Season each with small pinches of sea salt and pepper. Taste and adjust the seasonings. Cover each bowl and refrigerate for 8 hours or more.

To serve, put a ladle in each container of soup. Hold a soup bowl at a 30-degree angle to the table. Ladle a half portion of one soup (about 4 to 6 ounces) into the bowl. Carefully begin to ladle a half portion of the other soup into the bowl. As the soup bowl fills with the second soup, begin to lower the bowl back to the table.

To present the soup, you can create designs by dragging a toothpick, spoon, or knife from one side of the bowl to the other. If you are feeling really adventurous, try gently spinning the bowl. (Practice with empty bowls before attempting to do this with full bowls of soup.) Assuming there is some soup left in the bowl after this, you will have created a yin-yang swirl.

Makes 8 servings.

Blueberry and Red Wine Soup

2 cups blueberries,
   preferably fresh
1 whole cinnamon stick
2 whole cloves
Pinch sea salt
1½ cups red wine, preferably
   a California Zinfandel
¼ cup sugar
1½ cups vegan sour
   cream or 12 ounces tofu,
   puréed with 2
   tablespoons lemon juice

Heat the blueberries, cinnamon, cloves, salt, and red wine to a boil in a 6-quart soup pot over medium-high heat. Reduce the heat to medium and simmer the soup until most of the blueberries have burst. Remove from the heat. Remove the cinnamon and cloves. Add the sugar and mix well. Let the mixture cool to room temperature. Purée about half of the blueberry mixture.

Stir in the sour cream or tofu. Refrigerate until chilled thoroughly. Adjust the seasonings. If the soup seems too tart, add sugar. If the soup seems cloying, add lemon juice. Garnish with fresh whole blueberries.

Makes 8 to 10 servings.

Strawberry Soup with Almond Milk

Packaged almond milk can be substituted, but the resulting soup won't be as thick and luxurious. You can also substitute a tablespoon or two of Grand Marnier, Cointreau, or framboise for the rosewater.

1 cup blanched almonds,
   coarsely ground
¼ cup sugar
1 pint ripe, full-flavored
   strawberries
4 ounces silken tofu
2 teaspoons rosewater
Pinch sea salt

Soak the almonds for 8 to 12 hours in 3 cups of water. Strain and rinse the nuts. In a blender, whirl the almonds, 4 cups of hot water, and sugar together for 3 minutes. Strain the mixture through cheesecloth, squeezing the cloth to get all of the liquid. You should have 4 cups of almond milk.

Hull the strawberries and purée them with the tofu. Mix the strawberry purée and the almond milk together. Add the rosewater and sea salt. Taste and adjust the flavorings.
(If the strawberries aren't at their ripest, a little more sweetener may be needed.) Refrigerate until thoroughly chilled.

Makes 4 to 6 servings.

Korean Seaweed Soup

½ ounce wakame seaweed
4 cups Vegetable Stock
   (page 65) or Asian
   Broth (page 68)
1 Japanese cucumber or
   small seedless cucumber
1 green onion, thinly sliced
1 teaspoon toasted white
   sesame seeds
1 small fresh red chili,
   thinly sliced, or ⅛
   teaspoon cayenne
3 tablespoons soy sauce
1 tablespoon rice wine
   vinegar
1 teaspoon sesame oil

In a small bowl, pour very hot water over the wakame until it is covered by 2 inches. Put a lid on the bowl and let the wakame stand for 20 minutes. Lift the wakame out of the bowl, being careful to leave any grit in the bottom of the bowl. Squeeze as much water as you can out of it and chop coarsely.

In a small soup pot, bring the stock to a boil. Add the wakame and reduce the heat to medium. Simmer the wakame until tender, 30 minutes to 1 hour.

Toward the end of the wakame's cooking time, cut the cucumber into halves lengthwise and cut the lengths into ¼-inch slices. Toss with the remaining ingredients. Let the cucumbers marinate just until they begin to soften, about 15 minutes.

Add the cucumbers and marinade to the seaweed soup. Adjust the seasonings. Refrigerate the soup to chill thoroughly.

Makes 4 servings.

Avocado Soup

I prefer Hass avocados, the ones with the alligator-like skins, for their consistent flavor. Smooth-skinned Florida avocados are less dependable. Either variety works well.

8 ripe Hass avocados or 5
   large Florida avocados
Zest and juice of 1 lemon
1 teaspoon minced garlic
1 small onion, finely diced
1 jalapeño, seeded and
   minced
¼ cup chopped fresh cilantro
1 tablespoon chopped
   fresh basil
Salt and pepper
1 tomato, seeded and diced
Whole cilantro leaves (optional)

Peel and seed the avocados. In a 3-quart bowl, mash the avocados. Stir in the lemon juice, garlic, onion, jalapeño, chopped cilantro, and basil. Whisk in cold water until the desired consistency is reached, about 3 cups. Season with salt and pepper.

Just before serving, toss the tomato with half the lemon zest. Season the tomato mixture with salt and pepper. Add the remaining zest to the soup. Ladle the soup into bowls and garnish with the diced tomato mixture and, if desired, whole cilantro leaves.

Makes 8 servings.

Chilled Spring Pea Soup with Tarragon

6 cups Green Vegetable Stock (page 67)
2 fresh bay leaves (optional)
4 cups sugar snap peas, coarsely chopped, or 4 cups English peas, fresh or frozen
2 green onions, chopped
2 stalks celery, diced
1 shallot, minced
4 ounces vegan cream cheese
   or 4 ounces silken tofu
1 cup coarsely chopped spinach leaves
1 tablespoon chopped fresh tarragon
2 tablespoons chopped fresh parsley
1 teaspoon sea salt
1/4 teaspoon white pepper
Fresh whole tarragon leaves

Heat the stock and bay leaves to just barely boiling in a 6-quart soup pot over medium-high heat. Add the peas, green onions, celery, and shallot. Reduce the heat to medium. Cook until the vegetables are soft, about 15 minutes for English peas and 20 minutes for sugar snap peas. Crumble the cream cheese into the soup. Add the spinach, fresh herbs, salt, and pepper. Purée the soup. Strain the soup through a sieve to remove the tough fibers. Remove soup to a nonmetal container. Cover and chill thoroughly, preferably for 8 hours or more. Adjust the seasonings. Serve the soup garnished with fresh whole tarragon leaves.

Makes 8 to 10 servings.

Gazpacho: Two Variations

I offer two variations on this classic Spanish dish. The first is a quick food processor version that will leave you plenty of time to enjoy it outdoors on a summer day.

Quick Gazpacho

3   medium cucumbers
2   stalks celery, finely diced
1   medium green bell pepper, cut into 1/2-inch cubes
1   small red bell pepper, cut into 1/2-inch cubes
1   small yellow bell pepper, cut into 1/2-inch cubes
1/4   cup minced fresh parsley
1/4   cup finely diced onion
1   teaspoon minced garlic
3   cups fresh tomatoes, seeded and diced, or 1 22-ounce can diced plum tomatoes
1   26-ounce can tomato juice
1   tablespoon Tabasco sauce
Salt and pepper

Peel the cucumbers and remove the seeds. Cut the cucumbers into 1/2- to 1-inch cubes. If you are using canned tomatoes, drain them and reserve their juice. In a large bowl, combine the cucumber cubes with the celery, peppers, parsley, onion, garlic, and tomatoes. Pulse this mixture in small batches in a food processor until it is coarsely chopped. Put the chopped vegetables into a large bowl. Add the tomato juice and Tabasco sauce and mix well. Adjust the thickness with additional tomato juice or water. Season with salt and pepper.

Makes 8 servings.

Yellow Tomato Gazpacho

This recipe works well with any variety of yellow tomato, but I like it best with Lemon Boy. The skin of Lemon Boys can be a bit tough so it is important to remove them. Seeds left in the soup from either the tomatoes or the peppers can give it a bitter edge.

3   pounds yellow tomatoes (about 3 to 4 Yellow Wonder or 6 to 8 Lemon Boy)
1   small red bell pepper
1   small green bell pepper
1½ seedless cucumbers or 3 regular cucumbers
3   green onions, thinly sliced on the diagonal
1   tablespoon minced fresh garlic
½   cup white balsamic vinegar
⅓   cup fresh lime juice
⅓   cup extra virgin olive oil
⅓   cup chopped fresh cilantro
1   teaspoon Tabasco
1   teaspoon cumin
1   teaspoon salt
1   cup roasted red peppers (fresh or canned)
1   tablespoon chopped fresh basil
1   tablespoon fresh lime juice
⅓   cup extra virgin olive oil
Salt and pepper

To skin the tomatoes, bring a large pot of water to boil on the stove, cut a small X on the bottom of each tomato, and gently drop the tomatoes into the boiling water. Leave the tomatoes in the water for about 45 seconds (longer if they have a tough skin), and then remove to a bowl of ice water. When the tomatoes are cool enough to handle, the skin will peel off easily.

Cut the tomatoes into halves and squeeze gently to remove all the seeds. Coarsely chop two-thirds of the tomatoes and purée them in a food processor until very smooth. Cut the remaining tomatoes into ½-inch cubes.

Remove the seeds from the peppers and cut them into very small pieces. Cut the cucumbers into chunks and purée in a food processor until smooth. (Peel the cucumbers if the skin seems tough.) Cut the remaining cucumbers into ½-inch chunks.

Combine the tomatoes, red peppers, green peppers, cucumbers, green onions, garlic, balsamic vinegar, lime juice, olive oil, cilantro, Tabasco, cumin, and salt in a large bowl and mix well. Chill for at least 4 hours or overnight to allow flavors to meld. Taste and adjust the seasonings, adding sugar if necessary.

Combine the red peppers, basil, lime juice, olive oil, salt, and pepper in a bowl and mix well. Blend in small batches in a blender (not a food processor) until smooth. Reserve.

To serve, ladle the soup into chilled bowls. Drizzle the roasted red pepper mix over the top with the abandon of Jackson Pollack.

Makes 6 to 8 servings.

Chilled Beet and Cucumber Soup

2 pounds beets, trimmed
2 pounds cucumbers
  (about 3 seedless or
  4 medium salad
  cucumbers)
2 teaspoons grapeseed oil
3 green onions, chopped
1 teaspoon minced garlic
1 tablespoon fresh lemon
  juice
1 tablespoon chopped
  fresh dill
1 teaspoon sea salt
¼ teaspoon white pepper
Vegan sour cream (optional)
Sprigs of fresh dill

Bring a large pot of water to a boil and add the beets. Reduce the heat to low and cook until the beets are tender, about 30 minutes. Drain, reserving 2 cups of the cooking liquid. Run cold water over the beets until they are cool enough to handle. Peel the beets and cut into 1-inch chunks.

Peel and seed the cucumbers. Cut them into 1-inch chunks.

In a large pan over medium heat, heat oil and sauté the green onions and garlic for 2 minutes. Add the cucumbers and cook until they are wilted, about 3 minutes. Add 2 cups of water (not the beet water) to the pan and simmer the cucumbers until they are tender.

Purée the beets with the beet water. Purée the cucumber mixture. In a large bowl, combine the cucumber and beet mixtures. Add the lemon juice, chopped dill, salt, and pepper. Taste and adjust the seasonings. Refrigerate the soup until it is thoroughly chilled. Garnish with a dollop of vegan sour cream and sprigs of fresh dill.

Makes 4 to 6 servings.

salads & dressings

Salads

Arugula and Mushrooms with Pine Nuts

Caesar Salad

Baby Greens and Tofu with Sesame-Soy Vinaigrette

Mesclun with Almonds, Ginger, and Raspberries

Watercress and Spicy Glass Noodles

Roasted Vegetables with Balsamic Vinegar

Orange and Onion Salad

Italian Chopped Salad

Tempeh Niçoise

Apple-Fennel Salad

Poppy Seed Coleslaw

Asian Coleslaw

Almost-Traditional Potato Salad

French Potato Salad

Italian Potato Salad

Dressings

Basic Vinaigrette

Italian Vinaigrette

Balsamic Vinaigrette

Mustard-Sherry Vinaigrette

Raspberry Vinaigrette

Roasted Red Pepper and Basil Vinaigrette

Sesame-Soy Vinaigrette

Citrus Dressing

Tahini Dressing

Tofu-Dill Dressing

Tomato-Tarragon Dressing

Big Vegetable Dressing

The U.S. Food and Drug Administration's directive to eat three to five servings of vegetables a day can seem daunting. But salads can make it easy. One serving of vegetables is one cup of raw vegetables—and once you have discovered which salads excite and energize you, stopping at one cup may be difficult! The darker lettuces are a good source of calcium in the vegan diet. The lighter lettuces may have a role in colon cleansing.

Grocery stores now carry a wide array of greens—many of them pre-washed and ready for dressing. The most laborious step has been eliminated. Try buying greens at your local farmers' market for the freshest possible ingredients.

Salad greens include:

Crisp head lettuce: iceberg, romaine. These versatile lettuces provide a nice background for the flavors of the other salad ingredients and can take a heavy dressing without wilting or being overpowered. Red romaine tends to be more delicate than its green counterpart.

Bitter greens: arugula, dandelion, endive, chicory, escarole, radicchio, watercress. Every culture seems to have a special bitter green. These can be served raw, lightly steamed or sautéed, or wilted with a hot dressing. The bitterness of these greens pairs nicely with the sweetness of nuts, oranges, apples, pears, and full-flavored vinegars like raspberry, balsamic, and sherry.

Tender heads and leaves: baby spinach, green or red oakleaf, Boston, Bibb, and butter lettuces. These sweet greens require tender loving care. They tend to have a delicate flavor, particularly the head lettuces, so choose dressings and accompaniments that are light in flavor, such as raspberry vinaigrette, toasted almonds, cucumbers, teardrop tomatoes, julienned jicama, or carrots.

Mesclun: typically a mix of baby greens from all the other categories—the resulting taste is a mix of sweet and bitter. The leaves are small but fairly sturdy. The combination of lettuces changes with availability, though typically it will include frisée (curly endive), radicchio, arugula, red and green oakleaf, mâche (tat soi), mizuna (Japanese dandelion greens), and red and green romaine. The best thing about mesclun is that it comes washed and ready to use. Organic varieties are readily available in traditional grocery stores.

Here are some tips for washing salad greens:

- To wash very dirty lettuce, fill a 2-gallon pot or a clean sink with cold water. Add salt to the water to help carry the dirt down to the bottom faster. Cut or tear the lettuce into bite-size pieces. Submerge lettuce and gently swish, checking the rib portions for bugs and dirt. Let the lettuce sit for 2 minutes. Lift the lettuce out of the water, making sure not to stir up the dirt on the bottom. Place the lettuce in a colander. If the lettuce is exceedingly dirty, repeat with clean water.

- If the cold water coming from your faucet is not very cold, add some ice to it. Warm water will cause the lettuce to deteriorate quickly.
- Add a little lemon juice or vinegar to your wash water to prevent your lettuce from rusting—turning brown where it has been cut. (This is called acidulating the water.) Using this technique allows you to prepare enough lettuce for two or three days without much waste.
- Make sure that you lift the lettuce out of the washing water; don't pour it out into the colander because the dirt will come right with it.
- Lettuces bruise easily, so be gentle with that salad spinner. The NASCAR sounds it makes when revved up are amusing, but the vigorous movement can damage the tender leaves.
- To store your cleaned lettuce, put a dry paper towel in the bottom of an airtight container. Put the washed lettuce on top and keep the container tightly closed.

SALADS

Arugula and Mushrooms with Pine Nuts

If you buy your arugula at the grocery store, chances are good that it will have been cleaned once already. If you grow it yourself or purchase it at the farmers' market, it may be a little dirtier and require two or three washings to remove all the sand and grit.

2 tablespoons pine nuts
2 bunches arugula or 4 cups leaves
½ cup sliced white mushrooms
2 tablespoons roasted red peppers, cut into long strips
½ cup Balsamic Vinaigrette (page 111)

In a small heavy skillet over medium-low heat, toast the pine nuts until golden brown. Remove the pine nuts from the pan and let cool.

Remove the roots and any thick stems from the arugula. Separate the leaves and check for any large stones or pieces of sand before washing. Spin or pat the arugula dry.

Put the arugula, mushrooms, peppers, and 1 tablespoon of pine nuts into a 2-quart mixing bowl. Drizzle the dressing over the greens. Toss to combine. Divide the salad among 4 plates. The heavier ingredients tend to fall to the bottom of the bowl. If this happens, arrange them decoratively on top of the greens. Sprinkle each plate with some of the remaining pine nuts and serve.

Makes 4 servings.

Caesar Salad

To produce a thicker dressing, use a food processor or a hand-held mixer

2   cloves garlic
½   teaspoon salt
1   tablespoon Dijon
      mustard or ½ pommery
      and ½ Dijon
2   tablespoons lemon juice
1   teaspoon vegetarian
      Worcestershire sauce
      or 1 small pinch sour
      tamarind paste
      (optional)
1   tablespoon white wine
      or balsamic vinegar
½   cup olive oil or
      vegetable oil or a
      combination
2   tablespoons vegan
      Parmesan, if desired
1   teaspoon grated lemon
      zest
¼   teaspoon black pepper
1   head romaine lettuce
¼   cup croutons
¼   cup vegan Parmesan,
      prepared or homemade
      (recipe follows)

Crush the garlic in the bottom of a 2-quart mixing bowl or mince in a food processor. Add the salt and mix well. Allow the garlic and salt to sit together for 2 minutes. Add the mustard, lemon juice, Worcestershire or tamarind, and vinegar. While whisking vigorously or with the food processor running, drizzle in the oil very carefully—slowly at first, then a little faster as the oil is incorporated. The dressing should not be separated. Whisk or process in the 2 tablespoons of vegan Parmesan (if desired), lemon zest, and black pepper. (If you miss the taste of anchovies, try adding a little seaweed, softened in warm water.)

Remove and discard the tough outer leaves of the romaine. Cut or tear the dark green tops off the leaves and discard. Cut off the bottom 1 to 2 inches of the head. Cut the head in quarters lengthwise—sixths if the head of lettuce is big. Cut these sections into 1-inch pieces. Wash the lettuce. Spin or pat dry.

In a large bowl, mix the lettuce, croutons, and vegan Parmesan together. Add the dressing and toss to combine. Serve immediately.

Makes 4 to 6 servings.

Vegan Parmesan Substitute

2   tablespoons ground
      almonds
2   tablespoons nutritional
      yeast
Pinch salt

Combine ingredients in a small bowl.
   Makes ¼ cup.

Baby Greens and Tofu with Sesame-Soy Vinaigrette

4 ounces silken tofu, cut into ½-inch cubes
3 tablespoons Sesame-Soy Vinaigrette (page 113)
2 cups mesclun
1 teaspoon white sesame seeds, toasted

Toss the tofu with 1 tablespoon of the dressing. Allow the tofu to marinate 15 minutes.

In a small mixing bowl, toss the mesclun with the remaining 2 tablespoons of dressing. Divide onto 2 plates. Scatter the tofu on the greens and sprinkle the salads with the sesame seeds.

Makes 2 servings.

Mesclun with Almonds, Ginger, and Raspberries

Crystallized ginger is surprising to find on a salad. It is both sweet and spicy. Make sure to cut the ginger into pieces large enough for a guest to remove should they dislike it. Crystallized ginger can be found in most supermarkets.

¼ cup sliced almonds
2 tablespoons crystallized ginger or two large slices
4 cups mesclun greens
½ cup Raspberry Vinaigrette (page 112)
3 tablespoons fresh raspberries

Toast the almonds until golden in either a 300° oven for 5 to 8 minutes or in a sauté pan set over medium-low heat. Remove from the pan and reserve. Cut the crystallized ginger into long strips as thin as possible. If the knife becomes sticky, dip it into hot water.

In a 2-quart mixing bowl, toss the greens with the dressing. Divide the greens among 4 plates. Sprinkle the almonds and ginger on top of each salad. Arrange the fresh raspberries around the edge of the plates.

Makes 4 servings.

Watercress and Spicy Glass Noodles

The only oil in this salad comes from the 1½ teaspoons of sesame oil used to flavor the dressing. The sweetness of the glass or mung bean noodles, added sugar, and cucumber are sufficient to balance the vinegar and lime juice. Watercress is a much-neglected green that deserves a renaissance.

3   ounces glass noodles (cellophane noodles, mung bean noodles, or bean threads)
¼ cup soy sauce
1½ teaspoons sesame oil
½ teaspoon garlic chili paste
1   tablespoon sugar
½ cup rice wine vinegar
1   tablespoon lime juice (optional)
1   green onion, green and white parts, trimmed and cut into thin slices diagonally
2   teaspoons sesame seeds, toasted
2   bunches watercress, washed and trimmed

Cover the noodles with cold water and let soak for 20 minutes. Drain the noodles and put them in a pot of boiling water. Let the water return to a boil and boil for 1 minute. Drain, rinse with cold water, and chill.

Whisk the soy sauce, sesame oil, chili paste, sugar, vinegar, and lime juice. Toss the noodles with the dressing. Add the green onion and 1 teaspoon of the sesame seeds.

Divide the watercress among 6 plates. Divide the noodles among the plates. Sprinkle the salads with the remaining sesame seeds.

Makes 6 servings.

Roasted Vegetables with Balsamic Vinegar

Roasting the vegetables brings out their natural sugars. The cremini, or brown Italian mushrooms, add an earthy quality to the dish. Use whatever vegetables are on hand. Make sure to cut them into consistent-size pieces so they will cook in the same amount of time.

1   small eggplant
Salt
2   cups cremini or white
      mushrooms
1   small bulb fennel
1   medium zucchini, cut
      into 1½-inch cubes
1   medium yellow squash,
      cut into 1½-inch cubes
2   medium firm tomatoes,
      cored and cut into
      eighths
1   tablespoon minced garlic
1   teaspoon salt
⅔   cup seasoned oil
½   cup balsamic vinegar
¼   cup fresh basil leaves,
      coarsely chopped
Freshly ground pepper

Preheat the oven to 300°. If the eggplant is older and the skin is tough, peel it. Cut the eggplant into 1½- to 2-inch cubes. Liberally salt the cubes and put them in a colander. Allow the eggplant to drain for 15 minutes. Rinse the cubes under cold water and pat dry.

Remove the stems from the mushrooms if they seem woody. (Reserve them for making stock, if you wish.) Cut the mushrooms into quarters.

Cut the bottom and the long stalks off the fennel. (Reserve the stalks and the feathery leaves for making stock, if you wish.) Cut the fennel bulb into halves. Remove the core by cutting toward the middle of the bulb on either side of the core. Pop out a triangular piece of core. Trim away any core you may have missed. Cut the fennel into ¾-inch slices or strips.

In a 3-quart mixing bowl, combine all the vegetables. You should have about 7 cups. Toss the vegetables with the garlic and salt. Add the seasoned oil and mix thoroughly.

Arrange the vegetables in a single layer on a baking sheet. Roast in the oven for 30 minutes. Stir the vegetables gently and roast for another 15 minutes or until cooked through.

Put the vegetables into a 3-quart mixing bowl. Toss with the vinegar and basil. Season with black pepper. Serve warm or at room temperature.

Makes 8 servings.

Orange and Onion Salad

This salad stands on its own or can be served with a pile of bitter greens in the center of the plate. Arugula and watercress work particularly well. Soaking the onions tames their flavor. This step can be omitted if you are using Vidalia, Maui, or Oso Sweet onions. The peeling technique for the oranges can also be used with melons, pineapple, or tomatoes. Preparing the oranges this way gives you the classic presentation for this Catalonian salad.

2 tablespoons lemon juice
1 tablespoon sherry vinegar
¼ teaspoon salt
1 teaspoon sugar
3 tablespoons olive oil
1 tablespoon coarsely chopped fresh mint leaves
1 medium-large red onion
3 large navel oranges
Whole mint leaves for garnish

Whisk the lemon juice, vinegar, salt, and sugar until the sugar and salt are dissolved. Whisk in the olive oil. Add the chopped mint leaves. Reserve.

Cut the onion into rings as thin as possible with your knife, mandoline, food processor, or the side of your box grater. Soak the onion slices in ice water for 15 minutes. Drain and pat dry. Toss with 2 tablespoons of the reserved dressing and reserve.

While the onions are soaking, peel the oranges with a knife in the following fashion: Cut a slice from top and bottom of each orange so it is stable on the cutting board. Place your knife on the top of the orange at the point where the orange and white part meet. Carefully cut down the side of the orange, from top to bottom, following the curve of the fruit, cutting away both the peel and the pith to expose the orange pulp. Continue cutting around the orange until all the peel and pith are removed. Cut the oranges crosswise into ¼-inch-thick slices. Toss the orange slices with the remaining dressing.

Alternate the orange and onion slices in an overlapping pattern around the serving platter. (This is called shingling.) Garnish with whole mint leaves.

Makes 6 servings.

Italian Chopped Salad

This salad can be a catch-all for those slim pickin's from the early spring or late summer garden or a creative way to present the remnants of the week's vegetable purchases. The dressing is minimal, allowing the flavors of the vegetables to shine. Fresh basil, oregano, thyme, or marjoram are wonderful accents when judiciously added to the salad.

1   cup broccoli florets, blanched and coarsely chopped
2   ripe tomatoes, cut in ³/₄-inch cubes
1   medium or 2 small cucumbers, cut into ¹/₂-inch cubes
1   medium red pepper, cut into ¹/₂-inch cubes
1   small red onion, finely minced
4 or 5 radishes, trimmed and cut into very thin slices
¹/₂ head radicchio, cored and cut into 1-inch squares
2   cups romaine lettuce, washed and cut into 1¹/₂-inch squares
¹/₂ teaspoon sea salt
¹/₃ cup extra virgin olive oil
2   tablespoons lemon juice
Freshly ground pepper

Place all the vegetables in a 2-quart mixing bowl. Season with sea salt. Drizzle the olive oil on the vegetables and toss to combine. Add the lemon juice and toss again.

Divide among salad plates and season with freshly ground pepper.

Makes 6 salad-course servings or 4 main-dish servings.

Tempeh Niçoise

This is a classic composed salad—one in which each type of vegetable is arranged in a separate mound on the plate. Dressing each ingredient separately gives the best result. If you don't want to be so fussy, though, toss everything except the aioli together in a bowl and serve the aioli on the side.

- 1 pound fingerling or new potatoes, scrubbed and cut into quarters
- 1 cup Basic Vinaigrette (page 110)
- 8 ounces tempeh
- 1 teaspoon oil
- 8 red cherry tomatoes, cut into halves
- 8 yellow pear or cherry tomatoes, cut into halves
- 1/2 pound green beans, trimmed and cooked in boiling water for 1 minute
- 2 heads Boston or Bibb lettuce, washed, leaves separated
- 2 tablespoons Niçoise olives or other brine-cured or salt-cured olives
- 2 tablespoons Aioli (page 120)
- 1 cup Red Onion Pickles (page 126)
- 2 tablespoons capers

Rinse the potatoes well. Boil the potatoes in a pot of salted water until they are tender. Drain the potatoes and rinse gently with cold water to remove starch and avoid discoloration. Toss the warm potatoes with 1/4 cup of the basic vinaigrette. Let the potatoes cool completely.

Cut the tempeh into finger-size strips. In a medium sauté pan, heat the oil over high heat. Add the tempeh strips. Shake the pan or stir the tempeh strips until they begin to brown. When they are nicely browned, add 2 tablespoons of the vinaigrette to the pan. The vinaigrette will separate when it hits the pan. Stir briefly to glaze the tempeh and remove the pan from the heat. Lift the tempeh out of the pan, leaving the oil behind. Reserve.

Combine the tomatoes with 2 tablespoons vinaigrette and reserve. Combine the green beans with 2 tablespoons vinaigrette and reserve.

Line 4 large dinner plates with the lettuce leaves. Arrange one linear mound each of the potatoes, green beans, olives, tomatoes, and tempeh in a spoke pattern around the plate. Top each section of tempeh with some of the aioli. Mound some onion pickles in the center of each plate. Scatter the capers over the salads.

Makes 4 servings.

Apple-Fennel Salad

This is a quick and easy salad that showcases two of autumn's most delightful riches. If you are fortunate enough to live in an apple-producing area, go to a local orchard or farmers' market for the best selection of varieties.

1	tablespoon lemon juice
1	teaspoon sugar
½	cup soy mayonnaise
1	bulb fennel
3	medium-size tart apples, preferably York, Winesap, or Stayman

Whisk the lemon juice, sugar, and mayonnaise. Reserve.

Cut off the bottom and the long stalks of the fennel, reserving the stalks for stock, if you wish, and the feathery leaves for garnish. Cut the fennel bulb into halves. Remove the core by cutting toward the middle of the bulb on either side of the core. Pop out a triangular piece of core. Trim away any core you may have missed. Cut the fennel into ¼-inch slices or strips.

Cut the apples into quarters. Remove the core and seeds. Cut the apples into ⅓- to ½-inch half-moons.

In a 2-quart mixing bowl, toss the apples and fennel with the dressing. Adjust the seasonings with lemon juice, sugar, and salt.

Makes 6 servings.

Poppy Seed Coleslaw

If this salad sits for longer than 30 minutes, the green cabbage turns pink, which could be unappealing to some. If you prefer, you may omit the green cabbage entirely and use all red cabbage or vice versa.

⅔	cup brown rice syrup
1	cup raspberry vinegar
1	medium shallot, minced
1	tablespoon poppy seeds
¼	teaspoon salt
Pinch of white pepper (optional)	
¼	medium head red cabbage
¼	medium head green cabbage

Place the syrup in a mixing bowl. Whisk in the vinegar. Add the shallot and the poppy seeds. Season with salt. Add the white pepper. The flavors of the dressing should be fairly intense.

Slice the cabbage as thinly as possible with a chef's knife, a food processor, or the slicing side of a box grater.

Mix the cabbage with the dressing. Let stand for 30 minutes and then serve immediately.

Makes 8 servings.

Asian Coleslaw

I use regular green cabbage, which remains crisp for several hours in the dressing. If left overnight, the cabbage will become a little limp and the chilies will add some significant heat. Neither of these consequences is unpleasant, depending on your preference. If you substitute a more tender cabbage, like savoy or napa, the cabbage can be cut into ¼-inch slices, but the salad should be served on the same day it is made. For green cabbage, use your food processor, mandoline, or the side of your box grater to slice the cabbage as thinly as possible.

If you dislike cilantro, substitute Thai basil.

3 tablespoons lime juice
2 tablespoons rice wine vinegar
1 tablespoon sugar
½ teaspoon salt
2 dried red chilies, crumbled
4 cups thinly sliced green cabbage
1 small carrot, cut into small matchsticks or grated
2 shallots, thinly sliced
1 tablespoon fresh ginger, cut into matchsticks, or 2 teaspoons minced fresh ginger
1 tablespoon coarsely chopped fresh cilantro leaves
¼ cup unsalted peanuts, roasted and chopped
Whole cilantro leaves for garnish

Whisk the lime juice, vinegar, sugar, salt, and chilies in a 2-quart mixing bowl. Add the cabbage, carrot, shallots, ginger, and chopped cilantro. Mix all ingredients thoroughly. Let the coleslaw stand for 15 minutes to allow the flavors to develop.

Divide the salad among 4 plates. Sprinkle generously with chopped peanuts and garnish with whole cilantro leaves.

Makes 4 servings.

Almost-Traditional Potato Salad

There's no reason that vegans can't participate in the traditional backyard cookout, so bring this version of potato salad to your next neighborhood gathering—but don't give your secret away!

2 pounds new potatoes, scrubbed and cut into 1½-inch cubes
1 cup soy mayonnaise
1 tablespoon mustard
1 tablespoon red wine vinegar
2 teaspoons lemon juice
1 teaspoon sugar or 1 tablespoon sweet pickle relish
¼ teaspoon salt
2 stalks celery, thinly sliced
½ medium red onion, finely diced

Rinse the potatoes well. Boil the potatoes in a large pot of salted water to cover by 3 to 4 inches until they are tender. Drain the potatoes and rinse gently with cold water to remove starch and avoid discoloration. Let the potatoes cool completely.

In a 2-quart mixing bowl, whisk the mayonnaise, mustard, vinegar, lemon juice, sugar (or relish), and salt. Add the celery and onion and mix well. Add the potatoes and toss until they are well coated. Refrigerate if desired. Allow the flavors to blend for 30 minutes before serving.

Makes 6 servings.

French Potato Salad

2 pounds fingerling or new potatoes, scrubbed and cut into 1½-inch cubes
1 tablespoon capers
½ cup red wine vinegar
1 tablespoon grainy mustard
2 teaspoons lemon juice
1 shallot, minced
1 small clove garlic, minced
1 tablespoon minced fresh parsley
2 teaspoons minced fresh tarragon or basil
1 cup extra virgin olive oil
Freshly ground pepper
2 green onions, green and white parts, trimmed and cut into ½-inch pieces

Rinse the potatoes well. Boil the potatoes in a large pot of salted water to cover by 3 to 4 inches until they are tender. Drain the potatoes and rinse gently with cold water to remove starch and avoid discoloration. Let the potatoes cool completely.

Chop half of the capers coarsely and put in a 2-quart mixing bowl. Reserve the rest of the capers. Add the vinegar, mustard, lemon juice, shallot, garlic, and herbs and whisk to blend. Whisking vigorously, drizzle the oil into the vinegar mixture, slowly at first, then a little faster as the oil is incorporated. The dressing should be fairly thick. (The consistency should be thicker than Italian dressing but thinner than mayonnaise.)

Add the potatoes and the reserved capers and toss until all of the potatoes are well coated. Season with freshly ground pepper. Refrigerate, if desired. Allow the flavors to blend for 30 minutes before serving. Garnish with green onions just before serving.

Makes 6 servings.

Italian Potato Salad

Perhaps this is not an entirely authentic Italian dish. It was born of necessity one day when I had made too much roasted red pepper vinaigrette. It is, however, in the Italian spirit—and delicious. Oil-cured or kalamata olives work well.

2   pounds fingerling or new
    potatoes, scrubbed and
    cut into 1½-inch cubes
1   cup Roasted Red
    Pepper and Basil
    Vinaigrette (page 113)
1   medium red onion,
    finely diced
1   teaspoon minced garlic
½   cup roasted red peppers,
    cut into ⅓-inch strips
¼   cup fresh parsley, minced
¼   cup fresh basil leaves,
    cut into strips
2   cups whole arugula
    leaves, well washed
¼   cup pitted black olives,
    cut into quarters

Rinse the potatoes well. Boil them in a large pot of salted water to cover by 3 or 4 inches until tender. Drain the potatoes and rinse gently with cold water to remove starch and avoid discoloration.

In a large mixing bowl, toss the warm potatoes with the vinaigrette, onion, and garlic. Allow the salad to cool to room temperature. The warm potatoes will absorb the dressing. Before continuing, add more vinaigrette, if desired.

Add the peppers, parsley, and basil to the cooled salad. To serve, arrange the arugula around the edge of the serving platter. Pile the potato salad in the middle and scatter the olives around the salad.

Makes 8 servings.

DRESSINGS

Once you get the hang of making your own dressings, you'll wonder why you ever bought the expensive bottled ones—especially the ones with chemical additives you'd rather avoid. Homemade dressings with lots of vegetables, such as Big Vegetable Dressing and Tomato-Tarragon Dressing, will keep in the refrigerator for 3 to 4 days. Other dressings will stay fresh in the refrigerator for 7 to 14 days. See pages 26–29 for information on oils.

Basic Vinaigrette

Mustard is the magic ingredient that holds vinaigrettes together. This dressing will separate but will come back together with a quick whisking. Or you can make the vinaigrette in a jar with a tight-fitting lid and shake it whenever you are ready to use it.

Match the flavors of the vinegar and oil to the other ingredients you plan to use.

1   tablespoon Dijon
    mustard
½   teaspoon minced garlic
1   teaspoon minced shallot
½   teaspoon sugar
½   teaspoon salt
¼   teaspoon black pepper
½   cup red wine, white
    wine, or other vinegar
1   cup canola, grape seed,
    or olive oil, or a
    combination

In a 1-quart mixing bowl or a food processor, whisk the mustard, garlic, shallot, sugar, salt, pepper, and vinegar. Whisking vigorously, or with the food processor running, drizzle the oil into the vinegar base, slowly at first, then a little faster as the oil is incorporated. Taste and adjust seasonings.

Makes 1½ cups.

Italian Vinaigrette

A good basic dressing to have on hand, this also works nicely as a marinade for raw or lightly blanched vegetables. If you'd like to make a Greek dressing, add ¼ teaspoon oregano. If you'd like to make it creamy, reduce the oil to ½ cup, add 4 ounces of tofu, and purée.

½ cup red wine vinegar
1 tablespoon Dijon mustard
1½ teaspoons minced garlic
1 teaspoon finely minced shallot or red onion
¼ teaspoon dried basil
⅛ teaspoon dried thyme
½ teaspoon sugar
¼ teaspoon salt
1 generous pinch black pepper
1 tablespoon lemon juice
1 cup oil

In a 1-quart mixing bowl or a food processor, whisk the vinegar, mustard, garlic, onion, herbs, sugar, salt, pepper, and lemon juice. While whisking vigorously, or with the food processor running, drizzle the oil into the vinegar mixture very carefully—slowly at first, then a little faster as the oil is incorporated. This dressing may separate but can be brought back together by whisking.

Makes 1¾ cups.

Balsamic Vinaigrette

This is my favorite dressing for everyday eating. Make sure to use a good mellow balsamic vinegar from Modena, Italy, where all true balsamics originate. This dressing is particularly well suited to mesclun greens.

½ cup balsamic vinegar
1 tablespoon Dijon mustard
½ teaspoon minced garlic
⅓ teaspoon sugar
½ teaspoon sea salt
⅛ teaspoon ground black pepper
2 teaspoons lemon juice
1 cup olive oil, or ½ cup extra virgin olive oil and ½ cup canola or grapeseed oil

In a 1-quart mixing bowl or a food processor, whisk the vinegar, mustard, garlic, sugar, salt, pepper, and lemon juice. While whisking vigorously, or with the food processor running, drizzle the oil into the balsamic mixture very carefully—slowly at first, then a little faster as the oil is incorporated. This dressing should be fairly thick and will remain emulsified for several days.

Makes 1⅔ cups.

Mustard-Sherry Vinaigrette

The sweetness of the sherry in this simple dressing pairs well with mesclun or bitter greens. For added richness, purée a roasted shallot into the dressing.

1   teaspoon Dijon mustard
2   teaspoons minced shallot
1/8 teaspoon sugar
Generous pinch of sea salt
1/2 cup sherry vinegar
1   cup oil

In a 1-quart mixing bowl or a food processor, whisk the mustard, shallot, sugar, salt, and vinegar. While whisking vigorously, or with the food processor running, drizzle the oil into the vinegar mixture very carefully—slowly at first, then a little faster as the oil is incorporated. This dressing may separate but can be brought back together by whisking.

Makes 1 1/2 cups.

Raspberry Vinaigrette

This is a classic sweet-and-sour combination, which makes it suitable for most bitter greens. If raspberries are too expensive or unavailable, simply omit them from the recipe.

1   heaping teaspoon Dijon mustard
1   teaspoon minced shallot
2   teaspoons brown rice syrup or 2 teaspoons sugar
1/2 cup raspberry vinegar
1   tablespoon lemon juice
1/4 cup fresh or frozen raspberries
1   cup canola, grapeseed, or olive oil, or a blend

In the container of a blender or food processor, combine the mustard, shallot, syrup or sugar, vinegar, lemon juice, and raspberries. Purée the mixture. With the food processor or blender running, carefully drizzle the oil into the vinegar mixture—slowly at first, then a little faster as the oil is incorporated. Taste and adjust seasonings.

Makes 2 cups.

Roasted Red Pepper and Basil Vinaigrette

While this recipe is similar to the one for Balsamic Vinaigrette, the addition of sweet roasted red peppers and basil change its flavors dramatically. While the Balsamic Vinaigrette is best for greens, this dressing is best used with potatoes, pasta, rice, or blanched green vegetables like broccoli rabe or green beans.

You will get the best results using a food processor or immersion blender. If you are preparing this recipe by hand, finely mince the red peppers and basil called for in the first part of the recipe.

½ cup balsamic vinegar
½ cup roasted red peppers, fresh or canned
½ cup fresh basil, loosely packed and coarsely chopped
1 tablespoon Dijon mustard
1½ teaspoons minced garlic
⅓ teaspoon sugar
½ teaspoon sea salt
⅛ teaspoon ground black pepper
2 teaspoons lemon juice
1 cup oil

In your food processor or a 1-quart mixing bowl, purée or whisk the vinegar, half of the peppers, half of the basil, mustard, garlic, sugar, salt, pepper, and lemon juice. With the food processor or blender running or while whisking vigorously, drizzle the oil into the balsamic mixture very carefully—slowly at first, then a little faster as the oil is incorporated. This dressing should be fairly thick. Cut the remaining peppers into ¼-inch strips. Add to the dressing along with the remaining basil. Taste and adjust seasonings.

Makes 2½ cups.

Sesame-Soy Vinaigrette

This is a simple, elegant dressing. It is not emulsified so you will need to whisk or shake it before you use it. If you can't get rice wine vinegar, distilled white vinegar will do.

1 clove garlic
1 tablespoon soy sauce
¼ cup rice wine vinegar
1 teaspoon sesame oil
½ cup canola or grapeseed oil
1 teaspoon sesame seeds, toasted

Crush the garlic clove with the side of your knife. In a 1-quart mixing bowl, place the garlic, soy sauce, and vinegar. Whisk in the oils. Add the sesame seeds. Let the dressing stand for 15 minutes to allow the flavors to blend.

Makes ¾ cup.

Citrus Dressing

This dressing stays emulsified longer when made in a food processor or with an immersion blender. Should the dressing separate, however, a little vigorous whisking will combine it again. Try either blood orange juice or orange juice concentrate for a fuller flavor.

1	minced shallot
2	teaspoons Dijon mustard
1/4	cup orange juice
2	tablespoons Key lime juice
2	tablespoons lemon juice
1	teaspoon sugar
1	teaspoon salt
1	cup oil

In a 1-quart mixing bowl or a food processor, whisk the shallot, mustard, juices, sugar, and salt. While whisking vigorously, or with the food processor running, drizzle the oil into the juice mixture very carefully—slowly at first, then a little faster as the oil is incorporated. This dressing should be thick and will stay emulsified for 2 or 3 days.

Makes 1 1/2 cups.

Tahini Dressing

This is a delightfully simple dressing with a clean taste. Use on blanched vegetables like broccoli or some of the sturdier bitter greens or head lettuces. This recipe does not work well in the food processor, which tends to heat the tahini and cause the dressing to become stiff.

2	tablespoons extra virgin olive oil
1/2	cup tahini
1	teaspoon minced garlic
1/2	teaspoon ground cumin
1/4	teaspoon ground coriander
1/8	teaspoon fine sea salt
6	tablespoons lemon juice

In a 1-quart mixing bowl, whisk 1/3 cup of cold water and the olive oil into the tahini. Add the garlic, cumin, coriander, and salt. Drizzle the lemon juice into the tahini mixture while whisking continuously. The dressing may become stiff, but this is a temporary condition. Once the lemon juice begins to be incorporated, the dressing will become smooth again. Taste and adjust seasonings.

Makes 1 1/2 cups.

Tofu-Dill Dressing

This is a creamy low-fat dressing perfect for cucumbers, romaine, carrots, and most any salad combination.

8	ounces firm silken tofu
2	tablespoons coarsely chopped fresh dill weed
½	cup lemon juice
2	tablespoons rice wine vinegar
1	teaspoon minced garlic
2	tablespoons finely minced red onion
1	tablespoon light miso
1	cup water

Place the tofu, 1 tablespoon of dill leaves, lemon juice, vinegar, garlic, onion, and miso into the bowl of a food processor and purée. With the food processor running, add the water in a constant stream. Taste and adjust the seasonings. Adjust the consistency with water. Remove to a storage container and add the remaining dill leaves. Allow the flavors to develop for 15 minutes before using.

If using a blender, place the water, lemon juice, and vinegar in the cup of the blender first. Cut the tofu into small pieces and put them into the water. Add 1 tablespoon of dill leaves, garlic, onion, and miso. Pulse the mixture and then purée. Taste and adjust seasonings. Adjust the consistency with water. Remove to a storage container and add the remaining dill leaves. Allow the flavors to develop for 15 minutes before using.

Makes 2½ cups.

Tomato-Tarragon Dressing

For leafy green salads, I prefer to toss the fresh herbs with the greens. For head lettuces, putting the herbs in the dressing works better. This dressing is also delicious on green beans, asparagus, or pasta.

1	cup seeded, diced fresh tomato or 1 cup canned diced tomato, drained
2	tablespoons coarsely chopped fresh tarragon
1	minced shallot
½	teaspoon chopped garlic
2	tablespoons red wine vinegar
2	tablespoons lemon juice
1	cup oil

Place the tomato, 1 tablespoon of tarragon, shallot, garlic, vinegar, and lemon juice into the container of a blender or food processor and purée. With the motor running, drizzle the oil into the vinegar mixture very carefully—slowly at first, then a little faster. Remove to a storage container and add the remaining tarragon. Allow the flavors to develop for 15 minutes before using.

Makes 2½ cups.

Big Vegetable Dressing

This dressing is so similar to a popular buttermilk dressing that it may fool the kids! If you don't have a food processor, put the vegetables through a food grinder. This dressing will keep for 3 to 4 days in the refrigerator.

1   small carrot, peeled and cut into ¹/₂-inch coins
1   small green pepper, cut into 1-inch cubes
1   small red pepper, cut into 1-inch cubes
1   stalk celery, cut into ¹/₄-inch pieces
2   cloves garlic
8   ounces firm silken tofu
¹/₄ cup soymilk
2   tablespoons lemon juice
1   tablespoon apple cider vinegar
1   teaspoon dried dill weed
1   tablespoon chopped fresh parsley
2   teaspoons Mrs. Dash, Spike, or similar seasoning
¹/₈ teaspoon black pepper

Place the carrot, peppers, celery, and garlic into the bowl of a food processor. Pulse until the vegetables are coarsely chopped. Add the remaining ingredients and purée. Taste the dressing and adjust seasonings.

Makes 2¹/₂ cups.

condiments & sauces

Condiments

Tofu Mayonnaise

Basic Aioli

Stovetop Ketchup

Cranberry Ketchup

Hot Mustard

Apricot Mustard

Olive Relish

Red Onion and Rosemary Relish

Green Tomato Relish

Summer Tarragon Pickles

Okra Pickles

Red Onion Pickles

Basil Pesto

Sun-Dried Tomato Pesto

Mushroom Pesto

Cilantro Pesto

Romesco Sauce

Black Olive Tapenade

Green Olive Tapenade

Sauces

Roasted Red Pepper Coulis

Tomato Barbecue Sauce

Orange-Chipotle Barbecue Sauce

Chinese-Style Barbecue Sauce

Simple Asian Barbecue Sauce

Tahini Sauce

Rich Tahini Sauce

Peanut Sauce

Pico de Gallo

Salsa Cruda

Simple Soy Dipping Sauce

Sweet and Sour Dipping Sauce

Vietnamese Lime Dipping Sauce

Harissa Dipping Sauce

Meshwiya

Vegan Béchamel

Vegan Mornay Sauce

Velvety Vegetable Sauce

Vegan Demi-glace

Vegan Gravy

Sometimes the most memorable part of a meal is that perfect accompaniment, the little item on the plate that adds just the right note of sweet, sour, salty, or bitter to bring the whole meal into focus. This is the power of a condiment. Similarly, in a traditional restaurant meal, there is usually a piece of meat (or poultry or fish) that is cooked rather simply but served with some sauce that gives the meal definition. In vegan meals, where vegetables, grains, and beans take center stage, it is the sauce that coaxes the subtle essences from food and elevates eating to dining.

CONDIMENTS

Mayonnaise

I never understood the appeal of mayonnaise until I had some freshly made with fresh lemon juice and flavorful oil. This rich emulsion adds body and flavor to lean ingredients, which accounts for its use in potato salad, coleslaw, and salad dressings. Regular mayonnaise contains egg yolks and lots of oil. The good news is that in vegan mayonnaise, the egg yolks and most of the oil are replaced by tofu. Not only is the resulting sauce void of cholesterol, but it's also creamy, lower in fat, and tasty! Recipes using fresh herbs retain their vibrant flavors in the refrigerator for 4 to 5 days. Other recipes stay fresh for 2 weeks.

Tofu Mayonnaise

There are many commercially available soy mayonnaises, but it is easy to make your own at home, not to mention cheaper. This would be a good place to slip in some garlic flaxseed oil, if you are so inclined.

1   **pound tofu**
1   **tablespoon rice wine or white vinegar**
2   **tablespoons fresh lemon juice**
1   **teaspoon Dijon mustard**
2   **tablespoons to 1/4 cup extra virgin olive oil or other oil**
1   **teaspoon white miso or 1/2 teaspoon salt**

Crumble the tofu into a blender container or the bowl of a food processor. Add the remaining ingredients. Process until smooth. Refrigerate for 8 to 12 hours before using.

Makes 2 cups.

Aïoli

Aioli is a traditional Italian condiment that is, in essence, a garlic mayonnaise. Below are several versions, all based on the Tofu Mayonnaise (page 119), that can add new dimensions to simple foods. This recipe will produce a mild, all-purpose aioli. I like aïoli with a sharp garlic bite, however, so feel free to double the garlic for a zestier sauce. But remember that a little garlic can go a long way!

Basic Aïoli

2   cups Tofu Mayonnaise
     or prepared soy mayonnaise
1   teaspoon minced fresh garlic
1   teaspoon lemon juice (optional)

Mix all ingredients well.
Makes 2 cups.

Roasted Red Pepper Aïoli: To 1 cup of Basic Aioli add ¼ cup of chopped, roasted red peppers and purée or blend well.

Pesto Aïoli: To 1 cup of Basic Aioli, add 2 tablespoons of Basil Pesto (page 127) and mix well.

Chipotle Aïoli: To 2 cups of Basic Aioli, add one-half of a single chipotle chili, ¼ teaspoon of ground cumin, ¼ teaspoon of chili powder, and ⅛ teaspoon of ground coriander and purée or blend well.

Mustard-Dill Aïoli: Combine 2 cups of Basic Aioli, 1 tablespoon of grainy mustard, and 1 tablespoon of chopped fresh dill and mix well. Mustard-Dill Aioli is good on green beans.

Ketchup

A member of a family of sweet and sour sauces common to American cuisine, ketchup is most commonly made with tomatoes, though mushroom ketchup was once widely marketed and banana ketchup can be found in the Asian section of many grocery stores. Most ketchups are smooth, puréed sauces. The base for ketchup is usually a fruit (a tomato is a fruit), nut, or vegetable, with vinegar or citrus juice added, along with some spices. Ketchup can be blistering hot or quite mild. Many hot sauces employ carrots as a base and have a ketchup-like consistency. The ketchup recipes given here will stay fresh in the refrigerator for 2 to 3 weeks.

These condiments are great accompaniments to Tostones (page 51), Ginger-Fried Tempeh (page 251), or your favorite veggie burger. Ketchup is also used in many Asian dishes such as Nasi Goreng (page 180) or Pad Thai (page 198).

Stovetop Ketchup

A distinctly American condiment, ketchup doesn't have to come from the grocery store. Stovetop ketchup requires refrigeration and is best used within a week or two.

This recipe specifies canned tomatoes because they are already skinned and seeded.

1   teaspoon oil
1   medium onion, diced
1   teaspoon minced garlic
2   teaspoons salt
1/8 teaspoon ground cinnamon
1/8 teaspoon ground allspice
Pinch cloves
1   28-ounce can diced tomatoes
1/2 cup apple cider vinegar
1/2 cup sugar

Heat the oil in a small saucepan over medium heat. Sauté the onion, garlic, salt, and spices for 8 minutes or until the onion is very soft. Add the remaining ingredients. Turn the heat to medium-high and bring the mixture to a boil. Lower the heat to medium-low and simmer for 15 minutes. Let the mixture cool, and then purée it.

Adjust the seasoning with salt, sugar, or vinegar and the consistency with water.

Makes 3 cups.

Chipotle Ketchup: Add one-quarter to one-half of a single canned chipotle chili just before puréeing.

Curry Ketchup: Add 2 teaspoons of curry powder to the spice mixture.

Mango Ketchup: Replace all or some of the tomatoes with fresh mangoes or mango purée.

Cranberry Ketchup

Most dried fruits, including blueberries, papaya, and apricots, will work in this recipe, although I wouldn't try it with dates or figs. Different fruits may require some seasoning adjustments.

1 1/2 cups dried cranberries or cherries
1/2 cup cranberry juice
1/2 cup orange juice
2   tablespoons balsamic vinegar
2   tablespoons Succanat or brown sugar
1/8 teaspoon ground allspice
1/4 teaspoon ground ginger
1   shallot, minced

Combine all the ingredients in a small saucepan and bring to a boil over medium-high heat. Lower the heat to medium and simmer for 20 minutes or until the cranberries are very soft. Let the mixture cool, and then purée it. Adjust the seasoning with salt and sugar and the consistency with water or orange juice.

Makes about 2 cups.

Mustard

Whole mustard seeds come in white, brown and black. Black mustard seeds have a hot but mellow flavor, while brown are blistering hot and white a bit milder. Dry mustard loses its potency after opening so either keep it in the freezer or plan to use it within six months. White mustard seeds are found in most American prepared mustards, while English mustards contain both brown and white mustard seeds along with wheat flour. Chinese mustards normally contain brown seeds.

Mustard is often a humble ingredient in other sauces, like barbecue sauce or mayonnaise. In vegan recipes, it is often paired with nutritional yeast to produce a cheesy flavor. Hearty mustards, like the Apricot Mustard below, can stand on their own as accompaniments to veggie burgers, Panelle (page 54), or Ginger-Fried Tempeh (page 251). These mustards will keep indefinitely in the refrigerator.

Hot Mustard

For a different taste, try using beer for all or part of the liquid in this recipe. If you prefer a yellow color, add ¼ teaspoon of turmeric to the mustard powder.

¼ cup white wine
   (optional)
½ cup dry mustard

Reduce the wine by half. Add ½ cup of water and bring the mixture to a boil. Whisk the boiling water slowly into the dry mustard. Let the flavors develop for 15 minutes.
   Makes ¾ cup.

Apricot Mustard

5 dried apricots, cut into
   thin strips
2 tablespoons whole
   mustard seeds
¼ cup orange or apple juice
¼ cup dry mustard
½ teaspoon salt

In a small bowl cover the apricots with ¼ cup of boiling water. Cover the bowl and let stand for 10 minutes. In a food processor, blender, or spice mill, coarsely grind the mustard seeds. In a small saucepan, boil the juice. Whisk the juice into the dry mustard. Combine all of the ingredients in the saucepan, including the soaking liquid from the apricots. Cook the mixture over low heat for 5 to 10 minutes, until it is quite thick. Purée the mustard, adjusting the consistency with juice or water. Refrigerate the mustard for 8 to 12 hours before using to allow the flavors to develop.
   Makes 1 cup.

Relish

Relish typically refers to pickle relish, a condiment combining sweet, salty, and sour tastes, perhaps with a little hot pepper. Relishes are based on the same flavor principles as ketchups but have a chunky texture.

In addition to trying the recipes here, you can find all sorts of prepared relishes in the store. Chowchow, piccalilli, and kimchi are familiar but wildly different relishes. Chutneys are a subset of relishes but with some unique characteristics. East Indian chutneys tend to be more like salsa—raw or lightly cooked vegetables and fruits—but with the sweet note of relish. English chutneys are long-cooked and contain chunky fruits, vegetables, and spices. Another relish to look for is sambal, a spicy Indonesian condiment, served with rice or as a side dish. Sambals can be as simple as ground chilies with sugar and salt, or as elaborate as a combination of fruits, coconut, chilies, and lemongrass. Specialty stores often carry some very good packaged sambals.

Olive Relish

Olive Relish, a component of Muffuletta (page 150), is equally good topping Bruschetta (page 60) or tossed with tomatoes for an impromptu salad. This relish should be used within 1 week.

⅓ cup pitted green olives
⅓ cup pitted black olives (not canned ripe olives)
1 tablespoon capers
⅓ cup chopped roasted red peppers
¼ cup diced celery
½ teaspoon red pepper flakes
1 tablespoon chopped fresh basil
2 teaspoons chopped fresh parsley
1 teaspoon chopped fresh oregano
1 tablespoon fresh lemon juice
1 teaspoon minced fresh garlic
¼ cup minced red onion
¼ teaspoon black pepper
¼ cup red wine vinegar
¼ cup extra virgin olive oil

Chop the olives, capers, and red peppers coarsely with a knife or by pulsing in a food processor. Combine the olive mixture with the remaining ingredients. Let the mixture stand for at least two hours before using.

Makes about 1½ cups.

Red Onion and Rosemary Relish

Balsamic vinegar gives this relish a deep, rounded flavor. For a more piquant relish, use red wine vinegar. This condiment goes well with sturdy, earthy flavors such as lentils, kasha, tempeh, grilled vegetables (especially portobellos), or veggie burgers. This recipe is best used within 3 to 4 days.

1 tablespoon blended oil
3 large red onions, peeled, cut in $3/8$-inch slices, and separated into rings
4 cloves garlic, sliced thinly
$1/4$ cup balsamic vinegar
2 teaspoons sugar
$1/4$ teaspoon salt
$1/8$ teaspoon black pepper
$1/2$ teaspoon minced fresh rosemary

In a wide skillet, heat the oil over high heat. When the oil is quite hot (just below smoking), carefully add the onions to the pan. When the onions develop some color, after about 1 to 2 minutes, stir them. Add the garlic and reduce the heat to medium-high. Cook, stirring every 1 to 2 minutes, until the onions are wilted and are a deep brown color.

Add the balsamic vinegar and cook, stirring, until all the liquid has evaporated. Sprinkle the sugar over the onions and cook for 1 minute longer. Remove the pan from the heat. Add the salt, pepper, and rosemary and mix well.

Makes about 2 cups.

Green Tomato Relish

This is a quick relish, not meant for canning, that takes full advantage of the astringent quality of green tomatoes. It gives an added dimension to tofu pups. This relish will keep indefinitely in the refrigerator.

2 tablespoons salt
1 cup chopped green tomatoes
2 medium green bell peppers, finely diced
2 small jalapeños, seeded and finely diced
1 medium red bell pepper, finely diced
1 medium yellow bell pepper, finely diced
1 medium yellow onion, finely diced
3 tablespoons Succanat or brown sugar
2 teaspoons mustard seeds
$1/2$ teaspoon celery seeds
$1^1/3$ cups vinegar

In a large mixing bowl, sprinkle the salt over the vegetables and mix thoroughly. Let stand for 3 to 4 hours. Drain the vegetables in a colander and rinse under running water. Pat the vegetables dry and reserve.

In a large stainless steel saucepan, combine the sugar, mustard seeds, celery seeds, and vinegar. Simmer the mixture for 15 minutes. Add the vegetables and bring the mixture to a boil. Pack the hot mixture into a 1-quart jar. When the relish has cooled from hot to very warm, put the lid loosely on the jar. When the relish has cooled to room temperature, tighten the lid and refrigerate for 8 to 12 hours before using.

Makes 1 quart.

Pickles

Pickles can be sweet or sour, hot or mild. Sturdy vegetables, such as carrots, cauliflower, okra, zucchini, onions, corn, hot peppers, cactus paddles, or, of course, cucumbers, make wonderful pickles. Pickles can be a good vehicle for sneaking vegetables into the diet of a picky child.

Summer Tarragon Pickles

2   medium cucumbers, bias cut into 1-inch slices
1   medium carrot, bias cut into ½-inch slices
4   stalks celery, bias cut into 1-inch slices
1   medium onion, cut into 1-inch cubes
1   cup 1-inch chunks of red bell pepper
1   cup 1-inch chunks of green bell pepper
1   small cauliflower, broken into florets
½   cup salt
½   cup sugar
2   teaspoons mustard seeds
1   teaspoon celery seeds
2   tablespoons whole black peppercorns
1   cup tarragon white wine vinegar
4   sprigs tarragon

Combine the vegetables in a large bowl. Dissolve the salt in 6 cups of cold water and pour over the vegetables. Let stand for 8 to 12 hours in a cool place. Drain and rinse under running water. Drain thoroughly and reserve.

In a stainless steel saucepan, combine the sugar, mustard seeds, celery seeds, peppercorns, and vinegar. Simmer the mixture for 15 minutes. Add the vegetables and simmer for 5 minutes longer. Pack the vegetables into a 1-quart jar. Slide the tarragon sprigs into the jar. Pour the hot vinegar mixture over the vegetables, making sure to transfer all the spices to the jar.

When the pickles have cooled from hot to very warm, put the lid loosely on the jar. When the pickles have cooled to room temperature, tighten the lid and refrigerate for 8 to 18 hours before use.

Makes 1 quart.

Okra Pickles

Even people who hate cooked okra like okra pickles. For this recipe to work, the okra must be tender, so choose okra the size of your thumb or smaller. If it is more mature, simmer the okra with the vinegar and sugar for 5 minutes or until it's tender.

1   medium onion, cut into long, thin strips
1   pound young okra, trimmed
1¾ cups apple cider vinegar
1   tablespoon salt
¾   cup sugar
4   whole cloves
6   black peppercorns
2   teaspoons mustard seeds

Pack the onion and okra into a quart jar with a tight-fitting lid. In a stainless steel saucepan, bring the remaining ingredients to a boil. Pour over the okra and onions. When the mixture has cooled from hot to very warm, put the lid loosely on the jar. When the pickles have cooled to room temperature, tighten the lid and refrigerate for 8 to 12 hours before using.

Makes about 1 quart.

Red Onion Pickles

3   large red onions, peeled, cut into ⅜-inch slices, and separated into rings
½   cup plus 2 tablespoons red wine vinegar
¼   cup sugar
¼   teaspoon salt
1   whole clove
3   black peppercorns

Place the onions in a medium bowl. In a small saucepan, combine the vinegar, sugar, salt, clove, peppercorns, and ¼ cup of water. Bring the mixture to a boil. Pour the hot liquid over the onions and toss to blend. Let the onions marinate for 1 hour before using. Store the onions in the vinegar mixture in the refrigerator.

Makes 2 cups.

Pesto

Pesto is an uncooked, finely ground sauce usually made with fresh herbs, nuts, and oil. It can be the featured sauce for pasta, a marinade for roasted vegetables, or a flavoring agent for mayonnaise. Pesto showcases the brilliant, sharp flavors of fresh herbs and modulates them with the sweetness of nuts and oil.

Ready-made pestos available at the grocery store generally contain cheese. Vegan pestos tend to have more intense herb flavors and an oilier consistency. To thicken the pesto for use as a spread, add some breadcrumbs or matzoh meal.

Basil Pesto

Genoa is the home of pesto. Genovese basil has a bit of a spicy kick and makes the most authentic pesto. Look for basil with notched or serrated leaves and a deep green color. Sweet basil, whose leaves are smooth along the edges, has a mild, pleasing flavor but won't give you the bite of Genovese basil. For a different taste, use half sweet basil and half flavored basil, such as lemon basil or cinnamon basil.

Traditionally, pesto is made by crushing the ingredients together in a mortar with a pestle. Thank goodness for the food processor and the blender! If the blade on your food processor is not exceptionally sharp, you will want to coarsely chop the basil with a knife before putting it into the food processor.

1½ teaspoons minced garlic
½ teaspoon sea salt
1½ cups fresh basil leaves
3 tablespoons pine nuts
⅓ cup extra virgin olive oil

In the bowl of a food processor, mix the garlic and salt. Let stand for 2 minutes. Add the basil and pine nuts and process until a thick paste forms. With the motor running, drizzle the olive oil through the feed tube. Work quickly, as the heat of the food processor warms the mixture, possibly altering its flavor. Taste and adjust seasonings.

Makes about ⅔ cup.

Sun-Dried Tomato Pesto

If your food processor can effectively handle smaller volumes, this recipe may be halved.

½ cup hazelnuts, toasted
1 cup sun-dried tomatoes
  in oil, well-drained, oil
  reserved
1 teaspoon minced garlic
2 tablespoons minced
  fresh basil
Extra virgin olive oil
Salt and pepper

Coarsely chop the hazelnuts in a food processor. Add the sun-dried tomatoes and garlic and process until fairly smooth. Taste the oil from the sun-dried tomatoes. If you find the taste pleasing, you may use it in the next step. Add the basil and turn the machine on. Slowly drizzle either the reserved oil or extra virgin olive oil through the feed tube until a thick but spreadable paste is formed. Taste and add salt and pepper as desired. The amount of oil you need will vary depending on the sun-dried tomatoes you use.

Makes 1¾ cups.

Mushroom Pesto

5 medium portobello
  mushrooms, grilled or
  roasted, or 2 cups
  cremini mushrooms,
  roasted
2 teaspoons minced garlic
¼ teaspoon salt
⅛ teaspoon freshly ground
  black pepper
½ cup walnut halves and
  pieces
1 teaspoon finely chopped
  fresh rosemary
½ cup coarsely chopped
  flat-leaf parsley
½ cup extra virgin olive oil

Slice the mushrooms thinly and chop coarsely. In the bowl of a food processor, mix the garlic, salt, and pepper together. Let stand for 2 minutes. Add the mushrooms, walnuts, and herbs and process until a thick paste forms. With the motor running, drizzle the olive oil through the feed tube. Taste and adjust the seasonings.

Makes about 2 cups.

Cilantro Pesto

1½ teaspoons minced garlic
1   teaspoon sea salt
½   teaspoon chili powder, preferably ancho
¼   teaspoon chipotle powder, or one-half of a dried chipotle, or one-fourth of a canned chipotle
½   teaspoon ground cumin
¼   teaspoon cayenne
1½ cups fresh cilantro leaves
½   cup toasted pumpkin seeds
⅓   cup extra virgin olive oil

In the bowl of a food processor, combine the garlic, salt, chili powder, chipotle powder, cumin, and cayenne. Let stand for 2 minutes. Add the cilantro and pumpkin seeds and process until a thick paste forms. With the motor running, drizzle the olive oil through the feed tube. Work quickly, as the heat of the food processor warms the pesto, possibly altering its flavor.

Makes about 1 cup.

Romesco Sauce

Romesco sauce is very similar to pesto but comes from Catalonia in Spain. Traditionally, this sauce is served over grilled baby leeks. Adjust the heat to your liking by adding or omitting the red pepper flakes. Try using this sauce used as a sandwich filling, as in Mixed Vegetable Romesco Focaccia (page 153). Good Spanish paprika adds some lovely flavor undertones. Many gourmet shops carry a smoked Spanish paprika in both mild and hot varieties, which is especially nice. If your paprika is old, just omit it.

½   cup sliced or slivered almonds
¼   cup breadcrumbs or matzoh meal
2   teaspoons minced garlic
⅛   teaspoon red pepper flakes
⅛   teaspoon paprika
¼   teaspoon sea salt
⅛   teaspoon freshly ground black pepper
1   cup roasted red peppers
1   medium tomato, peeled and seeded (optional)
½   cup red wine vinegar
½   cup extra virgin olive oil

Process the almonds, breadcrumbs, garlic, pepper flakes, paprika, salt, and pepper in a food processor until the almonds are finely chopped. Do not allow a paste to form. Add the red peppers, tomato, and vinegar. Process until the mixture is smooth. With the machine running, drizzle the oil through the feed tube. Taste and adjust the seasonings.

Makes about 2 cups.

Tapenade

The people of Provence in the South of France created tapenade. There are thousands of variations on this olive paste. Many versions contain anchovies or even tuna. Some are thick and emulsified and some are thin and separated. However you prefer your tapenade, it makes a delightful dip for French bread, a delicious spread on sandwiches, or a lovely condiment with the grilled vegetables of late summer.

Double check for pits before placing the olives in the food processor! Unfortunately, tapenade does not fit into a low-salt diet.

Black Olive Tapenade

While it is not traditional, I like to use tomato juice in black olive tapenade. It helps to keep the mixture emulsified and allows me to use much less oil.

1 cup black olive paste or 1½ cups pitted black olives
¼ teaspoon red pepper flakes
1 tablespoon capers
2 tablespoons diced red onion
2 teaspoons minced garlic
2 tablespoons tomato juice
1 tablespoon lemon juice
2 tablespoons extra virgin olive oil
1 tablespoon coarsely chopped fresh basil

In a food processor, process the olives, red pepper flakes, capers, onion, and garlic in brief pulses until they are coarsely chopped. Add the tomato and lemon juices and pulse 2 or 3 times to mix. With the motor running (or while whisking), drizzle in the olive oil and add the basil. Do not overprocess.

If working by hand, finely chop or dice the olives, red pepper flakes, capers, onion, garlic, and basil. Add the tomato and lemon juices and mix well. Drizzle in the olive oil while whisking. Stir in the basil.

Makes about 2 cups.

Green Olive Tapenade

1½ cups green olives, pitted and finely chopped

¼ cup capers

2 tablespoons diced yellow onion

1 teaspoon minced garlic

Juice and zest of 1 lemon

3 tablespoons extra virgin olive oil

2 tablespoons coarsely chopped flat-leaf parsley

In a food processor, process the olives, capers, onion, and garlic in brief pulses until coarsely chopped. Add the lemon juice and zest and pulse 2 or 3 times to mix. With the motor running, drizzle in the olive oil and add the parsley. Do not overprocess.

If working by hand, finely chop or dice the olives, capers, onions, garlic, and parsley. Add the lemon zest and juice and mix well. Drizzle in the olive oil while whisking.

Makes about 2 cups.

SAUCES

Coulis

The word "coulis" may be unfamiliar to you, but it is merely a puréed sauce that highlights one prominent flavor with perhaps some subtle undertones or herbal accents.

Roasted Red Pepper Coulis

Here are basic and elaborate versions of a versatile, classic sauce.

Easy Roasted Red Pepper Coulis

This is a quick and easy sauce, assuming you have plenty of roasted red peppers on hand. Add a little spice with crushed red pepper or hot sauce.

1 cup roasted red peppers, prepared or homemade (page 232)

¼ teaspoon minced fresh garlic

1 tablespoon minced fresh basil (optional)

¼ cup extra virgin olive oil

Salt and pepper

Purée the roasted red peppers, garlic, and basil together. Add the olive oil. Taste and adjust the seasonings with salt and pepper. Adjust the thickness with water.

Makes 1¼ cups.

Elaborate Roasted Red Pepper Coulis

It may seem odd to include both oven-roasted peppers and roasted red peppers, but each contributes a different note to the sauce— much as the roasted onion and sautéed onion do. A good, fresh-tasting canned tomato is essential to this sauce.

This sauce, one of my favorites, is spectacular with Basic Polenta (page 172) and sautéed spinach, grilled portobellos, Roasted Vegetable Terrine (page 48), or plain pasta. This recipe makes a lot, but the sauce will keep for 2 weeks if well refrigerated. If you don't care to store that much, add some soymilk and additional fresh basil to make an easy, delicious soup.

1   or 2 fresh red peppers, cut in 1-inch wide strips
1   large onion, cut in ½-inch rings
2   tablespoons oil
1   small onion, diced
2   teaspoons minced fresh garlic
¼   teaspoon dried basil
⅛   teaspoon dried thyme
2   28-ounce cans diced tomatoes
1   15-ounce can tomato sauce
2   cups roasted red peppers, prepared or homemade (page 231–232)
1   teaspoon sugar
½   teaspoon salt
¼   cup thinly sliced fresh basil, packed

Preheat oven to 400°. Toss the sliced peppers and onion with 1 tablespoon of oil. Place the vegetables in a pan or on a baking sheet fitted with parchment. Roast the vegetables in the oven, turning every 10 minutes to ensure even cooking. Cook the vegetables until they are cooked through. The onions should be brown and the skins of the peppers will be slightly blackened.

In a heavy saucepan, sauté the diced onion, minced garlic, dried basil, and thyme in the remaining oil until the onion has softened. Add the roasted vegetables, diced tomatoes, tomato sauce, and prepared or homemade roasted red peppers. Cook the sauce for 15 to 20 minutes to allow the flavors to blend. Add the sugar, salt, and basil. Purée the sauce.

Makes 8 cups.

Barbecue Sauce

The perfect complement to grilled or roasted foods is barbecue sauce, with its sweet and sour flavors. Although ketchup is often used as a base, the spicing is more elaborate than that of ketchup, with onions, garlic, mustard, and chili powder added to the mix. Barbecue sauce with a high sugar content ensures a nice glaze. Soy sauce, especially mushroom soy sauce, imparts a rich brown color. Some very simple twists in flavoring can transport your barbecue sauce around the world—star anise and ginger bring you to China, chipotles and cilantro to Mexico, sesame and chili to Korea, cinnamon and cumin to the Middle East, red curry paste to Thailand, lemon and oregano to Greece. Barbecue sauces can be either completely smooth or have some chunky components in a smooth base.

Tempeh, tofu, and hearty vegetables such as eggplant, zucchini, corn, and mushrooms are all good candidates for grilling with barbecue sauce. If you can't grill outside, bake, braise, or broil your vegetables with the sauce.

To bake: prepare the vegetables as for roasting (page 206) and toss with barbecue sauce. Place the vegetables in a casserole with a little water to prevent burning. Bake until the vegetables are soft. If a crispy exterior is desired, broil the vegetables briefly.

To braise: prepare as for roasting (page 206), but place the vegetables and sauce in a heavy skillet or wide pan over medium-low heat. Cook until the vegetables are tender.

To broil: prepare the vegetables as for roasting (page 206), and blanch (cook briefly in boiling water, as described on page 205) until crisp-tender. Toss them with sauce and place in a single layer in a baking dish or on a parchment-lined baking sheet. Broil on one side about 2 minutes; turn the vegetables and broil on the other side for an additional 3 to 4 minutes or until nicely glazed.

Tomato Barbecue Sauce

1   tablespoon oil
1   medium onion, diced
2   teaspoons minced garlic
1   tablespoon chili powder
1   teaspoon dry mustard
    (optional)
1½ cups tomato ketchup
½   cup vinegar
1   tablespoon lemon juice
¼   cup soy sauce
2   tablespoons mushroom
    soy sauce
2   teaspoons molasses (optional)
⅓   cup sugar

Heat the oil in a saucepan over medium heat and sauté the onion, garlic, chili powder, and mustard for 5 minutes or until the onion is soft. Add the remaining ingredients, mix well, and simmer the sauce for 15 minutes.

Makes 2 cups.

133

Orange-Chipotle Barbecue Sauce

1   tablespoon oil
1   medium onion, diced
2   teaspoons minced garlic
1   cup orange juice
¼   cup lime juice
¼   cup rice wine vinegar
¼   cup sugar
1   teaspoon salt
Half of a chipotle chili,
    seeded and chopped
1   teaspoon garlic chili paste
1   teaspoon cornstarch
    dissolved in 1
    tablespoon water
1   tablespoon chopped
    fresh cilantro

Heat the oil in a saucepan over medium heat and sauté the onion and garlic for 5 minutes or until the onion is soft. Add the juices, vinegar, sugar, and salt and bring the mixture to a boil. Reduce the heat to low and add the chipotle, chili paste, and cornstarch mixture. Cook, stirring, until the sauce is slightly thickened. Add the cilantro.

Makes 2 cups.

Chinese-Style Barbecue Sauce

1   tablespoon fermented
    black beans
¼   cup dry sherry
1   teaspoon minced garlic
2   teaspoons grated fresh
    ginger
¼   cup soy sauce
¼   cup hoisin sauce
¼   cup ketchup
2   tablespoons rice wine
    vinegar
2   tablespoons sugar
1   teaspoon garlic chili paste
½   teaspoon five-spice
    powder or 2 star anise,
    ground

In a small bowl, cover the fermented beans with boiling water. Let stand 10 minutes. Drain and coarsely chop the beans. Whisk all the ingredients together in a bowl. Let stand for 1 hour before using to allow the flavors to develop.

Makes about 1½ cups.

Simple Asian Barbecue Sauce

2   tablespoons sesame oil
½   cup soy sauce
2   teaspoons mushroom
    soy sauce
1½ teaspoons chili garlic
    paste
1   tablespoon lime juice
1   tablespoon sugar

Whisk all ingredients together in a small bowl. Makes ¾ cup.

Tahini and Peanut Sauces

While you may associate tahini sauce only with falafel and peanut sauce only with soba noodles, these protein-rich sauces have many uses in vegan meals. Like mayonnaise, their rich oils give body to otherwise lean dishes. Try them with simple steamed vegetables, plain couscous, or seared tofu. Use them on grilled vegetables, crudité platters, or salads. For a quick meal, toss seitan or tempeh with one of these sauces and serve with blanched broccoli and brown rice.

Both peanut and tahini sauce can become very thick, especially when citrus juice or vinegar is added to them. Don't despair. The sauces will thin out again as oil or water is added.

Tahini Sauce

This sauce is simple and nutritious. Don't save it just for falafel!

½   cup tahini
¼   cup fresh lemon juice
¼   teaspoon ground cumin
2   teaspoons minced
    garlic
¼   teaspoon salt

In a medium bowl, whisk ⅓ cup of cold water into the tahini until smooth. Add the remaining ingredients and whisk to blend.
Makes about 1¼ cups.

Rich Tahini Sauce

The sweetness of the caramelized onions makes this a particularly good sauce for couscous served with some sautéed spinach or greens. For best results, have the patience to caramelize the onions thoroughly.

2	teaspoons oil
2	medium onions, cut into ½-inch rings
4	cloves garlic, sliced thinly
1	cup tahini
2	tablespoons lemon juice
½	teaspoon minced fresh garlic
½	cup extra virgin olive oil
½	teaspoon salt

Place the oil in a wide saucepan over high heat. Add the onions and sliced garlic. Lower the heat to medium-high and stir constantly until the onions develop a light, golden brown color. Place the onions in a food processor, blender, or food mill and purée. Add ½ cup of water to the onions. Add the tahini, lemon juice, and minced garlic and blend or mix well. The sauce may become thick at this point. Add the olive oil and salt and mix well. Adjust the thickness with water.

Makes 2½ cups.

Peanut Sauce

It seems that the people in love with the peanut butter and jelly sandwich have now fallen in love with Asian peanut sauces. This is a basic recipe that can be made spicier or milder, according to personal preference. Removing the seeds from the chilies will reduce their heat considerably.

Chopped peanuts, fresh cilantro leaves, and green onions are a natural garnish for any dish using this sauce.

1	cup smooth peanut butter
3	tablespoons rice wine vinegar
1	tablespoon lemon or lime juice
2	tablespoons soy sauce
2	teaspoons minced garlic
1	teaspoon grated fresh ginger
1	tablespoon sesame oil
1	small dried chili, crushed, or ½ teaspoon red pepper flakes

Place the peanut butter in a 1-quart mixing bowl. Whisk ½ cup of warm water into the peanut butter, slowly at first, then faster as the peanut butter begins to liquefy. Add the rest of the ingredients and mix well.

Makes 2 cups.

Salsas

Salsa simply means "sauce" in Italian or Spanish, but it has come to mean something so much more to many people. In the 1990s, sales of salsa began to outpace those of ketchup, a sign that our cuisine truly is an amalgam of many influences. Salsa, as the term is now used, refers to a chunky raw or lightly cooked tomato sauce, more sour and spicy than a relish.

These mainstay salsas are light and fresh and subject to change at the slightest whim of the cook. Try some of the suggestions or go wild with your own inventions.

Pico de Gallo

1   small red onion, diced
1   teaspoon minced garlic
2   cups seeded, diced
    fresh tomatoes
2   tablespoons lime juice
    or white vinegar
1/4 teaspoon salt
Freshly ground black
    pepper
2   tablespoons olive oil
1   tablespoon chopped
    fresh cilantro

Combine all ingredients in a bowl and toss to blend. Let stand for 15 minutes for the flavors to develop.

Makes about 2½ cups.

Corn and Black Bean Salsa: To the Pico de Gallo recipe, add 1 cup of corn kernels, ½ cup of cooked black beans, and 2 additional tablespoons of cilantro.

Mango Salsa: Prepare the Pico de Gallo recipe, but use only ½ of the onion. Add 1 large mango, peeled, pitted, and diced; 1 teaspoon of chili garlic paste; and 2 additional tablespoons of cilantro.

Chipotle Salsa: Sauté the onions and garlic briefly in some of the oil. Use canned tomatoes and add ⅛ teaspoon of ground cumin and half of a canned chipotle. Coarsely process all ingredients in a food processor.

Salsa Cruda

2 cups diced fresh
   tomatoes
1 teaspoon minced garlic
¼ cup extra virgin olive oil
1 tablespoon shredded
   fresh basil
Salt and freshly ground
   black pepper

Combine all ingredients together in a bowl and toss to blend. Let stand for 30 minutes for the flavors to develop. Makes about 2¼ cups.

Dipping Sauces

Dipping sauces are thin sauces with powerful flavors. The small amount that coats the dipped item is just enough of an accent.

Each of these sauces has a balance of sweet, sour, salty, and bitter components. They can accompany most anything—Fresh Spring Rolls (page 59), raw cabbage, fresh tofu, chilled noodles, or veggie wraps.

Simple Soy Dipping Sauce

2 tablespoons rice wine
   vinegar
3 tablespoons soy sauce
1 teaspoon sesame oil
1 teaspoon hot chili oil

Combine all ingredients in a cup or bowl and mix well. Makes about ⅓ cup.

Sweet and Sour Dipping Sauce

3 tablespoons orange
   juice
2 tablespoons rice wine
   vinegar
1 tablespoon lemon juice
2 teaspoons sugar
½ teaspoon salt

Combine all ingredients in a cup or bowl and mix well. Makes about ⅓ cup.

Vietnamese Lime Dipping Sauce

¼ cup rice wine vinegar
2 teaspoons lime juice
2 tablespoons water
2 teaspoons sugar
1 clove garlic, crushed
1 small chili, slivered
2 tablespoons long, fine carrot shreds
1 tablespoon whole fresh cilantro leaves
1 teaspoon crushed toasted peanuts

Combine all ingredients in a cup or bowl and mix well. Makes about ⅓ cup.

Harissa Dipping Sauce

Harissa, a fiery hot Tunisian paste, is a mix of chilies, spices, and olive oil. Often mixed with couscous, harissa can add a full-flavored heat to many dishes. Use this spicy sauce sparingly on Tostones (page 51), Sweet Potato Falafel (page 52), or Panelle (page 54).

2 tablespoons harissa
2 teaspoons lemon juice
¼ cup water
¼ teaspoon salt

Mix all ingredients together. Makes ⅓ cup.

Meshwiya

This Tunisian-style salsa is another spicy sauce, but with more body and less heat. It's best to wear gloves when working with the jalapeños. Use this as you would salsa, with tortilla chips, Panelle (page 54), or Chickpea Kibbeh (page 171).

4 medium tomatoes
1 large green bell pepper
1 or 2 jalapeño peppers or other hot peppers
2 teaspoons ground cumin
½ teaspoon ground coriander
1 tablespoon lemon or lime juice
1 teaspoon minced fresh garlic
¼ cup extra virgin olive oil

On the grill, with tongs over an open flame, or in a cast iron skillet, sear the tomatoes and green pepper until the skins are blistered and easy to peel. Seed the tomatoes and peppers and remove any white membrane. Chop the vegetables coarsely. Add the cumin, coriander, lemon or lime juice, garlic, and olive oil. Taste and adjust the seasonings.

Makes about 2¼ cups.

Classic Sauces

Adapting classic sauce recipes to a plant-only diet is challenging. While the texture of béchamel and beurre blanc is appealing, it is the richness of the butter and cream that makes people swoon. While these adaptations don't have the buttery richness of the originals, their smooth, creamy textures and rich clean flavors will win you over.

Vegan Béchamel

Also known as white or cream sauce, béchamel starts out with a roux—a mix of butter and flour—to which milk is added. This adaptation is easy if a rich, creamy soymilk is used. Cooking the flour is very important, as it eliminates the raw taste. Browning the flour adds a nutty flavor that is appealing in some recipes but not in others.

Serve cauliflower, brussel sprouts, or onions in this sauce to bring comfort to chilly winter evenings. Add sautéed mushrooms and tempeh to the sauce to make a hearty topping for rice.

2 tablespoons olive or canola oil
2 tablespoons flour
1 cup creamy soymilk, warm or at room temperature

Heat the oil in a small saucepan over medium heat. Whisk in the flour and cook for 3 minutes or until the flour comes together. Slowly whisk in the soymilk, taking care that no lumps form. Cook the sauce, whisking continuously, until it begins to thicken. Lower the heat and cook for 1 minute longer.

Makes about 1 cup.

Vegan Mornay Sauce

Mornay sauce is traditionally made by adding cheese to béchamel. You may wish to try adding chickpea purée, ground almonds, or ground cashews to the basic recipe below to give the sauce some additional body. Kitchen experimenters may also try adding ¼ teaspoon of guar or xanthan gum to the recipe to approximate the texture of cheese.

Use this sauce with blanched broccoli, pasta, or whole wheat toast topped with roasted vegetables.

¼ cup nutritional yeast
½ cup unbleached flour
2 cups soymilk, warm
1 tablespoon light miso
½ teaspoon garlic powder
¼ teaspoon paprika
¼ cup vegan margarine or
   ¼ cup grapeseed oil
2 teaspoons grainy
   mustard (optional)

In a medium saucepan over low heat, toast the yeast and flour just until the flour begins to take on some color and the yeast is lightly toasted. Carefully whisk the milk into the flour mixture, making sure no lumps form. Add the miso, garlic powder, and paprika. Whisk to blend thoroughly. Add the margarine and mustard. Taste and adjust seasonings.

Makes about 2 cups.

Velvety Vegetable Sauce

Reducing wine with minced shallot and then adding cold butter is the basic technique for beurre blanc, one of the classic French sauces. The result is velvety and rich—a definite crowd pleaser. While it's possible to substitute olive oil for butter and then thicken the sauce with cornstarch, the results are pale in comparison. And vegan margarine—with no whey protein—does not hold up like butter does in the sauce.

A better tasting and more healthful approach is to combine vegetable juice or purée with the reduced wine and then enrich with olive oil. To make vegetable purée, roast, blanch, or steam the vegetables until they are tender, but not discolored. Purée the vegetables and strain through a fine sieve. Straining is important with fibrous vegetables like asparagus, broccoli, or fennel.

Some vegetables that work well include leeks, carrots, fennel, onions, asparagus, edamame, peas, winter squash, or tomatoes. Cornstarch is used to thicken these sauces because of the acidity of the wine. (Flour cannot thicken sauces that have acidic components.) White bean purée and mashed potatoes may also be used to thicken the sauce. Keep the heat at medium or medium-low, as excess heat will cause the sauce to thin.

Herbs make a natural addition to this sauce. Refer to sections on individual vegetables in the "Vegetables" chapter (page 203) for pairings. Use this sauce to dress plain Jane rice or pasta and then top with roasted, steamed, or blanched vegetables; seared tempeh; or tofu.

½ cup dry white wine
1 tablespoon minced shallot
1 cup vegetable purée
⅛ teaspoon salt
Ground white or black pepper
2 tablespoons canola oil, grapeseed oil, or extra virgin olive oil (optional)
1 teaspoon cornstarch dissolved in 1 tablespoon water, or 2 tablespoons puréed white beans or mashed potatoes
1 teaspoon chopped fresh herbs (optional)

Heat the wine and shallot in a small saucepan. Reduce until only 1 tablespoon remains. (This step is very important to eliminate any raw wine flavor.) Whisk in the vegetable purée, salt, and pepper. Taste and add oil if desired. Cook the sauce until heated through. If the sauce is very thin, thicken it with the cornstarch mixture; otherwise, gently cook the sauce to the desired consistency. Add the herbs a few minutes before serving.

Makes 1¼ cups.

Vegan Demi-glace

Demi-glace is an intensely flavored, thick, brown sauce made from veal stock. In vegan cuisine, it may contain the water from soaking dried mushrooms or reduced balsamic vinegar to give it depth of flavor, and olive oil to give some richness. Cornstarch thickens the sauce and makes it glossy.

This is an all-purpose brown sauce for veggie cutlets, tempeh, portobellos, or Roasted Garlic Mashed Potatoes (page 233). For a lighter sauce, use white wine instead of balsamic vinegar and omit the black pepper. For a nutty flavor, add some nutritional yeast.

1 tablespoon olive oil
1 medium onion, diced
½ teaspoon minced garlic
4 stalks celery, diced
2 medium carrots, diced
2 bay leaves
½ cup aged balsamic vinegar
3 cups Roasted Vegetable Stock (page 66), or Mushroom Stock (page 67), or 2 bouillon cubes and 3 cups water
1 tablespoon cornstarch dissolved in 2 tablespoons water
1 tablespoon extra virgin olive oil (optional)
1 teaspoon black pepper (optional)

Heat the oil in a deep skillet over medium-high heat and sauté the onion until it begins to brown, about 8 to 10 minutes. Lower the heat to medium and add the garlic, celery, carrots, and bay leaves. Cook for 5 minutes longer, or until the carrots have begun to soften. Add the balsamic vinegar and reduce to 1 tablespoon, taking care not to let it burn. Add the stock and bring the mixture to a boil. Lower the heat and simmer the sauce for 10 minutes. Purée the vegetables. For a perfectly smooth sauce, strain through a fine sieve, pressing to release all the liquid.

Return the sauce to the pan and heat through. Whisk the cornstarch mixture into the sauce, then cook, whisking, until the sauce begins to thicken. When the sauce is thick enough to coat the back of a spoon, remove the pan from the heat. Taste and adjust the seasonings, adding the oil and pepper, if desired.

Makes about 3 cups.

Vegan Gravy

The Rice Milk recipe (page 317) can be decreased to ¼ cup of rice and 2 cups of water to give you just enough for this recipe. But I would suggest making lots of extra gravy because you may become hooked.

If you use prepared rice milk and it isn't thick, you may need to add 2 teaspoons of cornstarch dissolved in 2 tablespoons of water to thicken the gravy. No thickening is need for the Rice Milk recipe in this book.

This is a basic recipe to which you may add sautéed mushrooms, onions, celery, or carrots. It also works quite well as the basis for a quick stew, with the addition of some boiled potatoes and cooked veggies.

2   cups unsweetened rice milk, preferably homemade (page 317)

2   tablespoons nutritional yeast

½ tablespoon Marmite, Vegex, or yeast extract, or 1 tablespoon miso

1   teaspoon grainy Dijon mustard

⅛ teaspoon black pepper

Heat the rice milk. Whisk in the nutritional yeast, Marmite, mustard, and pepper.

Makes about 2 cups.

sandwiches

Cold Sandwiches

Tofu No-Egg Salad Pita

Hummus Sandwich

TLT: Tempeh or Tofu, Lettuce, and Tomato

Muffuletta

Greek Salad Pita

Italian Chopped Vegetable Pita

Mixed Vegetable Romesco Focaccia

Peanut Butter Variations

Tofu Boursin Lavosh

Burgers

Sun-Dried Tomato and Lentil Burgers

Black Bean Burgers

Portobello Mushroom Burgers

Broccoli-Almond Patties

Dress Up Your Veggie Burger

Hot Sandwiches

Vegetable Barbecue

Tempeh Reuben

What is a sandwich but a meal you can hold in your hand? It has a starch, a protein, and vegetables or fruit. The best sandwiches have varied textures that complement each other to provide a well-rounded, pleasant eating experience. But, of course, we don't think of it that way when we are scrambling to pack a lunch for the office or scraping the last bit of peanut butter from the jar.

The rise of fast food has conditioned us to eat on the run. Commercials and billboards entice us to visit the drive-through window and gobble something down to satisfy our immediate craving. The convenience and familiarity of fast food are tempting, so we need alternatives that are easy and appealing. That is why most of the sandwiches in this section are designed to parallel familiar sandwich selections. And while they may require some forethought and a shift in how you stock your refrigerator, they are designed to fit into a busy daily routine.

Here are a few pointers for creating a great-tasting sandwich that's also good for you:

- Experiment with breads. Good bread can turn an ordinary sandwich into a rapturous feast. Look for a combination of nutrition and flavor. Choose whole grains over refined grains. Select multigrain breads, which provide a variety of nutrients and fibers—and taste pretty darn good. Even traditional grocery stores often carry sprouted grain breads in the freezer section.
- Treat yourself to freshly baked bread, whether you make it yourself or buy it from a good bakery. A good bakery will make bread from scratch each day, and its bread will have very few preservatives or none at all. Ask at the counter. Be aware that many grocery-store bake shops use products that are either "par-baked," which means bread goes into the oven just to heat and develop some color, or "proof and bake," which means unrisen dough is allowed to rise and then baked. Some of these products contain stabilizers or preservatives that you may want to avoid. If you don't see any flour on the tables in the back, chances are good that the shop is using pre-made products.
- Match the bread to the style of sandwich you are making. It will be hard to make a delicate tea sandwich with a rustic peasant rye or to make muffuletta with a flimsy white sandwich loaf.
- Turn leftovers into lunch by spreading them on or rolling them into flexible flatbreads like pitas or flavored tortillas.
- Keep wet sandwich fillings, such as those for Greek Salad Pita (page 151) or Mixed Vegetable Romesco Focaccia (page 153), separate from the bread until you are ready to eat.

- Try the bean spreads found in "Appetizers and Snacks" as the spread for your sandwich (Tuscan White Bean Spread, page 43; Black Bean Dip, page 44; Refried Bean Dip, page 44; Curried Lentil Dip, page 45).
- Be adventurous with your sprout selection. Alfalfa sprouts are great, but try sunflower sprouts for a big crunch, radish sprouts for a peppery bite, or sprouted lentils for a nutty accent.

COLD SANDWICHES

Tofu No-Egg Salad Pita

If the firm tofu that you generally buy tends to be wet, weight it for several hours or wring it out to remove the excess water (for directions, see page 244). A pinch of cayenne helps liven up this dish, especially if your mustard is lackluster. Using a fork gives a better texture than a food processor in this dish.

1   pound firm tofu
¼   teaspoon turmeric
2   teaspoons Dijon or grainy mustard
¼   cup soy mayonnaise
¼   cup chopped celery
2   green onions, chopped
2   tablespoons chopped red onion
1   small green bell pepper, finely diced
2   tablespoons minced fresh parsley (optional)
2   6- to 8-inch whole wheat pitas (prepared or see page 271)
Shredded lettuce
1   tomato, sliced
1   cucumber, sliced

In a small mixing bowl, break the tofu into small chunks. Add the turmeric, mustard, and mayonnaise and mash the ingredients with a fork. Add the vegetables and parsley and stir gently until well mixed. Cut the pitas into halves. Carefully open the pockets. Divide the salad mixture evenly among the pita halves, stuffing it gently into the bread. Add lettuce, tomatoes, and cucumbers.

Makes 4 sandwiches.

Vegan Chilies Rellenos (page 58), Spinach and
Mushroom Quesadillas (page 53), Tostones (page 51).

Orrechiette with Butternut Squash and Thyme (page 187).

Chilled Soba Noodles on Painted Plates (page 200).

Top plate: Sweet Potato Falafel (page 52), Harissa Dipping Sauce (page 139).
Bottom plate: Chickpea Kibbeh (page 171), Curried Couscous (page 196).

Hummus Sandwich

Hummus, once relegated to bohemian potlucks and Middle Eastern restaurants, has come into the mainstream in grocery stores. You can find hummus with roasted red peppers, sun-dried tomatoes, caramelized onions, black olives and basil, pesto, and so on. My preference is for straightforward hummus topped with other ingredients, which give the sandwich additional flavors and a variety of textures.

If you have the time, you can make your own fresh hummus, which may have more protein and nutrients than the store-bought kind. Chickpeas, often labeled garbanzo beans, are a nutritional powerhouse—high in protein, calcium, and iron. Hummus will thicken considerably when it stands for several hours. The flavors will also develop and meld nicely.

2 slices sourdough bread
1/4 cup hummus, prepared or homemade (recipe follows)
4 to 6 1/4-inch cucumber slices
2 or 3 1/2-inch tomato slices
1/4 cup alfalfa sprouts
1 large lettuce leaf

Toast the bread, if desired. Spread the hummus evenly on both slices of bread. Layer the cucumbers, tomatoes, sprouts, and lettuce on one piece of hummus-laden bread. Top with the other piece of bread.

Makes 1 sandwich.

Hummus

To serve the hummus as a dip for an appetizer, dress it with a good fruity olive oil and some chopped fresh herbs and pair it with pita toasts or raw vegetables. (For Whole Wheat Pita Bread, see page 271.)

1 14-ounce can chickpeas, drained and rinsed
2 to 4 cloves garlic, minced
1/4 teaspoon ground coriander
2 tablespoons lemon juice
1/4 cup extra virgin olive oil
1/4 cup tahini
Sea salt

Purée the chickpeas in a food processor. Remove any tough skins that do not break down. Add the garlic, coriander, lemon juice, and oil and blend thoroughly. Add the tahini and pulse to blend. Adjust the texture with water. Taste and season with sea salt.

Makes about 2 cups.

Other Ideas for Hummus Sandwich Fillings

- Grilled or roasted portobello mushroom, caramelized onions, tomato, and arugula
- Sprinkle of ground cumin, toasted pumpkin seeds, cilantro, red bell pepper, tomato, and lettuce
- Marinated green beans, red bell pepper, thinly sliced red onion, and pine nuts
- Roasted red peppers, kalamata olives, radicchio, and fresh basil
- Avocado, thinly sliced red onion, radish sprouts, and tomato
- Capers, thinly sliced onion, black olives, tomato, and fresh oregano

TLT: Tempeh or Tofu, Lettuce, and Tomato

It seems that when people make the transition to a plant-based diet, the meats they crave most are the fatty, highly seasoned, and salty ones—bacon, sausage, fast food hamburgers, and lunchmeats. Highly processed soy products exist that try to replicate these flavors, but I recommend using a smoked and spiced tofu or tempeh. These tend to have few, if any, preservatives and plenty of flavor. Some grocery stores are now keeping these tofu products in the produce department.

Toasting the bread for this sandwich gives you the crunchy texture associated with a BLT. Garnish with a good dill pickle and some Almost-Traditional Potato Salad (page 108) and you'll feel like you are eating in your favorite greasy spoon without the grease.

2   slices mild-flavored whole wheat bread
Soy mayonnaise (optional)
3   ounces (½ package) smoked tofu or tempeh
2   thick slices ripe tomato
1   large leaf iceberg, green leaf, or other lettuce

Toast the bread. Spread each slice generously with soy mayonnaise. Cut the tofu or tempeh into halves to give you two flat pieces. Cut these pieces into 1½-inch strips, if desired. Arrange the tofu on the mayonnaise, and top with the tomatoes, then the lettuce. Cover with the second piece of toast. Cut the sandwich into halves.

Makes 1 sandwich.

Muffuletta

The flavor of this native of New Orleans improves if it is prepared several hours in advance and allowed to stand in the refrigerator. It is imperative that the bread be spongy enough to absorb the juices from the olive relish and vegetables but sturdy enough not to fall apart. A rustic Tuscan loaf or focaccia works well if you can't find a round country loaf. If you feel like baking, try the Big Fat Sandwich Loaf (page 262) or Focaccia (page 264).

Eggplants and portobello mushrooms are particularly good vegetables for this sandwich because they stand up to the assertive Olive Relish.

1   large round sandwich loaf (about 10 inches in diameter)
1   cup Olive Relish (page 123)
4   cups roasted or grilled vegetables
1   cup arugula leaves or other lettuce

Split the sandwich loaf in half horizontally. Spread each half with Olive Relish. Layer the vegetables on the bottom of the loaf. Top the vegetables with the arugula. Carefully place the top half of the bread on the sandwich. Replace any Olive Relish that falls out. Cover the sandwich for at least 15 minutes. Secure the top with toothpicks and cut the loaf into 6 wedges.

Makes 6 sandwiches.

Greek Salad Pita

I don't know if Greeks are familiar with this salad, but I do know that it has become a standard in diners. Make or buy vegan feta if you like, but be forewarned that the texture of vegan feta just barely approximates that of milk-based feta. A couple of dolmades, or stuffed grape leaves, makes this a heartier meal. When buying dolmades, read the ingredients carefully to make sure the grape leaves are filled with just rice and spices.

1	8-inch whole wheat pita (prepared or see page 271)
1½	cups chopped romaine lettuce
6	thin slices red onion
6	or 8 slices cucumber, ¼ inch thick
4	cherry tomatoes, cut into halves
4	pepperoncini or several rings pickled banana peppers
1	red radish, thinly sliced
4	pitted kalamata olives, cut into quarters
4	marinated artichoke hearts
3	ounces vegan feta (optional)
2	or 3 tablespoons Italian Vinaigrette (page 111)

Cut the pita into halves. Carefully open the pocket. In a medium mixing bowl, toss the vegetables, cheese, and dressing together. Divide the salad mixture between the pita halves, stuffing it gently into the bread.

Makes 2 sandwiches.

Italian Chopped Vegetable Pita

½ cup cooked kidney beans or chickpeas

½ cup quartered fresh button mushrooms

¼ cup Italian Vinaigrette (page 111) or Balsamic Vinaigrette (page 111)

1 cup shredded romaine lettuce

1 small red bell pepper, finely diced

1 small green bell pepper, finely diced

½ cucumber, seeded and finely diced

1 medium tomato, seeded and finely diced

2 green onions, thinly sliced

1 stalk celery, very thinly sliced

3 ounces tofu mozzarella or smoked tofu

1 6- to 8-inch whole wheat pita (prepared or see page 271)

In a small bowl or container, toss the beans and mushrooms with the dressing. Cover and refrigerate for 8 or more hours. In a medium mixing bowl, toss the vegetables and tofu with the bean mixture. Cut the pita into halves. Carefully open the pocket. Divide the salad mixture evenly among the pita halves, stuffing it gently into the bread.

Makes 2 sandwiches.

Mixed Vegetable Romesco Focaccia

This is a fantastic way to handle an overabundance of one vegetable or use up odds and ends of vegetables from the fridge. Romesco, the rich Catalan roasted red pepper pesto, is traditionally used on grilled vegetables. Green beans, fennel, zucchini, caramelized onions, and eggplant work particularly well with the Romesco Sauce and make an especially toothsome sandwich. You can buy focaccia or use the recipe on page 264. If you don't have focaccia, make sure to use a sturdy bread that will soak up some of the tasty sauce.

2   cups chopped grilled, roasted, or cooked vegetables
1   tablespoon chopped fresh basil
3/4 cup Romesco Sauce (page 129)
1   6-inch round focaccia or an 8x4-inch piece focaccia (prepared or see page 264)
1/2 cup arugula, mesclun, or similar bitter lettuce

Drain any liquid from the vegetables. In a medium bowl, combine the vegetables, basil, and Romesco Sauce. Let the mixture stand for at least 15 minutes or overnight.

Cut the focaccia into halves, then split each half horizontally. Divide the vegetable mixture evenly among the two bottom pieces of focaccia. Top each with half of the arugula, then the remaining focaccia. The sandwiches can stand at room temperature until the chill is off the vegetables.

Makes 2 sandwiches.

Peanut Butter Variations

Growing up a few miles away from the spot where George Washington Carver first cultivated peanuts sealed my fate as a peanut butter lover. Peanut butter seems to inspire odd combinations. While I've never heard of anyone else who loves peanut butter and ketchup the way that I do, these sandwich fillings, standard and exotic, are commonly paired with peanut butter.

- Sliced bananas
- Sliced apples
- Grated carrots
- Wheat germ

- Pineapple
- Dates
- Raisins
- Sunflower seeds

- Celery
- Radish slices
- Bread-and-butter or dill pickles

If the fat content of peanut butter concerns you, try puréeing 6 ounces of silken tofu and adding 2 tablespoons of peanut butter. Use this spread as-is or mix in your favorite peanut butter toppings to make a one-step spread.

Tofu Boursin Lavosh

Lavosh is a large, flexible, flat Armenian bread. Soaking the vegetables in salt water makes them flexible so the lavosh is easier to roll. If you can't find lavosh, use the large flour tortillas made for wraps.

1½ cups Tofu Boursin (recipe follows)
1   12-inch lavosh
½   English cucumber or 1 salad cucumber
2   medium carrots, peeled
1   medium zucchini
3   green onions, thinly sliced
4   small radishes, cut into paper-thin slices

Spread the tofu boursin evenly over the lavosh. If you are using a salad cucumber, peel it if the skin is tough and scoop out the seeds. Cut long, thin ribbons of cucumber, carrots, and zucchini. Soak the vegetables in salted water for 10 minutes. Drain and pat dry.

Layer the vegetables on the lavosh, alternating colors. It is not necessary that each vegetable cover the entire lavosh.

Roll the lavosh into a tight cylinder and wrap securely with plastic wrap. Cut into 3 pieces and serve immediately or refrigerate up to 4 hours.

Makes 3 sandwiches.

Tofu Boursin

If you add the fresh herbs to the food processor along with the cashews, the mixture will be an impressive, though perhaps not appetizing, green color.

Fresh herbs produce the best results, but if you need to use dried herbs in this recipe, place them in a small bowl, teacup, or custard cup and cover with a small amount of boiling water. Cover the bowl and let the herbs rehydrate. Drain the mixture before adding to the food processor.

1   cup cashews
4   cloves garlic, minced
½   teaspoon salt or 1 teaspoon white miso
⅛   teaspoon ground black pepper
1   pound medium tofu
2   tablespoons lemon juice
2   teaspoons each chopped fresh tarragon, basil, and parsley
1   teaspoon chopped fresh dill

Put the cashews in a 2-cup measure. Cover with hot water and let the nuts soak for 1 hour. Drain and rinse the cashews. Cover with hot water and let the nuts soak for 6 or more hours. Drain and rinse the cashews. Combine the cashews, garlic, salt, and pepper in the bowl of a food processor and pulse until the cashews are pasty. Crumble the tofu into the processor and add the lemon juice. Pulse until the mixture is blended well. Add the herbs and pulse until mixed well. Taste and adjust the seasonings with salt, pepper, and lemon juice.

Makes 3 cups.

BURGERS

Any of these burgers can be formed into small patties and served as appetizers or as part of a mezze-style dinner. These from-scratch burgers are designed to stand on their own in a hearty bun with a simple garnish of fresh tomato and lettuce, though you may want to get adventurous with the condiments.

Sun-Dried Tomato and Lentil Burgers

No need to drag the food processor out for this one. Mashing the lentils by hand retains their texture better. Substitute some leftover brown rice or bulgur for half of the lentils, if you like. If the mixture is too wet to hold together, add some breadcrumbs.

2   cups cooked brown, red, or yellow lentils

1   tablespoon oil

1   small onion, finely diced

1   teaspoon minced garlic

$1/4$ cup finely chopped walnuts

$1/4$ cup oil-pack sun-dried tomatoes, coarsely chopped

1   teaspoon chopped fresh sage or $1/3$ teaspoon ground sage

$1/2$ teaspoon fresh thyme leaves or $1/8$ teaspoon dried thyme

$1/8$ teaspoon black pepper

In a medium mixing bowl, mash the lentils with a potato masher or a fork. Heat 1 teaspoon of the oil in a skillet over medium-high heat. When the oil is hot, add the onion, garlic, and walnuts. Cook without stirring until the onion is browned. When the onion begins to color, reduce the heat to medium and cook until the onion is caramelized and the walnuts have begun to toast, about 4 minutes. Add the onion mixture to the lentils. Add the sun-dried tomatoes, herbs, and pepper to the lentils.

Form the lentil mixture into 4 patties. Heat 2 teaspoons of the oil in a skillet over medium-high heat. Fry the patties until they are nicely browned, about 5 minutes. Turn and fry the other side, about 4 minutes.

Makes 4 patties.

Black Bean Burgers

Serve these with fresh mango slices and salsa.

2   cups cooked black beans
1   tablespoon oil
1   small onion, finely diced
1   teaspoon minced garlic
1   red bell pepper, finely diced
1   jalapeño pepper, finely diced
½   teaspoon ground cumin
¼   teaspoon ground coriander
½   chipotle pepper, dried or canned
½   cup fresh or thawed corn kernels
2   tablespoons chopped fresh cilantro

In a medium mixing bowl, mash the black beans with a potato masher or a fork. Heat 1 teaspoon of the oil in a skillet over medium-high heat. When the oil is hot, add the onion, garlic, bell and jalapeño peppers, cumin, and coriander. Cook the vegetable mixture until the onion is soft. Add the vegetables to the black beans. Crumble the dried chipotle or mince the canned chipotle, add it to the bean mixture, and mix well. Stir in the corn and cilantro and mix well.

Form the bean mixture into 4 patties. Heat 2 teaspoons of the oil in a skillet over medium-high heat. Fry the patties until they are nicely browned, about 5 minutes. Turn and fry the other side for about 4 minutes.

Makes 4 patties.

Portobello Mushroom Burgers

The easiest mushroom burger involves a grilled or roasted portobello cap on a bun. I like to top it with roasted red peppers and some pesto. This recipe yields a more substantial burger. A combination of mushrooms works here as well—creminis, shiitakes, portobellos, and buttons.

4   teaspoons oil
1   pound portobello mushrooms, coarsely chopped
1   medium red onion, finely diced
1   teaspoon minced garlic
1/2   teaspoon dried thyme
1/4   teaspoon dried basil
1/8   teaspoon dried rubbed sage
1   tablespoon soy sauce, or 2 teaspoons soy sauce and 1 teaspoon mushroom soy sauce
1/4   cup red wine (optional)
1 1/2   cups cooked brown rice (preferably basmati) or 1 1/2 cups cooked bulgur
1/4   cup whole wheat or soy flour

In a wide skillet, heat 2 teaspoons of the oil over medium-high heat. Add the mushrooms, onion, garlic, and herbs. Cook until the mushrooms release their liquid, then until all of the liquid is evaporated. Add the soy sauce and wine and cook the mixture until it is dry. Cool the mixture in a medium mixing bowl. The mushrooms will release more liquid as they cool. Do not drain.

When the mushrooms are cool enough to handle, add the rice and flour. Stir to mix the ingredients. If the mixture does not come together, use a potato masher or pulse briefly in a food processor.

Form the mixture into 8 patties. Heat 2 teaspoons of the oil in a skillet over medium-high heat. Fry the patties until they are nicely browned, about 5 minutes. Turn and fry the other side for about 4 minutes.

Makes 8 patties.

Broccoli-Almond Patties

It seems impossible that these are so good! These can be enjoyed as a burger in a bun or an entrée with Roasted Red Pepper Coulis (page 131) or Mild Tomato Sauce (page 185). These are even good uncooked—just omit the wheat germ and the frying. Tahini, peanut butter, or cashew butter may be substituted for the almond butter.

2 cups chopped fresh broccoli florets and stems
½ cup sunflower sprouts, chopped fine
2 green onions, thinly sliced
¼ teaspoon minced garlic
½ cup almond butter
2 teaspoons kelp or salt-free Spike or Mrs. Dash
2 teaspoons chopped fresh sage or ½ teaspoon dried rubbed sage
1 teaspoon oil
½ cup wheat germ

In the bowl of a food processor, pulse the chopped broccoli, sprouts, green onions, and garlic until they are very finely chopped but have not begun to purée. (Alternatively, mix the broccoli, sprouts, onion, and garlic and put through a food grinder.) In a medium mixing bowl, combine the vegetable mixture with the almond butter, kelp, and sage. The mixture should hold together fairly well but not be too sticky or wet. Form into 4 patties.

Heat the oil in a wide skillet over medium-high heat. Dredge the patties in the wheat germ, patting the wheat germ so it will adhere. Fry the patties briefly until they are crisp on each side. Do not cook too long or they will become soggy.

Makes 4 patties.

Dress Up Your Veggie Burger

Commercially available veggie burgers are a quick and easy way to break the meat habit without feeling deprived. But a steady diet of them may get tiresome. Here are some ideas to give a little oomph to your new convenience food.

- Caramelized onions dressed with Orange-Chipotle Barbecue Sauce (page 134)
- Avocado slices, grapefruit sections, and mango salsa
- Pineapple rings glazed with brown sugar and lemon, and Asian Coleslaw (page 107)
- Caponata (page 46)
- Wasabi, pickled ginger, and Bibb lettuce
- Roasted red peppers, arugula, and pesto

HOT SANDWICHES

Vegetable Barbecue

You can use a prepared barbecue sauce or the recipes on pages 133–135. If you omit the peanuts, the Asian Coleslaw recipe on page 107 will work here.

1 medium red onion, peeled
2 cloves garlic, peeled
1 large red or green bell pepper, ribs and seeds removed
2 large portobello caps
1 medium zucchini, trimmed
2 teaspoons oil
1 cup barbecue sauce
4 whole wheat sandwich rolls
1 cup coleslaw (optional)

Cut the onion into halves vertically, from root to stem. Cut ¼-inch slices from each half. Slice the garlic as thinly as possible. Cut the pepper into ½-inch strips. Slice the portobello caps into long strips, ¼ inch wide. Using a box grater, vegetable peeler, or knife, make long, ¼-inch-thick ribbons of the zucchini.

In a wide skillet, heat the oil over medium heat. When the oil is hot, add the onion and garlic. Allow the onion to brown without stirring. When the onion has begun to brown, about 3 or 4 minutes, add the peppers and the portobellos. Sauté for 2 minutes. Add the zucchini ribbons to the pan. When the zucchini just begins to wilt, add the barbecue sauce to the pan. Heat the mixture thoroughly. The zucchini should be just beyond the crisp-tender stage.

Divide the barbecue between the 4 buns. Top with coleslaw.

Makes 4 sandwiches.

Tempeh Reuben

4   ounces tempeh
½   cup sauerkraut
2   slices rye bread
1   tablespoon vegan
     Russian dressing
     (recipe below)
2   slices vegan Swiss cheese
1   tablespoon oil

Cut the tempeh into halves horizontally so you have two thin, flat pieces. In a wide skillet, heat 1 teaspoon of the oil over medium heat. When the pan is hot, add the sauerkraut. Stir until the sauerkraut is warmed through. Remove from the pan and reserve.

Wipe the pan clean and add another teaspoon of the oil. When the pan is hot, sauté the tempeh until it is a little crispy on each side, about 5 minutes. Remove from the pan. Spread half of the dressing on each slice of bread. Put the tempeh on the bread. Top the tempeh with the sauerkraut and then the cheese. Heat the last teaspoon of the oil in the pan and grill the sandwich until nicely browned on each side.

Makes 1 sandwich.

Russian Dressing

2   teaspoons soy
     mayonnaise
1   teaspoon ketchup
¼   teaspoon pickle relish
2   or 3 drops lemon juice

Combine all ingredients in a very small bowl and mix well.

beans & grains

Beans

Savory Black-eyed Peas

Spaghetti with Lentil Tomato Sauce

Sweet and Sour Eggplant and Chickpea Stew

Seven-Bean Chili

Grains

Sesame Barley Pilaf

Bulgur Pilaf with Cashews and Oven-Roasted Tomatoes

Chickpea Kibbeh

Basic Polenta

Posole

Millet Paella

Stovetop Rice

Baked Rice

Dirty Rice

Lemon Zucchini Risotto

Nasi Goreng (Indonesian Fried Rice)

Beans and grains have been cultivated for ten thousand years. They have been deified, sacrificed, and used as the cornerstone of both civilizations and cuisines. Rice or corn, chickpeas or pasta, soybeans or black beans are some of the fundamental distinctions among the world's cuisines.

The recipes that follow will help you in using some provisions that may not be familiar to you, such as millet and bulgur, and give you some ideas on using old favorites such as lentils and hominy in new ways. And of course, many other recipes featuring beans and grains appear in other chapters throughout the book.

BEANS

Preparing Beans

A few simple steps can ensure safe, healthful, and tasty results.

Selecting: When buying beans, choose plump, smooth beans with bright colors. Avoid shriveled beans, which are old and have tough hulls. These give inconsistent results when cooked.

Rinsing: Prior to soaking or cooking, beans should always be rinsed under running water to remove dust and sorted to remove pebbles and damaged beans.

Soaking: Beans are full of complex sugars (oligosaccharides) that can cause flatulence. Fortunately, these hard-to-digest sugars are water soluble, meaning that soaking in water, especially boiling water, and discarding the water eliminate some or most of these sugars. (It is helpful to pair beans with onions and garlic, which are powerful carminatives, a polite way of saying that they help relieve gas. Particularly useful herbs with this property are sage, thyme, oregano, basil, fennel, parsley, cumin, cayenne, and cinnamon.) Note that lentils do not need to be soaked.

Quick soaking removes up to 90 percent of indigestible sugars, according to one study. Bring 2 cups of beans and 2 quarts of water to a boil in a large pot. Turn off the heat, cover the pot, and let the beans soak for at least 1 hour and up to 4 hours. Drain the beans and rinse thoroughly.

Long soaking is the more familiar technique, though it only removes about 20 percent of indigestible sugars. Soak the beans in a large amount of water for 8 to 12 hours. Drain the beans and rinse thoroughly.

Cooking: For plain beans, the ratio is 1 cup of beans to 4 cups of water. Combine them in a heavy pot and add a few bay leaves, sprigs of thyme, or oregano if you like.

It is very important that you do not salt the water. Salt causes the hulls to toughen and can prevent the beans from cooking. Bring to a boil, lower the heat to medium, and simmer until the beans are soft. Check the pot several times during cooking and add water as needed. Cooking times vary with the variety and age of the beans. Black turtle, Great Northern, red, and pink beans all take about 1 to 1½ hours. Kidney, dried lima, navy, and pinto beans take 2 to 2½ hours. Soybeans, chickpeas, and adzuki beans need about 3 to 3½ hours of cooking time.

Sprouting Beans and Grains

The popularity of bean sprouts waxes and wanes. Since reports of food-borne illnesses caused by bacteria in packaged sprouts, home sprouting once again has taken on a certain cachet. Years ago our sprouting equipment consisted of Mason jars topped with scraps left over from repairing the screen door. Now health food stores sell jars with color-coded tops and special seeds with guaranteed germination profiles.

Low tech or high tech, sprouting gives you another way of enjoying this nutrient-packed fare. Beans and grains are, after all, seeds. As the seeds sprout, they become more digestible. Sprouts can be enjoyed raw or quickly sautéed.

The basic procedure is the same for all:

- Rinse ½ cup of seeds in a colander, discarding any broken or blemished seeds. Put the seeds in a sterilized glass jar and cover with 4 inches of water.
- Soak the seeds for 12 to 24 hours, changing the water once.
- Drain the soak water from the seeds and discard the hulls, which will have risen to the top. Rinse the seeds 3 or 4 more times until the water runs clear.
- Set the jar at an angle in the dish drainer with the mouth down to allow the water to drain for 12 to 24 hours. Repeat the rinsing procedure once or twice a day until sprouts begin to appear. The seeds and sprouts should be kept out of direct sunlight and in an area that is not too cold.
- Set the jar in a sunny spot for several hours so the sprouts will turn green.

Lentils, chickpeas, black beans, mung beans, and wheat berries all produce sprouts in 3 to 4 days. Sunflowers and sesame seeds take only about 1 day. Alfalfa seeds take 3 to 6 days.

Black-eyed Peas

After migrating from China to Africa, black-eyed peas came to America with the slave trade. They made their home in soup pots all across the South and are essential eating on New Year's Day—they bring luck, and the small carrot "coins" or collard greens served with them bring money.

Savory Black-eyed Peas

Carl Lewis

10 ounces dried black-eyed peas
1 small onion, finely chopped
1 celery stalk, finely chopped
1/4 teaspoon red pepper flakes
1 tablespoon dried summer savory or marjoram
1 1/2 tablespoons olive oil
1 teaspoon sea salt
1/2 teaspoon black pepper

Place 4 cups of water and all ingredients except salt and pepper in an electric slow cooker. Turn the heat to medium. Check the beans after 30 minutes to see if they need more water. Cook the beans for another 40 minutes or until they are soft. Season with salt and pepper.

Makes 6 servings.

Lentils

Yellow, red, black, green, brown—lentils come in an amazing array of colors and textures. Sprouted, puréed, stewed, sautéed, or made into salads, lentils provide plenty of protein, potassium, magnesium, and folate.

Brown lentils, the type you are most likely to find in your grocery store, have a soft, creamy texture when cooked. These small lens-shaped pulses take about 15 to 20 minutes to cook, making them ideal for a fast supper.

Green lentils and black lentils, called French or le Puy and Beluga, respectively, are round and have a firmer texture when cooked. They are used in salads and sauces, where they hold their shape. They make excellent sprouts that can then be eaten raw or quickly sautéed for a peppery crunch.

Red and yellow lentils tend to fall apart on cooking, yielding a purée with a pleasant grainy texture. Current culinary trends use these purées as a low-fat alternative to traditional cream or butter sauces.

Spaghetti with Lentil Tomato Sauce
Carl Lewis

1   cup brown lentils
½   teaspoon dried thyme
½   teaspoon dried basil
2   cups tomato sauce
1   small onion, finely
    chopped
1½ teaspoons black pepper
½   teaspoon red pepper
    flakes
1   teaspoon dried oregano
1   teaspoon salt
8   ounces thin spaghetti
1½ teaspoons olive oil
3   or 4 sprigs parsley
    (optional)

Bring the lentils, thyme, basil, and 2 cups of water to boil in a medium saucepan over high heat. Reduce the heat to medium and cook until the lentils are al dente, about 12 to 15 minutes. Drain the lentils.

Combine the lentils, tomato sauce, onion, pepper, pepper flakes, oregano, and salt in a saucepan. Simmer over low heat for 30 minutes, stirring occasionally to prevent sticking.

Cook the spaghetti according to the package directions. Drain and rinse. In a large serving bowl, toss the spaghetti with the olive oil. Pour the sauce over the spaghetti. Garnish with parsley, if desired.

Makes 4 servings.

Chickpeas

A staple of the Mediterranean, chickpeas can be mashed, puréed, stewed, boiled, fried, dried, and ground. I love the convenience and consistency of canned chickpeas. People who hate beans often make an exception for chickpeas. With their slightly nutty flavor and crunchy-creamy texture, chickpeas are one of the most multitalented beans around.

Sweet and Sour Eggplant and Chickpea Stew

Serve this dish with some black Italian kale (bitter) and basmati rice (sweet) for an acrobatic flavor balance.

1½ pounds eggplant, cut into 1-inch cubes, salted, and drained (page 221)
1 tablespoon oil
1 large red onion, diced
2 teaspoons minced garlic
¼ teaspoon red pepper flakes (optional)
2 tablespoons tomato paste
1 20-ounce can diced tomatoes with juice
2 cups cooked chickpeas
2 tablespoons red, white, or tarragon wine vinegar
1 tablespoon Succanat or brown sugar
¼ cup coarsely chopped flat-leaf parsley
1 tablespoon chopped fresh basil
Salt and pepper

Rinse the eggplant and pat dry.

Heat the oil in a large skillet over medium heat. Sauté the onion, garlic, and pepper flakes for 4 minutes. Add the eggplant and cook, stirring, for about 5 minutes. Add the tomato paste and cook for 2 minutes longer, or until the paste is heated through. Stir in the tomatoes, chickpeas, vinegar, and sugar. Let the mixture stew for 10 minutes or until the eggplant is soft. Add the parsley and basil. Season with salt and pepper to taste.

Makes 6 to 8 servings.

Mixed Beans

Seven-Bean Chili

Carl Lewis

¼ cup dried pinto beans
¼ cup dried black turtle beans
¼ cup dried chickpeas
¼ cup dried soybeans
¼ cup dried kidney beans
¼ cup dried pinto or cranberry beans
¼ cup dried Great Northern beans
1 tablespoon cumin seeds, toasted
1 teaspoon dried oregano
2 bay leaves
2 teaspoons oil
1 medium onion, diced
1 teaspoon minced garlic
1 stalk celery, diced
1 medium red bell pepper, diced
1 medium green bell pepper, diced
1 teaspoon chili powder
¼ teaspoon red pepper flakes
1 teaspoon ground cumin
½ teaspoon ground coriander
1 cup diced tomatoes, fresh or canned
¼ cup red wine vinegar
Salt and pepper

Rinse and soak the beans as described on page 163. Put the beans in a heavy soup pot with 8 cups of fresh water and the cumin seeds, oregano, and bay leaves. Bring the beans to a boil, reduce the heat to medium, and simmer for 2 hours. Check the pot periodically and add more water as needed.

While the beans are cooking, heat the oil in a skillet over medium heat and sauté the onion, garlic, celery, peppers, chili powder, pepper flakes, cumin, and coriander for 5 to 7 minutes. Add the tomatoes and red wine vinegar and mix well. Cook the mixture until heated through.

Add the onion mixture to the soup pot when most of the beans seem tender (the soybeans will take the longest). Cook for 30 minutes. Remove and discard bay leaves. Season the chili with salt and pepper.

Makes 6 to 8 servings.

GRAINS

Barley

There are several types of barley available.

Pearled barley, the most widely available type, has been stripped of its bran, steamed, and polished. Although it is considerably lower in protein and mineral content than the other varieties, it is easily digestible and cooks quickly (15 to 20 minutes).

Hulled barley has had only the indigestible hull removed.

Scotch barley is hulled barley that has been lightly polished, removing most of the bran, and then coarsely ground.

Whole barley, while significantly more nutritious than the other types, takes much longer to cook (40 to 60 minutes) and has a stronger flavor that some may find less agreeable.

A little barley goes a long way. Who hasn't found their leftover mushroom barley soup turned into a mushroom barley brick after a day in the refrigerator? Toasting barley before cooking helps it retain its shape. When this is done, barley can be cooked much like risotto. Mushrooms are universally agreed to be barley's best partner. Other foods that harmonize well with barley include green beans, roasted red peppers, onions, tomatoes, arugula, almonds, and hazelnuts.

Sesame Barley Pilaf

1   cup barley
2   tablespoons canola oil
1   medium onion, diced
2   teaspoons minced garlic
2   medium carrots, cut into large matchsticks
4   stalks celery, cut diagonally into 1/2-inch pieces
2   teaspoons grated fresh ginger
1   cup blanched English or sugar snap peas
1   teaspoon mushroom soy sauce
2   teaspoons soy sauce
2   teaspoons sesame oil
1/4 cup toasted pine nuts

Heat a heavy skillet over medium heat. Add the barley and toast just until it begins to brown. Remove from the skillet and reserve the barley. Heat the oil in the skillet and sauté the onion, garlic, carrots, celery, and ginger until the onion begins to soften. Add the barley and cook 4 minutes longer. Add 3 cups of water, stir, cover, and simmer for 20 minutes. Add the peas, soy sauces, sesame oil, and pine nuts and cook for 5 to 10 minutes longer.

Makes 4 to 6 servings.

Bulgur

Sometimes confused with cracked wheat, bulgur consists of whole grains of wheat that have been steamed, dried, and milled.

Coarse-ground bulgur is similar to rice in texture and is used in pilafs, stews, stuffing, and as a side dish.
Medium bulgur is used in salads, the best known of which is probably tabbouleh.
Fine bulgur is used in patties, especially kibbeh, and some desserts.

All bulgur should be washed before cooking to remove any dust. Coarse bulgur is added to a pan of sautéed vegetables with twice its volume of water, then cooked for 20 minutes and allowed to steam, off the heat, for 20 minutes longer. Medium or fine bulgur should be soaked in at least twice its volume of water, then drained in a sieve and pressed to remove the excess water. One cup of raw bulgur yields 1½ cups cooked.

Bulgur Pilaf with Cashews and Oven-Roasted Tomatoes

2 tablespoons oil
2 medium onions, diced
1 teaspoon minced garlic
½ cup chopped toasted cashews
1 cup coarse bulgur, rinsed
½ teaspoon ground coriander
1 teaspoon salt
⅛ teaspoon black pepper
5 Oven-Roasted Tomatoes, chopped (page 239)
2 tablespoons chopped fresh basil, preferably lemon or cinnamon basil

Heat the oil in a wide, heavy skillet over medium-high heat. Sauté the onions, garlic, and half the cashews until the onions are soft. Add the bulgur, 2 cups of hot water, coriander, salt, pepper, and tomatoes and mix well. Cook, covered, over medium heat for 20 minutes. Remove the lid, quickly stir in the basil, cover the skillet, and remove from the heat. Let stand for 20 minutes so the bulgur can steam.

Alternatively, preheat the oven to 375°. Transfer the onion mixture to an ovenproof casserole. Add the bulgur, 2 cups of hot water, coriander, salt, pepper, and tomatoes. Cover the casserole tightly and bake for 30 minutes. Remove the casserole from the oven, stir in the basil, replace the cover, and let stand to allow the bulgur to steam for an additional 15 to 20 minutes.

Before serving, sprinkle the bulgur with the remaining cashews.

Makes 6 to 8 servings.

Chickpea Kibbeh

Kibbeh is a general term for a seasoned, shallow-fried patty. While fine bulgur is the base, most any combination of legumes, vegetables, and flour can be used. The mixture is usually flavored with a North African spice mix called raz al hanout, made with cumin, allspice, ginger, anise, cinnamon, and whatever else its creator decides to use. The sweet spices and the sharp edge of onion and garlic make for an interesting play of flavors. If you can find raz al hanout, substitute 1 teaspoon of it for the sweet spices in this recipe.

You can vary this recipe by substituting 12 ounces of tofu for the chickpeas, and thyme, basil, and oregano for the sweet spices. The result can be patted into patties or made into meatballs and fried. To reduce the fat, fit a baking sheet with parchment or spray it lightly with nonstick cooking spray, bake the patties or meatballs at 350° for 10 minutes, turn or rotate, and bake 7 minutes longer.

½ cup fine bulgur
1 cup cooked chickpeas
½ teaspoon pepper
1 small onion, chopped
1 teaspoon minced garlic
½ teaspoon ground cumin
½ teaspoon ground coriander
½ teaspoon ground allspice
Pinch ground cinnamon
⅛ teaspoon freshly ground black pepper
⅛ teaspoon cayenne
2 tablespoons finely chopped cilantro leaves
½ teaspoon salt
1 teaspoon baking powder
2 tablespoons nutritional yeast
¾ cup whole wheat flour
Oil for frying

Put the bulgur in a medium mixing bowl. Rinse twice with cold water. Pour 2 cups boiling water over the bulgur. Stir once or twice to mix. Cover the bowl and let stand for 10 minutes to allow the bulgur to absorb the water. Pour the bulgur into a sieve and press to remove any excess liquid.

Purée the chickpeas with the pepper, onion, and garlic. Add the bulgur, spices, cilantro, salt, baking powder, and yeast to the food processor and pulse until well blended. Transfer this mixture to a mixing bowl. Add the flour and mix until a workable dough is formed. If the dough is quite sticky, add more flour, 1 tablespoon at a time. The dough will be a little wetter than biscuit dough.

Heat up to ½ inch of oil in a wide, heavy skillet over medium-high heat. Form 2 tablespoons of the dough into patties ½ inch thick. Slide the patties into the oil and fry until lightly browned, about 2 minutes. Turn and brown the other side. Drain the kibbeh on paper towels.

Serve hot or cold. The kibbeh may be reheated or held in a warm oven.

Makes 16 patties, 8 appetizer servings or 4 main-course servings.

Corn

Corn is one of the few grains eaten both fresh and dried. Modern processing removes the hull and the germ, but stone-ground corn retains these and their nutrients. As with many whole products, the shelf life of stone-ground cornmeal and grits tends to be shorter than that of the more processed versions due to the rich, polyunsaturated oils in the germ. Keep cornmeal and grits refrigerated or buy only enough for a month or two at a time.

Basic Polenta

Polenta is a rustic Italian cornmeal porridge—basically mush. It can be served soft or firm. Firm polenta can be grilled, seared, or baked. Soft polenta will become firm polenta on cooling. Although polenta can be flavored with any number of additions, I prefer to flavor it simply with olive oil and garlic, saving the fancy accoutrements for use as toppings.

Long cooking is necessary to develop the rich flavors and texture of the corn. A fine-ground polenta will cook much faster than corn grits, but you won't get the same velvety texture. Some recipes call for cornmeal, but its quality is variable, with highly refined varieties resulting in a thin flavor. My favorite polenta is made from a particular whole-grain, stone-ground grit that takes four hours to fully cook. This is the love that polenta inspires.

When polenta is cooking, it is thick and hot, and when it bubbles, it splatters, which can cause very bad burns. Should the polenta "erupt," lower the heat and add more water.

Serve polenta with grilled or roasted vegetables, Lentil Tomato Sauce (page 166), Roasted Red Pepper Coulis (page 131), sautéed escarole or broccoli rabe, or nothing at all.

2	teaspoons salt
1½	cups polenta or yellow corn grits
⅓	cup extra virgin olive oil
¼	teaspoon black pepper
½	teaspoon minced garlic
1	tablespoon mashed Roasted Garlic (page 223)

In a medium saucepan over medium-high heat, bring 6 cups of water and the salt to a boil. Carefully whisk in the polenta, taking care that no lumps form. Cook, whisking, until the mixture becomes as thick as cream of wheat, about 5 to 8 minutes. Turn the heat to medium-low. Cook the polenta, stirring frequently with a spoon and adding water as needed, for at least 30 minutes, and up to 1½ hours for corn grits. The polenta should be thick but not too difficult to stir.

When the polenta is fully cooked, add the olive oil, pepper, and garlic. Adjust the seasonings with salt and pepper. Either serve the polenta immediately or spread in a lightly oiled jelly roll pan. Smooth the surface of the polenta and spread a small amount of oil over the top. Alternatively, pour the polenta into a lightly oiled loaf pan.

Makes 6 servings.

Posole

This Mexican dish features hominy, which is made from hard kernel corn that is left on the cob to dry, then treated with lye. Lye is a strong alkali made from wood ash and is also used in soap production. Why would someone put this on food? Processing corn this way makes the niacin available for absorption. Calcium, lysine, and tryptophan content are also increased. Hominy is also ground into grits and masa harina, the flour used to make tortillas. But mostly, those big white kernels are a wonderful comfort food. With this in mind, posole is not intended to be fiery hot, so choose your chilies based on your own tolerance. Because posole is a stew, it invites other ingredients you may have on hand. Try adding some chopped collard or mustard greens.

1   hot green chili, preferably jalapeño
2   poblano chilies
6   tomatillos or ½ cup prepared salsa verde
1   tablespoon oil
1   large onion, diced
3   cloves garlic
2   stalks celery, diced
2   pattypan squash, cut into ¾-inch chunks (optional)
½   teaspoon ground cumin
¼   teaspoon black pepper
1   teaspoon fresh lemon thyme leaves or ¼ teaspoon dried thyme
1   tablespoon fresh oregano, preferably Mexican, or 1 teaspoon dried oregano
2   15-ounce cans hominy, drained
1   15-ounce can Italian white beans (cannellini), drained
4   cups Vegetable Stock (page 65), or 1 vegan bouillon cube and 4 cups water
¼   cup chopped fresh cilantro
Avocado, green onions, lime wedges, shredded lettuce, corn bread, radishes, diced tomato, or chopped red or yellow bell peppers as accompaniments

Roast, seed, and coarsely chop the jalapeño and poblanos (page 231). Reserve.

Heat a heavy skillet over medium to medium-high heat. Remove the husks from the tomatillos. Sear the tomatillos in the hot skillet, moving them constantly. The skins should turn brown but not burn. The cooking time will vary. Remove the tomatillos from the pan. When they are cool enough to handle, coarsely chop them, reserving any liquid they release.

Heat the oil in a soup pot. Cook the onion, garlic, celery, squash, cumin, pepper, thyme, and oregano until the onion is soft. Add the chilies, tomatillos, hominy, and beans and mix well. Add the vegetable stock. Bring the stew to a boil, lower the heat, and simmer for 30 minutes to 1 hour, until the squash are soft and the flavors are blended. Stir the cilantro into the stew just before serving.

To serve, ladle the posole into deep soup bowls and garnish with any of the suggested accompaniments.

Makes 6 to 8 servings.

Millet

Millet's small size makes it easy to overlook. It's often the last grain left in the bird feeder, with even seed-eaters preferring to avoid it. Millet was first cultivated ten thousand years ago and may have been the first grain to be bred for improved size and yield. Perhaps its humble status is due to its tendency to become a gluey mass if not toasted before cooking. This may be why it is known as the "gruel of endurance" in the Old Testament. Millet is, however, one of China's five sacred crops, and was more important at one time than rice. The best millet recipes take advantage of its nutty flavor and pleasing texture.

Millet Paella

good – filling but not impressed w/millet

2   cups millet
2   tablespoons olive oil
A few saffron threads
1   medium onion, cut into halves and sliced ⅓ inch thick
2   teaspoons minced garlic
1   red bell pepper, diced
1   yellow bell pepper, diced
1   green bell pepper, diced
1   bulb fennel, trimmed (page 222) and sliced ⅓ inch thick
3   cups warm Vegetable Stock (page 65) or water
1   15-ounce can kidney beans, rinsed and drained, or 1 cup Seitan Chorizo (page 277), optional
1   cup diced tomatoes, fresh or canned
3   cups chopped escarole
½   cup peas, fresh or frozen, or 1 cup sugar snap peas or ½ cup edamame

Put a wide soup pot over medium heat. Add the millet to the pan and toast until it begins to brown, about 4 or 5 minutes. When the millet begins to pop, remove from the pan and reserve.

Heat the olive oil in the pot and add the saffron. When the saffron turns from bright red to slightly brown, add the onion, garlic, peppers, and fennel to the pot. Add the millet and mix well. Add the stock or water and reduce the heat to medium-low. Cook, covered, for 10 to 15 minutes. Add the beans or Seitan Chorizo, tomatoes, escarole, and peas to the stew. Cover and cook 5 minutes longer, or until the millet is soft but not mushy.

Makes 4 to 6 servings.

Rice

Half of the world's population is dependent on rice for sustenance. India saw the advent of rice cultivation about five thousand years ago. The spread of rice was slow but steady, and today rice is grown on every continent except Antarctica.

The nutrient content of rice has been enhanced through selective breeding. Most recently, a genetically modified rice containing beta-carotene has been developed to help combat vitamin A deficiency in countries where rice is a staple.

Your local grocer or health food store should be able to supply you with a rainbow of rice: purple, black, white, brown, red. The less polished varieties should be bought in small quantities that will be used up quickly, as the oils in the bran and germ will become rancid. Here is a quick overview of the types of rice generally found at the grocery:

Brown rice is the entire grain with only the indigestible husk removed. Brown rice takes longer to cook than white, but is much more nutritious, with more fiber, potassium, protein, phosphorus, riboflavin, and niacin than enriched white rice. Brown rice is available in many lengths and varieties. Try brown basmati rice; it has a distinctly nutty flavor and chewy texture. Quick and instant brown rice products are now available. These products have been "converted," which shortens the cooking time but adversely affects the texture.

Rice bran contains oil that is rich in polyunsaturated fats and vitamin E and has been shown to help reduce cholesterol. Since brown rice still has the bran attached, its shelf life is only 6 months. If you plan on keeping it longer than that, store the rice in the freezer or refrigerator.

White rice has had the husk, bran, and germ removed. When white rice, also known as polished rice, became common in Asia, the people there developed beriberi, a disease caused by a deficiency of thiamin, or vitamin B1, which is found in the bran of rice. Most white rice produced in the United States is now fortified with B vitamins and iron. These vitamins and minerals are sprayed on the surface of the rice. Rinsing the rice, as called for in some of the recipes that follow, removes many of these supplements.

Long-grain rice is four to five times longer than it is wide. With a relatively low starch content, cooked long-grain rice is light and dry, with separate grains. Basmati, jasmine, and California Rose are all long-grain rice varieties.

Short-grain rice has round, plump grains. It has a high starch content and when cooked it is sticky even when it is rinsed beforehand. Arborio is a short-grain rice variety, and sushi and mochi (Japanese rice cakes) are short-grain rice products.

Medium-grain rice has an appearance somewhere between that of the long- and short-grain varieties. When cooked, medium-grain rice is light and fluffy at first but gets sticky as it cools.

Converted or parboiled rice is soaked, then steamed under pressure, then dried. The white varieties are then milled. Steaming the whole grain helps infuse some of the bran and germ nutrients into the rice. The starch in the rice begins to bind together so that on final cooking, the grains are fluffy and separate.

Many varieties of rice are readily available. Should you happen to pick up a bag of imported rice with a decidedly shiny look, rinse thoroughly before cooking. This rice has been coated with a mixture of talc and glucose that acts as a preservative.

Jasmine rice is an aromatic long-grain variety from Thailand.

Basmati translates as "queen of fragrance." This long-grain rice is aged to reduce its moisture content, which enhances its nutty aroma.

Wehani rice is a basmati hybrid developed by Lundberg Farms in California. This brick red rice has the texture of wild rice and the fragrance of popcorn.

Arborio rice has short, plump grains; it is the most common rice used for risotto. Upon cooking, arborio releases its starch, which gives risotto its characteristic creamy texture.

Wild rice is not a rice at all, but a marsh grass native to the Great Lakes region. Its nutty flavor and chewy texture make it a perfect partner for classic autumn flavors such as hazelnuts, sage, mushrooms, and winter squash.

Stovetop Rice

There are several ways to prepare rice on the stovetop.

Absorption Method

This method works for a wide variety of rice. No nutrients are lost through rinsing or using excess water, making this the method of choice for enriched rice.

1 cup long-grain white rice
¾ teaspoon salt

Combine 2 cups of water, rice, and salt in a heavy-bottomed, 2-quart saucepan. Bring to a boil over high heat. Boil the rice, uncovered, until holes appear in the surface of the rice, about 7 minutes. Turn the heat to very low (or, if you have an electric burner, turn the heat off), cover the pot, and let the rice steam for 8 to 15 minutes. Separate the grains with a fork before serving.

Makes 4 servings.

Steaming Method

This is the same method that rice cookers employ. The measurements are inexact because the amount of water that the rice retains on rinsing varies. Once you've tried this method a few times, you'll know how to make the judgments. Jasmine and basmati rice are typically cooked without salt so their fragrant, nutty flavors can shine through.

2   cups jasmine or basmati
    rice

Put the rice in a heavy-bottomed 2-quart pot. Fill the pot with cold water. Agitate the rice in the water. When the rinse water is milky, pour it off and repeat the rinsing process. Continue rinsing the rice until the water is fairly clear, about 4 to 8 times.

Add enough clean water to the pot to cover the rice by about ¾ inch. Cover the pot and bring to a boil over high heat. Reduce the heat to very low and cook for 8 minutes. Turn the heat off and let the rice steam for 5 minutes. Separate the grains with a fork before serving.

Makes 8 servings.

Excess Water Method

The Absorption and Steaming Methods rely on steaming the rice in a specific quantity of water. This method just boils the rice in an excess of water until it is done. This is the preferred method of cooking starchy rice varieties to obtain a fluffy result, as the extra starch is drained with the cooking water. This method works well for short-grain brown rice and wild rice.

2   cups short-grain brown
    rice or wild rice

Bring a 2-quart pot of water to boil. Add the rice while stirring vigorously. Boil until the rice is tender, about 20 minutes for short-grain brown rice or 30 to 40 minutes for wild rice. Drain the rice into a strainer or colander. Rinse with running water if preparing the rice for salads or cold dishes.

Makes 8 servings.

Baked Rice

This method gives the rice several dimensions of flavor, especially if you choose to sauté some onions, garlic, celery, and seasonings with the rice.

2 cups long-grain white rice
2 tablespoons oil
2½ cups tepid water or Vegetable Stock (page 65)
1 teaspoon salt

Preheat the oven to 350°. Rinse the rice in several changes of water until the rinse water is clear, about 5 to 8 times. Heat the oil in an ovenproof pot. Sauté the rice in the oil until it just begins to brown, about 5 minutes. Add the tepid water or Vegetable Stock and salt to the rice. Cover the pot and place in the oven. Cook the rice for 30 minutes, or until the water is absorbed and the rice is tender.

If you prefer, you can sauté the rice in a skillet and then transfer it to a baking dish.

Makes 8 servings.

Dirty Rice

2 cups long-grain white rice
3 tablespoons oil
2 medium onions, diced
1 small green bell pepper, diced
1 small red bell pepper, diced
2 stalks celery, diced
2 teaspoons minced garlic
1 teaspoon ground cumin
½ teaspoon dried oregano
1 teaspoon dry mustard
½ teaspoon dried thyme
½ teaspoon cayenne
1 teaspoon paprika
1 teaspoon salt
¼ teaspoon freshly ground black pepper

Preheat the oven to 350°. Rinse the rice in several changes of water until the rinse water is clear, about 5 to 8 times. Lightly oil or spray a 9x13-inch baking dish.

Heat the oil in a wide skillet over medium-high heat, and sauté the rice and onions until the rice begins to brown, about 5 minutes. Add the remaining ingredients and mix well. Cook the mixture until the vegetables start to wilt, about 4 minutes. Transfer the mixture to the baking dish. Add 2½ cups of tepid water. Cover the dish tightly with foil and bake until the liquid is absorbed and the rice is tender, about 30 to 40 minutes.

Makes 8 servings.

Lemon Zucchini Risotto

Here's a dish that exploits the starchiness of the rice instead of rinsing it away. Risotto always uses a short-grain rice with a high starch content. Arborio is the easiest to find in the grocery store, though carnaroli or vialone nano are more forgiving, remaining al dente longer, should there be a delay in getting dinner on the table.

Risotto is not difficult, but it does require the cook's full attention. If you are an experienced risotto cook, you probably know that a little inattention can turn risotto into a burnt, gluey mass. Cooking time is generally 20 to 30 minutes. Most of the time is spent stirring and watching for the rice to absorb liquid.

The result should be creamy, with a consistency between that of soup and porridge. Most main course risotto is served in bowls. For risotto served as a side dish, allow the risotto to get just a bit thicker so it will sit nicely on a plate.

Fresh basil is preferable for this recipe, but dried also works well. Dried basil is added at the beginning of the cooking process to extract its full flavor. Fresh basil is added at the end.

6   cups Vegetable Stock (page 65)
2   tablespoons oil
1   small onion, diced
2 to 4 cloves garlic, thinly sliced
1½ cups arborio rice
3   tablespoons shredded fresh basil or 1 teaspoon dried basil
½ cup dry white wine
2   medium zucchini, cut into halves lengthwise, then into ½-inch slices
Zest and juice of 1 lemon
¼ cup extra virgin olive oil
¼ cup diced fresh tomatoes
Salt and white pepper

Heat the stock over low heat on a burner near the risotto pan. Have a ladle handy.

Heat the oil in a large, wide skillet over medium-high heat and sauté the onion, garlic, rice, and dried basil (but not fresh basil). Cook, stirring constantly, until the rice begins to brown. Do not let more than one-tenth of the rice brown. Add the wine and cook, stirring, until the rice absorbs the wine. Add 1 cup of the stock. Reduce the heat to medium. Cook, stirring, until most of the stock is absorbed. Do not allow the rice to brown or stick to the pan. Continue adding the stock, 1 cup at a time, and cook until it is nearly all absorbed. When adding the last cup of stock, add the zucchini.

When the stock is absorbed and the zucchini is just tender, remove the pan from the heat. Stir in the lemon juice, half the zest, 3 tablespoons of the olive oil, tomatoes, and 2 tablespoons of the fresh basil. Mix gently so the zucchini doesn't fall apart. Taste for seasoning and add salt and white pepper as needed.

Divide the risotto among four large, shallow bowls. Garnish with the reserved basil and top with some lemon zest. Drizzle a teaspoon or so of the extra virgin olive oil around the herbs. Serve immediately.

Makes 4 servings.

Nasi Goreng (Indonesian Fried Rice)

It is best to completely cool the rice before frying so that the grains remain separate when fried and take on all the different flavors. Serve with Ginger-Fried Tempeh (page 251) for a complete meal.

2   cups long-grain rice, brown or white
3   tablespoons peanut oil
1   small onion, very finely chopped
1 to 3 large fresh red chilies, seeded and thinly sliced
1   teaspoon grated fresh ginger
2   medium carrots, diced
4   ounces button mushrooms, quartered
2   teaspoons ketchup
1   tablespoon soy sauce
1/2 teaspoon salt
2   cups shredded cabbage (napa or green)
1/2 cucumber, sliced
1   bunch watercress

Cook the rice according to any of the stovetop directions above. Fluff it with a fork. Let it cool completely.

Heat the oil in a wok or wide, deep skillet over high heat. Add the onion, chilies, and ginger and stir-fry for 1 minute. Add the carrots and mushrooms and stir-fry for 2 minutes longer. Add the ketchup, soy sauce, and salt and mix well. Add the cabbage and stir-fry until it wilts, 1 to 2 minutes for napa, 4 to 6 minutes for green cabbage. Reduce the heat to medium-low.

Add the cold rice and mix thoroughly. Cook until the rice is heated through. Add a little water if the rice begins to stick or burn. Transfer the rice to a serving platter and garnish with cucumber slices and watercress.

Makes 4 servings.

pasta

European Pasta

Basic Tomato Sauce

Mild Tomato Sauce

Arrabiata Sauce

Puttanesca Sauce

Orecchiette with Butternut Squash and Thyme

Roasted Vegetable Lasagna

Pasta Ribbons with Cabbage and Apples

White Bean Ravioli with Caramelized Onion Sauce

Farfalle with Sun-Dried Tomatoes and Portobellos

Swiss Chard Cannelloni with Walnut Sauce

Macaroni and Cheeze

Middle Eastern Pasta

Basic Couscous

Couscous with Peas and Mint

Couscous with Raisins and Pine Nuts

Curried Couscous

Asian Pasta

Noodles and Broccoli with Spicy Peanut Sauce

Pad Thai

Chow Fun with Hot and Smoky Tofu

Chilled Soba Noodles on Painted Plates

People all over the world love pasta. While the origin of pasta is obscure, it seems to have arisen in several regions centuries ago, judging by its central role in widely disparate cuisines. Although many people think Marco Polo introduced pasta to Europe after his travels in China, this theory is suspect as he used an Italian name for pasta when writing about Chinese noodles. The ancient Romans thought pasta was a gift from Vulcan, the god of fire. Sicilian artifacts show that not only were flat noodles common three thousand years ago, but so were extruded pasta shapes like macaroni. Asian pastas have an equally impressive history.

While the debate on pasta's origin may rage, I am content to enjoy it in its varied shapes, flavors, and textures. Even if you are not a vegetarian, chances are you've had some meatless meals with pasta as the entrée. Pasta, with its nonassertive flavor and complex carbohydrates, is a natural for pairing with a wide variety of ingredients throughout the year.

EUROPEAN PASTA

While we are most familiar with the heavy, long-simmered tomato sauces, many Italian pasta sauces and dishes are quick and light, a veneration of the locally available products. Some of these dishes may seem dry if you are not used to them—particularly since they are not smothered with cheese. One secret is to include a little of the pasta water in the sauce, so don't be too thorough when draining the noodles.

Cooking pasta: Pasta, fresh or dried, should be cooked in an abundance of water at a full boil. When water is heating, bubbles appear at the bottom of the pan and then come to the surface. This is the water releasing dissolved air. If you can stir the water and stop the bubbling, then the water is not yet boiling. Adding pasta to water that is not rapidly boiling may make it mushy. Use at least 1 quart of water for every 4 ounces of pasta. Add the pasta to the water in batches so the water temperature doesn't drop too dramatically. Stir the pasta immediately with a long-handled spoon, being careful not to be burned by the steam. Stir frequently. If you use plenty of water, you will not need to add any oil, as oil is used primarily to keep the starchy foam from boiling over onto the stovetop. The oil will also coat the pasta and cause the sauce to slide off the noodles.

Most fresh pastas take 2 to 3 minutes to cook. Boxes of dried pasta usually give cooking times, but these should be thought of as guidelines only. A good rule of thumb is to cook the pasta 3 minutes less than indicated in the directions. Before draining, break one piece of pasta in half. There should be a small line or dot of white in the middle. The pasta will be al dente, or "to the tooth," at this point and perfect. If the pasta is to be baked in a casserole, consider cooking it a few minutes less.

Pasta being used for cold salads should be rinsed with cold water.

Pasta Sauces

Basic Tomato Sauce is a good standard sauce. I like to leave the seasonings fairly plain to increase the sauce's versatility. When you want a lighter sauce, try Mild Tomato Sauce. Arrabiata and Puttanesca are hearty, chunky sauces suitable for penne, spaghetti, radiatore, orrechiette—just about any type of pasta. They are easy to make for a large crowd and will generate quite a fan club for their cook.

Basic Tomato Sauce

Sometimes diced tomatoes give a better flavor to red sauce than crushed tomatoes or tomato sauce. You may want to try them—if you don't want a chunky sauce, you can purée it. Cooking the tomato paste gets rid of the tinned flavor. For a smoky flavor, let the tomato paste just begin to brown before adding the tomatoes and water.

1   tablespoon oil
1   medium yellow onion, diced
1   tablespoon minced garlic
2   tablespoons tomato paste
2   cups diced tomatoes, fresh or canned
1   teaspoon sugar
½   teaspoon salt
⅛   teaspoon ground black pepper
2   tablespoons chopped fresh basil

Heat the oil in a heavy saucepan over medium heat and cook the onion and garlic until the onion is soft, about 8 minutes. Add the tomato paste and cook, stirring, for 2 to 3 minutes or until the paste is heated through. Add the diced tomatoes, sugar, salt, and pepper. If using fresh tomatoes, add 1 cup of water. Loosely cover the pot and cook the sauce for about 20 minutes. Taste and adjust the seasonings. Add the basil. Purée if you prefer a smooth sauce.

Makes enough sauce for 8 ounces of pasta, or 4 servings.

Mild Tomato Sauce

This mild tomato sauce may be used in dishes where a light touch is desired, such as pasta tossed with spring vegetables, green beans with couscous, or baked fennel or artichokes stuffed with brown rice.

1   tablespoon olive oil
1   small yellow onion, diced
2   teaspoons minced garlic
1   28-ounce can diced tomatoes or 2 cups diced fresh tomatoes, seeded
1/2   teaspoon sugar
1/4   teaspoon salt
1   tablespoon chopped fresh basil
Freshly ground black pepper

Heat the oil in a saucepan over medium heat and sauté the onion and garlic until the onion is soft but not browned, about 7 minutes. Add the remaining ingredients and simmer for 15 minutes.

Makes about 2 cups.

Arrabiata Sauce

If you are not using fresh tomatoes, make sure that the canned tomatoes are of a very good quality.

1   tablespoon olive oil or other oil
1   teaspoon coarsely minced garlic
1   dried chili or 1/2 teaspoon red pepper flakes
3   cups diced tomatoes, fresh or canned
2   tablespoons chopped fresh parsley
Salt and pepper

Heat the oil in a saucepan over medium heat and sauté the garlic and peppers just until the peppers begin to brown. Add the tomatoes and their juice. If using fresh tomatoes, add 1/2 cup of water. Add the parsley, mix well, and heat through. Adjust the seasoning with salt and pepper.

Makes enough sauce for 8 ounces of pasta, or 4 servings.

Puttanesca Sauce

2 tablespoons canola oil and olive oil blend
1 tablespoon minced garlic
1 teaspoon fresh thyme or ½ teaspoon dried thyme
1 tablespoon chopped fresh basil or 1 teaspoon dried basil
½ teaspoon red pepper flakes
1 cup Basic Tomato Sauce (page 184) or prepared tomato sauce
6 cups diced tomatoes, fresh or canned
¾ cup pitted kalamata olives, quartered
2 tablespoons very small capers (often labeled "nonpareil")
½ cup chopped fresh parsley

Heat the oil in a saucepan over medium heat and add the garlic, dried herbs, and crushed red peppers. (Fresh herbs will be added later.) Do not brown the garlic. When the garlic mixture is hot, add the tomato sauce and tomatoes. If using fresh tomatoes, add 1 cup of water. Cook the sauce, stirring often, just until it bubbles. Add the olives, capers, parsley, and fresh herbs and reduce the heat to low. Allow the sauce to cook for 10 to 15 minutes longer for the flavors to develop.

Makes enough sauce for 1 pound of pasta, or 8 servings.

Pasta Dishes

Orecchiette with Butternut Squash and Thyme

Butternut squash are a challenge to peel, but here's a trick to greatly simplify the task. Microwave them, whole, for about 3 minutes. Let them cool. The cooking softens the skin slightly so the knife can get some traction.

The orecchiette, or little ears, hold plenty of sauce.

1	small butternut squash, peeled, seeded, and cut into 3/4-inch cubes
8	ounces orecchiette
2	teaspoons oil
1	large leek, white part only, cut into halves lengthwise, then sliced
4	cloves garlic, thinly sliced
1	cup moderately dry white wine
1/2	cup Vegetable Stock (page 65), Roasted Vegetable Stock (page 66), or 1 cup water from cooking the squash

Salt and pepper

2	tablespoons extra virgin olive oil
1	tablespoon fresh thyme or 1 teaspoon dried thyme

Bring 3 quarts of salted water to boil in a large pot. Add the squash cubes to the pot and cook just until they are tender, about 4 to 6 minutes. Drain the squash in a colander (reserving 1 cup of cooking water if you are using it in the sauce) and rinse lightly with cold water. Put the squash in a bowl and reserve.

Bring 3 quarts of water to a boil in a large pot. With the water rapidly boiling, add the pasta and stir. Let the pasta cook for 8 minutes or until the orecchiette are just al dente. Drain the pasta in a colander. Rinse lightly with cool water. Put the pasta into a large serving bowl and reserve.

Heat the oil in a wide skillet over medium-high heat and sauté the leek and garlic until the leek is soft. If you are using dried thyme, add it to the pan with the leeks. Turn the heat to high and add the white wine. Cook until the wine is reduced by two-thirds. Add the vegetable stock or cooking water from squash. Cook until the liquid is reduced by one-fourth. Add the squash to the pot. Reduce the heat to medium. Taste the sauce and adjust the seasoning with salt and pepper. Add the olive oil, fresh thyme, and orecchiette and mix well. Serve immediately or reserve in a warm oven.

Makes 4 servings.

Roasted Vegetable Lasagna

For baked pasta dishes, fresh uncooked pasta sheets work well as long as you thin the tomato sauce with a little extra water. If you can't get fresh pasta, cook 1 pound of the dry noodles and add only ½ cup of water to the tomato sauce.

To test that the lasagna is heated through, insert a dinner knife into the middle of the lasagna and hold it there for 5 to 10 seconds. If the tip of the knife isn't hot, then your lasagna isn't either. To avoid a false reading, make sure the knife isn't touching the bottom of the pan.

Salt
1   large eggplant, cut into ¾-inch slices
2   medium red onions, cut into ½-inch slices
1   medium red bell pepper, cut into halves and seeded
1   medium yellow bell pepper, cut into halves and seeded
1   medium green bell pepper, cut into halves and seeded
Seasoned oil or plain olive oil
2   medium zucchini, cut lengthwise into ¾-inch slices
2   medium yellow squash, cut lengthwise into ¾-inch slices
8   roma tomatoes, cut into halves
1   head broccoli, trimmed, separated into large florets, and blanched
3   cups Basic Tomato Sauce (page 184)
½   cup chopped fresh basil
2   teaspoons fresh thyme (optional)
1   teaspoon chopped fresh rosemary (optional)
1   teaspoon chopped fresh oregano (optional)
3   large pasta sheets, fresh or frozen

Liberally salt both sides of the eggplant slices and place them in a colander to drain. Let stand 30 minutes. When they have released a fair amount of liquid, rinse each slice briefly under cold water and pat dry.

Preheat the broiler to high or heat a grill plate or George Foreman grill. Do not separate the onion slices into rings or they may burn. Arrange the eggplant, onions, and peppers in a single layer on baking trays lined with parchment. Brush each vegetable slice lightly with oil. Broil them for 3 minutes on each side. Remove to a platter. Broil the zucchini, squash, and tomatoes until they are crisp-tender. If the skins have started to pull away from the peppers or tomatoes, discard them. Broil the broccoli until it is crisp-tender. Alternatively, grill the vegetables in batches until they are crisp-tender.

Turn the oven temperature down to 350° if you are using a glass baking dish and 375° if you are using a metal one.

If any liquid has accumulated from the cooked vegetables, put it in a 1-cup measure. Add enough water to make 1 cup and mix this liquid with the tomato sauce to thin it. Mix the herbs together in a small bowl.

Generously oil a large rectangular baking dish. Spread 1½ cups of the thinned tomato sauce over the bottom of the pan. Top the sauce with one sheet of pasta. Sprinkle with one-fourth the herb mixture and then spread with ½ cup of the tomato sauce. Layer half the vegetables on the pasta sheet. Sprinkle the vegetables with another fourth of the herb mixture and top with another pasta sheet. Sprinkle another fourth of the herb mixture on top of the second pasta sheet. Layer the rest of the vegetables on the pasta sheet and top with the remaining herbs. Place the last pasta sheet on top of the vegetables. Spread the last cup of tomato sauce on top of the third pasta sheet. Cover the lasagna with waxed paper and then with aluminum foil. Bake for 35 minutes or until it is quite bubbly and heated all the way through.

Makes 8 servings.

Pasta Ribbons with Cabbage and Apples

When is a noodle not a noodle? When it is vegan! All pastas labeled "noodles" are required to contain 5.5 percent egg solids. Savvy pasta companies have taken to labeling vegan noodles as pasta ribbons (see section on Asian pastas, page 196). If you can't find eggless noodles, use fettucini.

6	ounces wide eggless noodles
3	tablespoons oil
1	medium onion, cut into halves lengthwise, then into 1/2-inch half moons
2	cups shredded green cabbage or 4 cups shredded savoy or napa cabbage
1/2	teaspoon caraway seeds (optional)
1/2	cup sauerkraut
1	Granny Smith apple, cored and shredded
1/2	teaspoon freshly ground black pepper
3	tablespoons whole wheat breadcrumbs

Bring 3 quarts of water to a boil in a large pot and add the noodles. Cook according to package directions. Drain in a colander and rinse. Put the noodles in a large serving bowl and reserve.

In a wide skillet, heat 2 tablespoons of the oil over medium-high heat. Add the onion and cook for 3 minutes or until they begin to brown. Lower the heat to medium. Add the cabbage and caraway seeds and cook until the cabbage is wilted, about 4 to 8 minutes. Add the sauerkraut, apples, and pepper and mix well.

Add the cabbage mixture to the noodles in the bowl and mix well. Wipe out the skillet. Over medium heat, heat the remaining oil. Add the breadcrumbs and toast until they are browned. Top the noodles with the breadcrumbs. Serve immediately or reserve in a warm oven. If you are holding the noodles for more than 15 minutes, cover them loosely with aluminum foil and remove 10 minutes before serving.

Makes 4 servings.

White Bean Ravioli with Caramelized Onion Sauce

Use Tuscan White Bean Spread made from dried beans, as it is significantly thicker than that made with canned beans. A soft filling will make the pasta soggy, causing the ravioli to fall apart. Adding some breadcrumbs to the filling may be necessary to ensure success.

¾ cup Tuscan White Bean Spread (page 43)

50 round wonton or gyoza skins

2 teaspoons oil

4 red onions, cut into halves lengthwise and sliced

4 cloves garlic, thinly sliced

½ cup dry white wine

1 tablespoon balsamic vinegar

1 teaspoon mushroom soy sauce

1 cup Vegetable Stock (page 65)

1 teaspoon fresh thyme

½ teaspoon chopped fresh rosemary

⅛ teaspoon freshly ground black pepper

1 tablespoon extra virgin olive oil (optional)

½ cup toasted, chopped walnuts

4 sprigs fresh thyme or rosemary

Have a small bowl with water ready and a clean kitchen towel to dry your fingers. Place 1 teaspoon of the bean spread in the middle of the wonton skin. Brush the edges of the wonton skin lightly with water. Place a second skin directly over the first one. Working from the edge of the filling, press the pasta sheets together as you rotate the ravioli in your hand. Continue until the skins are pressed together with no air bubbles between the sheets. This may take some practice. On a baking sheet dusted lightly with semolina flour or cornstarch, arrange the finished ravioli in a single layer. Cover lightly with a clean, dry kitchen towel. Repeat until all the ravioli are made. Make a second layer of ravioli on the towel, if necessary.

Heat the oil in a wide skillet over medium-high heat. When the oil is quite hot, add the onions and garlic. Cook without stirring until the onions develop some color, about 1 to 2 minutes, and then stir. Cook, stirring every minute or two, until the onions turn a deep brown color and the aroma is pleasant. If the onions are blackening or smell like they are burning, reduce the heat to medium and watch closely. (If you are cooking on an electric stove, remove the skillet from the heat to allow both the burner and the skillet to cool down.) When most of the onions are a rich brown color, add the white wine and balsamic vinegar and reduce until the mixture is almost dry. Add the soy sauce and vegetable stock to the pan and cook until heated through. Add the thyme, rosemary, pepper, and olive oil and mix well. This sauce will be the consistency of broth.

In a Dutch oven or wide, deep pot, bring 4 quarts of salted water to a boil. Reduce the heat so the water is just simmering. Gently slide 12 ravioli into the water. Stir gently to prevent sticking to the bottom of the pot. Do not overcrowd the ravioli or they will break. Cook for 3 to 4 minutes, until the ravioli begin to rise to the surface. Remove them to a bowl as they rise. If there are a couple of stragglers, remove them from the pot anyway. Cook all the ravioli in this fashion.

Divide the ravioli among 4 pasta bowls. Place the onions from the sauce on top of the ravioli. Divide the broth among the four bowls. Sprinkle each serving with walnuts and garnish with fresh herbs.

Makes 6 side-dish servings or 4 main-course servings.

Farfalle with Sun-Dried Tomatoes and Portobellos

Lemon basil has a sharper, more assertive flavor than sweet basil, so it doesn't get lost in the other strong flavors in this dish. The little bow ties may even entice your younger diners to give it a taste test. Steamed broccoli or Broccoli Rabe with Sun-Dried Tomatoes and Pine Nuts (page 212) makes a nice accompaniment to this dish.

8   ounces farfalle (bow tie pasta)
2   teaspoons oil
1   medium red onion, cut into halves lengthwise, then into ½-inch half-moons
3   cloves garlic, thinly sliced
2   portobello mushrooms, stems removed, thinly sliced
1   cup Sun-Dried Tomato Pesto (page 128)
¼   cup thinly sliced lemon basil
1   teaspoon fresh thyme or lemon thyme

Bring 3 quarts of water to a rapid boil in a large pot and cook the farfalle according to the package directions. Drain in a colander and rinse. Put the pasta in a large serving bowl and reserve.

In a wide skillet, heat the oil over medium heat. Add the onion and garlic to the pan and sauté for 2 minutes or just until the onion begins to soften. Add the portobello strips to the pan and cook until they are soft, about 4 minutes. Stir gently to avoid breaking up the mushrooms. Add the pesto to the pan along with ½ cup of water. Add the farfalle, mix well, and heat through. Add the basil and thyme. Serve immediately or reserve in a warm oven.

Makes 4 servings.

Swiss Chard Cannelloni with Walnut Sauce

This is a lot of Swiss chard, but it cooks down to a reasonable volume. If you haven't developed a taste for chard, substitute spinach.

½ cup bulgur
½ cup golden raisins
2 pounds Swiss chard
2 teaspoons plus 1 tablespoon oil
2 leeks, white part only, washed, cut into halves lengthwise, and sliced
3 teaspoons minced garlic
Pinch ground nutmeg
Salt and pepper
¾ cup finely toasted, chopped walnuts (about 3 ounces)
1 cup fresh, soft breadcrumbs (no crusts, just the middle of the bread)
1 teaspoon chopped fresh marjoram
2 cups Vegetable Stock (page 65)
1 teaspoon grainy mustard
3 large pasta sheets, fresh or frozen
¼ cup coarsely chopped walnuts
2 tablespoons chopped fresh parsley

Put the bulgur in a 1-quart nonmetal bowl. Cover with 1 cup of boiling water. Cover the bowl with a plate or plastic wrap and let stand for 20 minutes or until all the liquid is absorbed.

Place the raisins in a small bowl. Pour just enough boiling water into the bowl to cover the raisins. Cover the bowl with a plate or plastic wrap.

Separate the stems from the leaves of the chard. Cut the stems into ½-inch pieces. Cut the leaves into bite-size pieces. Bring 1 cup of water to a boil in a large pot. Add the chard stems and cook for about 5 minutes. Add the leaves and cover the pot tightly. Steam the chard until it is tender, about 4 minutes, stirring occasionally. Drain the chard and place it in a strainer over a bowl. When it is cool enough to handle, squeeze out as much liquid as possible.

In a wide skillet, heat the oil over medium-high heat. Sauté the leeks and 2 teaspoons of the garlic for 2 minutes. Drain the water from the raisins into the skillet. Cook until all the water has evaporated. Add the bulgur, raisins, chard, and nutmeg to the pan and mix well. Taste the filling and adjust the seasoning with salt and pepper. Transfer the filling to a bowl and reserve. Wipe the skillet clean.

Preheat the oven to 350°. Heat the remaining oil in the skillet over medium heat and sauté the remaining garlic and walnuts until the walnuts are fragrant. Add the breadcrumbs to the skillet and sauté 3 minutes longer. Add the marjoram and vegetable stock. Bring the mixture to a boil to thicken it. If the mixture is getting too thick, add tepid water until the consistency is that of traditional pasta sauce. Stir in the mustard. Remove the sauce from the heat and reserve.

Cut the pasta sheets into 4-inch squares. Mound ⅓ cup of the filling along the bottom third of one pasta square. Roll the pasta into a tube enclosing the filling. Place the cannelloni in a greased rectangular baking pan. Roll the rest of the cannelloni in the same manner and neatly arrange them in the pan. Drizzle ½ cup of water over the cannelloni. Cover the cannelloni with the walnut sauce. Cover the baking dish with aluminum foil and bake for 25 minutes. Remove the pan from the oven and let stand for 10 minutes before serving. To serve, garnish the cannelloni with chopped walnuts and parsley.

Makes 6 side-dish servings or 4 main-course servings.

Macaroni and Cheeze

¼ cup nutritional yeast
½ cup all-purpose flour
1 tablespoon light miso
½ teaspoon garlic powder
¼ teaspoon paprika
¼ cup vegan margarine
　 or ¼ cup grapeseed oil
2 teaspoons grainy
　 mustard or ½ teaspoon
　 dried mustard
4 cups cooked macaroni

In a medium saucepan over low heat, toast the yeast and flour just until the flour begins to take on some color and the yeast is lightly toasted. Carefully whisk 2 cups of water (or soymilk) into the flour mixture, making sure no lumps form. Add the miso, garlic powder, and paprika and whisk to blend thoroughly. Gently cook the mixture until it is thick, about 8 to 10 minutes. Add the margarine and mustard and mix well. Taste and adjust the seasonings. Stir in the macaroni and heat through. Serve immediately or reserve in a warm oven.

Makes 4 servings.

MIDDLE EASTERN PASTA

Couscous is the pasta central to Middle Eastern cuisine. It is often referred to as a grain, but it is no more a grain than spaghetti is. Made of semolina flour, couscous is a pasta that traditionally was mixed with water and rubbed between the palms of the hands until the water was absorbed.

Modern cooks will certainly find it easier to cook couscous in boiling water. As with most pasta, the cooking time and the amount of water absorbed by couscous will vary depending on what type of wheat is used to make the couscous. Even the same brand may perform differently at different times. It's best to slightly undercook the pasta and complete the cooking when adding any vegetables or seasonings.

The small couscous that looks like yellow sand is called French couscous and the larger, whitish pellets are toasted Israeli couscous. The larger couscous is easy to overcook and will get gummy. If the couscous is not overcooked, it will keep in the refrigerator for several days.

Basic Couscous

2 cups couscous
2 tablespoons oil

Combine the couscous and oil in a large bowl and mix well. Bring a scant 2 cups of water to a boil in a pot with a tight-fitting lid. Stir in the couscous, remove from the heat, and cover tightly. Let stand for 15 minutes. The water should be completely absorbed. Using a fork or spoon, gently separate the grains of couscous and fluff them up.

Makes 4 cups.

Couscous with Peas and Mint

1/2 cup peas, fresh or frozen
1 1/2 cups cooked couscous, still warm
1 tablespoon chopped fresh mint
2 teaspoons fresh lemon juice
Salt and pepper

In a steamer, steam the peas until they are just tender. In a medium bowl, mix the peas with the warm couscous. Stir in the mint, lemon juice, and salt and pepper to taste.

Makes 2 servings.

Couscous with Raisins and Pine Nuts

Couscous can take on many personalities. Vary the seasonings according to the dishes it will be accompanying. Pine nuts can be expensive and hard to find, so substitute slivered almonds if you like.

¼ cup raisins
3 tablespoons pine nuts
2 teaspoons oil
1 medium onion, finely diced
½ teaspoon fresh thyme or lemon thyme
2 cups cooked couscous
Pinch ground nutmeg

Cover the raisins with boiling water in a small bowl or cup. Cover with a small plate or plastic wrap and let the raisins stand for 10 to 15 minutes.

Heat a skillet over medium heat. Add the pine nuts and cook, shaking the pan, until the pine nuts are evenly toasted, about 3 minutes. Remove the pine nuts to a plate and reserve.

Heat the oil in a skillet and sauté the onion until it is translucent. Turn the heat to low. Add the thyme, couscous, and nutmeg and mix well. Lift the raisins from the water and add to the couscous. If the mixture is too dry, add 2 tablespoons of the raisin liquid and stir until it is absorbed.

Makes 2 servings.

Curried Couscous

This versatile dish can be served hot, room temperature, or cold. In summer, it is good cold as the base of a composed salad with field greens and heirloom tomatoes, or hot with green beans and almonds. In winter, you may want to top it with some cauliflower with toasted cumin seeds or spicy chickpea stew.

1   tablespoon plus 1 teaspoon oil
1   medium onion, diced
2   teaspoons minced garlic
1   teaspoon grated fresh ginger
1   teaspoon curry powder
½   teaspoon ground cumin
½   teaspoon ground ginger
¼   teaspoon ground coriander
¼   teaspoon dry mustard or 1 teaspoon black mustard seeds (optional)
2   cups cooked couscous
2   carrots, finely diced
1   small green bell pepper, finely diced
½   red bell pepper, finely diced
1   tomato, seeded and finely diced, or 1 Granny Smith apple, finely diced
¼   cup toasted sliced almonds

In a wide skillet, heat 1 tablespoon of the oil over medium heat and sauté the onion, garlic, and ginger just until the onion begins to cook. Add the dry spices and mix well. The mixture will become stiff. If it begins to stick on the bottom, reduce the heat. Cook the mixture for 10 minutes, stirring occasionally. The mixture should be quite fragrant. Add the couscous to the skillet and mix well. Remove the couscous to a bowl and reserve.

Wipe the skillet clean. Heat the remaining teaspoon of oil over medium-high heat and sauté the carrots for 1 to 2 minutes. Add the peppers and sauté for 1 to 3 minutes longer. Mix the carrots, peppers, tomato or apple, and almonds with the couscous.

Make 2 servings.

ASIAN PASTA

Asian pastas can seem intimidating. Not only are unfamiliar ingredients used, like mung bean flour, but the translated names on packages—like "starch noodle" or "alimentary paste"—can give little indication of what type of noodle is inside. And the term "noodles" itself is often omitted now that the United States government requires that any product with that name contain at least 5.5 percent egg solids.

Mung bean noodles, also called glass, cellophane, or transparent noodles, are clear when cooked and can be found in both flat noodles and long, thin noodles.

Rice noodles have a delicate flavor and are susceptible to overcooking. They are found as flat, wide noodles and long, thin vermicelli (Italian for "little worms"). Some care must be taken when cooking these noodles so that they retain their shape throughout the stir-frying process.

Wheat and buckwheat noodles such as ramen and soba are sturdier than rice noodles, though they normally are only available in the thin, long-strand variety.

Noodles and Broccoli with Spicy Peanut Sauce

Noodles with peanut sauce, once thought to be a strange, exotic combination, is now a staple of take-out sections in many grocery and gourmet stores. Our love affair with peanut butter makes this an easy dish to embrace. If you are trying to eat more vegetables, add another cup of broccoli florets or peel and chop the stems and add them, too. Zucchini, red pepper, and blanched cauliflower work well in this dish also.

With delicate Asian pastas, it is important that the pasta water never really come to a boil. Therefore, cold water is added with the pasta to maintain a temperature just below boiling.

½ pound fresh wheat or rice vermicelli or 2 ounces dry noodles
1 tablespoon oil
1 medium onion, cut into halves vertically, then into thin half-moon slices
2 cloves garlic, thinly sliced
2 teaspoons grated fresh ginger
¼ teaspoon red pepper flakes
1 cup broccoli florets
1 cup Peanut Sauce (page 136)
1 tablespoon fresh lime or lemon juice
1 small cucumber, thinly sliced
¼ cup chopped fresh cilantro
2 tablespoons chopped, roasted peanuts

Bring 2 quarts of unsalted water to a boil in a large pot. Stir in the noodles. When the water returns to a full boil, add 3 cups of cold water. Reduce the heat to medium-high and continue to cook the noodles until they are al dente. Drain in a colander and rinse with cool water. Reserve.

In a wok or large, wide skillet, heat the oil over high heat, swirling to coat the bottom and side of the pan. Add the onion and garlic and cook, stirring constantly, until the onion begins to develop some color, about 2 minutes. Add the ginger, red pepper flakes, and broccoli. Stir-fry until the broccoli is crisp-tender, about 4 minutes. Add the peanut sauce and lime juice and heat through. Add the noodles and mix well. Garnish with cucumber slices, cilantro, and peanuts and serve immediately.

Makes 2 servings.

Pad Thai

There are as many versions of this Thai staple as there are cooks in Thailand. The sriracha sauce adds a distinctive, fiery bite. If you can't find it, use a hot sauce that's not too vinegary or use ½ teaspoon crushed red pepper. Add 2 tablespoons of diced pickled radish for an authentic touch.

8   ounces wide, flat rice
    noodles
2   tablespoons fresh lime
    or lemon juice
1   teaspoon soy sauce
2   tablepoons ketchup or
    chili sauce
1   teaspoon sriracha sauce
2   teaspoons oil
2   teaspoons minced garlic
1   teaspoon grated ginger
1   carrot, cut into
    matchsticks
3   green onions, cut on the
    diagonal into ³/₈-inch
    lengths
½   cup snow peas, cut into
    matchsticks
4   ounces firm tofu, cut
    into ½-inch cubes
¼   jicama, cut into
    matchsticks (optional)
¼   cup chopped peanuts
¼   cup sunflower or mung
    bean sprouts
1   tablespoon chopped
    fresh cilantro
1   tablespoon chopped
    Thai basil

Bring 3 quarts of water to a boil in a large pot. When the water boils, turn the heat off and add the noodles. Let the noodles soak in the water until they are barely tender, about 15 minutes. Drain the noodles in a colander and rinse with cold water. Reserve.

In a small bowl, combine the lime juice, soy sauce, ketchup, sriracha, and 2 tablespoons of water.

Heat the oil in a wide skillet or a wok over medium heat and sauté the garlic and ginger for 30 seconds. Add the carrot and green onions. Sauté for another 1 to 2 minutes, until the carrot is just barely crisp-tender. Add the snow peas, tofu, and jicama and stir briefly. Add the lime juice mixture and stir to coat the tofu and vegetables, being careful not to break the tofu up too much.

Add the noodles and toss or stir until they are fully cooked and heated through, about 2 minutes. Garnish with chopped peanuts, sprouts, cilantro, and basil.

Makes 4 servings.

Chow Fun with Hot and Smoky Tofu

This is another recipe for those flat, wide rice noodles. This Chinese Stir-fry is called chow fun. I like using a hot, smoky prepared tofu because it tastes so good with the caramelized pieces of noodles, which are my favorite part of the dish. Try to get fresh rice noodles from a local Asian grocery, but use dry if you must.

1   tablespoon mushroom soy sauce
2   tablespoons soy sauce
1   tablespoon Chinese sweet rice wine or sherry
2   teaspoons sugar
1   tablespoon hoisin sauce
8   ounces fresh wide, flat rice noodles or 2 ounces dry rice noodles
3   teaspoons vegetable oil
1   yellow onion, cut into halves and thinly sliced
1   teaspoon minced garlic
1   teaspoon grated fresh ginger
1   carrot, cut into matchsticks
6   shiitake mushrooms, stemmed and thinly sliced
½   cup broccoli florets
4   ounces seasoned baked tofu, cut into strips
1   red bell pepper, cut into thin strips
1   teaspoon toasted sesame oil
Dash white pepper
1   green onion, cut on the diagonal into very thin slices
2   tablespoons chopped fresh cilantro

In a small bowl, whisk the soy sauces, wine, sugar, and hoisin sauce. Reserve.

In a large pot of water just below the boiling point, cook fresh noodles for 2 minutes or dry noodles for 5 minutes. Drain the noodles in a colander, rinse with cold water, and reserve.

Heat a wok or large, wide skillet over high heat. Add 2 teaspoons oil and swirl the wok to coat the bottom and side. When the oil is hot, add the noodles and stir-fry for 2 to 3 minutes or until the noodles begin to take on some color. Remove the noodles to a serving platter and reserve.

Return the wok or skillet to the heat and add another teaspoon of oil. Add the onion, garlic, ginger, carrot, and mushrooms and cook, stirring constantly, for 2 to 3 minutes, or until the onion is translucent. Add the broccoli, tofu, and red pepper and stir-fry for 2 minutes longer, or until the broccoli is crisp-tender.

Add the soy sauce mixture, sesame oil, and pepper to the wok and gently stir to coat the tofu and vegetables, being careful not to break the tofu up too much. Add the noodles and toss or stir to mix everything well. Cook until the noodles are heated through and the sauce is reduced by half.

Mound the stir-fry on a serving platter and garnish with green onion and cilantro.

Makes 2 to 3 servings.

Chilled Soba Noodles on Painted Plates

Pasta salad may seem to us like an invention of the 1970s, but Japanese cuisine has been featuring chilled noodles for quite some time. This recipe is meant to dazzle both the eyes and the palate. It looks complicated, but with a little forethought it is quite easy to put together. When dividing the pasta among individual plates or serving on a large platter, make sure not to cover up your work of art.

Wasabi is the pungent green paste you get with sushi. Buy the powdered wasabi as opposed to the paste, since once the wasabi is mixed with water, it begins to lose its heat. It is sharp like horseradish and not to everyone's taste. If you don't know the heat tolerance of your guests, use wasabi sparingly, but have some extra wasabi oil available at the table.

A Japanese mandoline allows you to cut the vegetables so their shape mimics that of the noodles. If you don't have one, simply cut your vegetables into delicate strips. If taste, not presentation, is your concern, dice the vegetables and toss them with the pasta.

Soy Syrup (recipe follows)
Walnut Dipping Sauce
   (recipe follows)
Wasabi Oil (recipe follows)
8   ounces soba noodles
    (buckwheat or wheat)
1   bunch watercress, trimmed,
    or mesclun greens
2   sheets of nori or ¼ cup
    shredded nori
1   red bell pepper, cut into
    very thin strips
2   shiitake mushrooms
    reserved from Soy Syrup
    recipe (see below), cut
    into thin strips
1   3-inch piece daikon radish,
    peeled and cut into long
    strips
1   English or hothouse
    cucumber, peeled, seeded,
    and cut into long strips
2   green onions, cut on the
    diagonal into thin slices
¼   cup toasted sesame seeds

Make the Soy Syrup and Dipping Sauce several hours to a day in advance. Chill the plates or serving platter you will be using. Make the Wasabi Oil before beginning the noodles. Put the Soy Syrup and Wasabi Oil into squeeze bottles.

Bring 2 quarts of unsalted water to boil in a large pot. Add the noodles and stir. When the water returns to a full boil, add 3 cups of cold water. Reduce heat to medium-high and continue to cook the noodles until they are a little softer than al dente. Drain in a colander and rinse with cool water. Reserve.

Toast the nori either by holding it with tongs over the open flame of a gas stove, or by placing it in a dry cast iron skillet on the open flame, in a toaster oven on low heat, or under a broiler. The nori should be slightly fragrant and crisp. With sharp scissors, cut the nori into very thin strips and reserve.

Just before serving, remove the plates or platter from the refrigerator. Dry any condensation off the plates. Using sweeping motions, drizzle long lines of the Soy Syrup across the plates, all the way to the edge, in a pleasing pattern. In a random pattern, dot the plates with the Wasabi Oil, making your pattern all the way to the edge of the plate.

Place a small fan of watercress at 10 o'clock on each of four plates or a single large serving platter. Carefully mound the noodles on the watercress, piling them as high as possible so that much of your painting is still visible. Arrange the nori, red pepper, reserved shiitakes, and daikon around the noodles in a spoke pattern. Top the noodles with a tuft of the cucumber. Scatter the green onions on the noodles and the sesame seeds over the entire plate. Serve the dipping sauce in a small bowl. To eat, pick up some noodles and vegetables with your chopsticks. Drag your catch through the wasabi and soy syrup, and then dip into the dipping sauce and devour.

Makes 4 servings.

Soy Syrup

2   dried shiitake
    mushrooms
1   cup thin soy sauce
½   cup Chinese dim sum
    vinegar or ½ cup
    balsamic vinegar
2 ¼-inch slices fresh
    ginger
¼   cup brown sugar

In a small pot, soak the mushrooms in 1¼ cups water until they are soft, about 2 hours. Add the soy sauce, vinegar, ginger, and sugar. Simmer until the liquid is reduced by half. Remove the mushrooms and reserve.

Continue to cook the liquid until it is syrupy. Be careful to not to scorch the syrup or it will taste burnt. Cool to room temperature. Do not refrigerate.

Makes about 1½ cups.

Walnut Dipping Sauce

2   cups Japanese
    Seaweed Broth
    (page 68)
½   cup soy sauce
½   cup sake or dry sherry
½   cup rice wine vinegar
⅓   cup sugar
1   cup toasted, finely
    chopped walnuts

In a small pot, heat the stock, soy sauce, sake, vinegar, and sugar to boiling. Add the walnuts. Turn the heat off and let the sauce cool to room temperature. Chill for 2 to 24 hours.

Makes about 4 cups.

Wasabi Oil

3   tablespoons wasabi
    powder
1   tablespoon mirin
    (Japanese rice wine)
¼   cup grapeseed oil or other
    neutral oil

In a small bowl, mix the wasabi with 1 tablespoon of water until a thick paste forms. Cover and let stand for 10 minutes. Whisk the mirin and oil into the wasabi. Cover and chill the mixture.

Makes about ½ cup.

vegetables

Artichoke and Arugula Salad

Grilled Asparagus and Leeks with Almonds

Orange-Ginger Beets and Greens

Roasted Broccoli

Broccoli Rabe with Sun-Dried Tomatoes and Pine Nuts

Brussels Sprouts with Hazelnuts

Szechuan Cabbage

Cabbage Rolls with Kasha

Tunisian Carrot Salad

Cauliflower with Capers

Spicy Cauliflower

Spicy Corn on the Cob

Creamed Corn

Eggplant Rollatini

Fennel Baked with Olives and Tomatoes

Roasted Garlic

Green Beans with Almonds and Mustard

Peppery Mustard Greens

Leek Tomato Sauce

Shiitakes with Corn and Red Peppers

Okra with Tomatoes and Dill

Sweet Onion Caviar

Garden Peas with Saffron and Tomatoes

Roasted Peppers on the Run

Roasted Garlic Mashed Potatoes

Zucchini with Balsamic Vinegar and Mint

Acorn Squash Stuffed with Wild Rice and Winter Fruits

Sweet Potatoes with Pineapple and Peppers

Oven-Roasted Tomatoes

Fried Green Tomatoes

Turnips with Apples and Leeks

Now is the time to start your love affair with vegetables. Vegetables must be forgiven for whatever emotional trauma they caused in your childhood and embraced and appreciated for what they are. Vegetables are loaded with all the things your body needs and wants: protein, vitamins, minerals, fiber, and flavor.

Too often, vegetables are used as mere side dishes without respect for their nutritive value or main-course potential. The recipes in this chapter are designed to give you some new options for serving vegetables. Lots of people have eaten steamed artichokes or marinated artichoke hearts, but how many of us have tried them raw? Harvard beets may have been a standard at your mother's table, but have you tried roasting beets? Each recipe here is designed to bring out the best in a particular vegetable. You will also find tips and suggestions on preparing each vegetable that should inspire you to create your own delicious vegetable-centered meals. So eat your vegetables. And enjoy!

Cooking Methods

Most vegetables can be cooked by any of the following methods. Blanching hard vegetables, like corn, winter squash, cauliflower, and even green beans and asparagus will give you more options for preparation. Once they are partially cooked, they can be grilled or sautéed. Roasting is usually reserved for hard vegetables like potatoes and winter squash, but asparagus, broccoli, and zucchini are all delightful roasted. Experimenting with new ways of cooking familiar foods can significantly expand your culinary repertoire.

When working with mixtures of vegetables, remember either to equalize the cooking time by cutting the long-cooking vegetables smaller than the quick-cooking vegetables, or to cook the vegetables separately and then mix them together. Some vegetables require specific preparation or cooking techniques. These are noted in their individual sections.

Blanching: Cook the vegetables in barely boiling water until the vegetable is crisp-tender, usually 3 minutes or less. Rinse under cool water or plunge into ice water to stop the cooking. Often vegetables are blanched before using in a recipe to speed up cooking times. Vegetables that are frequently blanched include green beans, broccoli, broccoli rabe, bean sprouts, and many vegetables that will be grilled.

Steaming: This technique preserves the shapes and textures of vegetables. Steaming prevents loss of nutrients that might occur if the vegetables were submerged in boiling water. Place the vegetables in a steamer basket set over salted water. Keep the water at a low boil so the steam is consistent. Good vegetables for steaming include carrots, cabbage, cauliflower, green beans, zucchini, squash, cauliflower, broccoli, and broccoli rabe.

Roasting: The goal in roasting is a slightly crisp, browned exterior and a soft, moist interior. Brush or toss prepared vegetables with a little oil and any seasonings. Arrange the vegetables in a single layer on a baking sheet. Using parchment paper on the baking sheet will speed cleanup time and prevent the vegetables from sticking. Crowding the vegetables will cause them to steam instead of roast and will result in uneven cooking.

Roasting temperatures range from 325° to 400°. If roasting at a high temperature (400°), cut the vegetables in small chunks, about ¾ inch thick, so the inside cooks before the outside burns. Roasting at lower temperatures (325°) intensifies the flavors of the vegetables and prevents burning. Rotate the pan at least once and turn the vegetables with a spatula. Vegetables that are good roasted include summer squash, winter squash, broccoli, beets, garlic, leeks, onions, rutabagas, turnips, sweet potatoes, and potatoes.

Grilling: Prepare the vegetables as for roasting, but place on a clean, oiled grill over medium to medium-high heat. Some vegetables, such as eggplant and portobello mushrooms, can absorb a fair amount of oil. They have a tendency to release the oil as they get hot, and the oil drips onto the coals, smoking or even catching fire. If this happens, remove the vegetables immediately to prevent them from burning. Pat the excess oil off the vegetables with paper towels. Once the grill has calmed down, clean the grill rack to remove the soot and then start again. Patience is key to grilling. Cook the vegetables on one side until they are about 60 percent cooked before turning them over. This will help keep the vegetables moist. Vegetables that are good grilled include squash, eggplant, mushrooms, bell peppers, onions, leeks, and asparagus.

Baking: This method is used for potatoes and other vegetables that are cooked in their skins and also for mixtures of vegetables and wet ingredients. For vegetables cooked in their own skins, place either directly on the oven rack or on a baking tray and bake at a medium-low (325°) to medium-high (400°) temperature until the vegetable is easily pierced with a fork and the middle is cooked. Vegetables that benefit from baking include eggplant, sweet potatoes, potatoes, and beets. Almost any vegetable may be baked as part of a casserole.

Sautéing: Sautéing requires a medium to high heat and a little oil. Cooking times and temperatures will vary widely depending on the desired effect. For instance, when caramelizing onions, the onions are placed in the hot oil and allowed to sit for a minute or so to develop some color before stirring, but spinach needs a quick hand and careful attention since it is ruined if it develops a deep color. Since sautéing is generally quite fast, vegetables should either be cut into small enough pieces to allow for even cooking or blanched beforehand. Carrots, peppers, leeks, onions, broccoli, summer squash, mushrooms, fennel, and cabbage can all be cooked from the raw state. Winter squash, cauliflower, large asparagus, green beans, and brussels sprouts are normally blanched first.

Artichokes

Artichokes can be eaten raw or cooked. They can be baked, boiled, roasted, or steamed. Artichokes have such a luxurious flavor and texture that they need little more than lemon juice, olive oil, and salt. The artichoke supply and quality are best in the spring. Look for artichokes with very tight leaves.

While artichokes can easily stand on their own as part of a meal, they make convenient containers for a wide variety of grain dishes. Artichokes supply folate, fiber, and magnesium.

To trim: Cut the stem off the artichoke, and if it is tender, peel it and reserve for stuffing or another use. With a sharp knife, cut ½ to ¾ inch off the top of the artichoke. Trim the sharp points from the leaves with scissors. Rub the cut surfaces with lemon juice to keep them from discoloring.

To boil: Choose a stainless steel pot that will comfortably hold the artichokes in a single layer with no crowding. Bring enough salted water to a boil to completely cover the artichokes. Add 1 or 2 tablespoons of lemon juice to the water. Place the artichokes in the water and cover with a plate that is small enough to weigh down the artichokes but large enough not to fall into the water. Simmer the artichokes for 25 to 40 minutes (depending on size and age) or until a leaf in the middle can be pulled out easily. Drain the artichokes in a colander and refresh with some cold water (or drop into ice water if you plan to serve them cold). Arrange the artichokes upside-down in the colander to drain.

To steam: Place the artichokes in a steamer basket set over salted water. Steam for 30 to 40 minutes or until a leaf in the middle can be pulled out easily. Refresh with some cold water (or drop into ice water if you plan to serve them cold). Arrange the artichokes upside-down in a colander to drain.

To microwave: Cut an X into the bottom of each artichoke. Wrap each one in plastic wrap and put them on a plate, leaving at least 2 inches between artichokes. Microwave for 6 to 10 minutes or until a center leaf can be pulled out easily. Remove the plastic wrap carefully to avoid being burned by the steam. Drop the artichokes into ice water if you plan to serve them cold.

To serve: Carefully pull out the very center leaves to expose the hair-like choke. Using a small spoon, gently scrape the choke out, being careful not to take too much of the heart. Serve the artichokes as they are, fill them, or chill them for later use.

To roast: Preheat the oven to 350°. Cut each artichoke into sixths for large artichokes and quarters for medium ones. Cut out the hair-like choke. Rub all over with lemon juice, then olive oil and garlic, if desired. Place the artichokes in a roasting pan just large enough to hold them. Add a couple of sprigs of thyme and 2 tablespoons of dry white wine or water for each artichoke. Cover the pan with waxed paper then foil and bake for 40 minutes. Remove the waxed paper and foil and roast until browned, about 20 minutes longer.

To serve artichokes uncooked: Beginning near the stem, bend the leaves backwards and break off the green part, making sure the plump, light green nub remains attached to the heart. When the leaves are removed, gently pull the choke away from the heart. Trim the stem. Using a mandoline, the side of a box grater, or a revolving grater, cut the artichoke so it is paper-thin. Immediately toss with some lemon juice.

Artichoke and Arugula Salad

This salad has a lot of big, bitter flavors that are balanced by the sweetness of the pepper and mushrooms. Spinach or mixed baby greens can be substituted for the arugula.

2   tablespoons fresh lemon
    juice
¼   cup extra virgin olive oil
⅛   teaspoon salt
Freshly ground black pepper
2   large artichokes,
    prepared uncooked
    (see above)
1   red bell pepper, sliced
    into matchsticks
⅔   cup paper-thin slices of
    button or shiitake
    mushrooms
2   tablespoons shredded
    basil, preferably lemon
    basil or Thai basil
2   bunches arugula

Whisk the lemon juice, olive oil, salt, and pepper in a medium bowl. Drop the artichoke pieces into the dressing immediately after cutting them. Add the bell pepper and mushrooms to the bowl and toss to blend. Let the salad stand for 10 to 15 minutes.

Just before serving, add the basil and toss again. Divide the arugula among 4 salad plates and top with the artichoke salad.

Makes 4 servings.

Asparagus

Asparagus is the quintessential spring vegetable. The early crop can be a little pricey, but asparagus becomes more affordable as the season progresses. Enjoy it while it lasts, through mid-June or so. While the asparagus sold in the grocery store is wonderful, it has been out of the ground for a few days. Stores usually carry varieties that travel well and are not quite as tender as those grown for immediate consumption. I like asparagus raw only if it is fresh from the garden or farmers' market. Asparagus is rich in vitamins A,C,E, and folate as well as potassium.

Although considered a tender and delicate vegetable, asparagus can stand up to assertive flavors. Its affinity for ginger, green onions, soy, and garlic make it a natural in Asian dishes. Mustard, onions, mushrooms, lemon, tomatoes, and orange are all good partners for asparagus. It is also glorious on its own—hot, warm, or cold.

To prepare asparagus for cooking: Snap the woody ends off the asparagus. (They are great for Vegetable Stock, page 65.) If the asparagus seems tough, use a vegetable peeler to remove the green skin and reveal the pale green flesh.

To blanch: Drop the asparagus into a pot of salted water, at just below boiling. Cook for 3 to 6 minutes, depending on thickness. Drain the asparagus carefully so as not to snap the tips. Refresh with cold water if serving chilled or using in another dish.

To steam: Put the asparagus in a steamer basket over salted water and steam for 4 to 8 minutes or until crisp-tender.

Grilled Asparagus and Leeks with Almonds

1   large or 2 small leeks, trimmed
1   pound asparagus, blanched (see instructions above)
1   tablespoon seasoned oil
Salt and pepper
¼   cup Mustard-Sherry Vinaigrette (page 112), at room temperature
¼   cup sliced almonds, toasted

In a wide, deep skillet, simmer the leeks in salted water until they are crisp-tender, about 3 to 5 minutes. Rinse the leeks under cool water and pat dry. Cut the leeks into halves lengthwise. Rinse under cool water if there seems to be any sand in the leeks. Dry thoroughly. Rub the asparagus and leeks with the oil and lightly salt and pepper them. Grill the leeks, cut side down, for several minutes until heated all the way through. Turn them over and grill the other side. Grill the asparagus until they develop good color. Arrange the vegetables on a serving platter. Drizzle with vinaigrette and top with toasted almonds. Serve immediately.

Makes 4 servings.

Beets

Beets can be found almost any time of year. In the spring, their tender greens are a vegetable unto themselves. Look in farmers' markets or specialty produce stores for the exciting candy stripe or yellow beet varieties. Keep in mind that beet juice stains linens and clothing. It stains hands, too, so wear latex gloves when working with beets.

Often the wallflower of the produce section, beets are wonderful partnered with onions, apples, ginger, orange, lemon, tarragon, or white beans. Beets hold their own, hot or cold, in soups (see Chunky Polish Borscht, page 76, and Chilled Beet and Cucumber Soup, page 94), salads, or side dishes. Beets are a good source of folate, magnesium, and potassium.

To roast: Almost any oven temperature will do for roasting beets. I prefer a cooler oven, around 300°, but if it is convenient to use 400°, that's fine. Just cut the chunks a bit smaller so the insides will cook before the outside burns.

Peel the beets and cut into large chunks. Toss with oil, salt, and pepper. Spread in a single layer on a baking sheet covered with parchment paper and roast until they are easily pierced with a fork.

To boil: Combine whole, unpeeled beets and enough water to cover by 3 inches in a pot. Bring the water to a gradual boil, then reduce the heat and simmer until a fork easily pierces the beets, about 20 minutes for small beets and 35 minutes for large beets. Rinse under cool water. When cool enough to handle, peel the beets.

To steam: Steam whole, unpeeled beets in a steamer basket. Cooking times for steamed beets are about the same as boiling times.

Orange-Ginger Beets and Greens

1   **bunch small beets with their greens**
2   **teaspoons oil**
1   **small red onion, cut into halves lengthwise and thinly sliced**
1½ **teaspoons grated ginger**
⅔ **cup orange juice**
2   **teaspoons rice wine vinegar**
1½ **teaspoons cornstarch**
Salt and pepper

Cut the greens off the beets. Trim the roots from the beets and steam or boil until just tender. Peel the beets. Very small beets should be left whole; larger beets should be cut into halves or quarters. Wash the beet greens well and cut the leaves crosswise into 1-inch ribbons.

Heat the oil in a wide skillet over medium heat. Sauté the onion until it begins to soften. Add the beet greens and sauté until they are wilted. Transfer to a serving dish.

Mix the ginger, orange juice, vinegar, and cornstarch in a small bowl. Add the beets to the skillet and turn the heat to medium-low. When the beets are warm, pour the orange juice mixture over them and cook, stirring, until the mixture just begins to thicken. Season with salt and pepper. Arrange the greens and onions around the edge of a serving dish and place the beets in the center of the plate.

Makes 4 side-dish servings.

Broccoli

It's hard to imagine Brooklyn as the birthplace of an agricultural craze. After realizing some commercial success from harvesting broccoli in Brooklyn, the D'Arrigo Brothers Company made a trial planting of broccoli in California. They shipped the produce back east to Boston, and by 1925 the American broccoli market was established. California continues to grow over 90 percent of the country's broccoli.

Broccoli, a member of the cabbage family, can be eaten raw or cooked; it can be blanched, boiled, stewed, or roasted. The stems can be peeled and grated for slaw-like salads. The trimmings make a fine addition to vegetable stocks. Broccoli and its cousin, broccoli rabe, have substantial amounts of vitamin C and calcium, along with vitamins K and A, folate, and fiber.

When blanching or steaming broccoli, be careful to cook until just crisp-tender. Overcooking makes broccoli mushy. Excess water will dilute sauces and thin the flavor of a dish.

Roasted Broccoli

This is my favorite way to eat broccoli. The roasting intensifies both the sweet and bitter qualities of the little trees and gives it a chewy texture and slightly smoky flavor that I find appealing. Serve with brown rice and Leek Tomato Sauce (page 226).

1   head broccoli, cut into
      3-inch florets
Olive oil
Salt and pepper

Preheat the oven to 300° to 350°. In a small bowl, toss the broccoli with enough oil to lightly coat it. Season the broccoli with salt and pepper. Arrange the broccoli in a single layer on a baking sheet and roast until the broccoli's edges begin to brown and the stems are tender, about 20 minutes, rotating the pan and stirring the broccoli halfway through cooking.

Makes 3 servings.

Broccoli Rabe

While broccoli looks like a little tree, broccoli rabe looks more like a shrub, with a slender stalk, buds on the verge of flowering, and copious leaves. While broccoli stems are tough and should be peeled, broccoli rabe stems are usually tender. Just cut off the dry base of the stalk. Like many popular Italian vegetables, broccoli rabe has a pleasant bitter taste and pairs well with slightly sweet ingredients such as nuts, sun-dried tomatoes, extra virgin olive oil, and raisins. Like its more muscular cousin, broccoli rabe packs a mighty nutritional wallop.

Though a little pricey at times, broccoli rabe is available year-round. It is at its peak in late fall through early spring.

Broccoli Rabe with Sun-Dried Tomatoes and Pine Nuts

2 tablespoons thinly sliced sun-dried tomatoes (use ¼ cup if oil packed)
2 teaspoons oil
1 teaspoon minced garlic
⅛ teaspoon red pepper flakes
2 bunches broccoli rabe, cut into 2-inch pieces
2 tablespoons pine nuts, toasted
1 tablespoon extra virgin olive oil
Sea salt and freshly ground black pepper

Cover the sun-dried tomatoes with boiling water in a very small bowl or custard cup. Let stand for 10 minutes, drain, and reserve. (If using oil-packed tomatoes, omit this step.)

Heat the oil in a wide skillet over medium heat. Add the garlic and pepper flakes and sauté until the garlic is fragrant, about 40 seconds. Add the broccoli rabe and cook until it turns a brilliant green. If the garlic begins to brown, add a few ounces of water to the pan. Add the pine nuts, tomatoes, olive oil, salt, and pepper and toss to mix thoroughly. Serve immediately or reserve in a warm oven for up to 20 minutes.

Makes 2 to 3 servings.

Brussels Sprouts

Yet another cabbage relative, brussels sprouts grow in tightly packed rows of tiny, cabbage-like heads on a single, sturdy stem. They are at their best in the early to late fall, though they are available throughout the winter. Brussels sprouts provide vitamin C, folate, and fiber.

Since overcooking releases the unpleasant-smelling sulfurous compounds that cause the "boiled cabbage" odor, stick with brief blanching. Brussels sprouts may be sautéed or roasted, but should be blanched beforehand to ensure even cooking.

Brussels Sprouts with Hazelnuts

This recipe has converted many a brussels sprout hater, accustomed to overcooked, gray-green blobs in cream sauce. This dish may be served hot, cold, or at room temperature.

1   pint brussels sprouts
2   tablespoons chopped
    hazelnuts, toasted
1½ tablespoons hazelnut
    oil (available in specialty
    food shops)
Salt

Remove any yellow leaves from the sprouts. Trim the base, cutting off any stem that has been left. Carefully cut the brussels sprouts into quarters. Cook the brussels sprouts in a small amount of boiling salted water until they turn bright green and are just tender, about 4 minutes for young sprouts, up to 10 minutes for older sprouts. Drain thoroughly. To serve cold, cool the brussels sprouts under cold running water or in ice water.

Toss the brussels sprouts with the hazelnuts, oil, and salt. Serve immediately or reserve in a warm oven for up to 15 minutes.

Makes 2 generous servings.

Cabbage

Perhaps its year-round availability and relatively low price have contributed to cabbage's reputation as a second-rate vegetable. More likely, it's the sulfurous smell of boiled cabbage that has relegated this versatile vegetable to the back of our refrigerators. It needn't be that way. Many recipes require only brief cooking. For long-simmered cabbage dishes the addition of onions, garlic, thyme, or bay leaves can mitigate the smell.

There is very little waste with cabbages. Head cabbages should have the core removed before cooking. To prepare leaf cabbages, cut out and discard the ribs from the outer leaves. One pound of cabbage yields 6 cups of shredded or cut cabbage, enough for 4 generous servings. Cabbage is an excellent source of vitamins C and K, fiber, and antioxidant phytochemicals.

The cabbage family encompasses some of our favorite vegetables—broccoli, cauliflower, brussels sprouts, kale, and kohlrabi. Cabbage itself comes in an assortment of shapes, textures, and flavors, from red and green cabbage with their tight round heads and waxy leaves to leafy green Chinese mustard cabbage with its peppery bite.

Green and red cabbage are the familiar heavy, round heads available year-round. They keep seemingly forever in the refrigerator.

Savoy is a loose head cabbage with crinkled leaves and a mild flavor. The leaves are thin and crisp and require a much shorter cooking time than ordinary green cabbage. Savoy cabbage has a shorter season than green cabbage. It is available in early spring, fall, and early winter but not in the summer or in the coldest months.

Bok choy, also called pak choy, is a mild, versatile vegetable with crunchy white stalks, tender, dark green leaves, and a flavor like Swiss chard. It resembles a bunch of wide-stalked celery with long, full leaves. Bok choy is related to napa cabbage but is not the same. Shanghai bok choy is slightly smaller, smoother, and greener than bok choy. The leaves and stems are tender and the flavor is mild.

Napa cabbage, also called Chinese cabbage, has a loose, oval head with crinkled, veined leaves that are white at the base and light green at the tip. The flavor is delicate and the leaves are thin and crisp. Use raw, or sauté, bake, or braise. Chinese cabbage is a good source of vitamin A, folic acid, and potassium.

Mustard cabbage (gai choy) is the vegetable of choice for pickling. Rarely found in regular grocery stores, it is more common in Asian markets. Gai choy can be added to long-simmered soups and stews.

Szechuan Cabbage

2   tablespoons soy sauce
2   teaspoons dry sherry
1   teaspoon sugar
2   teaspoons rice wine vinegar
1   teaspoon sesame oil
2   tablespoons oil
¼   teaspoon red pepper flakes
2   teaspoons grated ginger
1   teaspoon minced garlic
1   small head cabbage, cut into long, thin strips or 2-inch squares

In a small bowl, whisk the soy sauce, sherry, sugar, vinegar, and sesame oil until blended. Reserve.

Heat the oil in a wok or wide skillet over high heat. Working quickly, add the red pepper flakes, ginger, and garlic and stir-fry until the mixture is fragrant, about 30 to 45 seconds. Add the cabbage and mix well. Cook just until the cabbage begins to wilt, about 3 minutes for green or red cabbage and 1 minute for napa cabbage. Add the reserved sauce and mix well. Cook green or red cabbage until cooked through but not mushy, about 4 or 5 minutes longer. Cook napa cabbage until crisp-tender, about 2 minutes longer.

Makes 4 to 6 servings.

Cabbage Rolls with Kasha

Select cabbage leaves large enough to hold about ½ cup of filling. If the cabbage is small, you may need to blanch a few extra leaves and piece them together. You may wish to use Vegetable Stock (page 65) rather than water to swell the kasha, as it gives the filling a more complex flavor.

16 large cabbage leaves, savoy, green, or napa
2 cups kasha (buckwheat groats) or coarse bulgur
2 tablespoons oil
2 medium onions, diced
4 stalks celery, diced
1 medium carrot, diced (optional)
2 teaspoons minced garlic
2 cups sliced shiitake mushrooms
¼ cup toasted almond butter
4 ounces prepared seitan or tempeh (optional), crumbled
1 teaspoon fresh thyme leaves
Salt and pepper
2 cups tomato sauce
1 cup Mushroom Stock (page 67) or water

Blanch the cabbage leaves, a few at a time, in boiling salted water. When the leaves are pliable, remove from the water and cool under running water or in ice water. Green cabbage may take 2 to 4 minutes, savoy a bit less, and napa only a minute or less. Pat the leaves dry and reserve.

In a wide skillet over medium-low heat, toast the kasha until it is fragrant and just starting to brown. Transfer the kasha to a bowl and pour 3 cups of boiling water or vegetable stock over it. Cover the bowl and let stand for 15 minutes or until the water is absorbed.

Heat the oil in a skillet over medium heat and sauté the onions, celery, carrots, garlic, and shiitakes until the onions have softened. Turn the heat off and add the almond butter and seitan. Season with thyme, salt, and pepper and mix well. Add the kasha to the skillet and mix well. The mixture should just hold together. Add a little water or more almond butter to adjust the consistency.

Preheat the oven to 350°. Lightly oil or spray a 9x13-inch baking dish. Mix the tomato sauce and stock and pour half of it into the baking dish.

Mound ½ cup of the kasha mixture at the root end of each cabbage leaf. Fold the sides of the leaf over the filling and roll the leaf to enclose the filling and form a small packet. Arrange the cabbage rolls in the baking dish. Top the rolls with the reserved sauce. Cover with plastic or waxed paper, then with aluminum foil. Bake for 1 hour or until the sauce is bubbly and the rolls are heated through.

Makes 8 servings.

Carrots

Carrots are an amazingly adaptable vegetable. They can be juiced, puréed, boiled, blanched, steamed, sautéed, roasted, eaten raw, or fried plain as chips or in tempura batter. Generally, younger carrots tend to be sweeter and are favored by children. As with other sweet vegetables, they pair well with salty and acidic ingredients such as lemon juice, seaweed, and vinegar. Carrots are used in soups and casseroles to temper the bitterness of garlic, onions, and herbs.

Carrots are packed with beta-carotene, a precursor to vitamin A, as well as flavanoids and phytochemicals. They are readily available year-round.

Tunisian Carrot Salad

2   cloves garlic, crushed
1/8 teaspoon cayenne
1/2 teaspoon cumin seed, toasted
1/2 teaspoon ground coriander
2   tablespoons lemon juice
3   tablespoons extra virgin olive oil
4   carrots, shredded or cut into matchsticks
2   tablespoons chopped fresh cilantro
Salt and pepper
1   head butter lettuce, washed and trimmed
4   yellow pear tomatoes, cut into halves
4   cherry tomatoes, cut into halves

Mix the garlic, spices, lemon juice, and olive oil in a medium bowl. Add the carrots and cilantro and mix well. Let stand for 15 minutes for the flavors to develop. Taste the salad and season with salt and pepper. Arrange the lettuce on 4 salad plates. Top the lettuce with the carrots. Arrange the tomatoes on the salads.

Makes 4 servings.

Cauliflower

The snowy white florets of cauliflower, another member of the cabbage family, can be eaten raw, lightly blanched, steamed, stewed, or roasted. As with all cabbage relations, overcooking tends to release sulfurous odors that are not appetizing. Cauliflower comes into the market in late summer and is available through early spring. When selecting cauliflower, avoid heads with a grainy texture or yellow to brown color, indicators of age. Cauliflower is a good source of vitamins C and K.

Cauliflower with Capers

2 tablespoons lemon juice
1/4 cup extra virgin olive oil
2 tablespoons capers
1/8 teaspoon salt
1 tablespoon chopped fresh parsley (optional)
1 head cauliflower, cut into florets and steamed

Whisk the lemon juice, oil, capers, salt, and parsley together. Add the hot cauliflower and toss to mix well. Serve the cauliflower hot or room temperature.
Makes 4 servings.

Spicy Cauliflower

2 teaspoons oil
1/2 teaspoon cumin seeds
1/2 teaspoon black mustard seeds
1 small hot chili, seeded, or 1/4 teaspoon red pepper flakes
2 teaspoons grated fresh ginger or 1/2 teaspoon dried ginger
1/2 teaspoon chili powder
1/2 teaspoon ground coriander
1/4 teaspoon salt
Freshly ground black pepper
1 large head cauliflower, cut into florets and blanched
2 teaspoons lemon juice
2 tablespoons chopped fresh cilantro

Heat the oil in a wide skillet over medium heat. Add the cumin seeds, mustard seeds, and the chili. When the mustard seeds begin to pop, add the ginger, chili powder, coriander, salt, pepper, and cauliflower and mix well. Add 1/2 cup of water and cover the pan. Let the cauliflower steam for 3 or 4 minutes, until it is heated through. Add the lemon juice and cilantro and mix well.
Makes 4 servings.

Corn

Summertime would be canceled by popular demand if fresh corn were not the reward for enduring the long, hot season. Most varieties available in the supermarket are either "sweet," with 5 to 10 percent sugar, or supersweet, with 30 percent. The sweetness of older varieties of corn deteriorated quickly, with the sugar turning to starch. Selective breeding has slowed this process, dramatically improving the shelf life of fresh corn. The local farmers' market, however, remains your best bet for fresh corn.

Ripe corn has a milky white juice and tender kernels. If the juice runs clear, the kernels are immature and should be cut off and discarded. If you are not going to cook corn right away, leave it in the husk and keep refrigerated. Bring the corn to room temperature before shucking and cooking. Corn is a good source of folate, thiamin, vitamin K, and fiber. See page 172 for a discussion of the uses of corn as a grain.

To prepare corn for cooking: Pull the husks off the cob (that is, shuck the corn). Remove the silk. Trim and discard the stalk and any tough small kernels. If the silk end has some insect damage, cut away the damaged piece and wash the cob well.

To cut kernels from the cob: Shuck the corn but do not trim the silk end. Set a baking dish on a work surface. Hold the corn cob at an angle, with the silk end in the dish. Beginning at the stalk end, slide your knife between the kernels and the cob as far down the cob as you can without hitting the baking dish. Turn the cob and continue cutting until all the kernels are cut away. Scrape the cob with your knife to get the juices and cornstarch from the cob. Remove stubborn kernels with a paring knife.

Spicy Corn on the Cob

Do not salt the water, as this will toughen the corn. Because the corn comes into contact with direct heat, this recipe works best with tender, fresh corn.

2   ears corn, shucked and
     cut into 3-inch lengths
1   tablespoon oil
1   medium onion, cut into
     halves and thinly sliced
2   cloves garlic, very thinly
     sliced
¼   teaspoon red pepper flakes
¼   teaspoon ground cumin
     (optional)
¼   teaspoon chili powder
Sea salt and freshly ground
     black pepper

Bring a large pot of water to a boil, add the corn, and boil for 3 to 4 minutes. Meanwhile, heat the oil in a large, wide skillet over medium-high heat and sauté the onion, garlic, and spices until the onion is slightly browned. Remove the corn from the water with tongs and add it to the skillet. Stir to coat with oil. Cook the corn until some of the kernels are lightly browned. Transfer to a serving platter and pour the onions and any pan juices over the corn.

Makes 2 to 4 servings.

Creamed Corn

Did you know that creamed corn contains no cream? The corn's starch acts as a thickener for the juices. Make sure to scrape every drop of juice from the cobs for this recipe. (This recipe does not work with canned or frozen corn.)

3 or 4 ears fresh corn
Salt
**1   teaspoon sugar
     (optional)**

Cut the corn from the cobs using the method described on the preceding page. Be sure to scrape the cobs well to obtain all the starch and juice. Put the corn and all its juices in a small pot over medium heat and pour 1 cup of boiling water over it. Bring the mixture to a boil and cook, stirring, for 5 minutes or until thickened. Taste and adjust the seasonings with salt and sugar. Remove from the heat and let stand, covered, for 5 minutes before serving.

Makes 2 servings.

Eggplant

Eggplant presents itself in many guises: puréed in Baba Ganoush (page 47); cubed and dressed in Caponata (page 46); sliced, roasted, and rolled in rollatini. Anyway you cut it, eggplant is a treat. It is very low in calories, is a good source of potassium and magnesium, and contains some Vitamin A. Eggplants come in a variety of shapes, sizes, and colors. Japanese or Chinese eggplants are long and thin. These have a smooth, creamy flesh and thin skin. Italian white eggplants have a thick, white peel over a dense creamy interior.

When choosing eggplants, look for a smooth skin with no soft brown spots. The eggplant should give under slight pressure. Very hard eggplants are old and may be especially bitter.

Eggplant, especially the large variety, can be bitter, so it's always a safe bet to salt and drain it to ensure sweet, tender flesh. The exceptions are skinny Asian eggplants, very young eggplants, and those you have grown yourself.

When grilling or roasting slices of eggplant, the skin may be left on; for stews, soups, and casseroles, it is safer to peel the eggplant completely since the skin may become bitter on sitting. Eggplants have a spongy texture that easily absorbs liquid ingredients, so be sparing in the use of oil. Sauté eggplant cubes at medium-high temperatures to minimize the amount of oil absorbed.

To salt eggplant: Cut the eggplants into 1-inch-thick slices or chunks. Liberally sprinkle salt all over and lay the slices in a colander. Allow the eggplants to drain for 20 to 30 minutes. When the eggplants have released a fair amount of brown liquid, rinse each slice briefly under cold water and pat dry.

To cook chunks or slices: Brush eggplant slices sparingly with seasoned oil. Arrange the eggplant in a single layer on a baking sheet covered with parchment. Roast, grill, or broil the eggplant about 3 to 7 minutes on each side until cooked through, depending on your cooking method.

To bake whole eggplant: Rub the eggplant with oil and prick the skin in several places. Bake the eggplant on a baking sheet in a 400° oven. For recipes requiring a purée or custard-like texture, bake until the eggplant collapses on itself, about 40 minutes. For recipes where the flesh will be chopped and sautéed or stewed, bake until a fork easily pierces the flesh, about 25 minutes.

Eggplant Rollatini

¼ pan Roasted Garlic
Polenta (recipe follows),
at room temperature
2 medium eggplants
Salt
Seasoned oil
½ cup roasted red peppers
2 tablespoons chopped
fresh basil
2 cups tomato sauce,
warm

Preheat the oven to 350°. Lightly oil or spray a 9x13-inch glass or ceramic baking dish.

Cut the polenta into pieces 3 inches long and ¾ inch thick. Cut the eggplant lengthwise into long slices, ½ inch thick. Remove as much skin as possible from the first and last slices. Salt the slices and place them in a colander to drain for 30 minutes. Rinse and pat dry. Brush the slices with seasoned oil and grill or roast them until tender.

Arrange a strip of red pepper, a sprinkling of basil, and a piece of polenta at the narrow end of the eggplant. Fold the narrow end of the eggplant over the polenta and roll to enclose the filling. Repeat with the remaining eggplant slices. Spread the tomato sauce in the baking dish. Arrange the rollatini, seam side down, in the sauce. Bake for 20 minutes, or until the sauce is bubbling and the rollatini are heated through.

Makes 2 to 4 servings.

Roasted Garlic Polenta: Prepare Basic Polenta (page 172), adding the paste from 1 head of Roasted Garlic (page 223) along with the olive oil and raw garlic.

Fennel

Much loved in Italy and Provence, fennel is just beginning to come into its own in the rest of the world. The slightly sweet, anise-scented bulbs are quite versatile—they are good raw with a little olive oil and lemon juice, or baked, grilled, puréed, or stewed. Fennel and fennel seeds have a long history in folk medicine. Modern science finds fennel a good source of vitamin A; it also provides some calcium, potassium, and phosphorus.

To prepare fennel for cooking, cut off the stalks. Separate the delicate greens from the stalks and reserve them for garnish, or chop them and add them to the dish at the very end of cooking (so their color is retained). Reserve the stalks for stock. With a paring knife, cut any discoloration or bruises from the outer layer. If the fennel is being braised or grilled, cut the bulb into halves horizontally. For other dishes, quarter the bulb and remove the core. Fennel is structured like an onion, with layers that may be separated from one another. To get the most consistent cut, separate the layers and cut each one separately.

Fennel Baked with Olives and Tomatoes

Browning the fennel and onions before baking them significantly reduces the cooking time. The olives are salty, so use salt sparingly.

1	tablespoon oil
2	fennel bulbs, cut into halves horizontally
2	small red onions, cut into 1-inch chunks
Sea salt and freshly ground black pepper	
⅓	cup dry white wine
2	tablespoons lemon juice
8	cloves garlic, peeled
1	large sprig thyme
¼	cup oil-cured or kalamata olives, pitted and quartered
1	cup diced fresh tomatoes
2	tablespoons chopped fresh basil

Preheat the oven to 400°. Lightly oil or spray a 9x13-inch glass baking dish. In a wide skillet over medium-high heat, heat the oil until it is almost smoking. Carefully add the fennel and onions, cut side down. Do not separate the onions into rings. Allow the onions and fennel to brown in the skillet, about 3 to 4 minutes. Turn and brown the other side.

Carefully transfer the onions and fennel to the baking dish. Season with a little salt and lots of black pepper, if desired. Add the wine, lemon juice, garlic, thyme, and olives to the baking dish. Cover the dish with waxed paper, then tightly with aluminum foil. Bake for 30 minutes, until the fennel is soft but not mushy. Add the tomatoes to the baking dish and place it under the broiler until the edges of the fennel and onion are just crisped. Add the basil and toss to mix.

Makes 4 servings.

Garlic

Garlic thwarted Circe as she tried to turn Odysseus into a pig. It has prevented the spread of vampires and was eaten by the Israelites before fleeing from Egypt. The first known mention of garlic was four thousand years ago, and since then it has been alternately praised and vilified with great passion. In various cultures, garlic has been recommended as a cure for bee stings, tumors, and most ailments in between. However, in the Ayurvedic tradition of southern India it is considered an impure plant not worthy of offering to Krishna.

Garlic, like the onion, is a member of the lily family. It is a compound bulb made up of four to fifteen cloves. The papery skins can be a whitish tan or a striped purple. Purple garlic, which matures later than the tan type, has a sharper taste. Elephant garlic has cloves the size of brazil nuts and a very mild flavor.

Allicin, a sulfur compound, is responsible for both garlic's characteristic odor and its medicinal benefits. Cooking breaks down the allicin and softens the flavor of the garlic. Roasting garlic produces a sweet, creamy paste that is a wonderful addition to sauces and tastes great spread on Italian bread.

Roasted Garlic

1 whole head garlic
Olive oil

Cut off the stem end of the garlic to expose the tops of the cloves. Liberally rub the garlic with olive oil and wrap tightly in aluminum foil. Bake the garlic at a temperature between 300° and 400° (you can bake it while something else bakes) until it is quite soft and fragrant, about 20 minutes for a small head at 400° and up to an hour for a large head at 300°. Garlic that is roasted at 300° to 325° is sweetest.

Makes 1 head of roasted garlic.

Green Beans

Not long ago, green beans were commonly referred to as "string beans," a reminder of the tough string that ran down one or two sides of the bean. Now many varieties have no fibrous appendage—to prepare them, simply remove the stem end. Green beans are suited to steaming, sautéing, and even quick frying. Steaming green beans helps preserve their high vitamin C content. Green beans are also a good source of vitamin A and fiber. They go well with mushrooms, tomatoes, fennel, peppers, onions, walnuts, almonds, garlic, ginger, tarragon, and thyme. Green beans are equally satisfying whether prepared cold or hot, simply or lavishly.

Green Beans with Almonds and Mustard

1   pound green beans
1   tablespoon oil
1   small red onion, cut into halves and thinly sliced
½   teaspoon minced garlic
½   teaspoon grated fresh ginger
3   tablespoons grainy mustard
⅛   teaspoon sea salt
Pinch ground white pepper
¼   cup sliced almonds, toasted

Steam or blanch the green beans and keep warm. Heat the oil in a wide skillet over medium heat. Add the onion, garlic, and ginger to the pan and sauté until the onion wilts slightly, about 2 minutes. Add the mustard, salt, pepper, and ¼ cup of water to the pan and heat to boiling. Add the green beans and toss to coat with the sauce. Add half the almonds and mix well. Transfer the beans to a serving dish and garnish with the remaining almonds.

Makes 4 servings.

Greens

Large and leafy, greens are an important component of the vegan diet. Some are slightly bitter when raw but develop a certain sweetness with long cooking. Greens like arugula, frisée, watercress, and spinach are delightful raw. Others like kale and collards can be blanched before cooking to tone down their bitter nature. Their thick stalks can usually be cut and cooked alongside the leaves. Preparation of escarole, mustard greens, and chard depends on the age of the leaves. Young tender leaves can be quickly sautéed; older, tougher leaves may require blanching and long cooking. Young mustard or dandelion greens can be eaten raw in salads for a radish-like bite. Slow-cooking creates a mellow flavor.

Greens are high in folate, phytochemicals, vitamins A and C, and calcium. Long cooking will destroy some of the nutrients, especially vitamin C. Oxalates, which bind iron and calcium, are found in high concentration in spinach, Swiss chard, and beet greens. To optimize your calcium intake, cook greens in an excess of water to wash away the oxalates. To get as much vitamin C as possible, use a minimum amount of water or eat the greens raw.

For other ways of addings greens to your diet see Caldo Verde (page 74), Escarole and White Bean Soup (page 87), Watercress and Spicy Glass Noodles (page 101), or Swiss Chard Cannelloni (page 192).

Peppery Mustard Greens

Carl Lewis

4 to 5 bunches flat-leaf
    mustard greens
1   bunch spinach
1   bunch arugula
2   tablespoons olive oil
1   small onion, finely
    chopped
1   teaspoon sea salt
2   teaspoons lemon pepper
2   teaspoons garlic pepper
    or garlic powder
1   teaspoon black pepper

Wash all the greens. Reserve the spinach and arugula separately from the mustard greens. Cut the mustard greens into 1-inch strips, place in a large pot, and add ¾ cup of water. Cook over medium-high heat for 20 minutes, adding more water as needed. Heat the olive oil in a large, wide skillet over medium heat. Sauté the onion with the seasonings until the onion is tender. Add the onion mixture, spinach, and arugula to the mustard greens. Cook for an additional 20 minutes over medium-low heat.

Makes 6 servings.

Leeks

In A.D. 626, the Welsh king Cadwallon was defeated by Edwin of Northumbria and exiled to Ireland. On his return seven years later, he instructed his men to wear a leek in their helmets so he could easily identify them. The battle was won and the king repatriated, so the leek became the national symbol of Wales. (Cadwallon survived only a year before being killed by Oswald. Perhaps he had stopped eating leeks.)

Leeks have a rich flavor and texture. Like garlic and onions, leeks contain some vitamin C, along with, perhaps more importantly, the phytochemicals allicin and quercetin, which may boost the immune system. Leeks are suitable for grilling, braising, sautéing, and puréeing. They are available most of the year, with the best supplies in the fall. The flat leaves of leeks tend to capture a lot of the sandy soil that they are grown in, so it is important to clean them carefully. The cleaning method varies according to whether the leeks will be used whole, cut in halves, or sliced.

To trim leeks: The easiest method for trimming leeks is to cut straight across the leek where the leaves begin to turn from white to green. You can discard the tough green tops, but considering the steep price of leeks, you may want to try this: Cut off the green leaves of the leeks, leaving about 2 to 3 inches of green above the white part. With a sharp knife, pare the green outer leaves away. The center will be white or very pale green and tender enough to use. Some people reserve leek greens for soup stock, but I think they impart an unpleasant taste.

To clean and prepare whole leeks: Cut an X in the stem end (the opposite end from the root) of the leek. Place the leek perpendicular to swift running water and thoroughly rinse the leaves. (If you let the water run directly into the heart of the leek, any sand will become imbedded in the leek and be impossible to get out without cutting.) Shake the leaves out and rinse several more times. Cut off the root end.

To clean and prepare leek halves: Cut the leeks into halves lengthwise. Hold the leek by the root end and place the leek at a downward angle under running water. Separate the leaves to let water run through the layers and rinse thoroughly. Cut off the root end.

To clean and prepare sliced leeks: Trim the leeks, cut in half lengthwise, then slice to the desired thickness. Place the leek slices in a large bowl of cold water. Swirl the leeks in the water to loosen the sand. Make sure that the leeks are floating with a few inches of water below so the sand will settle to the bottom and not on the leeks. Lift the leeks out of the water and drain them in a colander. Discard the first wash water. If there is lots of sand in the bottom, repeat the rinsing until the leeks are clean.

Leek Tomato Sauce

This sauce is equally good tossed with pasta, on top of grilled vegetables, with Fried Green Tomatoes (page 240), or over tempeh with brown rice.

2 tablespoons oil
3 cloves garlic, thinly sliced
2 to 4 leeks, cleaned and cut
    into ¾-inch pieces
¼ cup dry white wine
6 roma tomatoes, seeded
    and chopped
1 teaspoon fresh thyme
    leaves
Sea salt and freshly ground
    black pepper

Heat the oil in a wide skillet over medium heat. Add the garlic and leeks and sauté until the leeks begin to wilt, about 2 minutes. Add the wine to the pan and cook until the liquid is reduced to 1 tablespoon. Add the tomatoes and thyme and cook until the tomatoes are just warmed through. Season the sauce with salt and pepper. The sauce will become more liquid the longer the tomatoes cook. For a fresh chunky sauce, remove the skillet from the heat at this point.

Makes 4 to 6 servings.

Mushrooms

The sudden appearance of mushrooms can be so mysterious that people once thought they were gifts from the gods. With their meaty texture and earthy flavors, mushrooms are a favorite ingredient in meatless meals. Of course, mushrooms are fungi, not vegetables, but they have the same role as vegetables in cuisines worldwide. They are adaptable to most cooking methods—except perhaps steaming.

With a water content of up to 90 percent and only 10 calories per $\frac{1}{2}$-cup serving, mushrooms are not normally eaten for their nutritional content. However, they contain a surprising amount of vitamin D, along with several trace minerals like copper and selenium. Shiitakes, along with maitake and wood ear mushrooms, have a long history in Asian medical traditions.

When buying mushrooms, look at the gills, the fan-like structures under the smooth cap. The gills should be tight and dry and have a pleasant, earthy smell. If the gills are matted or slimy, the mushroom has been mishandled. The more open the gills, the older the mushroom and the deeper the flavor. If you are looking for mushrooms to use raw in a salad, try to find young mushrooms with tight or unexposed gills.

White or button mushrooms are creamy white in color, with a mild, woodsy flavor. Young mushrooms have tender stems that can be prepared along with the caps. Older mushrooms with more open caps may have woody stems that should be discarded or used to make stock.

Cremini (Italian brown mushrooms) are related to button mushrooms, but have a deeper flavor.

Portobello mushrooms are creminis allowed to grow to full maturity. Their meaty texture has made them a favorite meat alternative. They are sturdy enough to stand up to extreme cooking procedures—grilling, marinating, and roasting. Trim the dirt from the bottom of the stem and discard. If the stem is tender, it may be chopped and prepared along with the cap. If the stem is woody, discard it or save it for stock. Some recipes may call for removing the gills. This is primarily an aesthetic preference.

Shiitake mushrooms have caps that are either flat or domed, with edges that curl under tightly to meet the gills. The mushrooms may be light or dark brown. Shiitakes have a rich, earthy flavor and firm texture, making them another favorite meat substitute. The stems of shiitakes are woody and should be cut off and used for stock or discarded.

Oyster mushrooms resemble soft gray fans flowing from a central base. The caps have tight gills on the undersides. The very bottom of the mushroom is woody, but the rest is edible, though it is generally not eaten raw. When cooked, oyster mushrooms have a silky texture and delicate flavor.

Shiitakes with Corn and Red Peppers

✓ good

Canned or frozen corn will work in this recipe, though fresh gives the dish a fuller flavor. Instead of flat-leaf parsley, you may use basil, thyme, or rosemary. However, I prefer flat-leaf parsley because it does not distract so much from the vegetables' flavor.

2　teaspoons oil
1　medium onion, cut into halves and thinly sliced
2　cloves garlic, thinly sliced
1　cup sliced shiitake mushrooms
1　large red bell pepper, cut into 1/3-inch strips
2　cups corn kernels, preferably fresh
1　tablespoon chopped flat-leaf parsley
Salt and pepper

Heat the oil in a wide skillet over medium heat. Add the onion and garlic and sauté until the onion begins to soften, about 2 minutes. Add the shiitakes and peppers and cook for 3 minutes longer. When the peppers have started to soften, add the corn. If the vegetables are sticking to the pan, add a little water. Cover the skillet, turn the heat to low, and simmer the mixture for 5 minutes. Stir in the parsley and season the mixture with salt and pepper.

Makes 4 servings.

Okra

Like corn, okra is a vegetable of high summer. Don't think of it as slimy—think of it as a thickener and use it as a stew ingredient with tomatoes or other acidic ingredients that counter its texture. Choose pods smaller than your thumb if possible, as the seeds of older okra are quite hard. When I was finally successful in growing okra, there was such an abundance I couldn't imagine eating any more—so a friend sliced it, tossed it with a little salt, and dehydrated it in a 250° oven, and we ate it for snacks. Okra has substantial amounts of vitamins A and C.

Okra with Tomatoes and Dill

1 teaspoon oil
1 medium onion, cut into halves and thinly sliced
1 teaspoon minced garlic
1 teaspoon turmeric
1 pound okra, cut into 1-inch pieces
1 28-ounce can diced tomatoes
1 12-ounce can chickpeas, drained or 1 cup cooked chickpeas
2 tablespoons chopped fresh dill
1 tablespoon chopped fresh parsley
Hot cooked rice

Heat the oil in a deep skillet over medium heat and sauté the onion, garlic, and turmeric until the onion begins to soften, about 2 minutes. Add the okra and cook for 2 minutes longer. Add the tomatoes, chickpeas, and dill and simmer the mixture for 15 minutes or until the okra is tender but not too soft. Stir in the parsley. Serve with rice.

Makes 4 main-course servings or 6 side-dish servings.

Onions

Onions are a magical food. They can take center stage or play a small supporting role for which they receive no credit. Raw, they have a sharp bite; caramelized, they have a nutty sweetness. Vidalia, SuperSweet, and OsoSweet onions can be almost candy-sweet and can be used raw. To dull their sharp bite, other onions should be soaked for 15 minutes in water with a little lemon juice before being added raw to a dish. Rosemary and thyme are especially good with onions. Onions provide some vitamin C, as well as the pytochemicals allicin and quercetin.

Sweet Onion Caviar

1 cup chopped sweet onion, such as Vidalia
1 cup cooked black-eyed peas
1 medium green bell pepper, diced
1 medium red bell pepper, diced
1/2 teaspoon minced garlic
1 tablespoon brown mustard
1 fresh jalapeño, minced
1/4 cup Basic Vinaigrette (see page 110)

In a medium serving bowl, combine all the ingredients and mix well. Refrigerate for several hours before serving. If a firmer consistency is desired, purée about one-fourth of the salad and then mix with the whole salad.

Makes 4 cups.

Peas

All peas belong to the legume family, which means they are technically beans. If the fresh green peas that we eat were allowed to mature fully, they would become dried pulses like chickpeas or lentils. Fortunately, they are harvested when they are tender and sweet. Peas are nice with tarragon, mushrooms, pearl onions, sage, marjoram, and savory. Several varieties of peas, all high in vitamin C, are readily available.

English peas, or common garden peas, grow in a pod and must be shelled. Young peas are tender and require only brief cooking time, just a minute or two in boiling water. Older peas will take a little longer. For most recipes, fresh young peas can be added toward the end of cooking. Frozen peas make an adequate substitute for fresh, especially in the winter.

Sugar snap peas have a sweet, edible, puffy pod. They require little preparation except for the occasional removal of tough strings on older pods. Sugar snaps are good raw or blanched very briefly to retain their characteristic crunch.

Snow peas are another pea with an edible pod. They are flat and tender with a subtle crunch. Snow peas are used quite often in stir-fried dishes.

Edamame, or young soybeans, are a crunchy, sweet variety of pea (see pages 20 and 249–250 for more on edamame).

Garden Peas with Saffron and Tomatoes

Since saffron is expensive and a little bit goes a long way, use it sparingly in this dish.

1 teaspoon oil
4 strands saffron
1/2 teaspoon minced garlic
1 small leek, washed (pages 225–226), cut into halves lengthwise, and sliced 1/3 inch thick
3 tablespoons orange juice
1/2 teaspoon sugar
1 cup fresh peas
1/2 cup diced fresh tomatoes
2 teaspoons chopped fresh dill
Sea salt and freshly ground black pepper

Heat the oil in a skillet over medium-low heat and add the saffron. When the saffron turns from bright red to slightly brown, add the garlic and leeks. Sauté until the leeks begin to wilt, about 3 to 4 minutes. Raise the heat to medium-high and add the orange juice and sugar. When the liquid has reduced by a third, add the peas, reduce the heat to medium-low, and cook just until the peas are tender, about 3 minutes. Add the tomatoes and dill and mix well. Season with salt and pepper.

Makes 2 servings.

Peppers

With the astonishing variety of peppers available, it's no wonder that this humble vegetable maintains a loyal following that produces cookbooks, magazines, and websites to sing its praises. Peppers can be eaten raw, pickled, roasted, or sautéed. They can be sweet, mild, or hotter than you thought possible. All peppers are a good source of vitamin C when raw. Vitamin A content increases as the peppers ripen from green to whatever hue they manifest on maturity. Peppers are also good sources of phytochemicals and flavanoids.

The following list describes the more popular and readily available peppers. For more recipes, see Vegan Chilies Rellenos (page 58), Romesco Sauce (page 129), Roasted Red Pepper Coulis (page 131), or Millet Paella (page 174).

Banana peppers, also called Hungarian peppers or wax peppers, are yellow peppers, 3 to 5 inches long, with a mild to medium hot flavor. They have few seeds and thick walls, making them well suited to pickling.

Bell peppers are green when immature, and most will turn red when left on the plant to ripen. Some varieties produce yellow, purple, "chocolate," or orange peppers. Each color has a slightly different flavor profile.

Chilies, or hot peppers, come in a dazzling array of colors and flavors. Some of the most widely used varieties are listed below.

Jalapeños, probably the best-known chilies, are two to three inches long, smooth and green, and relatively mild in flavor.

Serranos resemble a small jalapeño but are usually hotter and have a more distinctive flavor.

Poblanos are large, deep green, and mild with a full, earthy flavor. They are most commonly used for stuffing or are dried. When dried, they are known as ancho chilies and are commonly ground for chili powder.

Habaneros, available in orange, red, and green, resemble colorful paper lanterns. Their cheerful appearance belies their super-hot disposition.

When preparing peppers, make sure to remove the seeds and white membrane completely, as they can become bitter during cooking. Those who find the skins indigestible can use a vegetable peeler to remove the tough skins.

To handle chilies: It is best to use disposable gloves when handling hot chilies. If you are bare-handed, wash your hands with cold water and soap after handling the peppers. Use a knife to cut out the ribs and then tap the pepper to dislodge the seeds. Avoid touching your eyes or nose for at least an hour after working with hot peppers.

To roast bell peppers and chilies: Roasting peppers mellows the flavors, reduces the heat, and develops the sugars more fully. Lightly oil the skin. Hold the pepper over an open flame with a pair of tongs until most of the skin is blistered. Alternatively, broil the pepper on a pan under the broiler, turning frequently so the skin blackens evenly. Remove the peppers. Place large peppers in a paper or plastic bag and close it. Let stand 15 minutes. Remove and slip off the skins. Let the peppers cool and then cut open and scoop out the seeds and white pith.

Roasted Peppers on the Run

Carl Lewis

2	green bell peppers
2	red bell peppers
2	yellow bell peppers
4	banana peppers
24	button mushrooms
¼	cup olive oil
1	teaspoon lemon pepper
1	teaspoon dried basil
1	teaspoon dried parsley
1	teaspoon garlic pepper
4	sprigs fresh parsley

Cut off the tops of the peppers and remove the seeds and white membrane. Slice the peppers into 1-inch strips. Place vegetables on a greased baking pan, placing mushrooms between rows of peppers. Brush with olive oil. In a small bowl mix the lemon pepper, basil, dried parsley, and garlic pepper. Sprinkle on the vegetables. Broil on low for 5 to 6 minutes. Garnish with fresh parsley.

Makes 6 servings.

Potatoes

Potatoes were first brought to Europe in the middle of the sixteenth century by the Spaniards returning from South America. Members of the nightshade family, potatoes, like tomatoes, were thought to be poisonous, despite their long history of cultivation by the Incas in Peru. Where would the potato be if Sir Walter Raleigh had not championed its cause by planting a tract on land he held in Ireland? The Irish quickly embraced these delicious tubers and by the end of the seventeenth century, potatoes were a major crop in Ireland. A hundred years later, potatoes were a key crop throughout Europe, especially in Germany and England. The potato famine of the mid–nineteenth century, which sent thousands of Irish to Ellis Island, pointed to the need to maintain a diverse base in both diet and agriculture.

Potatoes are a good source of vitamin C, potassium, and folate. Their reputation for being fattening is undeserved: 100 grams of pure unadorned baked potato (half a large potato) has about 100 calories, $\frac{1}{10}$ gram of fat, and 8 milligrams of sodium. On the other hand, 100 grams of French fries (about 10 to 15 fries) has 342 calories, 18 grams of fat, and 198 milligrams of sodium. In potato chips, most of the water in the potato is replaced with fat. A 4-ounce bag (a little less than 100 grams of chips) contains about 536 calories, 35 grams of fat, and 1,275 grams of salt. Now, potato chips on an occasional basis do not pose a major health risk, but if you are going to incorporate one of the world's most adaptable foods into your diet, try a healthier option such as Skordalia (page 46), Potato Soup (page 77), or Italian Potato Salad (page 109).

Yellow potatoes: Yukon Gold and Yellow Fin are the two most popular of these thin-skinned boiling potatoes. These make excellent mashers.

New potatoes: Young potatoes of any variety are new potatoes, but generally groceries carry small, round, redskin potatoes. These young potatoes have a waxy texture and slightly sweet flavor. They can be boiled and either served hot or used in potato salad. New potatoes are also good for roasting, either whole or cut into wedges. These do not make the best mashed potatoes.

Russet potatoes: These potatoes are low in moisture and high in starch, which makes them the perfect baking potato. Often they are called Idaho potatoes, no matter where they come from. The skin is a rough brown and the flesh is fluffy white.

Fingerling potatoes: These small, elongated potatoes are becoming increasingly available in retail markets. They have thin skins and slightly waxy flesh. Fingerling potatoes can be boiled or roasted whole.

Roasted Garlic Mashed Potatoes

A potato masher or stand-up mixer makes good fluffy mashed potatoes. Using a food processor will give the potatoes a stringy, glue-like texture.

3 pounds potatoes, peeled and cut into 1- to 2-inch chunks
2 teaspoons salt
1 large head Roasted Garlic (page 223)
¼ cup olive oil
Sea salt and pepper

Combine the potatoes, salt, and water to cover by 3 inches in a large pot. Bring to a boil over high heat. Lower the temperature slightly and boil the potatoes for 10 minutes longer or until they are cooked through. Reserve 2 cups of the cooking liquid. Drain the potatoes and mash with a potato masher, ricer, or mixer.

Gently squeeze the garlic head to remove the cloves. Mash the potatoes with the garlic and olive oil. Slowly add back 1 cup of the cooking liquid or enough to give it a moist, fluffy consistency. Season with sea salt and pepper. If you are not planning on serving the potatoes right away, add a little extra water, cover the bowl loosely with foil, and reserve in a slightly warm oven. Whip the potatoes again just before serving.

Makes 6 servings.

Squash, Summer

Tender, quick cooking, and amazingly prolific, summer squash are versatile, showing up in salads, stews, muffins, and cakes. Their mild flavor and springy texture allow them to take on many roles. Summer squash can be sautéed, roasted, grilled, steamed, or boiled. Like many summer vegetables, squash is high in vitamins A and C, but squash also contains some niacin.

Zucchini are the most widely grown of the summer squashes. They have a thin green skin and white flesh. They are available almost all year from California, Florida, or Mexico. Zucchini are often hollowed out and used as baking vessels for grain-based fillings.

Yellow squash are the most inconsistent of the summer squashes. Their skin can be smooth and thin or warty and thick. The condition of their skin often indicates their age. Older squash have well-developed seeds that should be discarded before cooking because they are bitter and tough. Otherwise, they are prepared and used the same ways as zucchini.

Scallop or patty pan squash are pale green with creamy white flesh. Use them as you might portobello mushrooms, cutting them into slabs and sautéing them, though they are more subtly flavored than mushrooms. They also hold their shape and texture when cubed and added to stews. Of course, they are quite enjoyable simply sautéed in a little olive oil with salt and pepper.

Zucchini with Balsamic Vinegar and Mint

This dish requires a very quick hand. Have all your ingredients prepared and close by before beginning.

1   tablespoon olive oil
2   medium zucchini, cut into halves lengthwise and sliced $1/2$ inch thick
2   cloves garlic, thinly sliced
$1/8$ teaspoon sea salt
Pinch freshly ground black pepper
2   tablespoons aged balsamic vinegar
1   teaspoon minced fresh mint
1   teaspoon minced fresh basil, preferably Genovese or Thai basil

Heat the oil in a wide skillet over high heat. When the oil is hot, add the zucchini. It should begin to brown immediately. Toss or stir the zucchini for 1 minute. Add the garlic, salt, and pepper. Continue to cook the zucchini until it is evenly browned, about 3 minutes longer. Add the balsamic vinegar to the hot pan and allow it to reduce and lightly glaze the zucchini. Remove the pan from the heat and stir in the mint and basil.

Makes 2 servings.

Squash, Winter

Winter squash have thick, hard shells and well-developed seed cavities like melons. This is not surprising, since botanically, squash is a fruit, not a vegetable. The yellow-orange flesh of these squash hint at their high vitamin A, carotenoid, and phytochemical content. Squash with a deep orange flesh, like butternut, are usually high in vitamin C also.

The sweet, firm flesh of these hard-shell squash pairs nicely with the hot and spicy flavors of curry, chipotles, ancho chili powder, or black pepper; the tart flavors of lemons, oranges, or green apples; the sweet flavors of maple syrup, cinnamon, vanilla, ginger, brown sugar, apples, or pears; and the savory flavors of onions, garlic, rosemary, thyme, and sage. Squash also taste great with nuts, celery root, turnips, and rutabagas.

Butternut squash have deep orange flesh, with the seed cavity conveniently located at one end. Microwaving the squash for 3 minutes simplifies the peeling process.

Acorn squash cannot be peeled because of their thickly lobed sides; instead they should be steamed or baked. Use them as convenient containers for hot, spicy fillings, which complement the sweet flesh.

Spaghetti squash is a mysterious vegetable. There are no definitive answers to questions about its origin. It seemed to simply show up one day with very little fanfare or explanation. Use this squash as you would pasta. To prepare the "spaghetti," simply cut the squash into halves lengthwise (you may wish to microwave it for 2 to 3 minutes first), scoop out the seeds, and place in a baking dish with 1½ inches of water. Bake the squash at 350° for 40 minutes or until a fork easily pierces the skin. Remove the squash from the baking pan and place it on a clean surface, cut side up, to cool. Scrape the flesh with a fork to separate it into strings and remove it from the shell.

Acorn Squash Stuffed with Wild Rice and Winter Fruits

Steaming the squash prior to filling and baking ensures that the squash bakes evenly and the stuffing doesn't dry out. If you omit this step, clean the squash, fill with the wild rice mixture, add 1 inch of water to the baking pan, and bake the squash for 25 minutes covered with foil, then 35 minutes uncovered. Dried thyme has a mellow flavor that I enjoy in the winter.

2   small to medium acorn squash
6   dried apricots, thinly sliced
1   tablespoon dried cherries
1   tablespoon dried cranberries
1   tablespoon oil
1   medium onion, diced
1   teaspoon minced garlic
Pinch cayenne
4   stalks celery, diced
2   medium carrots, diced
1   teaspoon grated fresh ginger
1/4 teaspoon dried thyme
2   cups cooked wild rice
Sea salt and freshly ground pepper

Cut off the stem end of the squash. Cut a small piece off of the other end to allow the squash to sit upright. Scoop out the seeds. Place the squash, cut side down, in a steamer basket. Steam until the squash are about half-cooked, 10 to 20 minutes. Steam the tops of the squash separately. When the tops have cooled, scrape out the flesh, coarsely chop, and reserve.

Preheat the oven to 350°. Lightly oil or spray a non-aluminum baking dish just large enough to hold the squash.

In a small bowl, combine the dried fruits. Pour boiling water over the fruits so they are covered by 1 inch of water. Cover the bowl and reserve.

Heat the oil in a wide skillet over medium heat. Add the onion, garlic, cayenne, celery, carrots, ginger, and thyme. Cook the vegetables until the onion begins to soften, about 2 minutes. Add the fruits and their soaking liquid. Cook until the liquid is reduced by half. Add the wild rice and the reserved squash and mix well. Season with salt and pepper.

Fill the squash with the stuffing. Bake for 35 minutes or until the squash can easily be pierced with a fork.

Makes 2 servings.

Sweet Potatoes

Peanuts were not the only concern of nineteenth-century botanist George Washington Carver. In addition to his *How to Grow the Peanut and 105 Ways of Preparing It for Human Consumption*, he also published a treatise devoted to the sweet potato. In this pamphlet are recipes for sweet potato doughnuts, biscuits, flour, and candy. Carver was drawn to the tuber's high nutrient content and great flavor. One serving of cooked sweet potato is high in vitamins A, C, and E; folate; copper; and iron.

Sweet potatoes can be boiled, baked, steamed, or roasted. However, they have a higher moisture and sugar content than white potatoes, making them more difficult to fry. Before frying sweet potato slices, allow them to air-dry in a well-ventilated spot for 30 minutes to 1 hour or until the slices feel dry to the touch and are slightly white. Sweet potatoes for chips should be sliced as thinly as possible on a mandoline or the side of a box grater. Try lightly brushing the slices with oil, and drying them in 250° to 350° oven. The resulting chips will be crisp and fairly low in fat. Sprinkle the dried chips with salt or chili powder.

Sweet Potatoes with Pineapple and Peppers

Serve this as an accompaniment to beans and rice, or mix it with black beans and serve on top of a crisp corn tortilla.

1   teaspoon fine sea salt
1   teaspoon chili powder
½   teaspoon ground cumin
½   teaspoon ground coriander
½   teaspoon ground black pepper
¼   teaspoon cayenne
3   sweet potatoes, peeled and cut into ¾-inch chunks
3   tablespoons oil
1   medium onion, peeled and cut into 1-inch pieces
1   green bell pepper, seeded and cut into 1-inch pieces
1   red bell pepper, seeded and cut into 1-inch pieces
1   cup 1-inch chunks of fresh pineapple
½   teaspoon minced garlic

Preheat the oven to 375°. Fit 2 standard baking sheets with parchment paper.

Combine the salt, chili powder, cumin, coriander, black pepper, and cayenne in a small bowl and mix well. In a mixing bowl, toss the sweet potatoes with half the oil. Add the spice mixture a little at a time until the desired degree of hotness is reached. Arrange the potatoes in a single layer on one of the baking sheets. Combine the onion, peppers, pineapple, and garlic in the mixing bowl and toss with the remaining oil. Arrange the vegetables in a single layer on the other baking sheet. Roast the vegetables in the oven for 30 minutes or until the sweet potatoes and onions are soft. The sweet potatoes may take more time than the other vegetables. Rotate the pans and turn the vegetables once or twice during cooking. If the pans do not fit on the same rack in the oven, alternate the pans between racks every 10 minutes. This may add to your roasting time. Serve immediately or reserve in a warm oven.

Makes 2 to 4 servings.

Tomatoes

Botanically, tomatoes, like cucumbers and squash, are a fruit. Legally, they are a vegetable. In 1893, in the tariff dispute *Nix v. Hedden*, the Supreme Court declared that because tomatoes are "served at dinner in, with, or after the soup, fish or meats which constitute the principal part of the repast, and not, like fruits generally, as dessert" they are properly treated—and taxed—as a vegetable. Quite a controversy for a plant that was thought to be poisonous less than a century earlier. Thomas Jefferson pioneered the cultivation of tomatoes, growing them first as ornamentals. Today tomatoes are prized as nutritional powerhouses, supplying vitamin C, potassium, and iron. Several phytochemicals found in tomatoes—phenolic acid and carotenoids such as lycopene—are being studied for their antioxident properties. Tomatoes come in a broad range of sizes, shapes, colors, and flavors.

Slicing tomatoes are juicy and mild.

Beefsteak tomatoes are larger, with a meaty texture and a more robust flavor.

Roma tomatoes have fewer seeds and thicker walls of flesh. They are great for cutting into wedges and adding to salads or peeling, seeding, and cooking down to a sauce.

Green tomatoes are unripe and too astringent to be eaten uncooked. Cooking and pickling mellow the sharp flavor to an agreeable taste.

Cherry tomatoes are bite-sized—perfect for snacking, salads, or a quick sauté. Grape tomatoes are smaller than cherry tomatoes with a milder flavor and firmer flesh. A traditionally produced hybrid, grape tomatoes can be found in both red and green. Because they are lower in acid with less juice and fewer seeds, they are often more palatable than regular tomatoes to the younger set. Sungold tomatoes, a yellow cherry variety, are quite popular in England. They, too, have a lower acid content and a mild, pleasing flavor.

Heirloom tomatoes are varieties with histories that predate modern agribusiness. Many of them were bred by small farmers in the nineteenth century. Thankfully, through seed exchanges and as family heirlooms, they have survived into modern times. Heirloom tomatoes come in a wide array of colors, shapes, and flavors. Brandywine, Mortgage Lifter, and Black Krim are distinctly aromatic, with deep pink to maroon flesh. Yellow tomatoes include Lemon Boy, Sun Gold, or Rainbow. Yellow and pink tomatoes are lower in acid than their red cousins.

Sun-dried tomatoes are available either dry or packed in oil. Drying the tomatoes intensifies both the sweet and sour flavors and gives a substantial texture, in addition to concentrating the iron.

Tomatoes are marvelous raw, juiced, grilled, stewed, or puréed. The seeds and skins of tomatoes can become bitter when left in raw preparations for more than a few hours or in long-simmered dishes. Do not save tomato seeds for stock.

To skin tomatoes: Tough skins can sometimes be removed with a vegetable peeler. For more than one tomato, though, it's probably easier to use the boiling water method. Bring a large pot of water to a boil. Have a large bowl of ice water handy. Cut an X in the bottom of each tomato. Slide the tomatoes into the boiling water a few at a time. Do not crowd the pot. When the edges of the X begin to curl away from the flesh, lift the tomato out of the water. Ripe tomatoes may need only 15 seconds in the water; less ripe tomatoes may need almost a full minute. Plunge the tomatoes into the ice water. Coax the skins off with a paring knife. If the skins are stubborn, return the tomatoes to the water for an additional 15 to 30 seconds.

To remove seeds: Cut the tomato into halves horizontally. Using a small spoon, scoop the seeds out of the pockets. Squeezing the seeds out of the tomato is acceptable only if the final texture of the tomato is not important, for example, in a stew. When the tomatoes are to be eaten raw or only lightly cooked, squeezing them will give them a mushy texture.

To reconstitute sun-dried tomatoes: Cover dried tomatoes with boiling water in a small bowl. Cover the container and let the tomatoes absorb the water and become soft, about 15 minutes. Drain the tomatoes (the liquid can be used in stews, soups, and tomato sauces). Add a very small amount of minced garlic and some extra virgin olive oil to the tomatoes and mix well. Store in the refrigerator.

Oven-Roasted Tomatoes

An alternative to sun-dried tomatoes, oven-roasted tomatoes are semi-dry and have an "in-between" taste and texture. They do not have the insistent sweetness of sun-dried tomatoes or the astonishing acidity of fresh tomatoes. Their texture is not as firm as a fresh tomato or as runny as a cooked tomato. Use them in place of fresh or sun-dried tomatoes for a different twist. Try them in Bulgur Pilaf with Cashews and Oven-Roasted Tomatoes (page 170).

4   ripe medium tomatoes
Sea salt
2   tablespoons olive oil

Preheat the oven to 250°. Fit a rimmed baking sheet with parchment paper. Cut the tomatoes into 1-inch slices. Arrange the slices in a single, uncrowded layer on the baking sheet. Season the tomatoes lightly with sea salt and drizzle with olive oil. Bake the tomatoes for 2 to 3 hours or until they are wrinkled but not dried out. Let the tomatoes cool to room temperature. Store in the refrigerator.

Makes about 2 cups.

Fried Green Tomatoes

1 cup fine cornmeal
1/2 cup whole wheat pastry flour
1/2 teaspoon salt
1/2 teaspoon pepper
4 large green tomatoes, cut into 3/4-inch slices
1 cup creamy soymilk
Oil for frying

In a baking dish, whisk the cornmeal, flour, salt, and pepper. Dip the tomato slices one at time in the soymilk. Coat the tomatoes with the cornmeal mix. In a wide, deep skillet, heat 1/2 inch of oil over medium heat. Test the oil by dipping a rim of a tomato slice in the oil. If the tomato begins frying immediately, the oil is ready. Gently slide the tomatoes in the oil and fry until golden brown on one side, about 2 to 4 minutes. Turn the tomatoes and fry the other side, about 2 minutes longer.

Makes 4 servings.

Turnips/Rutabagas

These peppery roots are unfairly ignored. The turnip bulb provides lots of fiber and vitamin C, while the leaves provide carotenoids, iron, riboflavin, and calcium, with the calcium being more readily available than in most greens. Rutabagas are rich in vitamins A and C. Turnips are generally smaller and milder than rutabagas. Tender young turnips may not need peeling, whereas the thickly waxed rutabagas should have all of the waxy coating and fibrous rind removed. Both turnips and rutabagas can be boiled, steamed, roasted, or braised.

Turnips with Apples and Leeks

4 tablespoons vegan margarine
2 pounds turnips, peeled and cut into 3/4-inch cubes
2 leeks, cleaned (pages 225–226), halved, and sliced
2 firm, tart apples, cored and cut into wedges
1/2 cup fruity white wine, such as Riesling or Moscati
1 teaspoon Succanat or brown sugar
1 small sprig thyme
Pinch sea salt
Pinch ground white pepper

Melt the margarine in a wide skillet over medium heat. Add the turnips and sauté until they begin to brown, about 7 minutes. Add the leeks and cook for 3 minutes longer. When the leeks begin to soften, add the apples and cook for 2 minutes longer. Add the wine and cook until the liquid is reduced to 2 tablespoons. Add 1/2 cup of water, sugar, thyme, salt, and pepper and simmer until the turnips are nearly soft, about 5 to 10 minutes longer. Remove them to a bowl with a slotted spoon. Turn the heat to high and reduce the liquid until it is thick enough to coat the vegetables. Adjust the seasonings.

Makes 6 servings.

soy foods

Seared Tofu

Glazed Tofu

Baked Tofu

Baked Barbecued Tofu

Afghan Spinach and Tofu

Ma-Po Tofu

Curried Tofu in Acorn Squash

Edamame with Hijiki and Brown Rice

Edamame with Zucchini, Tomatoes, and Tarragon

Spicy Soy Nuts

Ginger-Fried Tempeh

Tempeh in Tomato Gravy

Tempeh Sauerbraten

No Sheep Shepherd's Pie

As evidence of its health benefits continues to grow, soy is being welcomed into more and more meals. What once seemed like a chore—trying to consume 25 to 30 grams of soy protein a day—is rapidly becoming a pleasure. Soymilk comes in vanilla, chocolate, coffee, and fruit flavors; in half-gallon containers or convenient "juice boxes." Tofu is available fresh, baked, smoked, or seasoned. Tempeh makes a convenient replacement for chicken or beef in many recipes, while soy protein granules substitute for ground beef. Edamame (fresh green soybeans), a popular bar snack in Japan, are finding their way into frozen entrées and salad bars.

While tofu and tempeh may be new to you, they are easy to work with and very forgiving. Since they are already fully cooked, undercooking isn't a problem, and if they are accidentally overcooked, they will lose some texture but no flavor. Dried soybeans can be sprouted and stir-fried or cooked like any other dried bean in soups, stews, or casseroles. (They do take longer than most beans to cook, about 2 to 3 hours.) Although the word "edamame" may be unfamiliar, if you've ever cooked lima beans or fava beans, you won't find anything mysterious in the preparation of these fresh, raw soybeans. The only mystery will be why you never tried them before!

The Versatile Soybean

Soy can be easily incorporated into any meal. For more information on soy, see pages 20–24. To illustrate the variety of dishes that can be made with soy, here are just a few examples of recipes from other chapters in this book. For more recipes, see the index.

- Miso Soup (page 70)
- Tofu No-Egg Salad Pita (page 148)
- Tempeh Reuben (page 160)
- Chow Fun with Hot and Smoky Tofu (page 199)
- Scrambled Tofu (page 275)

- Country-Style Tempeh Sausages (page 277)
- Cheesecake (page 296)
- Easy Chocolate Pudding (page 303)
- Chocolate Peanut Butter Shake (page 318).

Tofu

Think of tofu as you would a potato—a highly nutritious, versatile everyday food that can be baked, broiled, sautéed, or fried. Also like a potato, tofu has a flavor that on its own is a bit bland, making it a good partner for almost any other ingredient. However, tofu is high in protein and calcium whereas potatoes have lots of carbohydrates, vitamin C, potassium, and folate. You may need to try several different brands of tofu until you find one to your liking.

There is nothing quite like tofu in the Western culinary canon, so take some time to familiarize yourself with these easy procedures for making the most of this versatile ingredient.

Simmering tofu: This technique is used to firm the texture of silken tofu so it will hold its shape in cooked dishes. For 10 ounces of tofu, heat 4 cups of water and 1 teaspoon of salt in a small pot. When the water is on the verge of boiling, add the tofu and simmer for about 3 minutes—1 to 2 minutes for very small pieces and 5 to 7 minutes for very large pieces. Lift the tofu from the pot with a slotted spoon or a small strainer and blot on absorbent towels for a minute or two.

In addition to firming the tofu, simmering also salts it and heats it through so cooking time is decreased after the tofu is added to the dish. This helps prevent the tofu from breaking up when stirred.

Pressing tofu: Pressing tofu firms it, but it also displaces water so that the tofu can more readily accept the sauce around it. For recipes in which the tofu will be puréed or crumbled, it is often sufficient to press the tofu by hand, firmly but gently squeezing the water out.

Place the tofu on a plate. Elevate one end of the plate so the water can run off the tofu as it drains—preferably not onto the floor. Find a heavy object that will sit on the tofu without sliding off. Either wrap the tofu in a towel or place a towel between the tofu and the weight. Leave the tofu to drain for an hour or up to 12 hours.

Seared Tofu

While fried tofu is more traditional, it tends to absorb lots of oil and get quite chewy. Searing the tofu gives it a chewy exterior and creamy interior. It can be served simply with Peanut Sauce (page 136), gomaiso (a sesame-seaweed seasoning), or soy sauce. I like to cut the tofu in half to form two thinner slabs, then cut each slab into 2 triangles. Most any shape of tofu will do, but to ensure even cooking, your tofu should be less than 1½ inches thick.

6   ounces silken tofu
1   scant teaspoon oil

In a small pan over medium heat, simmer the tofu for 3 minutes in salted water. Gently lift the tofu onto an absorbent towel and let rest for a few minutes.

Heat the oil in a nonstick pan over high heat. Be careful not to let any water get into the oil or it will splatter. Sear the tofu until it is golden brown on one side, about 3 to 7 minutes. Turn the tofu and brown the other side. Serve immediately.

Makes 1 or 2 servings.

Clockwise from top: Hijiki, edamame in the pod and shelled, brown rice,
Edamame with Hijiki and Brown Rice (page 249).

Millet Paella (page 174).

Facing page: **Soy Foods**
Clockwise from top: Easy Chocolate Pudding (page 303), soymilk, dried soy beans,
Spicy Soy Nuts (page 250), Miso Soup (page 70), miso, soy lecithin granules, soy sauce,
soy flour, fermented black beans, barbecued tempeh (made with garden vegetable tempeh),
Ginger-Fried Tempeh (page 251; made with sea vegetable tempeh),
glazed tofu (white), seared tofu (brown).
Center, top to bottom: firm tofu, sea vegetable tempeh (triangle),
garden vegetable tempeh (square).

Top right to bottom left: Cauliflower with Capers (page 218),
Tunisian Carrot Salad (page 217), Spicy Corn on the Cob (page 219).

Glazed Tofu

This is a slight variation on seared tofu. Adding barbecue sauce (prepared or see page 133), thinned with a little water, works nicely, too.

2 teaspoons soy sauce
¼ teaspoon grated fresh ginger
⅛ teaspoon minced garlic
1 teaspoon sriracha or other hot sauce (optional)
1 scant teaspoon oil
6 ounces medium tofu
½ teaspoon sesame oil (optional)

Mix the soy sauce, ginger, garlic, and hot sauce with 1 teaspoon of water in a small bowl. Reserve.

Heat the oil in a nonstick pan over high heat. Sear the tofu until it is golden brown on one side, about 3 to 7 minutes. Turn the tofu and brown the other side. Add the reserved sauce. Turn the tofu to coat it completely with the sauce. Cook until the pan is dry and the sauce has glazed the tofu. Remove from heat. Drizzle with sesame oil. Serve immediately.

Makes 1 or 2 servings.

Baked Tofu

Some tofu is firm enough to be pressed gently with the hands. Some is quite dry and needs no pressing at all. If you are using silken tofu, you will need to press it as described on the preceding page. Baked tofu has a pleasant chewy texture—it's rather like fried tofu, but without all the fat.

1 10-ounce package medium to firm tofu
1 tablespoon soy sauce
1 teaspoon grated fresh ginger

Press the tofu for 30 to 60 minutes. Preheat the oven to 350°. Cut the tofu into cubes or desired shape. Toss the tofu with the soy sauce and ginger. Place the tofu on a baking sheet that is either fitted with parchment paper or lightly oiled. Bake the tofu for 15 to 30 minutes. Serve immediately.

Makes 2 to 3 servings.

245

Baked Barbecued Tofu

This is a simple variation on the baked tofu recipe. Any good barbecue sauce will work well. Try tossing some zucchini, red pepper, and onion in barbecue sauce and roasting them along with the tofu for a quick meal.

1   10-ounce package medium to firm tofu
¼   cup Orange-Chipotle Barbecue Sauce (page 134)

Press the tofu for 30 to 60 minutes, if desired. Preheat the oven to 350°. Cut the tofu into cubes or desired shapes. Thin the barbecue sauce with 2 tablespoons of water. Toss the tofu with the sauce. Place the tofu on a baking sheet that is either fitted with parchment paper or lightly oiled. Bake the tofu for 15 to 30 minutes. Serve immediately.

Makes 2 to 3 servings.

Afghan Spinach and Tofu

To cut the spinach into ribbons easily, stack several slices, then roll them into a thick green cigar. Cut slices off the cigar so you have ribbons of spinach.

3   tablespoons oil
2   medium onions, cut into ¼-inch slices
2   tablespoons grated fresh ginger
2   tablespoons minced garlic
2   teaspoons ground cumin
2   teaspoons ground coriander
½   teaspoon red pepper flakes
½   teaspoon ground cinnamon
3   cups Vegetable Stock (page 65)
1   pound firm silken tofu, cut into ¾-inch cubes
2   pounds fresh spinach, trimmed and cut into ribbons
2   tablespoons raisins
2   tablespoons soy sauce
4   teaspoons sesame oil
½   teaspoon sugar
¼   cup toasted pine nuts
Hot cooked basmati rice

Heat the oil in a soup pot over medium heat. Sauté the onions, ginger, garlic, and spices, stirring constantly. When the mixture becomes fragrant, lower the heat and cook for 10 minutes more. If the mixture begins to stick, add more oil.

Add the stock to the soup pot and bring to a boil over medium-high heat. Stir to loosen any bits that stick to the bottom of the pot. When the stock boils, lower the heat to medium and add the tofu. Simmer for 3 minutes.

Add the spinach and raisins to the soup pot and stir gently. Cover the pot and let the mixture stew for 10 minutes. Add the soy sauce, sesame oil, sugar, and pine nuts and mix well. Serve over basmati rice.

Makes 4 servings.

Ma-Po Tofu

I don't remember how I happened across my first bag of fermented black beans, but this discovery was soon followed by repeated experiments with Ma-Po Tofu. For years I thought these beans were black turtle beans. Imagine my surprise when I finally discovered that they were in fact a variety of soybean!

In Chinese restaurants, I have actively sought out the vegetarian versions of this Szechuan classic (which typically contains pork). Some have been spectacular, with melting, delicate, fresh tofu as a counterpoint to the sharp, salty fermented beans. Others were disappointing, with frozen peas and carrots that had been added at the last minute.

Ma-po tofu can be prepared with no vegetables, with peas, or with broccoli. I prefer broccoli to peas since it can absorb so much more sauce. Blanching the broccoli before stir-frying dramatically decreases the amount of oil needed to stir-fry it to doneness.

1   bunch broccoli
3   tablespoons fermented black beans
2   tablespoons soy sauce
2   tablespoons sherry
1   teaspoon sugar
1   pound firm silken tofu, cut into ³/₄-inch cubes
2   teaspoons oil
2   teaspoons minced garlic
1   dried chili
2   teaspoons grated fresh ginger
6   green onions, cut diagonally into ¹/₂-inch pieces
¹/₄ teaspoon ground Szechuan peppercorns (optional)
2   teaspoons garlic chili paste
1   teaspoon cornstarch dissolved in 1 tablespoon water (optional)
1   teaspoon sesame oil
Hot cooked rice

Separate the broccoli into florets about 1 inch thick. Peel the stems and slice ¹/₃ inch thick. Blanch the broccoli (page 205), refresh under cool water, and pat dry. Soak the beans in ¹/₂ cup of boiling water for 10 minutes. Drain the beans, reserving ¹/₄ cup of the liquid. Coarsely chop the beans. Reserve.

In a small bowl, mix the soy sauce, sherry, and sugar. Reserve. In a small pot, simmer the tofu in 4 cups of water for 3 minutes. Gently lift the tofu from the water and reserve.

In a wok or wide, deep skillet, heat the oil over high heat. When the oil is quite hot, stir-fry the garlic, chili, ginger, and green onions for 1 minute. Add the peppercorns and chili paste and stir-fry for 1 minute longer. Reduce the heat to medium.

Add the reserved bean water and the soy sauce mixture to the wok. Add the broccoli and stir-fry for 2 or 3 minutes, or until the broccoli is hot. Add the cornstarch mixture and cook, stirring, until thickened. If the sauce becomes too thick, add more water, 1 tablespoon at a time. Add the tofu and sesame oil and mix gently. Let the mixture simmer for 1 to 2 minutes, or until the tofu is heated through. Serve over rice.

Makes 4 servings.

Curried Tofu in Acorn Squash

Don't be afraid to make the tofu spicy—the sweetness of the squash will cool the palate. Serve each squash on a bed of Couscous with Raisins and Pine Nuts (page 195).

2	small to medium acorn squash
1	tablespoon oil
1	medium onion, diced
2	teaspoons minced garlic
2	teaspoons grated fresh ginger
2	teaspoons curry powder
1	teaspoon ground cumin
1/2	teaspoon ground coriander
1/4	teaspoon dry mustard
1	15-ounce package firm tofu, cut into 1/2-inch cubes
1	red bell pepper, cut into fine matchsticks
1	green bell pepper, cut into fine matchsticks
1	tablespoon chopped basil, preferably Thai or lemon basil

Cut off the stem end of the squash. Scoop out the seeds. Cut a small piece off the other end to allow the squash to stand upright. Place the squash, cut side down, in a steamer basket over boiling water. Steam until the squash are cooked through, 20 to 30 minutes. (Alternatively, place the squash, cut side down, in a baking dish with 1 inch of hot water. Bake the squash at 350° for 30 minutes.) Do not overcook the squash, as this will cause them to lose their shape.

Heat the oil in a skillet over medium heat and sauté the onion, garlic, ginger, and spices, stirring constantly, until the mixture is fragrant. Turn the heat to low and cook for 10 minutes longer. If the mixture sticks to the pan, add more oil.

In a small pot, simmer the tofu in 4 cups of water for 3 minutes. Gently lift the tofu from the water and add to the pan along with the peppers and half the basil. Toss or gently stir to mix well. Cook for 3 minutes longer. Stuff the tofu into the squash and garnish with the remaining basil.

Makes 2 servings.

Whole Soybeans

Fresh soybeans are called edamame (ə-da-MA-may). Similar in size to butter beans, fresh soybeans have a crunch and sweet taste something like English peas. They have a very high protein content, so they do not have the grainy, starchy texture of lima beans. Sold shelled or in the pod, edamame should be briefly blanched (page 205) and then refreshed in cold water before use. A good addition to salads and stir-fries, edamame can also be used much like English peas or fava beans—tossed into rice for a quick pilaf, strewn over a salad, or puréed.

Dried soybeans can be cooked like pinto beans and used in chilies, stews, and casseroles.

Edamame with Hijiki and Brown Rice

¼ cup hijiki or wakame seaweed
1 tablespoon soy sauce
2 teaspoons sesame oil
1 tablespoon lemon juice
2 tablespoons canola or grapeseed oil
2 cups cooked short-grain brown rice
½ teaspoon minced garlic
1 teaspoon grated fresh ginger
1 medium carrot, cut into matchsticks
4 green onions, cut diagonally into ¼-inch pieces
½ cup shelled edamame, fresh or thawed

In a small bowl, cover the hijiki with 2 inches of boiling water. Cover and let the seaweed soak for 10 minutes. Drain and reserve.

Whisk together the soy sauce, sesame oil, lemon juice, and oil in a small bowl.

Mix together the rice, garlic, ginger, carrot, green onions, edamame, hijiki, and soy sauce mixture. Let stand 20 minutes for the flavors to develop. Serve warm or at room temperature.

Makes 2 to 4 servings.

Edamame with Zucchini, Tomatoes, and Tarragon

2   teaspoons oil
1   small red onion, cut into halves and thinly sliced
1   clove garlic, thinly sliced
1   medium zucchini, chopped
¼   cup blanched edamame
½   cup diced tomatoes, preferably fresh
1   tablespoon minced fresh tarragon
Salt and pepper

Heat the oil in a skillet over medium heat. Sauté the onion and garlic for 2 minutes and add the zucchini. Cook the vegetables until the zucchini is crisp-tender, about 5 to 7 minutes. Add the edamame, tomatoes, and the tarragon and heat through. Season with salt and pepper.

Makes 2 servings.

Spicy Soy Nuts

Just about everyone likes something salty and crunchy every now and then. These easy treats compare more than favorably to potato chips, with 5 times the protein, 40 percent less fat, 6 times the calcium, and 5 times the folate.

2   cups dried soybeans
2   teaspoons chili powder
2   teaspoons ground cumin
1   teaspoon ground coriander
¼   teaspoon cayenne (optional)
¼   teaspoon smoked Spanish paprika (optional)
1   teaspoon salt
2   tablespoons canola oil

Soak the soybeans using either the quick- or long-soaking method (page 163).

Preheat the oven to 300°. Drain and rinse the beans and pat dry. In a small bowl, combine the chili powder, cumin, coriander, cayenne, paprika, and salt. In a large bowl, toss the beans with the canola oil. Sprinkle the spice mixture over the beans and mix well. Spread the beans in a single layer on a baking sheet. Bake in the center of the oven for about an hour, stirring the soybeans every 15 minutes or so. The beans are done when they just begin to brown and are dry all the way through.

Makes 3 cups

Tempeh

Originally from Indonesia, tempeh is a mixture of soybeans and grains that is fermented and then pressed into a cake. While the concept of fermented food may seem strange, remember that bread, coffee beans, cacao beans (used to make chocolate), and most alcoholic beverages are all fermented. The beans in tempeh are kept whole, giving it a substantial texture that can withstand most cooking methods.

Use tempeh as you might portobellos. It is particularly good barbecued and served with rice and grilled vegetables. If the tempeh feels quite hard, you may try simmering it in vegetable stock or water to which you've added onions, celery, carrots, salt and pepper. This will soften the beans and make the tempeh more digestible. Be careful not to boil the tempeh—it may fall apart.

Ginger-Fried Tempeh

This is a simple preparation that can accompany rice and vegetables as a meal or can be served as an appetizer with Apricot Mustard (page 122), Curry Ketchup (page 121), or Peanut Sauce (page 136).

1 tablespoon oil
1 clove garlic, crushed
1/2 inch fresh ginger, thinly sliced
8 ounces tempeh, cut crosswise into 1/3-inch slices

Heat the oil in a skillet over medium heat. Fry the garlic and ginger until they are fragrant and beginning to brown. Remove them from the pan and add the tempeh slices. Do not crowd the pan. Fry the tempeh in batches until golden brown, about 2 to 3 minutes on each side, adding oil as needed. Serve immediately or reserve in a warm oven.

Makes 2 servings.

Tempeh in Tomato Gravy

1 tablespoon oil
1/4 teaspoon yellow mustard seeds
1 large onion, cut into halves and sliced 1/4 inch thick
1/2 teaspoon chili powder
1/2 teaspoon ground turmeric
1 cup diced tomatoes, fresh or canned
1/2 teaspoon salt (optional)
1 8-ounce package tempeh, cut into 1/2-inch-thick slices
Hot cooked basmati rice
2 teaspoons chopped fresh cilantro

Heat the oil in a large skillet over medium heat. Add the mustard seeds. When the mustard seeds begin to pop, add the onion, chili powder, and turmeric. Cook this mixture for about 10 minutes. Add the tomatoes, salt, and tempeh. Cook the mixture until thickened, about 10 to 15 minutes. Serve over basmati rice and garnish with fresh cilantro.

Makes 2 servings.

Tempeh Sauerbraten

For a warming winter feast, serve this as the beef version is served, accompanied by potato pancakes, applesauce, and braised red cabbage.

3   teaspoons oil
1   medium onion, diced
3   stalks celery, diced
2   medium carrots, diced
⅛ teaspoon caraway seeds
5   black peppercorns
⅛ teaspoon ground ginger
½ teaspoon salt
3   8-ounce blocks tempeh,
    cut into halves
½ cup red wine
2   tablespoons red wine
    vinegar
½ cup Vegetable Stock
    (page 65)
1   teaspoon cornstarch
    mixed
    with 1 tablespoon water

Heat 2 teaspoons of the oil in a wide skillet over medium-high heat and sauté the onion, celery, carrots, and spices for 6 minutes or until the onion is soft. Move the vegetables to one side and add the tempeh to the pan. Drizzle another teaspoon or two of oil around the tempeh. Fry the tempeh until just browned on each side. Add the wine and vinegar and cook until reduced by half. Add the stock and mix the vegetables and the tempeh together. Reduce the heat to medium-low and simmer for 10 minutes. Add the cornstarch and mix well so no lumps form. Cook, stirring, until the sauce has thickened slightly. Serve immediately. To make the dish ahead of time, omit the cornstarch, reheat the tempeh and sauce, then add the cornstarch and cook until thickened just before serving.

Makes 4 to 6 servings.

Soy Protein

Usually called TVP or TSP, soy protein can include okara, the pulpy by-product of tofu or soymilk production, or can more simply be made from processed soy flour. All formulations are high in protein and fiber. Use it in chilies, burgers, lentil loaf, or spaghetti sauce.

To rehydrate soy protein, pour ¾ cup of boiling water over 1 cup of the protein. Cover and let stand for 15 minutes. Once rehydrated, it keeps in the refrigerator for 2 to 3 days.

No Sheep Shepherd's Pie

1½ cups soy protein
1 tablespoon oil
1 large onion, diced
1 teaspoon minced garlic
2 stalks celery, diced
2 medium carrots, diced
1 small eggplant, cubed, salted, drained, and rinsed (pages 220–221)
1 cup sliced mushrooms
1 cup Vegetable Stock (page 65) or Mushroom Stock (page 67)
2 teaspoons mushroom soy sauce
1 teaspoon chopped fresh rosemary
½ teaspoon fresh thyme leaves
1 cup diced tomatoes
3 cups mashed potatoes, warmed

Preheat the oven to 375°. Lightly oil or spray a 2-quart round baking dish. In a small mixing bowl, pour 1 cup of boiling water over the soy protein. Cover and let stand for 15 minutes. Meanwhile, in a large, wide skillet, heat the oil over medium-high heat and sauté the onion, garlic, celery, and carrots until the onion begins to soften, about 5 minutes. Add the eggplant and mushrooms and sauté for 4 minutes longer. Add the soy protein, stock, soy sauce, and herbs. Reduce the heat to medium and simmer the mixture for 20 minutes or until it is thick. Add the tomatoes and mix well. Pour into the prepared baking dish.

Spread the mashed potatoes over the soy mixture, making sure to seal the edges. Brush a small amount of olive oil on the potatoes. Bake for 35 to 40 minutes or until the stew is bubbly and the potatoes are browned.

Makes 8 servings.

breads

Quick Breads

Biscuits
Sweet Potato Biscuits
Corn Bread
Tofu Banana Bread
Pumpkin Bread
Whole Wheat Quick Bread

Yeast Breads

Potato Rolls
Big Fat Sandwich Loaf
Everything Bread
Focaccia

Flatbreads

Pizza Crust
Pizza Sauce
Potato and Rosemary Pizza
Bianca Pizza with Tofu Boursin
Two-Tone Tomato Pizza with Basil and Garlic
Vegetable Tofu Pizza
Torta Rustica
Whole Wheat Pita Bread
Green Onion Pancakes

Bread, the staff of life, is an integral part of the base of any food pyramid. Its carbohydrates give us energy to fuel our day, its proteins build our cells, and its vitamins and minerals sustain our body's chemistry. Bread can stand alone in muffins or sweet quick breads. It can act as a backdrop for simple sandwiches like peanut butter and jelly, or elaborate creations like torta rustica.

Any way you slice it, bread takes a central role in the vegan diet. The recipes in this chapter are both familiar and innovative. An array of textures are represented, from flaky biscuits to a chewy multigrain bread with lentils. For information on ingredients for baking, see pages 289–290.

QUICK BREADS

If you haven't done much baking, quick breads are a great way to start. There are two things to avoid: overworking the dough and working too slowly. Overworking the dough will develop the gluten too much and can turn a light, fluffy biscuit into a leaden mass. In addition, overmixing releases carbon dioxide from the batter and reduces leavening action. Working quickly optimizes the rising power of the baking powder and baking soda. The baking powder and soda release their carbon dioxide—the gas that gets trapped and makes baked goods rise—when liquid first hits them. Ideally, you should get batter breads into the oven shortly after the wet and dry ingredients have been mixed.

Biscuits

Biscuits do not contain any eggs so the transition to a vegan version is quite easy, requiring only the substitution of soymilk for cow's milk. You can also sour 1 cup of soymilk with 1 tablespoon lemon juice to substitute for buttermilk in your favorite recipe. Vegetable shortening produces a light, airy biscuit. For a lower fat biscuit, without shortening, see Sweet Potato Biscuits (page 258).

2   cups flour
1   tablespoon baking
    powder
1/2 teaspoon salt
1/4 cup shortening
3/4 to 1 cup soymilk

Preheat the oven to 450°. Sift the flour, baking powder, and salt into a bowl. Cut in the shortening with a pastry blender or two knives until the mixture resembles coarse crumbs. Stir in just enough soymilk to form a soft dough. Do not overmix. Place the dough on a lightly floured board and knead 3 or 4 times only. Roll the dough out to a thickness of 1/2 inch. Cut with a 2-inch round cookie cutter. Place on an ungreased baking sheet. Brush the tops with olive oil, if desired. Bake for 12 to 15 minutes.

Makes 12 biscuits.

257

Sweet Potato Biscuits

These biscuits contain no shortening so are relatively low in fat.

1   cup sifted bread flour
1   tablespoon baking powder
3/4 teaspoon salt
1/8 teaspoon cayenne
2   tablespoons olive oil
1   cup mashed sweet potatoes
1/4 cup diced red bell pepper
2   to 4 tablespoons soymilk

Preheat the oven to 450°. Combine the flour, baking powder, salt, and cayenne in a bowl. Add the olive oil, mashed potatoes, and peppers and mix until the mixture resembles a coarse meal. Stir in just enough soymilk to form a soft dough. Do not overmix. Place the dough on a lightly floured board and knead 3 or 4 times. Roll the dough out 3/4 inch thick and cut with a 2-inch round cookie cutter. Place 1/2 inch apart on an ungreased baking sheet. Brush the tops with olive oil, if desired. Bake for 12 to 15 minutes.

    Makes 12 biscuits.

Corn Bread

1   cup yellow cornmeal
1   cup flour
1 1/2 teaspoons baking powder
1/2 teaspoon baking soda
1/4 teaspoon salt
1/4 cup maple syrup
1/3 cup soymilk
1   tablespoon lemon juice
3   tablespoons oil

Preheat the oven to 375°. Grease a 9-inch square or round pan. Sift the dry ingredients together into a large bowl. Combine the syrup, soymilk, lemon juice, 3/4 cup of warm water, and warm oil. Stir into the dry mixture and beat until smooth. Pour into the prepared pan and bake for 25 minutes.

    Makes 8 servings.

Tofu Banana Bread

Carl Lewis

- ³/₄ cup (about 6 ounces) medium tofu
- 1 cup mashed ripe bananas
- 1 cup sugar
- ¹/₄ cup olive oil or canola oil
- 1 teaspoon vanilla extract
- 2 cups whole wheat pastry flour
- 1 teaspoon baking powder
- ¹/₂ teaspoon baking soda
- ¹/₄ teaspoon sea salt
- ³/₄ cup coarsely chopped walnuts

Preheat the oven to 350°. Grease a loaf pan. Puree the tofu with ¹/₂ cup of banana, sugar, olive oil, and vanilla. Stir in remaining banana. In a separate medium bowl, stir together the flour, baking powder, baking soda, and salt. Add the flour mixture to the tofu mixture and mix gently. Fold in the walnuts. Pour into the prepared pan. Bake for 45 to 50 minutes. When bread is cool enough to handle, remove from the pan and cool on a wire rack.

Makes 1 loaf.

Pumpkin Bread

The ingredient list is long but the recipe is quite easy. The spices can be replaced by 2 teaspoons of pumpkin pie spice. Try substituting an equal amount of mashed sweet potato for the pumpkin.

- 2 tablespoons flaxseeds
- 1¹/₂ cups sugar
- 1 cup pumpkin purée
- ¹/₂ cup applesauce
- 1¹/₃ cups all-purpose flour
- ¹/₃ cup whole wheat flour
- 1 teaspoon baking soda
- ¹/₂ teaspoon baking powder
- ³/₄ teaspoon salt
- 1 teaspoon ground cinnamon
- ¹/₂ teaspoon ground nutmeg
- ¹/₄ teaspoon ground cloves

Preheat the oven to 350°. Grease and flour a 9-inch loaf pan. In a blender or food processor, blend together the flaxseeds and 6 tablespoons of water until light and frothy. In a large mixing bowl, whisk together the flaxseed mixture, sugar, pumpkin, and applesauce.

Sift the flours, baking soda, baking powder, salt, cinnamon, nutmeg, and cloves into a bowl. Add to the pumpkin mixture and mix well. Pour the batter into the prepared pan. Bake in the center of the oven for 1 hour to 1 hour and 15 minutes. When bread is cool enough to handle, remove from the pan and cool on a wire rack.

Makes 1 loaf.

Whole Wheat Quick Bread

If you are intimidated by yeast breads or feel you don't have the time for them, try this amazingly fast recipe. It has a rustic taste and texture and is good for sopping up soups and stews.

1½ cups creamy soymilk
1   tablespoon lemon juice
2   cups whole wheat pastry flour
½ cup all-purpose flour or soy flour
1   teaspoon baking powder
1   teaspoon baking soda
1   teaspoon salt
¼ cup canola oil
¼ cup molasses

Preheat the oven to 375°. Grease and flour a 9-inch loaf pan. Mix the soymilk and lemon juice and let stand for 5 minutes or until the soymilk has curdled. Mix the flours, baking powder, baking soda, and salt in a bowl. Mix the soymilk with the oil and molasses. Add the wet ingredients to the dry and stir until blended. Pour the batter into the pan and bake for about 50 minutes. When the bread is cool enough to handle, remove from the pan and cool on a rack.

Makes 1 loaf.

YEAST BREADS

Many conventional yeast breads use few eggs or dairy products, so using or adapting your favorite recipes should be fairly simple. The recipes that follow are perennial favorites.

Bread baking falls somewhere between science and art. For more information on theory and practice, you should consult one of the many excellent bread books available. The following recipes include instructions for working the dough by hand or with a standing mixer. You may also use a food processor, if you have one that can handle bread dough. Of course, you may also use a bread machine, adapting the recipes to the manufacturer's instructions.

Potato Rolls

Since the dough for these rolls must be refrigerated for several hours, it is convenient to mix it up after dinner, using leftover mashed potatoes. This dough also makes a great base for cinnamon rolls or sticky buns.

1 teaspoon sugar or barley malt
1/2 cup warm water, about 110°
1 1/2 tablespoons (2 envelopes) dry active yeast
1/4 cup olive oil
1 teaspoon salt
1 cup mashed potatoes, at room temperature
4 1/2 cups all-purpose flour

In a large mixing bowl, dissolve the sugar in the water and sprinkle the yeast on the water. Let stand until foamy. Whisk in the oil, salt, and potatoes. Add half the flour and beat with a wooden spoon until a sticky batter forms. Add the remaining flour. Coat your hands with flour and knead the dough in the bowl until it forms a ball. Add a little extra water or flour as needed. Turn the dough out onto a lightly floured surface and knead the dough until it is quite elastic, about 12 to 15 minutes by hand or 8 to 10 minutes in a standing mixer fitted with a dough hook. Form the dough into a tight ball.

Place the dough in a lightly oiled bowl. Turn the dough to coat with oil all over. Cover the bowl with plastic wrap and let the dough rise in the refrigerator for 8 to 18 hours.

Remove the dough from the refrigerator 1 1/2 hours before you want to make the rolls. When the dough has come to room temperature, punch it down and turn it out onto a lightly floured surface. Knead the dough a few times to eliminate any large air pockets.

Divide the dough into 12 equal pieces. Shape the rolls and place them, seam side down, on a lightly oiled baking sheet. Cut a slash in the top of each roll and cover the rolls with a clean kitchen towel. Let the rolls rise until they have doubled in bulk, about 25 to 35 minutes.

Preheat the oven to 375°. Bake the rolls until the crusts just begin to brown and the rolls sound hollow when tapped. For a crunchy crust, spray the rolls with clean water from a clean spray bottle before putting them in the oven and then every 2 minutes for the first 8 minutes.

Makes 12 rolls.

Big Fat Sandwich Loaf

This is the perfect loaf for Muffuletta (page 150) or any large, communal sandwich. You may also make long Italian loaves with this dough. Just divide the dough into two equal pieces and shape into long loaves. Whole wheat pastry flour may be substituted for the all-purpose flour.

2¾ cups all-purpose flour
2½ cups bread flour
1 tablespoon sugar
1 cup warm water, 110°
1½ tablespoons (2 envelopes) dry active yeast
3 tablespoons oil
1 teaspoon salt
2 teaspoons oil
1 teaspoon sesame seeds

In a medium bowl, mix the all-purpose and the bread flours together. In a large mixing bowl, dissolve the sugar in the water. Sprinkle the yeast over the water and let it soften. Beat 2½ cups of the flour mixture into the yeast mixture. Cover the bowl and let the mixture (called a "sponge") rise until doubled in bulk, about 20 minutes.

Using a spoon or dough hook, beat the oil, salt, and remaining flours into the sponge. Knead until the dough is smooth and elastic, about 10 minutes in a mixer or 15 minutes by hand. This long kneading will give the bread a fine grain. The dough will be quite soft and easy to work.

Shape the dough into a ball and place it, seam side down, on a baking sheet lined with parchment or lightly greased. Preheat the oven to 375°. Let the bread rise for about 20 to 30 minutes or until it is puffy. Do not let it rise too long or it will fall during baking. Brush the top lightly with oil and sprinkle with sesame seeds. Bake for 20 to 25 minutes. If a crispy crust is desired, spray the bread with clean water from a clean spray bottle every 6 minutes.

Makes 1 big, fat loaf.

Everything Bread

Your local health food store may not carry millet and barley flours. If you can't find these, you can grind the grains in a coffee grinder. Millet is quite soft, so it grinds easily and even some food processors can handle grinding it into flour. Barley is harder and very few food processors are up to the job. The coffee grinder works well, but you'll need to grind it in small batches. I prefer to use whole barley rather than pearled barley for the added texture and nutrition, but pearled is much softer and easier to grind.

The water measurements in the recipe are not exact since everyone's lentils will be different. It is better for the dough to be a little wet than a little dry. This dough is relatively low in gluten, so it will not have that familiar elastic texture.

2   teaspoons (1 envelope) dry active yeast
2   cups spelt flour
3/4 cup barley flour
1/2 cup soy flour
1/4 cup millet flour
2   tablespoons rye flour
1/2 teaspoon dried thyme
1   teaspoon sea salt
1/2 cup cooked lentils, mashed
1   tablespoon olive oil

Sprinkle the yeast over 1/2 cup of warm water in a small bowl and let stand for 10 minutes.

Mix the flours, thyme, and salt in a bowl. In a large mixing bowl, blend the lentils and olive oil with 1/2 cup of warm water (1/4 cup if the lentils are really mushy). Add the yeast mixture and 2 cups of the flour mixture and mix well. Stir in the remaining flour and knead in the bowl until a smooth dough is formed. Alternatively, place the ingredients in a standing mixer fitted with a dough hook and mix on medium-low speed until a smooth dough is formed. Add a little extra water or flour, if needed, to form a dough that is soft but not too sticky. Shape the dough into a ball and place it in a bowl greased with olive oil. Turn the dough to coat with oil all over. Cover the bowl with a clean kitchen towel and let the dough rise until it is doubled in bulk, about 1 to 1 1/2 hours.

Grease a 9-inch loaf pan. Punch the dough down and knead lightly. Turn the dough out onto a lightly floured surface. Shape the dough into a loaf and put it into the prepared pan. Cover with a clean kitchen towel and let rise until it is doubled in bulk, about 1 hour. Preheat the oven to 375°. Bake the bread for an hour or until it sounds hollow when tapped.

Makes 1 loaf.

Focaccia

The glory of focaccia comes from the olive oil, so splurge on a rich, fruity extra virgin oil. Coarse salt and fresh rosemary are helpful also. You can top your focaccia like a pizza or use it for sandwiches (try Mixed Vegetable Romesco Focaccia, page 153), but I prefer it in its naked, oily glory.

Let the focaccia rise at room temperature, rather than in a very warm spot. The long rising time allows the gluten to develop, giving the bread its slightly chewy texture. The dough can be made the night before and refrigerated after its first rising or after shaping the final loaf. Make sure the dough comes to room temperature before you work with it.

1½ tablespoons (2 envelopes) dry active yeast
1¾ cups warm water, about 110°
¼ cup olive oil
4 cups all-purpose flour, or 2 cups all-purpose flour and 2 cups bread flour
3 teaspoons salt
¼ to ⅓ cup extra virgin olive oil
1 teaspoon kosher salt
1 tablespoon coarsely chopped fresh rosemary

In the bowl of a mixer or a large mixing bowl, sprinkle the yeast over ½ cup of the warm water. Let stand 5 minutes. Add the oil and remaining 1¼ cups of warm water. In another bowl, whisk the flour and salt together. Add half the flour mixture to the yeast mixture. Stir with a wooden spoon until a sticky dough forms. Add the remaining flour. With a mixer fitted with a dough hook, blend the flour into the dough on low speed until it comes together in a ball, about 2 minutes. Scrape the sides of the bowl and knead the dough with the dough hook until elastic, about 6 minutes. If working by hand, mix the remaining flour into the dough. Knead the dough in the bowl, adding a little extra water or flour as needed until the dough comes together in a ball and is soft but not sticky. Continue to knead the dough in the bowl until it is quite elastic, about 12 to 15 minutes.

Shape the dough into a ball and place in a medium mixing bowl lightly coated with olive oil. Turn the dough to coat with oil all over. Cover the bowl with a clean kitchen towel and let the dough rise until it is doubled in bulk, about 1 to 1½ hours.

Punch the dough down, fold it into thirds, and form it into a ball. Turn the ball to coat with oil. Cover the bowl with a clean kitchen towel and let the dough rise until it is doubled in bulk, about 45 minutes to an hour.

Turn the dough out onto a lightly floured surface. Starting from the middle of the dough, push the dough down and away from you with the palm of your hand.

Burst any bubbles that appear on the surface of the dough. Gently work the dough into a rectangle the size of a cookie sheet or a circle the size of a 12-inch pizza pan. Fold the shaped dough in half or thirds and lay it on a lightly oiled pan. Unfold the dough and shape it to the pan so the dough is uniform in thickness.

With clean fingers, poke deep dents all over the dough. Drizzle the olive oil evenly over the dough. Sprinkle the kosher salt and rosemary over the dough. Cover the focaccia lightly with plastic wrap (which won't absorb the precious oil) and let rise until double in height, about 1 hour.

Preheat the oven to 400°. Bake the focaccia in the center of the oven. For a crispy crust, spray the focaccia with clean water from a clean spray bottle every 3 minutes for the first 10 minutes. Then allow the focaccia to brown lightly, another 2 to 5 minutes.

Makes 12 servings.

FLATBREADS

Most cuisines have a particular flatbread that helps to define them. Some of these are not worth the trouble to prepare at home. While tortillas are not hard to make, it can be difficult to duplicate the results obtained from baking on a *comal*. Injera, an Ethiopian flatbread, is a fabulous light creation made from teff, a cousin of millet, but it takes three or four days to prepare by the traditional method. Fortunately, most groceries have a wide variety of flatbreads available—crackers, tortillas, lavosh, and Scandinavian flatbrod. In this section we include several recipes for an all-time favorite—pizza—because of its adaptability to the vegan diet and its ease of preparation.

Pizza Crust

Pizza crust is a scaled-down version of focaccia.

2 teaspoons (1 envelope) dry active yeast

1⅓ cups warm water, about 110°

2 tablespoons olive oil

4 cups all-purpose flour

2 teaspoons salt

¼ cup wheat bran (optional)

In the bowl of a mixer or a large mixing bowl, sprinkle the yeast over ⅓ cup of the warm water. Let stand 5 minutes, then add the oil and remaining 1 cup of warm water. In another bowl, whisk the flour and salt together. Add half the flour mixture to the yeast and water. Stir with a wooden spoon until a sticky dough is formed. Add the remaining flour and wheat bran. With a mixer fitted with a dough hook, blend the flour into the dough on low speed until it comes together in a ball, about 2 minutes. Scrape the bowl down, turn the mixer on medium, and knead the dough until elastic, about 6 minutes. If working by hand, mix the remaining flour into the dough. Knead the dough in the bowl, adding a little extra water or flour as needed until the dough comes together in a ball and is soft but not sticky. Continue to knead the dough in the bowl until it is quite elastic, about 12 to 15 minutes.

Place the ball of dough in a medium mixing bowl lightly coated with olive oil. Turn the dough to coat with oil all over. Cover the bowl with a clean kitchen towel and let rise until it is doubled in bulk, about 1 to 1½ hours.

Punch the dough down. Turn out onto a lightly floured surface. Divide the dough in half. Turn each ball of dough inside out, then form into a smooth ball with no air pockets. Take each dough ball and rotate it in a little clockwise circle on the countertop (this will makes the dough easier to roll out into a circle later). If you are making only one pizza, wrap the remaining dough tightly in plastic wrap and refrigerate. Cover the dough with a clean kitchen towel and let it rest for 20 to 45 minutes.

Preheat the oven to 400°. Place the dough on a lightly floured surface. Put the palm of your hand in the middle of the ball and flatten with a clockwise twist. Roll or press the dough into a circle or rectangle slightly larger than your pan, working from the center of the dough out to the edges in a clockwise direction. As you work, occasionally pick up the dough and re-flour the surface underneath so the dough doesn't stick. Fold the shaped dough in half or thirds and lay it on the pan. Unfold the dough and fit it into the pan. Pop any visible air bubbles. Top the pizza and bake for 10 to 15 minutes or until the crust just begins to brown and the toppings are bubbling.

Makes 2 12-inch pizza crusts.

Whole Wheat Pizza Crust: For the all-purpose flour, substitute 2 cups of all-purpose flour and 2 cups of whole wheat flour, or 4 cups of whole wheat pastry flour.

Pizza Sauce

Any bottled pizza or marinara sauce will work on your pizza, but I prefer this very simple sauce, which is barely cooked and somewhat chunky.

1 28-ounce can good quality diced tomatoes, preferably roma
2 tablespoons olive oil
1½ teaspoons minced garlic
⅛ teaspoon red pepper flakes (optional)
⅛ teaspoon sea salt
Pinch ground black pepper
1 tablespoon chopped fresh basil

Drain the tomatoes, reserving the juice for making Vegetable Stock (page 65), if desired. Heat the oil in a wide skillet. Sauté the garlic and pepper flakes with the salt and pepper. Do not brown the garlic. When the garlic is fragrant, add the tomatoes. Stir the tomatoes until they are barely warm and turn off the heat. Use a potato masher to crush the tomatoes. Add the basil and mix well. Taste and adjust the seasonings with salt and pepper.

Makes about 2 cups.

Potato and Rosemary Pizza

1 to 2 pounds new
   potatoes
   or Yukon Gold potatoes
1 12-inch Pizza Crust
   (page 266), unbaked
2 to 3 tablespoons extra
   virgin olive oil
1 teaspoon kosher salt
1½ tablespoons chopped
   fresh rosemary
Freshly ground black pepper

Steam, boil, or microwave the potatoes until they are about half-cooked. Let the potatoes cool completely. Slice the potatoes paper-thin on a mandoline or with the side of a box grater.

Brush the pizza crust with half of the olive oil. Sprinkle half the salt and 1 tablespoon of the rosemary on the oil. Grind a little black pepper over the crust.

Preheat the oven to 375°. Arrange the potato slices decoratively over the pizza to within ½ inch of the edge. The potatoes should overlap a bit but should be no more than 2 layers thick anywhere on the pizza. Do not use the thick end slices, as they will not cook at the same rate as the rest of the potatoes.

Brush the remaining olive oil on the potatoes and sprinkle them with the rest of the salt. Bake the pizza in the oven until the potatoes are tender and just starting to brown, about 12 to 15 minutes.

Sprinkle with the remaining rosemary and serve immediately.

Makes 12 appetizer servings or 4 main-course servings.

Bianca Pizza with Tofu Boursin

For many vegans, the bianca is a pizza favorite that's hard to give up. Fortunately, there's no need to deprive yourself.

1 12-inch Pizza Crust
   (page 266), unbaked
1½ tablespoons olive oil
¼ teaspoon salt
1 teaspoon minced fresh
   garlic
Freshly ground black pepper
2 cups Tofu Boursin
   (page 154)
1 tablespoon chopped
   fresh chives

Preheat the oven to 400°. Brush the pizza crust with half the olive oil. Sprinkle with half the salt and all the garlic. Grind a little pepper over the crust and spread the boursin to within ¾ inch of the edge. Brush the pizza with the remaining olive oil. Bake in the lower third of the oven until the crust just begins to brown, about 10 to 15 minutes. Sprinkle with the remaining salt and chives just before serving.

Makes 12 appetizer servings or 4 main-course servings.

Two-Tone Tomato Pizza with Basil and Garlic

Meaty tomatoes work best in this recipe, since juicy tomatoes can make for a soggy crust. For added visual appeal and flavor, just before serving, paint the top of the pizza with Soy Syrup (page 201) made with balsamic vinegar and without the ginger.

2 pounds ripe red tomatoes
2 pounds yellow, pink, or striped tomatoes
1 teaspoon kosher salt
1 12-inch Pizza Crust (page 266), unbaked
1 tablespoon olive oil
½ teaspoon minced garlic
Freshly ground black pepper
1 cup Pizza Sauce (page 267)
½ cup fresh whole basil leaves

Preheat the oven to 400°. Slice the tomatoes as thinly as possible. Sprinkle with half the salt and let the tomatoes drain in a colander while preparing the rest of the pizza.

Brush the pizza crust with half the olive oil. Sprinkle with the garlic. Grind a little black pepper over the crust and spread the pizza sauce to within ¾ inch of the edge. Arrange half the basil leaves on the pizza sauce. Arrange the tomatoes and remaining basil in a decorative pattern over the pizza. Sprinkle the remaining salt over the tomatoes and drizzle with the remaining olive oil. Bake the pizza until the crust begins to brown, about 12 to 15 minutes.

Makes 12 appetizer servings or 4 main-course servings.

Vegetable Tofu Pizza

Carl Lewis

1 12-inch Whole Wheat Pizza Crust (page 267), unbaked
1 cup Pizza Sauce (page 267)
½ cup sun-dried tomatoes, rehydrated and drained
2 medium tomatoes, thinly sliced
½ cup thinly sliced mushrooms
1 10-ounce package extra firm tofu, thinly sliced
⅓ cup sliced green olives
1 medium red onion, thinly sliced (optional)
⅓ cup spicy brown mustard (optional)

Preheat the oven to 375°. Place the pizza crust on a baking sheet or pizza pan. Spread the Pizza Sauce to within ¾ inch of the edge. Arrange the tomatoes, mushrooms, tofu, olives, and onion over the sauce. Bake the pizza until the crust just begins to brown, about 12 to 15 minutes. Serve with mustard, if desired.

Makes 12 appetizer servings or 4 main-course servings.

Torta Rustica

This is a great way to use up leftover grilled or roasted vegetables. Just about any assortment of veggies will do, but the ones listed below make for a stunning presentation.

Dough for 2 12-inch Pizza Crusts (page 266)

2 tablespoons chopped fresh basil

1 teaspoon chopped fresh rosemary

1 teaspoon fresh thyme leaves

2 tablespoons olive oil

1/4 teaspoon salt

1 teaspoon minced garlic

Freshly ground black pepper

1 medium eggplant, sliced and grilled or roasted

3/4 cup roasted peppers

1 cup Tofu Boursin (optional, page 154)

1 medium zucchini, sliced, and grilled or roasted

2 medium tomatoes, sliced

1 large bulb fennel, trimmed (page 222), thinly sliced, and grilled or roasted

Preheat the oven to 350°. Roll one pizza crust 12 inches in diameter and the other 14 inches. Place the 12-inch crust on a pizza pan or large, lightly oiled sheet pan.

Mix the basil, rosemary, and thyme in a small bowl. If any of the cooked vegetables have expressed any liquid, pat them dry with paper towels.

Brush the 12-inch crust with half the olive oil. Sprinkle the salt, garlic, and a third of the herbs on the crust. Grind a little black pepper over the crust. Arrange half the eggplant over the crust, leaving a 2-inch margin around the edge of the pizza. Top with half the roasted peppers and half the boursin. Layer on all the zucchini, then the tomatoes. Sprinkle with a third of the herbs. Top with all the fennel, the remaining roasted peppers, boursin, and eggplant. Sprinkle with the last of the herbs.

Carefully lay the 14-inch crust over the torta so that the dough comes to within 1/2 inch of the bottom's edge. Once the top crust is on, gently press down to remove any air pockets. Try to shape the torta so it is a uniform height and straight-sided. Fold the bottom crust over the top crust and crimp them together so an air-tight seal is formed all around the torta. Brush all over with the rest of the olive oil.

Cover the torta loosely with aluminum foil to prevent overbrowning and bake for 15 minutes. Uncover and bake for 15 to 25 minutes longer.

Makes 6 to 8 main-course servings.

Whole Wheat Pita Bread

If these pitas are baked at the right temperature, they will form pockets like those found in the store.

2   teaspoons sugar
2   cups warm water,
     about 110°
1½ tablespoons (2 envelopes)
     dry active yeast
2   cups whole wheat flour
3   cups all-purpose flour
1   teaspoon salt

In a large mixing bowl, combine the sugar with ½ cup of the warm water, sprinkle the yeast on top, and let stand until foamy, about 5 to 8 minutes. Mix the flours and salt together. Add the rest of the water to the yeast mixture and beat in half the flour mixture until a thick, smooth batter is formed. Add the rest of the flour and knead until the dough is smooth and elastic, about 10 minutes by hand or 6 minutes in a standing mixer fitted with a dough hook. Put the dough into a bowl lightly coated with olive oil. Turn the dough to coat with oil all over. Cover the dough with a clean kitchen towel and let rise until doubled in bulk, about 1 hour.

Preheat the oven to 450°. Punch the dough down and let rest for 15 minutes. Divide the dough into 8 pieces. On a lightly floured surface, roll each piece of dough into 6- to 8-inch circles. (Alternatively, with lightly floured hands, slap the dough from palm to palm until the circle is formed.) Keep the edges of the pitas thicker than the middles (to prevent sandwich filling leakage later). For best results preheat 2 baking sheets for 5 minutes. Place the pitas on the hot baking sheets and bake in the center of the oven for 10 to 12 minutes, or until lightly browned and puffy in the middle.

Makes 8 pitas.

Green Onion Pancakes

Try serving these tasty pancakes with Simple Soy Dipping Sauce (page 138), Sweet and Sour Dipping Sauce (page 138), or Vietnamese Lime Dipping Sauce (page 139).

2　cups all-purpose flour, or 1 cup all-purpose flour and 1 cup cake flour
2　teaspoons salt
1　tablespoon peanut, blended, or canola oil
1　cup boiling water
1　teaspoon sesame oil
½　cup very thinly sliced green onions
Peanut oil, for frying

Combine the flour and salt in a large mixing bowl. Add the oil and stir with a wooden spoon while gradually pouring in the boiling water. Beat until a dough forms. When the dough is cool enough to handle, knead it for 10 minutes by hand or 6 minutes with a standing mixer fitted with a dough hook, or until the dough is elastic. Place dough in a bowl and cover with a clean, damp kitchen towel for 30 minutes.

Roll the dough out to a 10x15-inch rectangle that is about ¼ inch thick. Brush the sesame oil evenly over the dough. Sprinkle the green onions over the dough. Roll up the dough jelly-roll style. Cut the roll into 8 thick slices. Flatten each slice slightly with your hand. Roll out each piece, turning it to keep it circular, until it is ¼ inch thick and about 6 inches in diameter. Keep the finished pancakes covered with a damp towel while you work.

Heat a skillet over high heat. When it is hot, pour in oil to a depth of ¼ inch. When the oil is hot, turn the heat to medium-low. Cook the pancakes in the oil, one at a time, for about 2 to 3 minutes on each side, until they are golden. Replenish the oil as needed.

Makes 8 pancakes.

breakfast

Adults seem to have a love-hate relationship with breakfast—either it is a nuisance to be disposed of as quickly as possible with coffee and a doughnut or it evokes nostalgic reminiscences of a simpler time when someone else fed us a wholesome morning meal. In making the decision to adopt a plant-based diet, you've made a commitment to be the one nurturing your body, so it's time to make breakfast a healthy, enjoyable part of your day.

The following recipes closely parallel the most familiar breakfast choices. But don't let your old notions of breakfast limit your options. Instead of using soymilk on your granola, try orange juice. Why not have a Sun-Dried Tomato and Lentil Burger (page 155) or some Caponata (pages 46) with a crusty roll? Check out the smoothies in "Beverages" (pages 317–320) for quick liquid pick-me-ups.

And don't forget the easiest recipe for health: "1 apple, washed. Eat. Makes 1 serving."

Scrambled Tofu

The health food sections of most grocery stores carry pre-packaged mixes for scrambling tofu, but it is so easy to do yourself. The turmeric is more for color than flavor, in case you are trying to fool the kids or a reluctant spouse. If you are too bleary-eyed in the morning to be wielding a knife, substitute ½ teaspoon of onion powder and ¼ teaspoon of garlic powder for the vegetables.

2	teaspoons oil
1	small onion, diced
1	teaspoon minced garlic
1	small green bell pepper
8	ounces tofu
1	tablespoon nutritional yeast
¼	teaspoon ground turmeric
2	teaspoons soy sauce

Heat the oil in a skillet over medium heat. Sauté the onion, garlic, and green pepper until the onion is soft. Crumble the tofu into the vegetables. Add the yeast, turmeric, and soy sauce. Mix thoroughly and heat through.

Makes 2 servings.

Migas

Migas means rags in Spanish and refers to the shreds of tortilla that are scrambled along with whatever snippets of vegetables may be lurking in the fridge. Despite its humble name, this is a dish with extravagant flavors. For a quick meal on the go, roll the migas in a whole wheat tortilla. Serve migas with a light salsa.

2   teaspoons oil
1   medium onion, diced
2   teaspoons minced garlic
1   small jalapeño, minced (optional)
1   medium green bell pepper, diced
1   medium red bell pepper, diced
1   teaspoon ground turmeric
¼   teaspoon ground cumin
1   pound tofu
1   tablespoon nutritional yeast
1   medium tomato, diced
2   tablespoons chopped fresh cilantro
1   tablespoon soy sauce
2   6-inch uncooked corn tortillas, cut into strips, or ½ cup tortilla chip crumbs

Heat the oil in a skillet over medium heat. Sauté the onion, garlic, and peppers until the onion is soft. Mix the turmeric and cumin into the vegetables. Crumble the tofu into the vegetables. Add the yeast, tomato, cilantro, and soy sauce and mix well. Add the tortillas and heat through.

Makes 4 servings.

Seitan Chorizo

This spicy Spanish sausage can be served for breakfast or used in casseroles such as Millet Paella (page 174). The flaxseed in this recipe will help to hold the sausage together and give a more sausage-like texture, but the recipe works well without it also.

1   tablespoon flaxseed (optional)
2   tablespoons canola oil
½   cup finely diced yellow onion
2   teaspoons minced garlic
1   teaspoon cayenne
1   teaspoon ground cumin
2   teaspoons paprika, preferably smoked paprika
2   teaspoons black pepper
½   teaspoon fennel seed
¼   teaspoon dried oregano
1   pound seitan, chopped fine
½   cup dry red wine
1   tablespoon soy sauce

In a blender or small food processor, grind the flaxseed with ¼ cup of water. Pour into a small bowl and cover.

Heat the oil in a wide skillet over medium heat. Sauté the onion, garlic, and dry spices until the onion is soft and a hearty aroma rises from the pan. Add the seitan and heat through. Add the wine and soy sauce to the pan and cook until the mixture is dry. Remove the pan from the heat. Stir in the reserved flaxseed. Adjust the seasonings.

When the mixture is cool enough to handle, shape the sausage into patties or links. Cook the formed sausages in a clean skillet over medium heat with more canola oil until well browned, about 5 to 7 minutes on each side. (Since this sausage is so lean, it may require more oil.) Sausages may be cooked and frozen for later use.

Makes 4 servings.

Country-Style Tempeh Sausages

2   8-ounce packages tempeh, cut into 1-inch cubes
½   teaspoon dried thyme
1½ teaspoons rubbed sage
¼   teaspoon dried savory
½   teaspoon red pepper flakes
¼   teaspoon pepper
½   cup whole wheat flour
1   tablespoon soy sauce
¼   cup olive oil
Canola oil for frying

Steam the tempeh in a steamer basket over simmering water for 15 minutes. Alternatively, microwave the tempeh, covered by plastic wrap, for 1 or 2 minutes, or put the tempeh cubes into a mixing bowl and pour 2 cups of boiling water over them. Cover the bowl and let rest for 15 minutes. Drain.

Crumble the tempeh, add the dry spices, and mix well. Add the flour, soy sauce, and oil and mix well. Let the sausage rest for 10 minutes. With moistened hands, form the sausage into 8 patties. Put the patties onto a baking sheet lined with waxed paper or parchment. Chill for 1 hour.

Cook the formed sausages in a clean skillet over medium heat with canola oil until well browned, about 5 to 7 minutes on each side. (Since this sausage is so lean, it may require more oil.) Sausages may be cooked and frozen for later use.

Makes 4 servings.

Hash Browns

There are endless variations on this morning favorite. I prefer to slice the potatoes rather than grate them, but either method works. The secret is not to rush. Let the onions caramelize and the potatoes get crispy before turning. And use a metal spatula, not a spoon. (If using a nonstick pan, use a rubber spatula.) I like to use Yukon Gold potatoes here for their waxy texture, but just about any potato will do.

1½ pounds potatoes
1   medium onion
3   cloves garlic, peeled
Oil
Sea salt and freshly ground
    black pepper

Scrub the potatoes. Place the potatoes in a pot of cold, salted water. Bring the water to a boil and cook the potatoes until they are about half done. Cool. Remove the skins if desired and cut into ½-inch slices.

Peel the onion and discard the root end. Cut the onion into halves and slice ¼ inch thick. Slice the garlic cloves as thinly as possible.

Heat 1 tablespoon of oil in a wide skillet over medium heat. Add the onions and garlic in an even layer on the bottom of the pan. Top the vegetables with the potato slices. Season the potatoes with salt and pepper. Cook the potatoes undisturbed for 5 to 10 minutes. When the onions have begun to caramelize in the bottom of the pan, gently turn the mixture over so the potatoes are on the bottom and the onions are approximately on top. This will not form a cake, so it's fine if the mix has fallen apart.

Cook the potatoes undisturbed for another 5 to 10 minutes or until they begin to brown, adding more oil as needed. Continue cooking the potatoes, stirring more frequently, until they are done to your liking.

Makes 4 servings.

Congee

Eaten sweet or savory, congee, or rice soup, is a healing, comforting way to begin your day. The strength of congee is said to increase with cooking time, so try cooking this in an electric slow cooker overnight.

½ cup short grain rice
2 ¼-inch slices fresh ginger
1 2-inch square of kombu
   or other seaweed

SWEET TOPPINGS
Almond milk
Cinnamon
Cane juice sweetener

SAVORY TOPPINGS
2 tablespoons sliced
   green onions
3 teaspoons chopped
   peanuts
4 teaspoons chopped
   fresh cilantro
2 tablespoons Asian
   pickled vegetables

Electric slow cooker method: Place the rice, ginger, and seaweed in a slow cooker with 3 cups of water. Cook at high setting for 30 minutes, and then reduce the heat to low. Let cook for 8 or more hours.

Stovetop method: Place all ingredients (except toppings) in a heavy pot and bring to a boil. Reduce the heat to very low and cook for 2 hours or until the rice has fallen apart.

Remove the ginger before serving. Pour into two bowls. For sweet congee, drizzle with almond milk, sprinkle with cinnamon, and add cane juice sweetener. For savory congee, top each bowl with green onions, peanuts, cilantro, and pickled vegetables.
Makes 2 servings.

Pancakes

Derived from various flatbreads, pancakes have taken on a life of their own as a breakfast food. When buying a mix, check the ingredients carefully for dried eggs or dairy products.

2 cups all-purpose flour
2 teaspoons baking powder
½ teaspoon baking soda
¼ teaspoon salt
2 tablespoons applesauce
   or mashed banana
1 tablespoon maple syrup
1 cup soymilk
½ cup apple juice
2 tablespoons canola oil
Nonstick cooking spray or
   additional oil

Combine the flour, baking powder, baking soda, and salt in a medium mixing bowl. Add the applesauce, maple syrup, soymilk, apple juice, and canola oil and stir just until blended.

Heat a heavy skillet or griddle over medium to medium-high heat. Brush lightly with oil or coat with nonstick cooking spray. When the griddle is hot, drop the batter by spoonfuls. Do not crowd the pan. Cook the pancakes until bubbles form on the tops and the edges appear firm. Turn the pancakes with a spatula and cook on the other side until they are puffed and are golden on the bottom.

Serve immediately or reserve in a warm oven.
Makes 4 servings.

Crepes

The secret to making good crepes is to make the batter the night before you plan to cook them. This gives the gluten time to develop and keeps the crepes from breaking.

A crepe pan should have sloping sides so that when you are rotating the batter in the pan the bottom is evenly covered. Pans 6 to 8 inches in diameter are comfortable for most people, though the adventurous can try using a 10-inch pan. A nonstick pan and a heat-resistant rubber spatula simplify crepe making.

Roll these crepes around Strawberries Romanoff (page 283), maple-sweetened whipped tofu, or even creamed tempeh and shiitakes.

1   tablespoon potato starch or gluten flour
1   cup all-purpose flour
½   teaspoon salt
2   tablespoons vegan margarine, melted
½   cup soymilk
Oil or nonstick cooking spray

Food processor method: Place the dry ingredients in the bowl of a food processor. With the motor running, drizzle ¾ cup of water through the feed tube until a paste forms. Add the margarine and soymilk—the texture of the batter should be between those of pancake batter and soymilk. Put the batter into a bowl, cover, and let rest at least 2 hours at room temperature or for 8 hours or more in the refrigerator.

Manual method: Combine the dry ingredients in a medium mixing bowl. With a wooden spoon, stir ¾ cup of water into the dry ingredients, being careful not to form lumps. The dough will be stiff and a little hard to work. Persevere because it is this step that develops the gluten. Beat the margarine into the dough. Gradually add the soymilk. When the dough has become a thick batter, whisk until smooth. If the batter is lumpy, strain it through a fine wire sieve, discarding any hard bits of dough. Cover the batter and let rest at least 2 hours at room temperature or for 8 hours or more in the refrigerator.

To cook the crepes, heat the pan over medium heat for a few minutes Set the batter in a convenient spot near the pan and place a small ladle in it. When the pan is hot, turn the heat to high. Lightly brush the bottom of the pan with oil or coat with cooking spray. Hold the pan at a 45° angle to the stove. Place a ladleful of batter at the bottom of the pan. Quickly tilt the pan with a circular motion to distribute the batter evenly. The batter will be cooking as it hits the pan. When an even layer of batter covers the bottom of the pan, put the pan back on the heat. Cook the crepe until small bubbles form on the top, about 2 to 3 minutes. Flip the crepe with a rubber spatula or superior pan-flipping technique, and cook on the other side for about a minute or until just lightly browned. It may take a couple of tries to get the pan temperature, amount of batter, and wrist action just right. Don't be discouraged. Just eat your mistakes and try again.

Place the cooked crepes on a dinner plate and cover with a clean kitchen towel to keep them warm.

Makes 24 crepes.

Buckwheat Cakes

This make-ahead batter is perfect for those mornings when time is limited but hunger is not. Use a nonmetal bowl or container that can hold 8 cups because the batter will expand in the night. The dough will keep for 2 or 3 days before it becomes sour.

2   tablespoons molasses
2   teaspoons (1 package) dry active yeast
1   cup soymilk
2   cups buckwheat flour
1   cup all-purpose flour
1   teaspoon salt
Oil or nonstick cooking spray

Dissolve the molasses in 2 cups of warm water. Sprinkle the yeast on top of the water. Let yeast stand for 5 to 10 minutes or until it is foamy. Whisk the soymilk into the yeast, breaking up any lumps that may have formed. Stir in the flours and salt. Combine thoroughly but do not overmix. Cover and refrigerate for 8 or more hours.

When ready to cook, remove the dough from the refrigerator and stir it down. Heat a heavy skillet or griddle over medium to medium-high heat. Brush lightly with oil or coat with nonstick cooking spray. When the griddle is hot, drop the batter by tablespoonfuls. Do not crowd the pan. Cook the pancakes until bubbles form on the tops and the edges appear firm. Turn the pancakes with a spatula and cook on the other side until they are puffed and are golden brown on the bottom.

Serve immediately or reserve in a warm oven.

Makes 6 servings.

Waffles

1 tablespoon egg replacer
   mixed with ¼ cup water
1 cup soymilk
2 tablespoons oil
1 cup whole wheat pastry
   flour
½ cup all-purpose flour
1 tablespoon baking powder
2 teaspoons sugar
½ teaspoon salt
Nonstick cooking spray or
   additional oil

Whisk the egg replacer, soymilk, and oil together. Stir in the dry ingredients and mix until blended. Heat the waffle iron and spray with cooking spray or brush with oil. Pour in just enough batter to fill the iron. Close and bake until the waffle has puffed up and steam stops coming from the sides.

Makes 6 to 8 waffles.

Toppings for Pancakes, Crepes, and Waffles

Raspberry Sauce

½ cup seedless raspberry
   preserves (preferably an
   all-fruit variety)
2 tablespoons Framboise
   liqueur or water
Tiniest pinch salt
¼ cup fresh or frozen
   raspberries

In a small saucepan, thin the preserves with the liqueur or water and warm all the way through. Add the salt. Just before serving, add the raspberries. Heat thoroughly and serve.

Makes ¾ cup.

Spiced Blueberry Sauce

1 pint fresh blueberries
½ cup sugar
1 stick cinnamon
1 whole clove
Pinch salt
2 teaspoons cornstarch
2 tablespoons lemon juice

Place the fresh blueberries in a small saucepan with the sugar. Add the cinnamon, clove, and salt. Add enough water to cover the blueberries by 1 inch. Turn the heat to high. When the blueberries have just begun to burst, remove the pan from the heat. Dissolve the cornstarch in the lemon juice. Add to the hot blueberries. If the mixture doesn't thicken right away, return the pan to a low heat and cook with occasional stirring for 3 to 5 minutes. Remove cinnamon stick and clove before serving.

Makes about 2 cups.

Strawberries Romanoff

1 pint of fresh
   strawberries
¼ to ½ cup sugar
1 teaspoon fresh orange
   zest
½ cup Cointreau or orange
   liquer

Wash and hull the strawberries. Cut the strawberries into quarters (or smaller if they are large). Add the sugar, orange zest, and Cointreau or orange liqueur. Allow the fruit to macerate overnight.

Makes about 2 cups.

Spiced Apple Maple Sauce

1 tart apple
1 teaspoon oil
½ cup maple syrup
½ cup applesauce
1 teaspoon lemon juice
¼ teaspoon ground
   cinnamon
⅛ teaspoon ground nutmeg
Pinch salt

Cut the apple into ½-inch chunks. Heat the oil in a small saucepan over medium heat. When the pan is hot, put the apples in the pan and allow them to cook until they caramelize slightly. In a bowl, whisk the maple syrup with applesauce, ¼ cup of water, lemon juice, cinnamon, nutmeg, and salt. Add to the pan and cook until the apples are crisp-tender.

Makes about 2 cups.

Coffee Cake

⅓ cup brown sugar
⅓ cup whole wheat flour
½ teaspoon ground cinnamon
⅓ cup chopped nuts
   (optional)
2 tablespoons canola oil
1 cup all-purpose flour
⅔ cup sugar
¾ teaspoon baking soda
½ teaspoon ground
   cinnamon
¼ teaspoon ground nutmeg
¼ teaspoon salt
⅔ cup vegan sour cream or
   6 ounces silken tofu
   blended with 1 tablespoon
   lemon juice and 1
   tablespoon oil
2 teaspoons vanilla extract

Mix the brown sugar, whole wheat flour, cinnamon, and nuts. Add the oil and blend. If the mixture is too crumbly to make a good streusel, add 1 tablespoon of water and blend until it resembles coarse crumbs.

Grease an 8-inch square baking dish. Preheat the oven to 350°.

Mix the all-purpose flour, sugar, baking soda, cinnamon, nutmeg, and salt in a medium bowl. Stir in the sour cream and vanilla. Stir just until the mixture is blended. Pour the batter into the prepared pan. Top evenly with the streusel mixture. Bake for 25 to 30 minutes.

Makes 8 servings.

Scones

This is a basic recipe. Blueberries, chocolate chips, or diced apricots can easily be substituted for the currants. If you are using a very moist fruit, reduce the soymilk. For best results, cut the margarine into small cubes and chill well in the refrigerator or freezer.

2 cups all-purpose flour
1 tablespoon baking
   powder
¼ cup sugar
⅛ teaspoon salt
4 tablespoons vegan
   margarine
¼ cup currants or chopped
   raisins
1 cup soymilk
Soymilk for brushing

Preheat the oven to 375°. Combine the flour, baking powder, sugar, and salt in a large bowl and mix well. Cut in the margarine with a pastry cutter, two knives, or in a food processor until the mixture resembles a coarse meal. Add the currants and mix well. Add the soymilk and stir just until the dough holds together. Put the dough on a floured surface and knead 10 times. Over-kneading will make the scones tough.

Roll the dough into a square about 1 inch thick. Cut the square into quarters. Cut the resulting squares into halves to form triangles. Place the scones 1 inch apart on an ungreased baking sheet. Brush the tops of the scones with soymilk if desired. Bake for 15 minutes or until golden brown.

Makes 8 scones.

Date-Oat Bran Scones

1 cup oat bran
1½ cups all-purpose flour
1 tablespoon baking powder
½ teaspoon baking soda
½ teaspoon salt
½ teaspoon ground
   cardamom
⅛ teaspoon ground cinnamon
⅛ teaspoon ground nutmeg
8 ounces pitted date pieces
½ cup cold vegan
   margarine, cut into cubes
¾ cup soymilk or rice milk
1 teaspoon vanilla extract
Soymilk for brushing
2 tablespoons rolled oats

Preheat the oven to 375°.

Mix the oat bran, flour, baking powder, baking soda, spices, and dates together. Cut the margarine into the flour mixture with a pastry cutter, two knives, or in a food processor until it resembles coarse meal. Add the soymilk and vanilla. Mix just until the dough holds together. Put the dough on a floured surface and knead 10 times. Overkneading will make the scones tough.

Roll the dough into a circle about 1 inch thick. Cut the circle into 8 wedges. Place the scones 1 inch apart on an ungreased baking sheet. Brush the scones with soymilk and sprinkle with the rolled oats. Bake for 15 minutes or until golden brown.

Makes 8 scones.

Good Morning Muffins

These muffins will give you a jump start on eating right for the day.

1   cup whole wheat pastry
    flour
1/4 cup soy flour
1   cup all-purpose flour
1   tablespoon baking
    powder
1/2 teaspoon ground
    cinnamon
1/4 teaspoon ground nutmeg
1/4 teaspoon ground
    allspice or mace
1/2 teaspoon salt
1/2 cup sugar
1/2 cup raisins
2   tablespoons flaxseeds
1/4 cup molasses
1/2 cup applesauce
1   cup soymilk
1/4 cup oil

Preheat the oven to 375°. Spray a 12-cup muffin tin with nonstick cooking spray and fit paper liners into the cups if desired.

In a medium mixing bowl, combine the flours, baking powder, cinnamon, nutmeg, allspice, salt, and sugar. Add the raisins and toss to coat with the flour mixture. Purée the flaxseeds with 2 tablespoons of water. In a small bowl, whisk the molasses, puréed flaxseeds, and applesauce until well blended. Whisk the soymilk and oil into the applesauce mixture.

Add the wet ingredients to the dry ingredients and stir just until the mixture is blended. Fill the muffin tins two-thirds full. Bake for 20 to 25 minutes.

Makes 12 muffins.

Polka Dot Muffins

Can't get the kids to eat hot cream of wheat? They'll never suspect that these charming little muffins are packed with iron. Use a chunky jam for this one—jelly will make a mess. If you are using oil instead of margarine, reduce the soymilk to ¾ of a cup and add an extra ¼ cup of flour.

1¼ cups all-purpose flour
1   cup uncooked cream of
    wheat
1/2 cup sugar
1   tablespoon plus 2
    teaspoons baking
    powder
1/2 teaspoon salt
1   cup soymilk
3/4 cup vegan margarine,
    melted
1   teaspoon vanilla extract
12 teaspoons jam

Preheat the oven to 375°. Spray a 12-cup muffin tin with nonstick cooking spray and fit paper liners into the cups if desired.

In a medium bowl, combine the flour, cream of wheat, sugar, baking powder, and salt and mix well. Add the soymilk, margarine, and vanilla. Stir just until the ingredients are blended.

Divide the batter among the 12 muffin cups. Poke a small indentation into the top of each muffin. Drop 1 teaspoon of jam into each indentation. Bake for 35 minutes.

Makes 12 muffins.

Blueberry Bran Muffins

Do you feel deprived when you choose a bran muffin over a blueberry one, but do you feel guilty if you just get the blueberry? Don't hurt your brain like that in the morning! These muffins give you the best of both worlds. Use a bran cereal that is fortified with vitamin B-12.

If you are using frozen blueberries, do not defrost them before mixing them into the batter—unless you like blue food.

1   cup All-Bran cereal
1   cup raw wheat germ
½ cup oil
1   cup soy-gurt
1   cup soymilk
1   teaspoon vanilla
      extract
1   cup all-purpose flour
½ cup soy flour
1   tablespoon baking
      powder
1   teaspoon baking soda
½ teaspoon salt
1   cup sugar
1½ cups blueberries, fresh
      or frozen

Preheat the oven to 375°. Spray a 12-cup muffin tin with nonstick cooking spray and fit paper liners into the cups if desired.

In a medium bowl, mix the cereal, wheat germ, oil, soy-gurt, milk, and vanilla. Let the mixture stand for a few minutes while you assemble the dry ingredients.

In a large bowl, mix the flours, baking powder, baking soda, salt, and sugar. Add the wet ingredients to the dry ingredients and stir just until they are blended. Gently fold in the blueberries, being careful that they don't burst. Fill the muffin tins about two-thirds full. Bake for 25 to 30 minutes.

Makes 12 muffins.

desserts

Cakes

Everyday Chocolate Cake
Company Chocolate Cake
Chocolate Raspberry Torte
Yellow Cake

Carrot Cake
Gingerbread
Cheesecake

Frostings

Chocolate Icing
Chocolate Glaze
Thin Chocolate Ganache
Thick Chocolate Ganache

Fluffy White Icing
Tofu Walnut Frosting
Lemon Glaze

Bars, Cookies, and Candy

Brownies
Oatmeal Ginger Bars
Linzer Cookie Squares
Chocolate Chip Cookies

Sugar Cookies
Chocolate Raisin Fudge
Peanut Butter Candy

Puddings

Easy Chocolate Pudding
Vanilla Pudding
Lebanese Rice Pudding

Mango Tapioca Pudding
Coconut Flan

Pies and Fruit Crisps

Shortening Crust
Oil Crust
Mango Cream Pie

Apple Cranberry Pie
Easy Peach Crisp
Pear Betty

Frozen Desserts

Soft-Serve Ice Cream
Strawberry-Banana Blast Ice Cream

Watermelon Ice

Learning to make your favorite desserts without butter or eggs can be a challenge. Fortunately, with a little planning you can still indulge your taste for sweets. Here are some tips on equipment, ingredients, and baking techniques that will help you create mouth-watering vegan desserts.

Pans: Vegan baked goods stick and burn more easily because they lack the lecithin found in eggs and because they use oil instead of butter. Therefore, I highly recommend that you invest in a heavy-gauge, insulated, air-bake cake pan and cookie sheet—especially if your oven has uneven temperature control. These pans are more forgiving than other types of pans.

To help prevent baked goods from sticking, add a small amount of liquid lecithin to a dough or batter or to the oil or shortening used to grease the pans. You can also line the pans with parchment or waxed paper, then grease the paper before baking. For cakes, sprinkle flour on the oiled parchment, shake until it is evenly distributed, then tap out the excess.

Shortening and margarine: Use shortenings and margarines which do not contain hydrogenated fats. There are a few brands on the market which use expeller pressed palm oil to produce a neutral, white shortening which is great for vegan baking.

When substituting shortening for butter, add 1 tablespoon of water to the recipe for each $\frac{1}{2}$ cup of shortening.

When substituting margarine for butter, use an equal amount. When substituting margarine for shortening, reduce the liquid in the recipe by $1\frac{1}{2}$ tablespoons for each $\frac{1}{2}$ cup (or stick) of margarine used. See the discussion of fats and oils for more details, pages 24–29.

Egg replacers: Eggs provide leavening, strengthen gluten to provide elasticity, retain moisture, give a good "crumb," and help distribute fat evenly throughout the product. Don't be fooled by those cartons of egg replacers in the dairy section: they are all based on eggs themselves, usually the whites.

EnerG makes an easy-to-use egg replacement powder. Mix $1\frac{1}{2}$ teaspoons of powder with 2 tablespoons of water to make a reasonable substitution for one whole egg (in baking, not over-easy or in quiche). One package replaces $9\frac{1}{2}$ dozen eggs, which explains the hefty price tag.

For most recipes in which eggs are not a major ingredient, you can use $1\frac{1}{2}$ tablespoons of oil, $1\frac{1}{2}$ tablespoons of water, 1 teaspoon of baking powder, and a tiny drizzle of liquid soy lecithin in place of one egg. If you want to reduce the fat content of the recipe, you may substitute 3 tablespoons applesauce, mashed banana, or mashed potato plus 1 teaspoon baking powder for one egg. One tablespoon flaxseed blended with 1 tablespoon of water makes an acceptable substitute, though you may need to add more leavening. See the discussion of flaxseed oil on page 27.

To date, there is no good substitute for egg whites.

Flours: In most recipes, a good quality, soft whole wheat pastry flour can substitute for the all purpose flour. One-fourth of the all-purpose flour can be replaced by soy flour with no additional adjustments. If you are using whole soy flour (not de-fatted), make sure the flour smells fresh before using it. Compared to wheat flour, most other flours have a low gluten content. Gluten forms the structure of the baked good. Guar gum and xanthan gum improve the quality of gluten-free baked goods by helping to trap air, binding water, and improving elasticity. To substitute a low-gluten flour for wheat flour, use $3/4$ cup of alternate flour, $1/4$ cup of potato starch, and $1/4$ teaspoon of guar or xanthan gum.

Technique: You probably don't realize it, but when you are beating margarine and sugar together or puréeing tofu with oil and sugar, you are helping to form the air pockets that will keep your baked goods light. That is why it is very important that you take some care with this step. Margarine and shortening should be soft enough to beat with a spoon but not so soft that they are runny or don't hold a shape when the sugar is incorporated. Cut the cold margarine into small cubes and sprinkle the sugar over it before you beat them together. Beat them thoroughly, until the mixture is pale and fluffy. Introducing air mechanically allows you to use less chemical leavening.

Most chemical leavening agents release their carbon dioxide—the gas that gets trapped and makes baked goods rise—when liquid first hits them. This is why so many recipes admonish you to work quickly, stirring just until all ingredients are mixed before pouring into a prepared pan. Overmixing releases the carbon dioxide from the batter and significantly reduces the leavening action.

CAKES

Where there's a cake, there's a celebration— even if you're just celebrating the end of a meal. I'm not sure that cakes can ever be considered healthful in the same way salads are, but omitting them from our celebrations of life's major milestones would certainly be harmful to our mental health.

Everyday Chocolate Cake

Most people would not consider changing their eating habits if it meant giving up chocolate cake. So thank goodness there are plenty of recipes for vegan chocolate cake—even The Joy of Cooking *has one.*

This is a quick, easy cake. It's not terribly sophisticated, but it certainly hits the chocolate spot. This cake is moist enough to eat plain or sprinkled with confectioners' sugar, but who's going to argue with chocolate icing?

¾ cup boiling water
½ cup cocoa powder
1 tablespoon instant coffee powder
1 cup soy mayonnaise (see the note below for a substitution)
2 teaspoons vanilla extract
2½ cups flour
2 teaspoons baking soda
1 cup sugar
1 recipe Chocolate Icing (page 297, optional)

Preheat the oven to 350°. Cut 2 8-inch rounds of waxed or parchment paper. Lightly grease the bottoms of 2 8-inch round cake pans. Fit the waxed paper into the bottoms of the cake pans. Grease and flour the sides and bottoms.

In a small bowl, whisk the boiling water into the cocoa powder and instant coffee. Allow the mixture to cool. Whisk the mayonnaise and vanilla extract into the cocoa mixture. Mix the flour, soda, and sugar together. Add the cocoa mixture and ½ cup of cold water to the dry ingredients and stir just until the ingredients are blended but with no large lumps. Pour the batter into the prepared pan and bake for 25 to 30 minutes. The cake will not pull away from the side of the pan until after it begins cooling, so touch the top of the cake to determine doneness. Allow the cakes to cool in the pans and invert to remove them.

If icing the cake, when the cake is cool, trim the rounded tops off the layers so they will be even. Place one layer, bottom up, on a cake plate. (This will help prevent crumbs from mixing in with the icing.) Spread one-third of the icing to within 1 inch of the cake's edge. Place the second cake layer, bottom up, on top of the first. Spread most of the remaining icing on the top of the cake, leaving a thick border of icing around the edge. Carefully work the icing from the edge, down the side of the cake. Rotate the cake and continue until there is an even layer of icing covering the whole cake.

Makes 8 to 12 servings (2 8-inch cake layers).

Note: You may make your own substitute for soy mayonnaise by combining 6 ounces of tofu, 2 teaspoons of lime juice, 1 teaspoon of lecithin, 1 tablespoon of vegetable oil, and ½ teaspoon of salt in a blender.

Company Chocolate Cake

This is a more refined cake, with a more delicate crumb, than the Everyday Chocolate Cake above. It requires a quick hand and a watchful eye but is well worth the attention. If your oven is temperamental, as my home oven is, keep a close eye on it during the first 10 minutes of baking. If the oven is too hot, the cake will rise too quickly and then fall.

This recipe requires vegetable shortening. The margarines I tried were not able to retain enough air during the beating process. So while it's desirable to avoid hydrogenated fats, you can make an exception for this cake as long as you don't eat the whole thing in one sitting.

2 ounces unsweetened chocolate
$\frac{1}{2}$ cup (8 tablespoons) vegetable shortening
$1\frac{1}{2}$ cups sugar
1 tablespoon oil
2 teaspoons vanilla extract
$2\frac{1}{2}$ cups cake flour
$1\frac{1}{2}$ teaspoons baking powder
$1\frac{1}{2}$ teaspoons baking soda
1 recipe Chocolate Icing (page 297) or Thin Chocolate Ganache (page 298)

Preheat the oven to 350°. Cut 2 8-inch rounds of waxed or parchment paper. Lightly grease the bottom of 2 8-inch round cake pans. Fit the waxed paper into the bottom of the cake pans. Grease and flour the sides and bottoms of the pans.

Melt the chocolate and cool to room temperature. Beat the shortening and sugar until well blended. Add the oil and beat until the mixture is quite fluffy and forms a ball. Beat in the cooled chocolate. (Do not add the chocolate warm.) Beat in the vanilla extract. Add the flour, baking powder, baking soda, and $1\frac{1}{2}$ cups of cold water. Working very quickly, beat all the ingredients together just until they are mixed. The batter will be a bit stiff. Divide the batter between the prepared pans and smooth the tops. Bake on the center rack of the oven for 20 to 30 minutes or just until the cakes begin to pull away from the sides of the pans and the centers feel set. Allow the cakes to cool in the pans and invert to remove them.

When the cake is cool, trim the rounded tops off of the layers so they are even. Place one layer, bottom up, on a cake plate. (This will help prevent crumbs from mixing in with the icing.) Spread one-third of the icing (or ganache) to within 1 inch of the cake's edge. Place the second cake layer, bottom up, on top of the first. Spread most of the remaining icing on the top of the cake, leaving a thick border of icing around the edge. Carefully work the icing from the edge down the side of the cake. Rotate the cake and continue until there is an even layer of icing covering the whole cake. Use any leftover icing to patch any remaining bare spots.

Makes 8 to 12 servings (2 8-inch cake layers).

Chocolate Raspberry Torte

This recipe uses Company Chocolate Cake, Thin Chocolate Ganache, and Thick Chocolate Raspberry Ganache to create a sophisticated dessert. If you do not plan to decorate the top of the cake with the Thick Chocolate Raspberry Ganache, one recipe will be enough to fill the cake.

The jam layer prevents the cake from absorbing the Thick Chocolate Raspberry Ganache. When left overnight, the cake will absorb much of the Thin Chocolate Ganache topping. If you are concerned about presentation, you may want to use the Chocolate Glaze instead. When preparing this recipe, be sure to make the ganaches or glaze in the order described in the method.

2   Company Chocolate Cake layers, unfrosted (page 292)
1   12-ounce jar seedless raspberry preserves
¼   cup raspberry liqueur
2   recipes Thick Chocolate Raspberry Ganache (page 298)
1   generous pint fresh raspberries
1   recipe Thin Chocolate Ganache (page 298) or 2 recipes Chocolate Glaze (page 297)

When the cake layers are cool, trim the rounded tops off of the layers to make them flat. Cut each layer into halves horizontally. You may do this with a long knife, or use a long length of dental floss as a saw to cut the layers. Melt the raspberry preserves with the raspberry liqueur. Brush each of the four layers with the warm raspberry preserves. Reserve the flattest, most uniform layer for the top of the cake.

Make the Thick Chocolate Raspberry Ganache and spoon ½ cup of it into a pastry bag fitted with a decorative tip and reserve in a cool place. Evenly divide the remaining ganache among the three bottom layers and spread evenly.

Reserve 12 beautiful raspberries for garnishing the top of the cake. Divide the remaining raspberries evenly among the bottom three layers of the cake.

Assemble the torte, placing the reserved layer, cut side down, on top of the bottom layers. Make the Thin Chocolate Ganache or Chocolate Glaze after the cake has been assembled. Immediately frost the cake. Allow the frosting to cool. Use the pastry bag filled with Thick Chocolate Raspberry Ganache to pipe 12 swirls around the top edge of the cake. If the ganache in the pastry bag doesn't hold its shape on piping, refrigerate briefly until it does. Place a raspberry on each swirl. Chill the cake for an hour or so or until the icings have set.

Makes 12 servings.

Yellow Cake

1½ cups flour
1 cup sugar
1 teaspoon baking soda
½ teaspoon salt
½ cup oil
1 cup soymilk
1 tablespoon vanilla extract
1 tablespoon vinegar
1 recipe Fluffy White Icing (page 299)

Preheat the oven to 350°. Cut an 8-inch round of waxed or parchment paper. Lightly grease the bottom of an 8-inch round cake pan. Fit the waxed paper into the bottom of the cake pan. Grease and flour the side and bottom of the pan.

In a medium mixing bowl, whisk the flour, sugar, baking soda, and salt together. Add the oil, soymilk, and vanilla extract to the flour mixture and whisk until smooth. Add the vinegar to the batter, mix briefly, and immediately pour into the prepared pan. Bake on the center rack of the oven for 20 to 30 minutes or just until the cake begins to pull away from the side of the pan and the center of the cake feels set. Let cool in the pan for 2 minutes and invert onto a serving plate. Fill and frost with Fluffy White Icing.

Makes 6 servings (1 8-inch cake layer).

Carrot Cake

1¾ cups whole wheat flour
½ cup soy flour
¼ cup shredded coconut
¾ cup walnuts (optional)
½ teaspoon salt
1½ teaspoons baking powder
1 teaspoon ground cinnamon
¼ teaspoon ground nutmeg
¼ teaspoon ground allspice
Zest of 1 lemon
3 tablespoons oil
1 cup maple syrup
¼ cup molasses
¼ cup raisins
2½ cups grated carrots
1 recipe Tofu Walnut Frosting (page 299)

Preheat the oven to 350°. Grease and flour 2 9-inch round cake pans or 1 9x13-inch pan. Combine the flours, coconut, walnuts, salt, baking powder, cinnamon, nutmeg, allspice, and lemon zest in a large bowl and mix well. Combine the oil, syrup, molasses, ¼ cup of water, raisins, and carrots in a large bowl and beat until light. Add the flour mixture and mix just until blended. Do not overmix. Pour the batter into the pans and smooth the tops. Bake for 30 to 40 minutes or until a wooden toothpick inserted in the center comes out clean. Let cool in the pan for 2 minutes and invert onto a serving plate. Frost with Tofu Walnut Frosting.

Makes 12 servings.

Gingerbread

Serve this perennial favorite plain, with applesauce, or topped with Lemon Glaze (page 299) or Fluffy White Icing (page 299).

1   stick vegan margarine
1   cup sugar
2   teaspoons grated fresh
    ginger
1/2   cup molasses
2 1/2 cups whole wheat
    pastry flour
1   tablespoon baking soda
1/2   teaspoon salt
2   teaspoons powdered
    ginger

Preheat the oven to 350°. Cut an 8-inch round of waxed or parchment paper. Lightly grease the bottom of an 8-inch round cake pan. Fit the waxed paper into the bottom of the cake pan. Grease and flour the side and bottom of the pan.

In a large bowl, beat the margarine, sugar, and fresh ginger together until the mixture is light and fluffy. In a separate small bowl, mix the molasses with 1/2 cup of warm water. In another bowl, mix the flour, baking soda, salt, and powdered ginger together. Add the molasses mixture to the margarine-and-sugar mixture. Add the flour mixture and stir just until the ingredients are blended but with no large lumps. Pour the batter into the prepared pan and bake for 35 minutes or until a toothpick comes out clean. Allow the gingerbread to cool in the pan and invert to remove.

Makes 8 servings.

Cheesecake

Cheesecake can be tricky. I regulate the oven temperature by cracking the oven door if the cake seems to be cooking too quickly. This cake does not brown at all, so if it begins to develop color in the first 15 minutes of baking, your oven temperature is too high. You may also bake the cake in a water bath. Place the cheesecake pan in a baking dish large enough to hold it with at least an inch all around. Pull the center rack of the oven out halfway and set the pans in the center. Pour boiling water in the bottom pan until the water reaches halfway up the side of the cheesecake pan. Cooking time may or may not be affected, depending on your oven.

½ cup whole wheat pastry flour
¼ cup toasted wheat germ
½ cup ground almonds
2 tablespoons vegan margarine, softened
2 tablespoons oil
Pinch salt
2 pounds silken tofu
1 cup sugar
½ cup maple syrup
¼ cup oil
½ cup soymilk
2 tablespoons cornstarch or ¼ cup all-purpose flour
1½ tablespoons lemon juice
2 tablespoons orange juice or water
Zest of 1 orange or lemon
2 tablespoons Grand Marnier
1½ teaspoons vanilla extract

Preheat the oven to 275°. Combine the flour, wheat germ, ground almonds, margarine, oil, and salt in a medium bowl and mix until the mixture resembles crumbs. Press the mixture into the bottom of an 8- or 9-inch springform pan or a cake pan. Lightly grease the sides of the pan.

Squeeze the tofu to remove excess water. In a blender or food processor, purée the tofu, sugar, maple syrup, and oil. When the mixture is quite smooth, add the remaining ingredients and purée again until quite smooth. Pour the batter over the crust and bake in the center of the oven for 15 minutes. Insert a dinner knife between the cake and the pan. Slide the knife around the perimeter of the pan to separate the cake from the side of the pan. This will simplify the removal of the cake from the pan later. Repeat this procedure a couple more times during baking and again when you remove the cake from the oven. The cake is done when it stops jiggling in the center when shaken, about 1¼ to 1½ hours total baking time. Allow the cheesecake to cool completely in the pan. If the cake does not begin to fall out of the pan when you carefully invert it, place the pan on the burner at *very* low heat for 30 seconds and then try again.

Makes 8 to 12 servings.

Chocolate Cheesecake: Melt ⅔ cup of semisweet chocolate chips, cool them to room temperature, and add to the batter just before pouring into the shell.

FROSTINGS

Chocolate Icing

This is just like the icings we used to make when I was a child. The only difference is the use of vegan margarine and 10X sugar. If you can't locate vegan 10X sugar, process 2 cups of vegan sugar with 1 tablespoon cornstarch in a food processor until the sugar is quite fine. If the blades on your food processor are not sharp enough, process the sugar in batches in a coffee grinder or blender.

⅓ cup semisweet vegan chocolate chips
1 stick (8 tablespoons) vegan margarine
3 cups 10X confectioners' sugar
2 tablespoons soymilk
Pinch salt
1 teaspoon vanilla extract

Melt the chocolate and cool to room temperature. Beat the margarine, sugar, soymilk, salt, and vanilla extract together until the icing is quite fluffy. Beat the cooled chocolate into the icing.

Makes enough to frost 2 8-inch cake layers.

Chocolate Glaze

3 ounces semisweet vegan chocolate chips
1 tablespoon vegan margarine
1 tablespoon corn syrup

Melt the chocolate chips in a small bowl or pan. While the chocolate is still hot, add the margarine and syrup. Stir until ingredients are well blended. Immediately pour over cake and allow to drip over the sides.

Makes enough to drizzle over 1 8-inch cake layer.

Thin Chocolate Ganache

Ganache is a thin, rich chocolate icing. This version can be spread over a warm cake to give an elegant, glossy finish. This recipe has a higher water content than traditional ganache, so it will be absorbed over time by baked goods. However, the fat content of this ganache is significantly lower—and I prefer the taste and texture. If you are icing a cake ahead of time and want a more attractive appearance, you may opt for the Chocolate Glaze (page 297).

⅓ cup semisweet vegan chocolate chips
2 ounces tofu, at room temperature
1 tablespoon maple syrup
1 small dribble lecithin
1 teaspoon vanilla extract
2 tablespoons vegan margarine, softened

Melt the chocolate chips. Blend the tofu, syrup, lecithin, vanilla extract, 2 tablespoons of hot water, and margarine until smooth. Add the melted chocolate while still warm and blend thoroughly. Spread over a warm cake. If the ganache has hardened or the cake is cold, spread the ganache as much as you can, then place the plate with the half-iced cake in a slightly warm oven until the ganache becomes workable. Remove the cake from the oven and spread the ganache over the cake.

Makes enough to glaze 2 8-inch cake layers.

Thick Chocolate Ganache

This is the type of ganache used as filling. Any rum or liqueur can be used.

½ cup semisweet vegan chocolate chips
2 ounces tofu, at room temperature
1 tablespoon maple syrup
1 small dribble lecithin
1 teaspoon vanilla extract
2 tablespoons vegan margarine, softened
1 tablespoon liqueur or dark rum, or 2 teaspoons vanilla extract or rum extract

Melt the chocolate chips. Blend the tofu, syrup, lecithin, vanilla extract, and margarine together in a food processor or blender. Add the melted chocolate while still warm. Allow the ganache to cool in the processor or blender. When the ganache seems fairly stiff, add the liqueur or extract and blend until it is light and fluffy.

Makes enough to generously fill an 8-inch, 2-layer cake.

Thick Chocolate Raspberry Ganache: For the liqueur, rum, or extract, sustitute 1 tablespoon of Framboise, raspberry brandy, or raspberry extract.

Fluffy White Icing

4 ounces firm tofu, at
    room temperature
1 tablespoon maple syrup
2 cups 10X confectioners'
    sugar
1 small dribble lecithin
1 tablespoon lemon juice
Pinch salt
3 tablespoons vegan
    margarine, softened
2 teaspoons vanilla extract

Squeeze the excess water from the tofu. Combine all the ingredients in a blender or food processor and purée. Let the icing rest in the blender or food processor for 5 to 20 minutes, until the mixture seems fairly thick. If you are using a blender, put the icing in a bowl and chill slightly during the resting time. When the icing seems fairly stiff, whisk or process again until the icing is light and fluffy.

Makes enough to generously frost 1 8-inch cake layer.

Tofu Walnut Frosting

¾ cup walnuts
1 pound tofu
⅓ cup maple syrup
¼ cup coconut
1 tablespoon vanilla
    extract
1 cup coarsely chopped
    walnuts

Process the ¾ cup of walnuts in a food processor until they are a fine powder but have not become pasty. Add the tofu and blend thoroughly. Add the maple syrup, coconut, and vanilla extract and process until thoroughly blended. Add a little soymilk if the mixture seems too thick.

Spread the icing evenly over the cooled cake. Press the chopped walnuts into the side of the cake or sprinkle on top.

Makes enough to frost and fill 2 9-inch cake layers.

Lemon Glaze

1 cup 10X confectioners'
    sugar
2 teaspoons lemon juice

Whisk all the ingredients and 2 tablespoons of water in a bowl until there are no lumps. Use immediately.

Makes enough to glaze 1 9-inch cake layer.

BARS, COOKIES, AND CANDY

Most people can't resist a chewy chocolate brownie or warm chocolate chip cookie. Cookies are an anytime treat. Eaten from your hand, they don't require a plate, fork, or knife, though you may want a napkin for the crumbs at the edge of your mouth.

Brownies

½ cup very hot espresso or strong coffee
⅓ cup cocoa
1 cup sugar
1 teaspoon vanilla extract
⅓ cup vegetable oil, preferably grapeseed or canola
1¼ cups all-purpose flour
1 teaspoon baking powder
¼ teaspoon salt

Preheat the oven to 350°. Grease an 8-inch square baking pan. Whisk the hot coffee into the cocoa and sugar until smooth. Add the vanilla extract and oil and whisk to blend thoroughly. Stir in the remaining ingredients just until blended. Excessive stirring will toughen the brownies.

Pour the batter into the pan. Bake for 35 minutes. Let the brownies cool to room temperature before cutting.

Makes 12 brownies.

Oatmeal Ginger Bars

2 cups rolled oats
1½ cups flour
1 teaspoon baking powder
1 teaspoon ground ginger
1 cup sugar
½ teaspoon salt
¼ cup crystallized ginger, finely chopped
1 cup applesauce
½ cup vegetable oil
1 recipe Lemon Glaze (page 299)

Preheat the oven to 350°. Combine the oats, flour, baking powder, ginger, sugar, salt, and crystallized ginger. Add the applesauce and oil and stir just until blended. Pour the mixture into a greased and floured 9x13-inch pan. Bake for 20 to 25 minutes or until the bars feel set in the center. (The toothpick test is not reliable with applesauce-based baked goods.) When the cake is still slightly warm, cut it into bars and drizzle with Lemon Glaze.

Makes 24 bars.

Linzer Cookie Squares

These are easier to make and lower in fat than traditional Linzertorten, but have just as much flavor. Most any thick jam will work for the filling. All-fruit jams will run more during baking, so to avoid an unpleasant burnt jam mess, make sure the bottom layer of dough seals the pan tightly.

4 tablespoons vegan margarine
2 tablespoons oil
1/2 cup corn syrup or barley malt
1 1/2 cups flour
1/2 cup ground almonds
1 tablespoon baking powder
1 1/2 teaspoons salt
1/4 teaspoon ground nutmeg
1/4 teaspoon ground allspice
1/2 cup water or soymilk
1/2 teaspoon almond extract
1 teaspoon vanilla extract
3/4 cup raspberry jam, preferably seedless
1/2 cup sliced almonds (optional)

Preheat the oven to 375°. Grease an 11x7-inch baking pan. Beat the margarine, oil, and syrup until light and fluffy. Combine the flour, almonds, baking powder, salt, and spices in a bowl and mix well. Cut the dry ingredients into the margarine mixture until it resembles a coarse meal. Add the water or soymilk, almond extract, and vanilla extract and mix until a dough forms.

Press half the dough into the pan, making sure there are no cracks. Spread the jam over the dough. Crumble the remaining dough into tiny pieces over the jam. Press the dough together to form a solid layer of dough over the jam. Sprinkle the sliced almonds over the dough and gently press into the dough. Bake for 20 to 25 minutes. Let the bars cool before cutting them.

Makes 24 bars.

Chocolate Chip Cookies

2 sticks vegan margarine
1 1/2 cups Succanat or brown sugar
1 teaspoon vanilla extract
1/2 cup whole wheat pastry flour
1 1/2 cups all-purpose flour
1 teaspoon baking powder
1 teaspoon baking soda
1/8 teaspoon salt
2 cups vegan chocolate chips
1 cup chopped nuts (optional)

Preheat the oven to 375°. Lightly grease 2 cookie sheets or fit with parchment paper. In a large bowl, beat the margarine, sugar, and vanilla until the mixture is light and fluffy. Beat in 2 tablespoons of cold water. In a separate bowl, combine the flours, baking powder, soda, and salt. Stir the flour mixture into the margarine-sugar mixture. Add the chocolate chips and nuts.

Drop by heaping tablespoonfuls onto the prepared cookie sheets. Flatten the cookies slightly with your fingertips. Bake the cookies for 8 to 10 minutes or until the edges just begin to brown. Remove from the cookie sheet immediately and place on a cooling rack.

Make 36 cookies.

Sugar Cookies

2/3 cup sugar
3 tablespoons vegan margarine
2 tablespoons oil
1 tablespoon lemon juice
1 1/2 cups all-purpose flour
1/2 teaspoon baking soda

Preheat the oven to 375°. Cover 2 cookie sheets with parchment or spray with nonstick cooking spray. Beat the sugar with the margarine. Add the oil and lemon juice and beat until the mixture is light and fluffy. Add the flour and baking soda and mix until the dough forms a ball. Cover the dough with plastic wrap or waxed paper and refrigerate until thoroughly chilled.

Working on a lightly floured board, roll out half the dough to a thickness of about 1/8 to 1/4 inch. Cut out shapes with cookie cutters dipped into flour. Place the cookies on the prepared cookie sheets and bake for 8 to 10 minutes or until the edges of the cookies just begin to brown. You may use all of the dough or refrigerate a portion of the dough, wrapped in plastic wrap or waxed paper, for later use.

Make about 24 cookies.

Chocolate Raisin Fudge

2 cups semisweet vegan chocolate chips
1/2 cup raisins
12 ounces firm tofu, at room temperature
1/2 cup brown rice syrup
1 small dribble lecithin
1 teaspoon vanilla extract
1 stick vegan margarine, softened
1/2 cup chopped, toasted peanuts or hazelnuts

Oil an 8-inch square pan. Melt the chocolate chips. Soak the raisins in 3/4 cup of hot water for 10 minutes. Blend the tofu, syrup, lecithin, vanilla extract, and margarine together in a blender or food processor. Add the melted chocolate while still warm and process until smooth. Transfer the tofu mixture to a small mixing bowl. Drain the raisins. Stir in the raisins and nuts. Spread into the prepared pan. Let the fudge cool completely and then refrigerate for several hours.

Makes 16 squares.

Peanut Butter Candy

½ cup smooth peanut butter
½ cup brown rice syrup
1 cup toasted wheat germ
½ cup unsweetened shredded coconut or chopped nuts

Mix the peanut butter, syrup, and wheat germ. The mixture should be stiff enough to hold its shape but a bit sticky. Form the mixture into small balls. Roll the candies in the coconut or nuts and pat firmly.
    Makes 24 candies.

Chocolate Peanut Butter Candy: Add ½ cup of melted vegan chocolate chips to the initial mixture.

PUDDINGS

I find the cool, creamy texture of puddings, custards, and flan to be very soothing. There are several vegan pudding mixes for tofu available that are fast and easy. Even without a mix, tofu puddings are as easy as puréeing tofu with a little sweetener and enough soymilk to get the consistency you like, and perhaps adding a little vanilla or orange zest.
    When storing puddings, cover with plastic wrap touching the surface to prevent formation of a tough skin.

Easy Chocolate Pudding

12 ounces soft tofu
1 small banana
¼ to ½ cup vanilla soymilk
2 or 3 tablespoons chocolate syrup
1 teaspoon vanilla extract
Pinch salt

Purée all ingredients together in a blender or food processor. Pour into individual dessert glasses and chill.
    Makes 4 servings.

Vanilla Pudding

Use a full-flavored soymilk for this dessert. If the soymilk looks thin and watery, blend a couple of ounces of silken tofu into it. If you are using vanilla soymilk, reduce the sugar and use just 1 teaspoon of vanilla extract.

1/3 cup sugar
2 1/2 tablespoons cornstarch
1/8 teaspoon salt
2 cups creamy soymilk
2 teaspoons vanilla extract
2 tablespoons vegan margarine (optional)

In a heavy-bottomed, medium saucepan, mix the sugar, cornstarch, and salt. Whisk in the soymilk slowly so no lumps form. Cook the mixture over medium heat, stirring constantly, until it begins to thicken. Lower the heat and continue cooking for another minute or so until it is fairly thick. Add the vanilla extract and margarine. Pour the pudding into a bowl or 4 individual cups. Cover with plastic wrap, pressing the wrap so that it touches the surface of the pudding. (This will prevent the formation of a tough skin.) Refrigerate the pudding for several hours.

Makes 4 servings.

Lebanese Rice Pudding

2/3 cup cream of rice cereal, uncooked
2 cups water
1 cup soymilk (or 1 additional cup water)
1/2 cup Sugar Syrup (recipe follows) or 1/4 cup sugar
1/2 teaspoon cardamom
1/2 teaspoon ground cinnamon
1/2 teaspoon ground ginger
1/2 cup sugar syrup (recipe on page 305)
1 tablespoon chopped pistachios (optional)

Mix the cream of rice, water, and soymilk in a pan until smooth. Slowly bring to a simmer, and then cook over low heat, stirring constantly, until quite thick, about 15 minutes. Add the Sugar Syrup or sugar, cardamom, cinnamon, and ginger to the cream of rice and mix well.

Pour the pudding into 4 lightly oiled custard cups or 1 quart bowl. Tamp the cups or bowl against a counter to remove air bubbles and chill until set. Turn the puddings out onto dessert plates. Pour Sugar Syrup around the pudding and top with chopped nuts.

Makes 4 servings.

Sugar Syrup

1 cup sugar
¼ teaspoon orange blossom or rose water

Heat the sugar and ⅔ cup of water in a small pot over low heat, stirring, until the sugar melts. Bring the syrup to a boil with no further stirring. Wash down any sugar crystals that may form on the side of the pan with some cold water and a pastry brush. When the syrup has boiled for about 3 minutes, remove it from the heat and let cool to lukewarm. Add the orange blossom water (or rosewater), mix well, and chill thoroughly.

Makes about 1 cup.

Mango Tapioca Pudding

If you can't find mangoes, replace the water with mango or apricot nectar. In fact most fruit juices will work well here.

Mangoes can be intimidating if you are not accustomed to them. Examine the fruit to determine where the large flat seed is located. Then, using a sharp chef's knife, cut the mango halves away from the flat sides of the seed. Cut a checkerboard pattern into the flesh of each mango half with a paring knife, taking care not to cut through the skin. Place the mango half skin-side-down on a cutting board. Flatten the mango against the board. Slip the knife between the skin and the flesh to cut the pieces of flesh away from the skin. With a paring knife, peel the skin from the remaining flesh on the seed. Cut the flesh from the seed and cut into cubes. This may take some practice but once mastered, you will have many years of mango happiness. The cook's reward is that the pit can be gnawed and sucked to release the last of its goodness.

Don't pass by those small mangoes in your supermarket. Often these are much sweeter and less stringy than their larger cousins.

⅓ cup sugar
3 tablespoons quick-cooking tapioca
Pinch salt
1 large or 2 small mangoes, peeled, seeded, and chopped or puréed
½ cup fresh raspberries

Mix the sugar, tapioca, and salt in a medium saucepan. Whisk in 2 cups of water. Cover and let stand for 5 minutes.

Bring the mixture to a boil over medium heat. Cook for two minutes and remove from heat. Let cool to warm. Add the mango. Divide the pudding among 4 serving cups and chill. Just before serving, garnish with fresh raspberries.

Makes 4 servings.

Coconut Flan

If your agar is in a light, puffy block or long, thin strands, crumble well before using.

¾ cup sugar
1 14-ounce can unsweetened coconut milk
1¾ cups almond milk
½ cup sugar
1 tablespoon agar

Put the sugar in a small, heavy saucepan. Drizzle 2 tablespoons of water over the sugar. Do not stir. Place the pan over medium heat. When the sugar begins to melt, gently swirl the pan. If any sugar crystals stick to the sides, brush them down with a pastry brush dipped in a very small amount of cold water. When the sugar turns a very light amber color, remove from the stove. The sugar will continue to darken, so work quickly. Pour the caramel into ungreased custard cups or a 1-quart serving bowl and swirl to coat the bottom and a portion of the side with caramel. Do not pour caramel into all 4 custard cups at once or it may harden before you have a chance to swirl it.

Mix the coconut milk, almond milk, sugar, and agar in a small saucepan. Stir to dissolve the sugar; the agar may not fully dissolve until heated. Bring the mixture to a boil over medium heat. Reduce the heat to medium-low and simmer for 6 minutes, making sure that all of the agar has dissolved. Pour the flan into a bowl set over ice. Stir the flan until it has cooled from hot to warm (about 100°). Pour the flan on top of the caramelized sugar. Let stand for at least 2 hours or overnight.

Makes 4 servings.

PIES AND FRUIT CRISPS

Finding just the right touch with piecrust dough takes some experience. If dough is worked too much when mixing or handling, the gluten will develop and the crust will be tough. If it is not mixed enough, the fat won't be evenly distributed and the texture will be uneven.

I was lucky enough to be able to observe my mother as she rolled out perfect crusts every time. Practice makes perfect so get rolling! And if you're pressed for time or just feeling lazy, try a fruit crisp. These desserts combine the "pastry" with the fruit and are relatively quick and easy.

Here are general instructions for rolling and baking perfect piecrust.

Rolling the crust: On a lightly floured board, begin in the middle and lightly roll the dough into a circle, turning the dough as you go. If the dough sticks, run a floured hand under the crust. The dough circle should be 1 inch larger in diameter than the top of your pie pan and have an even thickness.

Fold the dough in half or roll it up onto the rolling pin and lay it over the pie pan. Gently fit the dough into the pan. Trim any dough so that 1 inch of dough hangs over the edge of the pan.

The top crust should be rolled out in the same fashion—perhaps a little thinner if the pie filling is voluminous, as in apple pies.

Blind baking: Crusts are prebaked for fully cooked fillings. "Blind" baking means that the crust is hidden from sight when it's being cooked. Just keep an eye on the edges and the middle will take care of itself. Preheat the oven to 400°. Prick the bottom of the piecrust all over with a fork. Place a piece of parchment or waxed paper over the crust. Fill the pie with weights or beans. Bake the crust until the edges just begin to brown, about 15 minutes, checking frequently to make sure that it is not browning too quickly.

Shortening Crust

This is an old-standby recipe. Shortening produces a crisp, flaky crust that is hard to match. Chilling your shortening will produce a tender crust.

2 cups flour
1 teaspoon salt
¾ cup vegetable shortening

Mix the flour and salt together. Using a food processor, a pastry cutter, or two knives, cut the shortening into the flour until it resembles very coarse meal. Sprinkle 5 tablespoons of cold water over the flour and pulse in a food processor or mix with a fork until the dough just holds together in a ball. If it is sticky, dust with a little flour.

Cut the ball in half with a knife and, with lightly floured hands, form each half into a 6-inch disc. Wrap the discs in plastic or waxed paper and refrigerate until ready to use.

Remove the dough from the refrigerator 15 minutes before using it.

Makes enough dough for 2 piecrusts.

Oil Crust

This crust will not have the flaky texture of a shortening crust, but it also won't have the saturated fat or trans–fatty acid content. Because this dough is so lean, take care not to overmix it or handle it too much, as it can easily grow tough.

2 cups flour
1 teaspoon salt
½ cup oil
¼ cup soymilk

Mix all the ingredients together with a fork or pulse in the food processor just until blended. Shape the dough into 2 6-inch discs and refrigerate for 10 minutes before using.

Makes enough dough for 2 piecrusts.

Clockwise from top:
Apple Energizer (page 319),
Chocolate Peanut Butter Shake
(page 318),
Strawberry-Banana Smoothie (page 318),
Creamy Dreamy Orange Smoothie
(page 318), V-5 (page 320).

Hash Browns (page 278), Scrambled Tofu (page 275),
Country-Style Tempeh Sausages (page 277).

Clockwise from top:
Apple Energizer (page 319),
Chocolate Peanut Butter Shake
(page 318),
Strawberry-Banana Smoothie (page 318),
Creamy Dreamy Orange Smoothie
(page 318), V-5 (page 320).

Hash Browns (page 278), Scrambled Tofu (page 275),
Country-Style Tempeh Sausages (page 277).

Company Chocolate Cake (page 292) with Chocolate Icing (page 297) and toasted almonds.

Large plate on left: Peanut Butter Candy (page 303),
Chocolate Peanut Butter Candy (page 303),
Brownies (page 300), Lebanese Rice Pudding (page 304).
Small plate in back: Coconut Flan (page 306).
Small plate in front: Chocolate Raisin Fudge (page 302).

Mango Cream Pie

½ recipe Shortening Crust (page 308)
1 15-ounce package firm silken tofu, at room temperature
2 large mangoes, peeled, seeded, and diced (page 305)
1 teaspoon guar gum (optional)
⅓ cup sugar
2 teaspoons lime juice
Tofu Cream (recipe follows)

Roll the dough and bake the piecrust according to the directions on page 307. Purée the tofu with the mangoes. Add the guar gum, sugar, and lime juice and purée until the mixture is quite smooth. Pour the filling into the prepared crust. Cover the pie and refrigerate until well chilled, about 2 hours. Top with Tofu Cream.

Makes 8 servings.

Tofu Cream

6 ounces firm silken tofu
2 tablespoons soymilk
½ teaspoon guar gum
2 tablespoons maple syrup or 3 tablespoons sugar
1 teaspoon lime juice
1 tablespoon oil or softened vegan margarine
1 teaspoon vanilla extract
Pinch sea salt

Purée all the ingredients together. Let the mixture stand for 15 minutes, and whisk or whip again until light and fluffy.

Makes about 1 cup.

Apple Cranberry Pie

Fruit pie recipes often call for adding flour to the filling to thicken the fruit juices. My mother taught me to replace flour with tapioca, which doesn't obscure the pure fruit flavors the way flour can.

If you are using sweetened, dried cranberries, reduce the sugar to ¾ cup.

1   recipe Oil Crust (page 308)
4   Granny Smith apples, peeled, cored, and cut into thick slices
⅔   cup cranberries, dried or fresh
2   tablespoons thinly sliced crystallized ginger
1   cup sugar
3   tablespoons tapioca
Pinch sea salt
2   tablespoons oil, preferably canola (optional)

Roll the dough according to the directions on page 307. Fit one crust in the pie pan. Preheat the oven to 350°. In a large bowl, toss the apples, cranberries, ginger, sugar, tapioca, salt, and oil until well blended. Mound the apple-cranberry mixture in the piecrust. Cover the filling with the second piecrust and press the edges together with a fork, or pinch decoratively. Cut a few small vent holes in the upper crust. Set the pie on a baking sheet in the oven and bake until the apples are tender and the crust has browned, about 1 hour. Cool the pie before cutting, about 30 minutes. Serve warm or at room temperature.

Makes 8 servings.

Easy Peach Crisp

6   cups frozen peaches
2   teaspoons lemon juice
½   cup sugar
¼   teaspoon salt
½   teaspoon ground cinnamon
¼   teaspoon ground ginger
⅛   teaspoon ground nutmeg
1½ cups granola, preferably gingersnap
2   tablespoons vegan margarine, melted

Preheat the oven to 350°. Oil an 8-inch square glass baking dish.

Toss the peaches with the lemon juice, sugar, salt, and spices. Put the peaches in the prepared pan and top with the granola. Cover the pan with aluminum foil and bake for 30 minutes or until the peaches are very tender. Remove the foil. Drizzle the granola with the margarine. Place the pan under the broiler and gently brown the granola. Serve hot or at room temperature.

Makes 8 servings.

Pear Betty

1 cup rolled oats
½ cup all-purpose flour
1¼ cups Succanat or
   brown sugar
⅓ cup toasted sliced
   almonds or hazelnuts
½ teaspoon ground
   cinnamon
¼ teaspoon ground ginger
Pinch sea salt
4 tablespoons vegan
   margarine or ¼ cup oil
4 pounds ripe pears, cored
   and cut into wedges
2 tablespoons fresh
   lemon juice
½ cup raisins

Preheat the oven to 400°. Lightly oil or spray a 9x13-inch baking dish. Combine the oats, flour, ½ cup of sugar, nuts, spices, and salt in a bowl and mix well. Work the margarine or oil into the dry ingredients until it resembles coarse crumbs. Sprinkle ⅓ cup of cold water over the mixture and stir to incorporate. Reserve.

Toss the pears with the lemon juice, remaining ¾ cup of sugar, and raisins. Pour the fruit in the baking dish. Top with the oat mixture. Bake until the pears soften and the topping is golden, about 40 minutes. Cool on a rack for at least 15 minutes before serving.

Makes 8 servings.

FROZEN DESSERTS

On a hot summer day, nothing is more refreshing than fruit ices or ice cream. Fruit ices, of course, don't need to be adapted for a vegan diet. Ice cream obviously requires some modification, but with some soymilk and tofu, you can make a tasty frozen treat. The total preparation time for frozen desserts is much reduced if all the ingredients are chilled. For more frozen dessert ideas, check out the smoothie recipes in "Beverages" (pages 317–320).

Soft-Serve Ice Cream

If you have a small ice cream maker, this recipe may be processed into a more traditional ice cream. The blender method, however, produces a nostalgic treat.

1 cup flavored soymilk
1 10-ounce package silken
   tofu
2 teaspoons vanilla extract
Pinch sea salt

Process all the ingredients in a blender or food processor until smooth. Freeze the mixture in ice cube trays. When the cubes are frozen, grind them in the food processor until smooth and airy, adding more soymilk if needed. Serve immediately.

Makes 2 to 4 servings.

Strawberry-Banana Blast Ice Cream

2 cups soymilk
1 tablespoon agar flakes
16 ounces silken tofu
1 pint strawberries, hulled
2 bananas
1 6-ounce can orange juice concentrate
1 tablespoon vanilla extract

Heat the soymilk in a small pan. Add the agar and bring to a boil. Reduce the heat and simmer for 5 minutes or until the flakes have dissolved. Let cool to room temperature. Blend the tofu, strawberries, bananas, juice concentrate, and vanilla extract in a food processor. Add the soymilk and blend again. Freeze the mixture in an ice cream freezer.

Makes 8 to 10 servings.

Watermelon Ice

4 cups 1-inch watermelon cubes, seeds removed
1 teaspoon fresh lime juice (optional)
1 teaspoon chopped fresh mint leaves
Pinch sea salt

Combine all the ingredients in a bowl and toss to blend. Transfer the mixture to a flat-bottomed, glass or ceramic baking dish. Cover the dish tightly and freeze for about 2 hours or until the watermelon is frozen solid. Process half of the frozen watermelon in a food processor until grainy. Repeat with the remaining watermelon. Spoon the mixture back into the container. Cover the container tightly and freeze. Stir after 30 minutes. Return to the freezer and stir again after another 30 minutes. Freeze for 1 hour or until frozen solid. With an ice cream scoop, using long, scraping strokes, shave the watermelon ice and put into chilled glasses. For a smoother consistency, process the mixture again in a food processor. Serve immediately or cover the glasses and freeze the watermelon ice until ready to serve.

Makes 2 to 4 servings.

beverages

Milks

Banana Milk

Oatmeal Banana Milk

Almond Milk

Rice Milk

Smoothies

Chocolate Peanut Butter Shake

Strawberry-Banana Smoothie

Creamy Dreamy Orange Smoothie

Piña Colada Smoothie

Apple Energizer

Mango Lassi

V-5

Ginger Mint Julep

Ades and Teas

Strawberry-Basil Lemonade

Easy Soda

Hibiscus Tea

Chai Concentrate

Water is essential to life, so my initial inclination was to have only one recipe in this chapter: "Water: Drink cold, hot, or room temperature. Catch on the tongue during a spring shower, or eat as fresh snow."

But variety is the spice of life, so here are some refreshing beverages that will let you increase your water intake in style. In addition to being thirst quenching, many of these drinks provide a nutritional boost as well. For the best results, use fresh ingredients with filtered or spring water.

MILKS

While you can make soymilk at home, it is a long, tedious process with results that are often inferior to the soymilk sold at the grocery store. It's hard to improve on commercial soymilk, which has a pleasant flavor and texture and is fortified with vitamins A, D, and E, riboflavin (B-2), and calcium.

However, there are other delicious milk drinks that you can efficiently prepare yourself. To add body to the milk, substitute brown rice or corn syrup for sugar. Carageenan, xanthan gum, or guar gum will also thicken the milk. If you want to experiment with these additives, start with a very small amount, $\frac{1}{8}$ teaspoon for 2 cups of water, since they do impart a slight taste.

Banana Milk

This is a quick answer to the question, "What am I going to put on my cereal?"

1	banana
1	cup water
$\frac{1}{2}$	teaspoon vanilla extract

Blend all ingredients in a blender or food processor until smooth. Drink or use immediately, as the banana will discolor in a short time.

Makes about $1\frac{1}{2}$ cups.

Oatmeal Banana Milk

1   banana
1   cup cooked oatmeal
2   cups water
½   teaspoon lemon juice
1   teaspoon vanilla extract
    (optional)

Blend all ingredients in a blender or food processor until smooth. Use immediately or refrigerate for up to 2 days.

Makes about 3¼ cups.

Almond Milk

Nut milks are particularly good as the bases for sauces. If you are using this as a beverage, a little vanilla, nutmeg, and sweetener are tasty additions. Almonds make the most pleasing beverage, but cashews may be used also.

1 cup raw blanched almonds

Soak the almonds for 8 to 12 hours in 3 cups of water. Strain and rinse the nuts. In a blender or food processor, purée the almonds with 4 cups of hot water. Purée for 3 minutes or until the mixture is as smooth as possible. Strain the milk through cheesecloth, squeezing out all the liquid. Sweeten if desired. Use immediately or refrigerate for up to 5 days.

Makes about 4 cups.

Rice Milk

Aromatic rice, such as jasmine or basmati, produces flavorful results, but almost any rice will do. However, if you choose to use brown rice, the Rice Milk will take 2 to 3 hours to cook. If you omit the cashews and sweeteners, you will have made congee, or Chinese rice porridge. Congee (page 279) is served with various toppings for breakfast or lunch. Make sure to save some unsweetened Rice Milk for Vegan Gravy (page 144). Rice Milk keeps for 5 days in the refrigerator.

3/4 cup raw white rice
1/4 cup cashews or almonds
6 cups water
1/4 cup Succanat or sugar (optional)
1 teaspoon vanilla extract
1/8 teaspoon salt

Place the rice in a large pot and cover with cold water. Agitate the rice to release any debris. Drain the rinse water and add the cashews and 6 cups of water to the pot. Bring the rice to a boil. Reduce the heat to medium-low and simmer for 2 hours. Check the pot periodically and add water, typically 2 to 3 cups more, to maintain the same level of water in the pot. The rice should be falling apart and the liquid quite milky. Cover the pot and allow it to cool to room temperature.

Add sugar, vanilla, and salt. Blend the milk with an immersion blender. Keep refrigerated.

Makes about 2 quarts.

SMOOTHIES

Smoothies are often spontaneous concoctions, with bits and pieces of fruits, flavorings, and fillers coming together in serendipitous harmony. My favorite smoothies are made from fresh fruits in season—when the price is the lowest and I can indulge with abandon.

Thickeners for smoothies: To add body and improve the texture in combinations with little bulk, add tofu, almonds, cashews, tahini, bananas, peanut butter, cooked oatmeal, or ice. Use frozen fruit or frozen juice to provide the texture of ice along with intense flavor. Individually quick-frozen fruit (often labeled IQF) works best since it has no added sugars.

Plan ahead for your spontaneous treats by cutting peeled bananas into chunks, wrapping them in plastic wrap, and freezing them like ice cubes. You can also freeze fruit juice in ice cube trays.

Healthful additions: Since smoothies often replace a regular meal, it's a good idea to try packing in some added nutrition. Remember that blending or puréeing retains all of the vegetable fiber that would be left behind in a juicer. For a healthy boost, try adding wheat germ, flaxseed, flaxseed oil, kelp, parsley, ginger, parsley, or miso.

Chocolate Peanut Butter Shake

3   tablespoons smooth
    peanut butter
1   cup soymilk
2   tablespoons chocolate
    syrup
Ice cubes

Combine the peanut butter and a little soymilk to thin the peanut butter; this will ensure even processing. Blend the peanut butter, soymilk, and chocolate syrup in a blender or food processor until smooth. Add ice cubes and process until it is thick and frosty.

Makes 1 serving.

Strawberry-Banana Smoothie

1   banana, peeled
1   cup pineapple juice or
    vanilla soymilk
1   cup individually quick-
    frozen (IQF) strawberries

Blend all ingredients together in a blender or food processor, adding the strawberries last. Adjust the consistency with soymilk, water, juice, or ice.

Makes 1 to 2 servings.

Creamy Dreamy Orange Smoothie

2   cups vanilla soymilk
1   16-ounce can frozen
    orange juice
    concentrate
1   teaspoon vanilla
    extract
1   tray ice cubes

Blend all ingredients together in a blender or food processor, adding the ice last. Adjust the consistency with soymilk, water, juice, or ice.

Makes 2 servings.

Piña Colada Smoothie

2 bananas
1 cup pineapple, fresh or canned
1 14-ounce can unsweetened coconut milk
4 ounces silken tofu
2 tablespoons maple syrup
Ice cubes

Blend all ingredients together in a blender or food processor, adding the ice last. Adjust the consistency with soymilk, water, juice, or ice.

Makes 2 servings.

Apple Energizer

I like using Granny Smith apples for their bright green color. For the best presentation, add the carrot at the end of blending. You'll get bright orange flecks suspended in the beautiful pale green smoothie.

2 small apples, cored and cut into chunks
1 stalk celery, thinly sliced
2 thin slices peeled ginger
1 cup water or orange juice
8 sprigs parsley
1 small carrot, peeled and thinly sliced

Blend all ingredients together in a blender or food processor until puréed. Adjust the consistency with soymilk, water, juice, or ice.

Makes 2 servings.

Mango Lassi

1 mango, peeled, seeded and diced
1 cup soy-gurt or kefir, or 1 cup soymilk and 2 teaspoons lime juice
2 tablespoons sugar (omit if using vanilla yogurt or soymilk)
Ice cubes

Blend all ingredients together in a blender or food processor, adding the ice last. Adjust the consistency with soymilk, water, juice, or ice.

Makes 2 servings.

V-5

2 cups water or tomato juice
2 medium-size ripe tomatoes
1 stalk celery, thinly sliced
¼ medium green bell pepper, thinly sliced
1 green onion, thinly sliced
8 sprigs parsley or basil
½ teaspoon kelp powder or 2 teaspoons miso

Blend all ingredients together in a blender or food processor until puréed. Adjust the consistency with water, juice, or ice.

Makes 2 servings.

Ginger Mint Julep

2 cups water
2 cups sugar
2 inches fresh ginger, thinly sliced
1 cup loosely packed mint leaves
Bourbon (optional)

In a small saucepan, boil the water, sugar, and ginger for 5 minutes. Turn off the heat. Add the mint leaves to the syrup. Cover the pan and let the syrup cool to room temperature. Strain the syrup, pressing the mint leaves to release all the liquid. Store in the refrigerator. Keeps for 1 week.

To serve, mix equal parts syrup and water or bourbon and serve over crushed ice. Alternatively, place the water and syrup in a blender and add 1 glassful of ice cubes.

Makes about 2½ cups syrup, enough for 12 bourbon or 6 virgin juleps.

ADES AND TEAS

There are times when water simply doesn't slake a thirst. Our bodies are calling for something more refreshing. Ades and teas can give you that extra little something your body is calling for, keeping you hydrated and happy at the same time.

Strawberry-Basil Lemonade

1¼ cups strawberries, fresh or individually quick-frozen
12 fresh basil leaves
½ cup sugar
1½ cups fresh lemon juice from 6 to 9 lemons
5 to 6 cups water

Purée the strawberries and basil with the sugar. Combine the strawberry mixture, lemon juice, and water in a pitcher and mix well. Taste and adjust the sweetness with additional sugar. Serve over ice.

Makes 2 quarts.

Easy Soda

Making your own soda can eliminate the preservatives and artificial colors found in so many packaged drinks. These can be of particular concern to parents of children with chemical sensitivities. If you are adventurous, try buying a soda siphon. This will allow you to carbonate almost any beverage.

1 can all-fruit juice concentrate
2 liters seltzer water

Combine the concentrate and seltzer water in a pitcher and mix well. Serve immediately over ice.

Makes 2½ quarts.

Hibiscus Tea

This is a traditional rehydration drink. Look for hibiscus flowers in Caribbean markets.

4 cups boiling water
4 ounces dried hibiscus flowers, also called dried sorrel
1 tablespoon grated fresh ginger
2 whole cloves
Zest of 1 lime
Zest of 1 orange
½ cup sweetener

Pour the water over the hibiscus, ginger, cloves, and zests. Cover the tea and steep for 12 to 24 hours. Strain the tea concentrate and sweeten to taste.

To serve, mix the concentrate with an equal volume of water. Add ice and serve with a wedge of lime.

Makes enough for 2 quarts of tea.

Chai Concentrate

I don't remember the circumstances of my first cup of chai, but I do remember the enchantment of the heady spices, strong tea, and rich milk. If your only experience of this North Indian specialty is at your local coffee shop (which is probably using a concentrate), try making your own. You can adapt the spice blend to your personal taste, increasing the ginger in winter to help ward off the sniffles.

If you use ground cinnamon instead of cinnamon sticks, remember that a little goes a long way.

4   cups water
2   cinnamon sticks or ground cinnamon
4   cardamom pods, lightly crushed to break pods
6   whole cloves
1   inch fresh ginger, thinly sliced
7 or 8 black, pink, or white peppercorns
Pinch fennel seeds
3   tablespoons loose leaf tea, preferably Assam
½   cup sugar
4   cups soymilk

Bring the water to a boil in a saucepan. Reduce the heat and add the spices. Simmer for 10 minutes. Add the tea and steep for 5 minutes. Strain the tea and add the sugar. Let cool and then refrigerate.

To serve, warm equal parts soymilk and tea. Sweeten as desired.

Makes enough for 8 to 10 cups tea.

treats
for kids

Ants on a Log

Red Ant Attack

Birds' Nests

Cinnamon Monster Fingers

Sunflower Salad

Dirt Pudding

Special-Occasion Crispy Rice Bars

Popcorn Balls

Sometimes we have to trick children into eating what's healthy for them. Nutritious food can be a hard sell to a generation constantly bombarded by images of empty calories. To entice your kids, try presenting healthy food in fun ways. Children can help with most of these recipes. It can be a little messy, but it's fun—for the child, at least.

Ants on a Log

2 stalks celery
1 tablespoon peanut butter
1 tablespoon raisins

Fill the celery stalks with peanut butter. Arrange raisin "ants" in a line on top. For ants on a tree, use stalks that still have the leaves attached.
Makes 2 servings.

Red Ant Attack

Here is a good way to disguise tofu. The acid from the pineapple thickens the tofu a bit, but depending on the brand you are using, you may want to add a few raw, ground cashews to give this a slightly better texture.

2 ounces firm tofu or cream cheese substitute
2 tablespoons crushed pineapple
1 teaspoon brown rice syrup
2 stalks celery
1 tablespoon dried cranberries

Mash or purée the tofu, pineapple, and brown rice syrup together until well blended. Fill the celery stalks with the tofu mixture. Arrange dried cranberry "ants" in a line on top of the pineapple mixture.
Makes 2 servings.

Birds' Nests

Use fortified bran cereal to add a nutritional boost to snack time. Shredded carrots, apples, or coconut may be added to make nests for different species. Any small round fruit will work here. Use a dried apricot half for an ostrich egg or fresh blueberries for robins' eggs.

2   slices whole wheat bread
2   tablespoons peanut
     butter
1   tablespoon jam or jelly
1/3 cup bran cereal
2   teaspoons raisins

Using a biscuit cutter, cut 2 3-inch rounds from the bread and spread peanut butter on them. In a small pan on the stove or in the microwave, melt the jelly over low heat. Mix the bran cereal with the jelly. Using a spoon, arrange the bran cereal around the edge of the bread to resemble the twigs of a nest. Arrange the raisin "eggs" in the center of the nest. Let the nest cool completely before giving it to your child.

Makes 2 servings.

Cinnamon Monster Fingers

This just may be the way to get your kids to eat whole grain bread. Use a moist whole grain bread like Everything Bread (page 263) to get a crunchy outside and chewy inside that closely resembles the texture of a monster.

If turbinado sugar is your sweetener of choice, be warned that it is usually too coarse for this recipe. You may wish to grind it to a finer texture in a food processor or coffee grinder. Cinnamon sugar is normally 1 part ground cinnamon to 4 parts sugar.

1   loaf whole grain bread,
     unsliced
Softened vegan margarine
About 2/3 cup cinnamon
     sugar

Preheat the broiler. Cut the bread into 1¼-inch slices. Cut off the crusts. Cut each slice into 1¼-inch strips. Place the bread fingers on a baking sheet and broil until the fingers are lightly toasted, turning once. Generously spread the softened margarine on the fingers and roll them in cinnamon sugar. Return to the broiler and broil until the sugar is bubbly. Sprinkle with a little more cinnamon sugar if necessary. Let the fingers cool slightly before giving them to children.

Makes about 24 pieces.

Sunflower Salad

1	tablespoon dried dates
2	tablespoons raisins
1	orange
2	tablespoons sunflower
	seeds
Mint sprigs

Place the dates and raisins in a small bowl. Pour 2 tablespoons of boiling water over the fruit, and cover with a plate or plastic wrap. Alternatively, put the raisins, dates, and 2 tablespoons of water in a small microwave-safe bowl and microwave them until the mixture is warm but not boiling.

Cut away the pith and peel of the orange to expose the pulp. Cut the sections out of the membrane. Drain any excess water from the dates and raisins. Squeeze the juice from the orange membrane over the dates and raisins.

In a food processor, pulse the dates, raisins, and 1 tablespoon of sunflower seeds together. Put this mixture in the middle of a plate. Arrange the remaining sunflower seeds on top to resemble the middle of a blooming sunflower. Arrange the orange "petals" around the center. Construct a stem and leaves from the mint sprigs.

Makes 2 child-size servings.

Dirt Pudding

The Everyday Chocolate Cake recipe can be halved successfully, but it can't be quartered successfully. I recommend that you halve the recipe and freeze the unused portion of the cooked cake for another day. Serve the pudding in colorful paper party cups for easy cleanup.

¼	Everyday Chocolate
	Cake (page 291)
2	recipes Vanilla Pudding
	(page 304)
1	6- or 8-ounce package
	Gummi Worms (make
	sure the brand you
	choose is made
	with cornstarch, not
	gelatin)

Crumble the cake into small pieces. Layer a third of the crumbs in a large serving bowl or individual 8-ounce custard cups. Cover cake crumbs with half the pudding. Layer another third of the cake crumbs on the pudding, followed by the rest of the pudding. Crumble half of the remaining cake crumbs on top of the pudding. Randomly distribute the worms over the surface, burying them in the "dirt" at different levels. Sprinkle the remaining cake crumbs over the worms.

Makes 6 to 8 servings.

Special-Occasion Crispy Rice Bars

Log Cabin makes a cinnamon syrup meant for pancakes that can substitute for the corn syrup to add a kick to these treats.

1 cup smooth peanut butter
1 cup corn syrup
1 cup sugar
1 tablespoon vegan margarine
7 cups crispy rice cereal
1 cup vegan butterscotch chips
1 cup vegan chocolate chips

In a Dutch oven or large, wide pot, melt the peanut butter, syrup, sugar, and margarine together. When the sugar is dissolved and the mixture is warm, add the rice cereal and mix well. Oil your hands slightly and pat the mixture into a 9-inch square pan. Melt the butterscotch chips in the microwave and spread over the bars. Melt the chocolate chips in the microwave and spread over the butterscotch layer. Refrigerate until the chocolate layer hardens slightly. Cut the mixture into bars before the chocolate layer becomes really hard. If the chocolate or butterscotch cracks when you try to cut the bars, heat a sharp knife under hot water before cutting.

Makes 9 1-inch bars.

Popcorn Balls

If possible, have someone help you form the popcorn balls because speed is of the essence. Keep a bowl of cold water and a hand towel close by to cool your hands. You can try adding a tablespoon of nutritional yeast to the corn before mixing with the syrup. The yeast will add a nutty flavor and lots of good B vitamins.

8 cups unsalted popped popcorn
1 cup sugar
1/2 cup molasses
2 teaspoons vinegar
1/4 teaspoon salt
1 tablespoon vegan margarine
1/2 cup peanuts

Put the popcorn into a large bowl and keep warm. Whisk the sugar, molasses, 1/4 cup of water, and vinegar in a small saucepan. When the sugar is dissolved, bring the syrup to a boil over medium heat. Cook the syrup to 270° (hard ball stage) or until a bit of it dropped into cold water turns brittle. Remove from the heat and stir in the margarine and peanuts. Drizzle the syrup over the popcorn and quickly toss with a fork until it is evenly mixed. Oil your hands slightly and quickly form the mixture into balls. When they are completely cool, wrap each in plastic wrap and decorate with curling ribbon.

Makes 8 to 12 large balls or 16 to 18 small balls.

Index

329